How to De-Program Yourself

from All the Blasphemous Ideas
You Learned in Public School

Should you pull your children out of the public schools? There are plenty of man-centered reasons to, including a dumbed-down curriculum that encourages mediocrity and is anti-American, anti-family, anti-God, pro-homosexual and pro-Marxist. Other books have discussed these issues, but only **How to De-Program Yourself** *discusses God's reasons for exiting your children from such indoctrination. When we began our school 43 years ago we didn't have the advantage of a resource like this, but you do, so make certain that you take advantage of it. Your children will love you for it because it will show them not only to have a heart for God, but how to have the mind of Christ!* **How to De-Program Yourself** *explains how to think like God wants us to think. Indeed, how to think like America's founders who gave us such biblical principles as pro-family self-government, instead of anti-family central government.*

—Bobbie H. Ames, Senior Administrator
and David P. Ames, Headmaster
Emerald Mountain Christian School
Montgomery, AL 36124

Scripture quotations are from the *New Geneva Study Bible*, *NKJV*, 1995, Thomas Nelson, Inc.

©2009
Hanson Group
2 Windsor Drive • Tuscaloosa, Alabama 35404
205.454.1442
bhanson@graceandlaw.com • www.graceandlaw.com

ISBN-0-9771773-5-1
Printed and bound in the United States of America

Table of Contents

• PART ONE •
Cutting the Strings from Your Non-Christian Puppet Master

First Cut: Education
Questions 1–17

Second Cut: Civil Government
Questions 18–26

Third Cut: Worldview & Lifestyle
Questions 27–44

Fourth Cut: Decision-Making
Questions 45 – 50

Fifth Cut: Eliminating Rationalizations & Pragmatism

• *PART TWO* •
Building Your Own Spiritual Musical Instrument

Replacement String 1

Replacement String 2

Replacement String 3

Replacement String 4

Replacement String 5

Music Maestro, Please!

Charts

Think You're Ready to Make Your Decision on How to Educate Your Child?

If so, what are you going to say when the phone rings
and the caller asks:

"Why don't you pass the time by playing a little solitaire?" *

Make this your answer:

"Bug off, Satan, I'm giving my children a Christian education!"

---

* *In the Manchurian Candidate the suggestion to play solitaire was an irresistible command to Sergeant Raymond Shaw. When he saw the Queen of Diamonds, it compelled him to follow the orders of his Communist brainwashers to assassinate the nominee for President of the U.S. Today, such a suggestion could be Satan's code to have us rationalize, "The public school my children go to is not like all the other public schools. Their teachers are kind and caring Christians who, together with my children, are being 'salt and light' to other students." This is Satan's attempt to have your children be his unwilling pawns in bringing honor to him, instead of to Jesus, as they make their daily decisions.*

Preface

Picture this: The war is over and you return home a hero. You are a Major and your platoon has received accolades for bravery with one member receiving the Medal of Honor for single-handedly saving the lives of all but two members of your platoon. Everything appears to be going well until you begin having nightmares that include flashbacks of very disturbing scenes in which the Medal of Honor recipient kills two members of your platoon. You wake up screaming, and begin to think you are losing your mind, because when someone asks you about the Medal of Honor winner Sergeant Raymond Shaw, your answer is:

Raymond Shaw is the bravest, kindest, warmest, most wonderful human being I've ever met in my life.

As these words come tumbling out of your mouth, you wonder why you would say that about a person that you and the other members of the platoon greatly disliked: a person who even admits that he is not a very likable person. Still, the nightmares continue and when you discover that another member of your platoon is having similar nightmares, you set out to solve the mystery. What you don't know is that Sergeant Shaw is receiving phone calls in which the caller says, "Raymond, why don't you pass the time by playing a little solitaire?" After a few minutes the phone rings again. "Did you see the Red Queen? This is what I want you to do. Tomorrow, go to such and such a place and kill so-and-so." Shaw, unaware of the trigger word "Red Queen," would then proceed, zombie like, to his prescribed destination and carry out his orders.

To make a long (and dramatic) story short, the Communists plan to use Sergeant Shaw as a sleeper agent to kill the nominee for President of the United States, so that his step-father, the Vice Presidential candidate can become the Presidential nominee. The trigger word "Red Queen," which turns out to be the Queen of Diamonds, causes him to turn his focus on the brainwashing that he and the other members of the platoon underwent. As the truth begins to unfold, you remember that instead of the reported heroics of Raymond Shaw, your platoon was captured, then brainwashed to believe that Shaw saved you from the communists. During this process the Queen of Diamonds was used to focus his thoughts upon following the orders of his Communist handlers, *without knowing why he is doing it*!

Richard Condon's 1959 thriller novel, *The Manchurian Candidate*, was adapted in a classic film that popularized the concept of brainwashing a person to do sinister activities. The idea of a person or group of persons being "programmed" to automatically act in a particular manner captivated movie goers in 1962, and again when it was re-made in 2004. This begs the question: "If the Communists can do that to mature military personnel, why couldn't someone do this to the immature and unsuspecting minds of public school* children?"

"No way, Hanson!" you say. "There's absolutely no way our public schools could motivate students from Christian homes to automatically make decisions that fly in the face of their religion, *and then not even realize what they were doing*! Besides, I came through the public (government) schools without having my Christian worldview negatively impacted."

My response to that is "Not so fast!" Before concluding that your worldview hasn't been implanted with suggestions to serve yourself with your daily decisions, instead of serving God and others, check your

---

* *Public schools are not really "public" at all. The "public" has no say in the curriculum, the school their children must attend or the discipline (or lack of it) in that school. Instead the civil government teaches an anti-Christian worldview that totally omits the Christian roots of American history, and self-government. Instead of depending upon individual initiative and self-government, today's curriculum promotes a tyrannical, central governing nanny state. In addition, there is no instruction provided to support the reality of absolute truth (since, if there were, the children would know who they are, how they got here, what they are supposed to do, and how they are to do it, instead the curriculum is designed to "dumb the students down" so that they will become good "wards of the state." Indeed, the government schools teach the "religion" of the state, and serve as its "churches," or should we say, "synagogues of the state."*

premise with the following list of "Trigger Words," and see if your typical response mirrors the "conditioned response" Satan prefers, or whether it mirrors the "conditioned response" that Jesus prefers.

The Power of Suggestion

"Trigger" Words	Satan's Conditioned Response	Jesus' Conditioned Response
Jesus	Savior	Savior, Lord, & King
God's Word	True, but has a few contradictions.	Inerrant and no contradictions.
Purpose of God's Word	To comfort us during Satan's domination of the earth.	To instruct us in how to live and govern ourselves and complete the defeat of Satan.
Christ's Kingdom	Church	The entire earth.
Our duty	Evangelism	Evangelism & discipleship
Our attitude	Be nicer than non-Christians, but not confrontational.	Personal holiness, which includes rebuking unholy acts.
Worldview	Live according to God's principles *inside* our homes and churches ("religious realm"), and according to man's principles *outside* in the "real life" realm.	Live according to God's principles in *all* situations in *all* circumstances, because God has given us *one* ethical standard to be used at all times.

How did you do? If you found that your worldview is unscathed by your years spent in civil government indoctrination, pat your self on the back, because research indicates that only *five percent* of adult Christians have a Christian worldview. Compare that to the statistic that approximately *95 percent* of adult Christians were "educated" (perhaps I should say "indoctrinated") in the government schools and you will have the first of several "hmmm moments" as you go through these pages.

How you react to them will give you a good indication of whether your profession of faith is real and you are indeed a Christian, or whether it is based upon some misinformation and you are merely a person who is attempting to live a moral lifestyle. Remember the conditioned response that the "Manchurian Candidates" automatically said when asked about Sergeant Shaw?

> *Raymond Shaw is the bravest, kindest, warmest,*
> *most wonderful human being I've ever met in my life.*

Just for fun, let's string together the individual portions of Satan's preferred conditioned response and compare it to the conditioned response preferred by Jesus. In both cases we will be responding to the question of what we, as Christians, believe and stand for. In other words, "What makes Christians tick?"

Satan's Preferred "Conditioned Response"

Jesus is the Son of God and came to earth to rescue us from our sins by doing what it is impossible for us to do: live a perfectly sinless life. His Word is true and only contains a few contradictions and it comforts us with thoughts about how wonderful it will be in heaven when we are once and for all free from Satan's domination of the earth.

In the meantime we should do our best to present a testimony that we are "nice" law-abiding people, but we should be careful not to be confrontational by "imposing" our beliefs on others.

Our duty as Christians is to tell the Gospel message to as many people as we can, because we increase Christ's Kingdom whenever we add new members to the church. When we are *inside* our homes and churches, we tell each other about God's Word, but when we are *outside*, in the "real life" realm of life, we respect other people's beliefs by not forcing Christian principles into the workplace or school room.

Jesus' Preferred "Conditioned Response"

Jesus is the Son of God and came to earth to rescue us from our sins by doing what it is impossible for us to do: live a perfectly sinless life. In addition to being our Savior, He is also our Lord (boss) and King (ruling over our civil rulers). The Bible is without error and is our instruction book on how to live and govern ourselves according to God's will, because it is our duty to "take dominion" of the earth (Gen. 1.26-28), and eventually "crushing" Satan's head" (Gen. 3.15; Rom. 16.20). Jesus assures us that He is now ruling the earth from heaven at the right hand of God the Father where He promises to "reign till He has put all enemies under His feet." (1 Cor. 15.25)

Since God has given us *one* ethical standard to be used in *all* situations and in *all* circumstances, we are presenting a Godly antithesis to the cultural agenda of non-Christians. This means that we should not only tell the Gospel to others, but help each other grow in God's grace and knowledge through discipleship. (Matt.28.18-20)

Both of these "conditioned responses," or "life scripts" are lengthy and would not be used in every response or in deciding every decision, but they do provide a working framework for how to respond to the various situations that present themselves to us on a daily basis. So as you think about which "response," or "script" most accurately describes the way in which you are currently living, remember that it was only when the Manchurian Candidates began to realize that someone was "pulling their strings" that they were able to correctly deal with their situation. This is the purpose of *How to De-Program Yourself from All of the Blasphemous Ideas You Learned in Public School.*

It's been said that "the road to hell is paved with good intentions," and unless and until we realize that, with the best of intentions, we are doing a much better job of serving Satan than Jesus, we will have no reason to make any corrections in our lifestyles.

Former college and professional football coach Lou Holtz says, "Life is 10 percent what happens to you and 90 percent how you react," and my prayer is that your reaction to your everyday situations and circumstances reflect Jesus' preferred "conditioned response, rather than Satan's.

Speaking of football, one of the most valuable teaching tools of coaches is game films, because "the films don't lie." A player who does not believe that he is incorrectly performing a particular technique can see on the game tape that he didn't execute a play properly because he failed to perform the technique correctly. No player sets out to mess up a play, just as none of us sets out to make bad decisions, but the game tape is unbending in its depiction of the truth. Players learn to check their egos at the door of the film room, and that is just what we need to do when we encounter a biblical principle that challenges our current way of making decisions.

The Format

The first five chapters, (named "Cuts" to remind you that your "non-Christian conditioned strings" are being cut) explain the answers to the "Personal Worldview Checkup:"

First Cut	Education
Second Cut	Civil Government
Third Cut	Worldview & Lifestyle
Fourth Cut	Decision-Making
Fifth Cut	Eliminating Rationalizations & Pragmatism

The second five chapters, (named "Replacement Strings") provide explicit explanations on how to tune yourself up to play some sanctified soul music, by incorporating *biblical ethics* into your *daily decision-making*. The fifth "Replacement String" is a seminar in print that divides the Christian lifestyle into Seven Days, so you can see which "Day" you're on and what you need to do to move to the next day. You won't want to miss this, but resist the temptation to turn to it now. It will make more sense if you work your way toward it by reading the preceding chapters.

Upon completing the text you will have "cut" the man-honoring non-Christian strings which may be currently influencing your daily decision-making and lifestyle, and replaced them with God-honoring Christian strings. The logical next step is to live a "perfectly" obedient Christian lifestyle. Is that a possibility? Jesus thinks so, and Appendix One. "Be Ye Therefore *Perfect...*" explains how to do it.

Along the way there are helpful charts and illustrations. There is even a "Biblical Filter for Any Christian Curriculum (Home School, or Christian Day School) on the Parents Resource Page in the Fifth Cut, so you can make certain that your child's education is *Christian,* and not merely *conservative.*

You should be able to make good use of the previous descriptions of Satan's and Jesus' preferred conditioned responses,* plus your answers to the "Personal Worldview Checkup" in determining just whose "life's script" you are following. The main goal of the Checkup is to reveal the CAUSE behind your DECISIONS. Your daily decisions don't happen in a vacuum. Something is motivating your approach to life, and the five topical areas of the Checkup will help you clarify what that motivation is. To go back to our sports analogy, if you have ever played in a team sport, you can probably recall a particular player who was, at best, having only average success at a position until the coach moved him to another position, and all of a sudden his success rate increased dramatically. This could also be a benefit of taking the Checkup. You may discover that where you are currently spending the majority of your time and efforts could be better used in another vocation, because God has given you gifts that are better suited for that area.

WARNING: The manner in which some of the questions on the Personal Worldview Checkup are phrased give away the correct answer, but be honest with yourself and answer each question according to what your current worldview and lifestyle reflects. After all, you're the only one who is going to see your answer sheet! This will provide you with as accurate analysis of your worldview as possible. The correct answer to each question will be discussed in the following chapters, so take a deep breath, hang on and enjoy the journey!

---

* *You may well have some additions and/or deletions to my generic "conditioned responses," and if so please send them to me. I would very much like to see them (and perhaps even use them!).*

Your Very Own, Self-Administered, Personal Worldview Checkup[*]

First Cut | Education

1. **What is man?**
   a. A biological accident.
   b. A special creature made by God.

2. **Should instruction be exclusively based upon absolute truth?**
   a. No.
   b. Yes.

3. **Should teachers instruct students in "basic and relative ethics" facts," or in "basic facts and absolute ethics?"**
   a. Relative Ethics.
   b. Absolute Ethics.

4. **Should students be taught the principles of self-government, or should they be instructed in how to work in groups to form a "consensus" or a "synthesis" of opinions through "Group Think?"**
   a. Consensus and/or synthesis
   b. Self-government

5. **The teaching of history**
   a. Actual history should be revised to fit a politicized view that all cultures, at bottom are identical, since all religions are, at bottom, equally irrelevant.
   b. The actual history of Western civilization (which is based upon biblical ethics) is contrasted with the history of Eastern civilization (which is based upon non-biblical ethics), because *only* God's Word gives the correct principles on how to live and govern ourselves.

---

[*] *Appendix Two has a "clean copy" of the Personal Worldview Checkup. Feel free mark your answers on this one and to make copies of that one and give it to your friends.*

6. Is there such a thing as a "mind," or are the only things "real," those that can be "touched, seen, smelled, or objectively measured?"
   a. There is no "mind."
   b. There is a "mind."

7. Should the curriculum be child-centered, or Christ-centered?
   a. Child-centered
   b. Christ-centered

8. Students should be taught how to bring "glory and honor to God" in everything they do.
   a. False
   b. True

9. Christian education is:
   a. An optional add-on to a child's worldview.
   b. It is an essential part of The Great Commission.
      (Matthew 22.37; 28.18-20)

10. How does a person become "wise?"
    a. Be a good student; go to the best schools and sit under the best teachers, and learn from our experiences.
    b. Study the Word of God.

11. What is the purpose of an education?
    a. Prepare us for a paycheck.
    b. Prepare us for life.

12. Who is responsible for the education of children?
    a. The state
    b. Parents

13. Where is the best place to educate students?
    a. In a structured classroom.
    b. Wherever we "sit, walk, lie down, and rise up."
       (Deuteronomy 6.7)

14. Should teachers get to know the worldview of their students, or should they stick to the curriculum?
    a. Stick to the curriculum.
    b. Learn the worldview of the students.

15. Teachers should pray with and for their students.
    a. False
    b. True

16. When it comes to the issue of Christian education:
    a. Pastors should approach this in a pragmatic manner by not addressing it because it is a divisive issue and they will lose members (or their job!). Besides many churches have members (including officers) who are affiliated with the public schools and/or who send their children to the public schools.
    b. Pastors should approach this in a pious manner by obeying God's clear commands and thoroughly explain the sin of sending Christian children to schools that hate God and only promote the worship of false religions. (Deuteronomy 6.4-7; Isaiah 36.9; 2 Corinthians 6.14; Matthew 15.14, etc.) In the process of doing this, the pastors are providing a testimony to their members that they practice what they preach by trusting-in and relying-upon God's sovereign control of His creation to honor our obedience and curse our disobedience.

17. Is it a sin to submit our children to programs and policies of non-Christians, and/or to join with non-Christians in business ventures?
    a. No
    b. Yes

Second Cut | Civil Government

18. What does the separation of church and state mean?
    a. The church shouldn't have anything to do with the state, and the state shouldn't have anything to do with the church. Both should be entirely separate.

b. God gave each self-governing sphere (individual, family, church, state) particular responsibilities, and neither sphere should usurp any responsibilities of the other.

19. **Should we depend upon the civil government to "legislate" us out of our cultural problems, or should we "self-govern" ourselves out of our cultural problems?**
    a. Legislate
    b. Self-govern

20. **Our civil laws:**
    a. Should be based upon man's opinions and "best guesses," which means sometimes there will be some "gray" areas when the courts administer justice.
    b. Should be based upon God's absolute ethics as revealed on the in errant pages of the Bible, which means there are only "black and white" areas of right and wrong behavior.

21. **Our elected representatives should govern as:**
    a. Politicians
    b. Statesmen

22. **When we vote:**
    a. Do we vote for the "lesser of two evils," or
    b. Do we vote to "overcome evil with good?" (Romans 12.21)

23. **Which economic policies do you favor?**
    a. Those which promote the socialistic "heavy hand" of civil government? or
    b. Those which promote biblical capitalistic principles of self-government?

24. **Do you see the role of civil government as:**
    a. Providing a wide array of social programs, including education? or
    b. Defending us against attack and keeping our communities safe for us to live, work, play and raise our families the way we want?

25. **We should "Render to Caesar:"**
    a. Everything he asks, because Jesus says so.
    b. Only the things that are Caesar's, because Jesus says so.

26. **Should Christians be involved in civil government?**
    a. No, all politicians are crooks, and we should not dirty our hands in that field.
    b. Yes, a Christian can bring honor and glory to God in all areas of life, and since God has given only *one* ethical code by which to live, Christian statesmen can help ensure that only biblical legislation takes place.

Third Cut | Worldview & Lifestyle

27. **What does having a Christian worldview mean to you?**
    a. It helps me to know the differences between how Christians and non-Christians view the world.
    b. It helps me to know the *descriptions* of the differences between a Christian and non-Christian worldview, plus it helps me know God's *prescriptions* for how to deal with the various cultural issues.

28. **In order to have a satisfying lifestyle:**
    a. We can depend upon our self-sufficiency, personal initiative, education and the practical application of our knowledge to an ever-changing value standard of relative ethics, or
    b. We can depend upon God's Word to sufficiently provide us with all the wisdom needed to live and govern ourselves successfully in accordance with an absolute and unchanging value standard.

29. **When it comes to one's worldview and lifestyle:**
    a. There two ethical value standards: a "religious" one to be used in our homes and churches, and a "real life" one to be used in our vocations and/or with non-Christians?
    b. There is only one absolute and unchanging ethical standard for all areas of our life and for all the situations and circumstances in which we may find ourselves?

30. Is your worldview and lifestyle based upon:
    a. The 2nd Table of God's Law: Commandments 5-10 (honor those in authority, don't kill, cheat, steal, lie or be jealous)? Or
    b. Upon both the 2nd Table *and* the 1st Table of God's Law: Commandments 1-4 (worship only the one true God of the Bible, don't make idols, or misuse the name of the Lord, and to keep the Lord's Day holy)?

31. When God tells us to "walk in all the ways that I have commanded you, so that it may be well with you," (Jeremiah 7.23) what does this verse mean to you?
    a. God made a mistake, He really didn't mean it, and we won't be punished if we only make an effort to obey those parts of the Bible that conform to our current worldview and lifestyle. After all, nobody is perfect!
    b. Even though we are imperfect and will never be able to obey God perfectly, we should strive to do that because God never makes mistakes and means what He says. We should put forth our best effort, knowing that we will blessed if we obey God, and cursed if we disobey Him.

32. I believe that:
    a. God exists for us.
    b. We exist for God.

33. Who's "running the show?" Who's in charge of planet earth?
    a. Satan
    b. Jesus

34. As Christians do we have a
    a. Hope to cope?
       Or a
    b. Hope to conquer?

35. It is said that a "text without a context is a pretext," and so is a "worldview and lifestyle without a biblical reference point, pointless." This is why we should always ask before making any decision, or addressing any cultural issue:
    a. Is the *context* of my decision-making man's word?
    b. Is the *context* of my decision-making God's Word?

36. Which statement correctly describes the Christian attitude?
    a. We should keep in our place and not impose our religion on others.
    b. We should "boldly" and "confidently" live by God's ethics at *all* times and in *all* places.

37. Which group of people controls history?
    a. Non-Christians
    b. Christians

38. Are the times in which we are living "normal," or "abnormal?"
    a. Normal
    b. Abnormal

39. God's Word is:
    a. Something soothing for our troubled mind.
    b. A lamp to our feet.

40. How do we "enlarge the place of Christ's tent?" (Isaiah 54.2)
    a. Be seeker-friendly and water down God's Word so that we won't offend non-Christians by using words such as "sin," and "hell."
    b. Teach the whole counsel of God's Word and trust in God's sovereign control to bless the preaching of His Word.

41. Our duty as Christians:
    a. Rely-upon and trust-in the advice of *others* when they tell us that we are supposed to live and interpret the Bible within the frame work of current events.
    b. Trust-in and rely-upon God's Word to guide and direct our daily actions.

42. Are we:
    a. Armed with God's perfect counsel, and not dangerous?
    b. Dangerous because we have the potential for changing our culture with God's ethics, but don't know *how* to go about it because many of our pastors have done a poor job of teaching us?

43. Is your daily testimony (lifestyle):
    a. About the same as the lifestyle of your non-Christian neighbors.
    b. Significantly different than that of your non-Christian neighbors.

44. Do we live in an orderly, cause-and-effect universe, or in a universe where events happen randomly?
    a. A random universe.
    b. An orderly universe.

Fourth Cut | Decision-Making

45. Is it possible for us to make correct decisions by depending upon our own wisdom and common sense?
    a. Yes, after all, God has given us a brain and the ability to communicate.
    b. No, because Adam and Eve's disobedience impaired our ability to reason correctly. This is why we need to filter all of our decisions through a gird of biblical ethics. Thinking God's thoughts after Him is the only way we can be confident that we will arrive at correct decisions.

46. What is your opinion regarding God's Word?
    a. I have *respect* for it.
    b. I have a *reverential fear* of it.

47. What is the "Chief Influencer" of your daily decisions?
    a. What's in it for *Me?* or
    b. What's in it for *God?*

48. What's the Context of Your Worldview?
   a. It's pretty much the ethics of commandments 5-10: Honor those in authority, don't murder, cheat, steal, lie or covet.
   b. It is a combination of all Ten Commandments, plus the application of the Case Laws that follow them, whereby Moses tells us how to live and govern ourselves.

49. What are the criteria you use to make your best decisions?
   a. The "prevailing opinion" of other Christians, plus my common sense and logic.
   b. God's Word is the primary authority, but for those topics about which I haven't studied, I comply with the counsel of other Christians.

50. Do you lean on your understanding, or upon God's?
   a. Are you going to mirror the way non-Christians live, making your daily decisions according to your wisdom, while *adding* moralistic ethics to your lifestyle in an external effort to win points with God? Or,
   b. Are you going to mirror the way the Bible commands you to live, with your external actions founded on the internal motivations of your new spiritual heart.

Total of "A" answers   _____
Total of "B" answers   _____

Multiply the "B" answers by 2
to get a numerical score.   _____

Relax, there's no "pass or fail" score. As you have probably figured out, the "B" answers reflect a Christian worldview. Since each of us is completely "justified" in God's sight as soon as we repent and turn from living according to our rules, and begin living in accordance to His rules, and since each of us is gradually "sanctified" (made more holy) throughout the remainder of our life on earth, there is no "pass" or "fail" score for this test. The only thing that counts is to identify those areas of our worldview and lifestyle that need repenting of, and then to do so. This is the only way to bring glory and honor to our Lord, Savior and King, Jesus Christ, and it is also the only way to present a godly antithesis to the ungodly cultural agenda of our non-Christian neighbors. They *think* that they know how to live, but we, through the grace of the Holy Spirit who has removed the veil from our eyes[1] *do know* how to live and govern ourselves and we are commanded to provide a daily testimony of how to do just that.[2]

Each one of us grows at our own speed. So, instead of focusing on a particular *score*, we should be concentrating on the *process* of improving our current score so that we can be more consistent and effective servants of Jesus. This percentage score simply indicates to you the amount of biblically correct answers you selected. Your two-pronged strategy for walking in a more consistent manner with your Creator is to keep your strong areas strong ("B" answers), and to strengthen your weak areas ("A" answers).

A friend of mine says, "You never know what you look like until you get your picture taken." And now that you have had your spiritual "picture taken," and know your "score," are you so quick to dismiss the idea that up to now you may have been an unwilling *sleeper agent* for advancing the non-Christian cultural agenda by rarely, if ever, stepping back from your daily decision-making process to consider whether your daily decisions will honor man, rather than God?

God's Theological Coin

We are all quick to say, "God's Word is *true*," [3] but we are slow to turn that theological coin over and admit what's inscribed on the other side: Man's word is *false*." However, there is no such thing as a one-sided coin, so we must remind ourselves that if our decisions do not conform to Scripture, they are false and won't work, no matter how much time, effort or resources we devote toward them. This will be discussed more in Replacement String 4, but for now let's proceed to the explanation of the answers to your Personal Worldview Checkup.

In your *process* of becoming more sanctified (holy), periodically ask yourself:

- ✔ Am I doing what I can to grow in God's grace and knowledge?
- ✔ Am I weeding out misunderstandings about what I believe the Bible to be teaching?
- ✔ Am I approaching Bible study with a "no holds barred" attitude of allowing God's Word to take me wherever it will?

God's Practical Application Coin

NOTES
1   2 Corinthians 3.14
2   1 Corinthians 10.31; Colossians 3.17
3   Psalm 119.160; John 17.17

Introduction

Christians agree that:

- ❖ "We are more than conquerors." Romans 8.37
- ❖ God's will "will be done on earth as it is in heaven."
  Matthew 6.10
- ❖ "He who is in you is greater than he who is in the world."
  1 John 4.4
- ❖ "The earth will be filled with the knowledge of the glory of the
  LORD, as the waters cover the sea." Habakkuk 2.14 And,
- ❖ "The kingdoms of this world have become the kingdoms of our
  Lord and of His Christ and He shall reign forever and ever."
  Revelation 11.15

Yet, the vast majority of us *live* as though none of these glorious truths are in the Bible and that we are merely a bunch of nice and polite cultural losers! Something is out of sync. Could it be our definitions? And could our definitions be different because of our *presuppositions*? Everybody is a *presuppositionalist*. You may be thinking, "Not only did I not know that I am a presuppositionalist; I'm not certain that I even know what that word means!" That's a fair response. A presuppositionalist is a person who presupposes a *conclusion* about a particular set of facts. For example, all Christians presuppose that God's Word is true, because to not do so would be to invent a false religion, whereby they or someone else would be the ultimate determiner of truth. However, among Christians there are sub groups that presuppose certain *conclusions* regarding God's Word. A large group, for example, presupposes that Satan rules the earth, so anytime they come across one of the numerous passages that describe how Christians will be blessed for living according to God's agenda instead of their agenda, they say something to the effect: "This is a true statement, because all of God's Word is true, but this particular passage is meant for a future (or past) generation." They explain their presupposition by stating: "Just look at today's events, how could anything good come out of all of the evil that is currently going on!"

Another group of Christian presuppositionalists approach such optimistic verses in the Bible with the attitude, "God's Word is true, and I have been called to obey it, not edit it, so if His Word tells me that I can expect blessings from obeying it, and curses from disobeying it, I take that at face value and let God determine when He will bring about His intended results and when and how I and my family and community will be blessed. After all, *He* is in complete control of His creation and Jesus says that He came to 'defeat the works of the devil.'[1] In other words, I am going to let God's Word interpret God's Word, not current events, or best-selling end times books, or TV preachers!"

There you have it: Two sets of Christians, both with the best of intentions, yet the worldview and lifestyle of one group is pessimistic about making a positive difference in their culture, and the worldview and lifestyle of the other group is optimistic about restoring culture to reflect biblical ethics. If this were a book about the end times, this would be the perfect place to begin that discussion, but this book is about *carrying out our calling* in Christ's Kingdom, and how we should, as God's chosen people, conduct ourselves in order to provide a godly testimony to our non-Christian neighbors. Each of us would agree that we have been miraculously rescued from an unholy worldview and lifestyle. The discussions of the various answers in the Third Cut—Worldview & Lifestyle, provide detailed descriptions of how we should go about our daily duties in a God-honoring manner. This book is not about *when* Jesus will return or *what* He is going to do when that happens, but *how we should live between now and then*. Despite what you may hear from the pulpit, or from TV, or in best-selling books, the Bible gives no definitive answer to *when* Jesus will return. Jesus Himself states, "But of that day and hour no one knows, not even the angels of heaven, but My Father only."[2] This means that anyone who thinks they might have a clue about Jesus' return is only making a subjective *speculation*. On the other hand, God has caused His inerrant Word to be given and preserved through the centuries because it provides us with objective *revelation* about how we should live and govern ourselves. The question facing each of us is whether we're spending the vast majority of our time basing our worldview and lifestyle upon objective *revelation*, or upon subjective *speculation*.

Let's put this in terms of preparing for an upcoming game. We *know* the strengths and weaknesses of our opponent, because they are *revealed* in the films we have of their previous games. But we can *speculate* that they may put in a few new plays for their game against us. QUESTION: Would you prefer that your coaching staff spend most of this week's practice preparing us for what our opponent *might do*, or upon what we *know* our opponent *will do*? The answer is obvious isn't it? We could enter the game prepared for virtually every trick play in the book, and get blown away because we were neither prepared to defend the strengths of our opponent, nor to attack their weaknesses.

You may know all of the "Christian" things to say, but if what you *say* does not reflect what you are *thinking*, be assured that sooner or later, *your actions will betray your thoughts*. Each of us wants to be successful. Nobody sets out to make a wrong decision, which means that if, in your heart of hearts, you trust in *your* word and *agenda*, instead of in *God's* Word and *agenda*, your decisions will reflect that. The purpose of *How to De-Program Yourself from All of the Blasphemous Ideas You Learned in Public School* is to assist you in making decisions that will reflect your trust in God's Word and His agenda.

> Nothing could be more pleasing to Satan than for us to be so consumed by speculating on when Jesus will return, that we neglect to do the very things that will lead to his ultimate demise.

Do you think that it could be possible that you make your daily decisions as though you were a puppet on a string? "No way!" you reply. "I am an independent and self-reliant person." While that may well be your personality, consider the fact that none of us has the time to think through every decision we make. Instead we depend upon a *framework* of experience and learning through which we can filter our many daily decisions. However, think back to how you developed your decision making *framework*. After all, it didn't just appear in your brain. Slowly and surely you developed it as you formed friendships and learned which actions were acceptable to them, and you also spent large chunks of your time sitting in a classroom where you were constantly bombarded with ideas and points of view that probably contradicted the ethical values you learned at home. But since they were coming from a respected source of information, you tended to accept them without questioning their validity. As you became a teenager, you began to incorporate these ideas and philosophies into your daily actions and found that your parents were very much out-of-date. So you rebelled against their ethics. Welcome to the wacky worldviews of non-Christian teenagers!

By the time you got to college, you were determined to change the world with your *new-fashioned* ideas, because obviously your parents' *old-fashioned* ideas weren't working very well. But, then as the years passed, you grew tired of rubbing up against ethical brick walls, and discarded your liberal ideas and became a respected conservative member of society by pretty much "going with the flow" of events and not bothering to "rock the boat." However, as you've progressed from conservative child, to liberal young adult to conservative adult, you have maintained your decision-making frame of reference. Your days of picketing the administration building on campus may be a pleasant memory, but your method of arriving at what's good or bad behavior is still in tact. As sad as surrendering your idealism for the blandness of the status quo is, you are now doing something even more inglorious by attempting to live a God-honoring lifestyle while making decisions like a non-Christian! No wonder you are having trouble "putting off your old, unholy garments and putting on new holy garments!" [3]

The basic elements of our decision-making frame of reference have been tightly wound around us by public education. Even many of the administrators of Christian Day schools have received their masters and doctorate degrees from non-Christian colleges and universities. The question is what steps have they taken to eliminate the non-Christian principles of philosophy and psychology that they learned as "gospel" in their God-hating graduate schools? And, are the books they use the same as the ones public schools use? Simply "baptizing" public curriculum with a morning prayer is not in any way, shape or form Christian education.

And what about some of the elements of *your* decision-making frame of reference? Elements that seem to you too correct to question, but which nevertheless, are inaccurate? Things such as:

- A better education will result in better citizens and less crime.
- Everyone should chip in through their taxes so that the civil government can "solve" our social problems.
- We shouldn't bother getting involved in the political process because Satan is "alive and well on planet earth," and any "improvement" we might bring about would only delay Jesus' return.
- Since our pastor is such a nice guy, we can completely trust him to teach us the truth and don't need to take time to meditatively study the Bible.
- Our constitution was written so long ago, that we need to view it as a "living document" that changes with the times.
- We shouldn't be judgmental because all of us are sinners.
- The only thing that really counts is whether a person is saved.

Again, are your decision-making strings being surreptitiously pulled by a "Queen of Diamonds," as was the case for the *Manchurian Candidate*? Or, are they being intentionally pulled by the "King of the Earth," our very own Lord, Savior and King, Jesus Christ?

If any of the items on the following "More or Less" chart appear to go against the grain of what you have been thinking as true, your decision-making frame of reference has some defects that need eliminating. Let's look at a brief explanation of each of them:

M-1: Non-Christians believe that people act in the wrong manner because they are ignorant of how to act in the right manner. Hence, they believe that the *more education* a person has, the better he will act. Listen to what Horace Mann, the godfather of America's public schools, said in 1841:

> *Let the Common School be expanded to its capabilities, let*
> *it be worked with the efficiency of which it is susceptible,*
> *and nine tenths of the crimes in the penal code would become*
> *obsolete; the long catalogue of human ills would be abridged;*
> *men would walk more safely by day; every pillow would be*
> *more inviolate by night; property, life, and character held*
> *by a stronger tenure; all rational hopes respecting the future*
> *brightened.* MICHIGAN EDUCATION REPORT, SUMMER 2005

More or Less

Have you ever wondered why:

M-1: The more money that is spent on public education, the less likely it is to improve?

M-2: The more our taxes are increased to pay for social programs provided by the civil government, the less effective they are?

M-3: The more politicians lie to us in their campaign promises, the less they do when we elect them?

M-4: The more credit we give to Satan for his influence on our culture, the less "Christian" it becomes?

M-5: The more we depend upon other Christians to tell us what the Bible says, the less effective we are in presenting a holy lifestyle to our non-Christian neighbors?

M-6: The more we allow our legislative representatives to tax us, the less personal liberty we have?

M-7: The more we disregard God's absolute cultural ethics, the less court decisions are based upon the law and the more they are based upon legal technicalities?

M-8: The more hours we spend on our careers, the less harmonious our families become?

M-9: The more we spend preaching and teaching that personal salvation is the "single reason" that Jesus died, the less influence we have on our culture?

L-1: The less we instruct our children about the responsibility of every citizen to be self-governing, the more they demand that we provide for them?

L-2: The less our pastors tell us God's prescriptions for improving our culture, the more our culture disintegrates?

L-3: The less we judge ourselves and our neighbors by God's ethical standard, the more we become a disorderly culture?

L-4: The less attention we pay to Jesus' command to not be "unequally yoked" with non-Christians, the more we are influenced by their worldview and lifestyle?

By the 1850s, Mann's idealism was reflected in the popular slogan: "Build a school, close a jail." Here we are, more than a century and a half later and obviously things haven't quite turned out the way the proponents of a mandatory public school system planned. Christians should have known that such platitudes promising a virtually crime free environment were lies, because the Bible says we sin not because we are ignorant, but because we're *sinners*! A better education won't solve our problems, but only a better heart ...a new supernaturally implanted spiritual heart. [4]

M-2: No matter how high taxes are raised to pay the civil government to provide the wide range of social programs, the amount of the needs seems to continue to increase exponentially. The result of this is that with each increase in our taxes, the amount of our personal liberty is decreased, because we are prohibited from spending our money as we would choose. The well-intended efforts by non-Christians are all for naught because God instructs us to handle the social service needs of a community through His self-governing spheres of the individual, family and church. The only responsibilities He commands the state are to defend us against attack, and to police communities so that crime will be reduced and we will have the liberty to live, work, play and raise our families according to God's instructions.

M-3: *Politicians* lie because they don't believe in absolute truth, so for them words have no intrinsic value and are used only to help them accomplish what they want. We should not be surprised at their lies, because by their own definition, *politicians* are liars. What should concern us is to be careful to elect *statesmen* to be our civil rulers so that they will legislate in accordance with what is right, and not according to what is expedient to keeping them in office.

M-4: When we erroneously define Paul's description of Satan as being "the god of this age" [5] to mean that Satan is controlling the actions of both non-Christians *and* Christians, instead of controlling *only* the actions of non-Christians, we are being disobedient as well as disrespectful to Jesus who came to earth to "defeat the works of the devil." [6] Throughout Scripture, we read that we will be blessed when we obey God's Word, and cursed when we don't. [7]

M-5: Being lazy in our approach to Bible study is not an indication that we are recipients of a supernatural heart transplant. The sons of Korah proclaim, "As the deer pants for the water brooks, so pants my soul for You, O God." [8] Jesus tells us that we will keep His commandments "if we love Him." [9] It's pretty hard to keep His commandments when we don't even care enough to find out what they are. Such a disinterest in God will tempt us to seek out Bible teachers who teach us things we want to hear, whether it is true or not! The consequence of such disobedient behavior is that our lifestyles will resemble the chaotic and confusing worldview of our non-Christian neighbors. By attempting to demote and confine God to the inside of our homes and churches, we end up living schizophrenic double lives where we have one set of ethics for the imagined "real world," and another set of ethics for the imagined "religious world." The truth, of course, is that God created a *uni*verse, not a *bi*verse and that His ethics apply to *all* of our situations and circumstances.

M-6: As will be discussed, the civil government is one of the four God-appointed self-governing spheres, but to allow it to usurp responsibilities that God has assigned to the individual, family and church spheres, will result in continuing losses of personal liberties. The reason for this is that instead of following the perfect and self-liberating rules of our Creator, we are forced to follow the personally limiting rules of the state, because the less personal liberty we have, the more the state has, and for non-Christians "power" is synonymous with "success."

M-7: Once we dismiss the idea of absolute ethics, the words in our law books become worthless. This means that winning the case becomes more important than bringing about justice. So lawyers (and judges) look for legal technicalities, rather than the rightness or wrongness of the charges. The comic strip character Pogo once stated, "When everybody is somebody, then nobody is anybody." In the same way, once absolute ethics are dismissed, all ethics are up for grabs and the person with the most resources will usually determine the court's outcome according to his or her preferred agenda.

M-8: It's not nice to fool around with the instructions from the tri-une Godhead. Fathers are to rule their families and oversee the education of their children. It's impossible to do that when he leaves for work before his children get up and returns after they go to bed. Obviously, such behavior not only affects his children, but his relationship with his wife. As the saying goes, "Money can't buy happiness."

M-9: While there is no doubt that our personal salvation is the single most valuable blessing we have, we greatly err if we believe that "being saved," is the only purpose for our life. To the contrary, our salvation is only the *first step* of our walk with Christ. Doesn't Jesus command us to pray that His Father's will "will be done *on earth* as it is in heaven?!"[10] And just who do you suppose will be responsible for bringing about His Father's will if it isn't *us?* Certainly we shouldn't imagine that *non-Christians* will bring it about! While salvation is a gift, and we cannot earn it by our good works, once we are saved, we are expected to produce good works. Doesn't Paul tell us that we are "created in Christ Jesus for good works?" [11] Even Jesus' half-brother James tells us "Faith without works is dead." [12] By incorporating biblical ethics into our situations and circumstances we are enabled to "take dominion" over our culture. [13] Conversely, by not living out our faith, we allow non-Christians to "take dominion" over us.

L-1: The apostle Paul proclaims, "If anyone will not work, neither shall he eat." [14] Certainly this does not mean that we should shove our children out of the house if they are not bringing in some income, but it does teach that we should instruct them that we have worked to produce the revenue to provide for our home, groceries, clothes, and that whatever their dreams are, they should be prepared to work to provide the capital to fund their own lifestyle, and not expect other people to help as in a socialistic economic system. The Bible invented self-governing capitalism.

L-2: During the early years of the American republic, pastors were the most influential people in their community. They preached the whole council of God and prepared their members to incorporate biblical ethics into all of their situations and circumstances. Sadly, too many of today's pastors are more content to incorporate their church to the state, than teach their congregations to incorporate their beliefs into their everyday actions. They timidly and shamefully hide behind the myth that they must incorporate with the state, when the first amendment to the U.S. Constitution says that any church is automatically tax-exempt without incorporating to the state. As will be explained, each of us makes decisions based upon what we trust-in, and pastors who readily incorporate their churches to the state are doing so because it provides them "cover" from having to instruct their congregation in the whole counsel of God's Word. They fear their congregations more than they fear God, so they have no trust in God to grow their church. They believe that only their ingenuity can do that. Their day of reckoning is coming, and so could be your day of reckoning, if you stay in such a church and continue to be deceived by their incomplete and erroneous teaching.

L-3: Our non-Christian neighbors insist that America is a religiously pluralistic country, where all gods are equally irrelevant. This is only natural for them to say, since they neither believe in the triune God of the Bible, nor in absolute truth, which would prove to them that our country did begin as an explicitly Christian country. Early America provided the freedom to worship any god a person wanted, but our civil laws only reflected the Bible's ethics. The pluralism myth has been so widely taught that many Christians conclude that it is wrong for anyone to judge anyone else. The question that must be asked of them, is if that is the case, why did God bother presenting and preserving the Bible for us with all of its information on how to live and govern ourselves?!

L-4: We continue to demonstrate daily that we have a very low regard for God's Word. Hence, we don't think twice about aligning ourselves with non-Christians in various projects.[15] Then we wonder why these relationships don't work out, or why we have been cheated, or taken advantage of. God is not fooling around. His Word is truth, and He means for us to live in accordance to it.

NOTES

1 1 John 3.8
2 Matthew 24.36
3 Colossians 3.9-10
4 Ezekiel 11.19-21; 2 Corinthians 5.17
5 2 Corinthians 4.4
6 1 John 3.8
7 Leviticus 26, Deuteronomy 28
8 Psalm 42.1
9 John 14.15
10 Matthew 6.10
11 Ephesians 2.9
12 James 2.17
13 Genesis 1.26-28
14 2 Thessalonians 3.10
15 2 Corinthians 6.14

PART ONE

**Cutting the Strings
From Your Non-Christian
Puppet Master**

First Cut

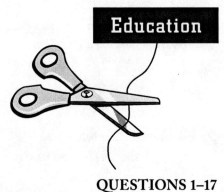

Education

QUESTIONS 1–17

Question 1. What is man?

a. A biological accident.
b. A special creature made by God.

Are we autonomous beings who are capable of determining "good and evil," as Eve attempted to do? Or, are we dependent upon God for giving us the correct wisdom on how to live and govern ourselves? In other words, are we "biological accidents living in a random universe, or special creations of God living in a meaningful and orderly universe? When Eve decided to disobey God by eating of the tree of "the knowledge of good and evil," she was, in essence, saying:

> *It's OK to sin a little, because I am smart enough to control the consequences of my disobedience, as long as it's a "small" sin.*

Today, we might add, "What could be so wrong with a particular decision, when practically everybody I know agrees with my actions?" While such logic may sound very pragmatic, it nevertheless is unbiblical. We cannot evaluate our obedience to God based upon the majority

3

opinion of our friends and neighbors, but only upon the inerrant Word of God. Besides, if God, in fact, gave us a "gene" that makes us smarter than He is, why doesn't He use it to instruct us? The answer is, "He doesn't give us that gene, He kept it for Himself, but He does, indeed, instruct us with it. Paul warns us to:

> *Let no one deceive you with empty words, for because of such things God's wrath comes on those who are disobedient.*
>
> EPHESIANS 5.6

He adds,

> *Do you not know that the wicked will not inherit the kingdom of God?* 1 CORINTHIANS 6.9

As creatures who have been made in the image of God, how are we "imaging" Him by sending our children to schools who hate Him? Schools, which, indeed, are willing to worship any god but Him?

> *Thus says the LORD: "Do not learn the way of the Gentiles; do not be dismayed at the signs of heaven, for the Gentiles are dismayed at them. For the customs of the peoples are futile.*
>
> JEREMIAH 10.2

Paul tells us:

> *Not to be conformed to this world, but be transformed by the renewing of your mind, that you may prove what is that good and acceptable and perfect will of God.* ROMANS 12.2

He adds that we should:

> *Not provoke our children to wrath, but bring them up in the training and admonition of the Lord.* EPHESIANS 6.4

Finally, we must consider the all-important question: "Who's evangelizing, and discipling whom?" No less than Jesus, Himself, warns us of the influence that a teacher will have on his students:

> *A disciple is not above his teacher, but everyone who is*
> *perfectly trained will be like his teacher.* LUKE 6.40

May we make certain that we don't trade, "thus says the Lord," for "thus says man."

Question 2. Should instruction be exclusively based upon absolute truth?

a. No.
b. Yes.

Since God's Word is true and man's word is false, the only way to impart a true education is to base it upon biblical ethics. In terms of ethics, there are only two categories: right and wrong. Jesus, in His Great Commission, commands us to "teach them all things I have commanded you."[1]

Is this what is being taught daily in the public schools? For example, how about the "Fruit of the Spirit: love, joy, peace, long-suffering, kindness, gentleness, self-control."[2] Do you remember receiving any instruction on these during your school days? Of course not, and even when "values" are taught, they are taught as if they are "common sense," and are not given the authority of being based upon God's Word (i.e., the first four of the Ten Commandments). And, speaking of the Ten Commandments, the first one says:

> *You shall have no other gods before Me ... For I, the LORD*
> *your God, am a jealous God..."* EXODUS 20.3,5

It should be clear from this that the public schools are founded upon the principle of breaking this commandment, so our Christian brothers and sisters who say we should not "abandon" the schools, but "reform" them, should be asked: "Upon what basis do you hope to reform them since their leaders will not allow you to bring biblical ethics into the picture?" Long story short, God did not ordain government school, and He won't allow it to be reformed according to man's wisdom.

Whether as an individual, family, community, state or nation, we can ill afford to continue to disregard God's counsel. The words or warning that Jehovah spoke through the prophet Hosea to Israel's Northern Kingdom more than 2,700 years ago apply equally to us in 21st century America:

> *My people are destroyed for lack of knowledge. Because you have rejected knowledge, I also will reject you from being priest for Me; Because you have forgotten the law of your God, I also will forget your children.* HOSEA 4.6

Approximately 400 years earlier Jehovah spoke similar words to Israel's priest Eli:

> *I said indeed that your house and the house of your father would walk before Me forever. But now the LORD says: "Far be it from Me; for those who honor Me I will honor, and those who despise Me shall be lightly esteemed."*
> 1 SAMUEL 2.30

The most fundamental element in education is the fear of the Lord. [3] Fear is the part of one's character that respects God as sovereign. True education must have Christ at its foundation. Education is more than being equipped to read the classics. It includes teaching students to think about what they read. Such thinking must include determining whether the author is describing right or wrong behavior and in order to determine this, a biblical standard of truth must be adhered to.

The question is: "Are public school teachers likely to teach God's Word, or *criticize* it?" The answer should be obvious. Not only will they hide behind the "pluralism" myth that states "All religions take you to heaven," but they will use the "neutrality" myth: "We can't endorse any particular religious belief, because that would cause some students who have different beliefs to be uncomfortable."

The former Professor in Systematic Theology at Princeton Seminary, A. A. Hodge, made these prophetic remarks when the move for public schools were beginning to gain momentum:

> *I am as sure as I am of the fact of Christ's reign that a comprehensive and centralized system of national education, separated from religion, as is now commonly proposed, will prove the most appalling enginery for the propagation of anti-Christian and atheistic unbelief, which this sin-rent world has ever seen... It is capable of exact demonstration that if every party in the State has the right of excluding from the public schools whatever he does not believe to be true, then he that believes the least must give way to him that believes absolutely nothing, no matter how small a minority the atheists or the agnostics may be. It is self-evident that on this scheme, if it is carried out in all parts of the country, the United States' system of national popular education will be the most efficient and wide instrument for the propagation of atheism which the world has ever seen."* [4]

Neither pluralism nor neutrality is a biblical alternative. So, even though public schools profess to be "neutral," we know they are lying, because Genesis 3.15 states that non-Christians "hate" biblical ethics and those who hold to them.

In recognizing the critical importance of basing a curriculum on the absolute truth of the Bible, 17th century British poet John Milton states, "The end of learning is to repair the ruins of our first parents." [5] Our "first parents" were, of course, Adam and Eve and their "ruin" was to attempt to live according to their rules, and not God's rules. Therefore, the only way for us to "repair those ruins," is to base our instruction upon God's Word!

Q. 2 NOTES

1 Matthew 28.20
2 Galatians 5.22
3 Proverbs 9.10

4 A. A. Hodge, "Popular Lectures on Theological Themes," 1889, pp. 281-283
5 *On Education*, John Milton

6 Cited in *Finding Dewey in the Foxfire Approach*, Starnes, Paris, & Stevens, 1999

Public education's idol John Dewey didn't agree with Milton, since he didn't believe there is such a thing as absolute truth. His view was that teachers were not "instructors," but "facilitators" who "guide" students as they try out various pragmatic strategies in an effort to discover "what works for them." [6] Dewey's ideas reflect the non-Christian hallucination that there is no absolute truth, therefore there is no way to absolutely teach students. This is why public schools instruct students to construct their own knowledge according to their own self-serving delusions!

By now, it should be clear that the curriculum of the public (government) school system is 180-degrees different than a Christian curriculum. They teach according to what *they* think, while we should teach according to what *God* thinks.

Question 3. Should teachers instruct students in "basic facts and relative ethics," or in "basic facts and absolute ethics?"

a. Relative Ethics.
b. Absolute Ethics.

In case you've ever considered asking your public school which "values" your children are being taught, so you can judge whether they mirror the values you teach them in the home, the answer is: "We do not teach 'values.' We don't teach students to become a bunch of narrow-minded, bigoted, judgmental citizens!"

As mentioned, the basic premise of the public schools is that there is no such thing as absolute truth, but instead of this meaning that they are "neutral" in their approach to ethics, what this really means is that they have no definitive clue about how a person should live and govern himself. In a manner similar to Dragnet's Sergeant Friday, they "Just want the facts, maim." So, not only will your children not be taught the values you teach them at home, they will be taught to disrespect them because they are indoctrinated with the ungodly idea that there is no way to know whether one person's values are any better or worse than those of another person. Instead of basing their worldview and decision-making upon the Rock of God's Word (MATTHEW 16.18) they base their worldview and lifestyle on the ever-shifting sand of the latest fads of behavior as reflected in the newest opinion polls. In short, an educational curriculum based

8

upon "relative ethics" will ultimately wind up teaching that somehow, the student's experience will tell him what he is experiencing!

Question 4. Should students be taught the principles of self-government, or should they be instructed in how to work in groups to form a "consensus" or a "synthesis" of opinions through "Group Think?"

    a. Consensus and/or synthesis.
    b. Self-government.

Once absolute truth (God's Word) is disrespected and rejected, the only thing left is mass ignorance, better known as democracy. With no definitive principles to guide and direct our behavior, we fall prey to the collective opinion of the group. God's principle of personally liberating self-government is replaced by man's pragmatic principle of tyrannical central governing. Dewey writes, "When it comes to practical matters circumstances compel us to compromise." [1] Socio-psychologist Richard Paul, a disciple of Dewey, adds

> *The classroom environment should be structured so that students feel encouraged to decide for themselves …teachers should shield their students from the pressure to conform to peers or the community [parents, ministers, police, etc.]."* [2]

Such a view of reasoning was popularized by the 18th Century German philosopher Georg Wilhelm Friedrich Hegel whose writings were a major influence upon Karl Marx. Hegel held that person "A" would put forth a thesis, person "B" would present an antithesis, and person "C" would present a synthesis, which would be a win-win situation for all persons. This ungodly reasoning completely omits the idea of there being a transcendent truth from a sovereign, omnipotent Creator God and relegates the bottom line to a person's reasoning as what they feel is right, and what the majority decrees as acceptable behavior. One of the major problems with this type of decision-making is groups don't think, individuals do. In the words of former British Prime Minister Margaret Thatcher, "Consensus is the negation of leadership."

9

The delusion behind such reasoning by non-Christians is that they are omnipotent and sovereign, as though they created themselves by their very thoughts. Such was the position of "The Founder of Modern Philosophy," Rene Descartes, who during the 17th Century proclaimed, "I think therefore I am." However, as Christians we know that God created us, therefore we "are." In addition, we know that we enter this world with an inability to come to the truth of a matter unless the Holy Spirit gives us a new spiritual heart, and writes God's law on it.[3] Instead of bouncing around from church to church until we find someone presenting us a god who fits our imagination of who He is we need only read His clear and easy-to-understand Word. This won't tickle our ears, but it will give us the truth. Listen to the insightful words of Martin Luther

> *Miserable Christians, whose words and faith still depend on the interpretations of men and who expect clarification from them! This is frivolous and ungodly. The Scriptures are common to all, and are clear enough in respect to what is necessary for salvation and are also obscure enough for inquiring minds ... let us reject the word of man.* [4]

Question 5. The teaching of history
a. Actual history should be revised to fit a politicized view that all cultures, at bottom are identical, since all religions are, at bottom, equally irrelevant.
b. The actual history of Western civilization (which is based upon biblical ethics) is contrasted with the history of Eastern civilization (which is based upon non-biblical ethics), because only God's Word gives the correct principles on how to live and govern ourselves.

Q. 4 NOTES
1 John Dewey, *Experience & Education*, p. 17
2 Paul, Richard, *Critical Thinking: What Every Person Needs To Survive In A Rapidly Changing World*, p. 113
3 Jeremiah 31.33; Ezekiel 36.26-27; 2 Corinthians 3.3; Hebrews 8.9-10
4 Martin Luther, *Luther's Works*, V.32, p. 217

Public schools emphasize multi-culturalism at the expense of American/Western culture. The goal is to revise history to fit a politicized view of reality. Without a thorough understanding of the past, we can be easily manipulated. To the non-Christian, the present is all that matters, and without a belief in absolute truth, the events of history are seen as a meaningless repetition of events.

Christian education, which does believe in absolute truths, teaches true history and points out the lessons history has for us, so that we won't make the same mistakes as previous civilizations, and suffer similar consequences. The Christian goal is to teach the student to connect the present with the past.

Question 6. Is there such a thing as a "mind," or are the only things "real" those that can be "touched, seen, smelled, or objectively measured?"

    a. There is no "mind."
    b. There is a "mind."

The public schools don't believe in anything that cannot be "touched, seen, smelled or objectively measured," which is a pretty good reason that the curriculum of the public schools is "mindless." With no fixed standard of truth, the public schools substitute random facts for God's orderly principles.

Christian education emphasizes the importance of our mind, but stresses the necessity of developing the "mind of Christ," (PHILIPPIANS 2.5) whereby we re-think God's thoughts before making our daily decisions.

This means that subjects can be taught, discussed and debated in a moral framework with a fixed standard of right and wrong that can be universally applied so students learn that their actions will result in either good or bad consequences.

Question 7. Should the curriculum be child-centered, or Christ-centered?

    a. Child-centered.
    b. Christ-centered.

Public schools educate students according to man's wisdom, which is the opposite of how teachers are commanded to teach them. King Solomon admonishes us to "acknowledge God in all of our ways, and He shall direct our paths." (PROVERBS 3.6) Therefore to present any instruction that doesn't "acknowledge God" is to disobey our commanded duty. The reason that public schools ignore God's counsel in their instruction is that their top priority is to eliminate the Christian worldview through a systematic curriculum approach that can be best described as "Christian ethic cleansing."

The ungodly *child-centered* curriculum focuses on self-esteem, social promotion, "doing our own thing," and bringing glory and honor to ourselves. In contrast to this, the *Christ-centered* approach focuses on the truth that we are born sinners and need His salvation so we can image Him by bringing glory and honor to Him in all we do.

While Christian education is the acquisition of true wisdom and true knowledge, non-Christian educators, who don't know what truth is, (or even if it exists), can do no better with their definition than to say it is "socializing students." We must realize that we have a wonderful and most meaningful *truth* to present to our children. It's so much better than the *fiction* the state-mandated schools are presenting.

God's four self-governing spheres (Individual, Family, Church and State) and the responsibilities of each, should be thoroughly explained so that students will not only know their accountabilities to God, but also know the personal liberty that results from this divine division of labor since no God—ordained sphere should attempt to usurp the responsibilities of the others.

Reason, logic, literature rhetoric, history, capitalism, should be included in the curriculum, plus the following topics:

- Walk in the Spirit: Galatians 5.16-20
- Put on the Whole Armor of God: Ephesians 6.10-20
- Godly Behavior in the Home: Colossians 3.18-25
- Walk in Christ's "Light": Ephesians 5.18-24
- How to Defend the Faith: 2 Corinthians 10.5-6; 1 Peter 3.15
- The Sermon on the Mount Principles of Behavior: Matthew 5.1-27

- Responsibilities and Attitude toward Civil Rulers: Romans 13.1-7
- Loving our Enemies: Matthew 5.38-48

When in the public school curriculum will children be taught these pivotal character traits?!

Question 8. Students should be taught how to bring "glory and honor to God" in everything they do.

    a. False.
    b. True.

While it has been pointed out that one of the distinctive differences between a public school (false) education, and a Christian (true) education is that the former is concerned about how individuals can bring glory and honor to themselves, while the latter is concerned with bringing glory and honor to our Lord Savior and King, Jesus Christ.

This eternal distinction between how Christians and non-Christians should live was pointed out by the prophet Jeremiah more than 2,500 years ago:

> *Then the LORD said to me, "Proclaim all these words in the cities of Judah and in the streets of Jerusalem, saying: 'Hear the words of this covenant and do them. For I earnestly exhorted your fathers in the day I brought them up out of the land of Egypt, until this day, rising early and saying, Obey My voice.'"* **JEREMIAH 11.6-7; 23.21-22; 25.5-7**

It should be noteworthy to us that the word "hear" is synonymous with the word "do." Christian teachers, therefore, should be concerned with what their students are doing as a result of the instruction they are receiving. Of course, this lesson extends to each of us. It can probably be safely said that most of us read too much and reflect too little. Since the way we live reflects the way we think about God, it is important that the teacher know what his students are thinking about God.

13

Question 9. Christian education is

   a. An optional add-on to a child's worldview.

   b. It is an essential part of The Great Commission.
      (Matthew 22.37; 28.18-20)

Public schools were established to de-Christianize America so that their graduates would image the worldview and lifestyle of Satan. Yes, upstanding, law-abiding citizens are among the public school graduates, and yes many of them profess to be Christians. But, measure any lifestyle issue and compare the statistics of Christians with non-Christians and you will find no discernible difference in their behaviors. Crime, divorce rate, drug usage, gambling, you name it and you will find it just as prevalent among those inside the church as you will among those outside the church. The only discernible difference is in what those who profess to be Christians say they believe, and those who don't profess to be Christians say they believe. Yet, the difference among what Christians and non-Christians say seems to be as transparent as the difference between what Republicans and Democrats say.

Ultimately, there are only two possible answers to this dilemma. Either a well-meaning person is not a Christian, and doesn't know it because the spineless church in which he is a member prefers for its congregation to "feel good" about themselves, rather than know that they are worthless sinners who need to repent and turn their lives over to God who will then lead them in the truth. Or, a person is a Christian, but his worldview and lifestyle has been subverted by all of the blasphemous instruction he has learned in the public schools.

John Dewey, the "god" of the public school curriculum, makes his agenda very clear by stating that teachers are "the prophets of the true God and the usherer of the true kingdom of God." In case you're wondering why the public schools are so anti-American, Karl Marx provides the answer: "Take away the heritage of a people and they are easily persuaded." Even President Abraham Lincoln saw the critical consequence of what is being taught: "The philosophy of the classroom shall become the philosophy of the government in the next generation."

Approximately 400 years ago, the Protestant Reformer Martin Luther made the following prophetic observation:

14

I am much afraid that schools will prove to be great gates of Hell unless they diligently labor in explaining the Holy Scriptures, engraving them in the hearts of youth. I advise no one to place his child where the Scriptures do not reign paramountly. Every institution in which men are not increasingly occupied with the Word of God must become corrupt.

Needless to say, the education a person receives becomes the framework for his worldview, so we are doing a most severe disservice to our children by sending them into the courts of hell for six hours a day for 12+ years. If you doubt this, ask yourself how you're doing so far on this Personal Worldview Checkup. Even though its early in the Checkup, you've probably already had several "hmmm moments," and the question is, "Why would you want to force your child to have to learn all of the wrong (untrue) things you did, only to have to unlearn them later in life?" Why not give them a jumpstart on their service to Jesus by having them learn the truth from the beginning?

Question 10. How does a person become "wise?"

    a. Be a good student; go to the best schools and sit under the best teachers, and learn from our experiences.

    b. Study the Word of God and incorporate its ethics into our worldview and lifestyle.

In the Old Testament we read where "the Word of the LORD came" to the prophets, and they, in turn proclaimed that word to the intended listeners. This is why Isaiah exclaims:

> *How beautiful upon the mountains are the feet of him who brings good news, who proclaims peace, who brings glad tidings of good things, who proclaims salvation, who says to Zion, "Your God reigns!"*   **ISAIAH 52.7**

Of course, today, we have God's Word revealed to us on the pages of our Bible, so there is no need to wait for the "Word of the Lord" to come to us with His instructions on how to live. This means that in order for

15

us to find out what God would have us to do with our life, we need to pick up the Bible and begin seriously reading it and then thinking about how what we have just read can be incorporated into our worldview and lifestyle.

We also read in the Old Testament of Jehovah bringing judgment upon the disobedient Jews through invading armies, storms, and famines. Approximately 2,800 years ago, Jehovah announces through the prophet Amos the coming of the most terrible famine imaginable: a famine of God's Word.

> *"Behold, the days are coming," says the Lord GOD, "That I will send a famine on the land, not a famine of bread, nor a thirst for water, but of hearing the words of the LORD. They shall wander from sea to sea, and from north to east; they shall run to and fro, seeking the word of the LORD, but shall not find it.* AMOS 9.11-12

The reason the threat of a famine of God's Word is so terrible is because without it, we would have no way of knowing how to live and govern ourselves. A famine of food will result in physical death, but it won't prevent a person from living for God while he remains alive. But a famine of God's Word would result in people merely existing for themselves with no purpose or direction to their lifestyles. Of course, this is not to mention that a physical death that is not preceded by an encounter with God's Word will result in eternal torment in hell. King Solomon makes it perfectly clear: The only successful way to live successfully is to

> *Trust in the LORD with all your heart, and lean not on your own understanding; in all your ways acknowledge Him, and He shall direct your paths.* PROVERBS 3.5-6

Solomon adds that "there is more hope for a fool" than for the person who is "wise in his own eyes." [1] He also states "there is more hope for a fool" than for the person who neglects to take the time to compare a potential decision with biblical ethics. [2] Luke provides an example of this kind of ungodly thinking.

16

The Pharisee stood and prayed thus with himself, "God,
I thank You that I am not like other men—extortioners,
unjust, adulterers, or even as this tax collector. I fast twice a
week; I give tithes of all that I possess."   LUKE 18.11-12

Such people are self-satisfied with their ethical behavior and see no need repent and give their whole heart to following Jesus. This results in their "Christianity" being "lukewarm, and neither cold nor hot," which will cause Jesus to "vomit them out of His mouth." Jesus gives this warning to the first century's church at Laodicea (and to anyone else with their worldview):

Because you say, "I am rich, have become wealthy, and have
need of nothing"—and do not know that you are wretched,
miserable, poor, blind, and naked —I counsel you to buy
from Me gold refined in the fire, that you may be rich; and
white garments, that you may be clothed, that the shame of
your nakedness may not be revealed; and anoint your eyes
with eye salve, that you may see. As many as I love, I rebuke
and chasten. Therefore be zealous and repent. Behold, I
stand at the door and knock. If anyone hears My voice and
opens the door I will come in to him and dine with him, and
he with Me.   REVELATION 3.16-20

In Scripture, the word "wisdom" is synonymous with the Holy Spirit being in a person's heart. [3] Unless and until that happens non-Christians only have an accumulation of random facts, with no way to relate them to an over-arching view of "truth." In other words, they are in desperate need of some Supernatural Glue* to hold together all of the random facts they accumulate in their education, because without that they have no wisdom. Our prayer should be the same as King Solomon's

Now give me wisdom and knowledge, that I may go out and
come in before this people; for who can judge this great people
of Yours?"   2 CHRONICLES 1.10

17

Since "all the treasures of wisdom and knowledge" are hid in Jesus, [4] and since He "gives it to all who ask Him," [5] we should not cease to ask that He give wisdom not only to us, but to others, as well.[6] Job's friend, Elphaz, minced no words when he questioned him:

> *Are you the first man who was born? Or were you made before the hills? Have you heard the counsel of God? Do you limit wisdom to yourself? What do you know that we do not know?* JOB 15.7-9

In Job's discourse on wisdom, He asks:

> *But where can wisdom be found? And where is the place of understanding?* JOB 28.12

He later answers his own question

> *Behold, the fear of the Lord, that is wisdom, and to depart from evil is understanding.*
> JOB 28.28; ALSO PSALM 110.10;
> PROVERBS 1.7; 9.10; 15.33

Job was soon to discover that whenever you ask God a question, brace yourself for an unvarnished answer:

> *Then the LORD answered Job out of the whirlwind, and said: "Who is this who darkens counsel by words without knowledge? Now prepare yourself like a man; I will question you, and you shall answer Me. "Where were you when I laid the foundations of the earth? Tell Me, if you have understanding. Who determined its measurements? Surely you know! Or who stretched the line upon it? To what were its foundations fastened? Or who laid its cornerstone, when the morning stars sang together, and all the sons of God*

---

* See "Parents Resource Page," in the Fifth Cut.

18

*shouted for joy? Who has put wisdom in the mind? Or who
has given understanding to the heart? Who can number the
clouds by wisdom? Or who can pour out the bottles of heaven.*
                                        JOB 38.1-7, 36-37

King Solomon states that the goal of biblical wisdom is to provide
man with the knowledge of how to conform his worldview and lifestyle
to the principles of God's Word.

*My son, if you receive my words, and treasure my commands
within you, So that you incline your ear to wisdom, and
apply your heart to understanding; yes, if you cry out for
discernment, and lift up your voice for understanding, if you
seek her as silver, and search for her as for hidden treasures;
then you will understand the fear of the LORD, and find the
knowledge of God.*   PROVERBS 2.1-5

Solomon continues by pointing to the benefits of Godly wisdom:

*When wisdom enters your heart, and knowledge is pleasant
to your soul, discretion will preserve you; understanding will
keep you, to deliver you from the way of evil, from the man
who speaks perverse things, from those who leave the paths
of uprightness to walk in the ways of darkness; who rejoice in
doing evil, and delight in the perversity of the wicked.*
                                        PROVERBS 2.10-14

In light of this, does it come as a surprise that Solomon's conclusion
is for everyone to "get wisdom, and in our getting, get understanding?" [7]
Who among us would not want to re-think the thoughts of our Creator
God who "changes the times and the seasons. Who removes kings and
raises up kings. Who gives wisdom to the wise and knowledge to those
who have understanding." [8] Clearly, not to take advantage of His perfect
counsel when making our decisions, is to act the fool. [9]

Of course, non-Christians will accuse us of being hopelessly
outdated by making our daily decisions conform to God's Word, and

instructing our children to do so, but as the saying goes, "the proof is in the pudding," and a person's "wisdom" will be justified by the results it brings.[10] God gives His perfect, inerrant and unchanging Word that decisions based upon biblical ethics will be successful. What assurance can a non-Christian provide that decisions based upon the ever-changing winds of the latest public opinion poll will lead to successful results?!

Question 11. What is the purpose of an education?

    a. Prepare us for a paycheck.
    b. Prepare us for life.

If Karl Marx were right in proclaiming, "Man is the creature of the natural universe only," then it could be said that the purpose of education is to prepare the student for a paycheck. After all, if we were merely biological accidents, why shouldn't we turn to material possessions in an effort to achieve happiness and satisfaction? Fortunately, we are much more than "economic units," or "Worker Bees," who have no substantial purpose for our existence other than being tax payers to fund the whims of tyrannical central governing politicians.

Instead of being biological accidents we are special creations of God who have been mercifully rescued from our sins to bring glory and honor to Him in all we think, say and do. This is why the overall purpose of education should be to prepare students for life, by explaining their need to repent and live according to God's rules, instead of according to their rules. 17th Century British poet John Milton provides this definition of the purpose of an education:

> *The end of all knowledge is to know God, and out of that knowledge to love and imitate Him.* [1]

Q. 10 NOTES

1   Proverbs 26.12
2   Proverbs 29.20
3   Exodus 28.3; 31.3, 6; 35.26, 31; 36.2; 1 Kings 4.29; Ezra 7.25; Proverbs 2.6; 1 Corinthians 12.8; Ephesians 1.17; 2 Peter 3.15
4   Colossians 2.3
5   James 1.5
6   Colossians 1.9
7   Proverbs 4.7
8   Daniel 2.20-21
9   Jeremiah 8.8-9; Proverbs 14.8
10 Matthew 11.19

Paul tells us that "all the treasures of wisdom and knowledge" are hidden in Christ, and that we should be "rooted and built up in Him and established in the faith." [2]

In addition to being taught biblical ethics, students should be instructed in how to incorporate them into their daily decision-making so they, in effect, will be "missionaries" to their non-Christian neighbors. The psalmist Asaph vividly describes the consequences of a generation that does not receive a Christian education:

> *Give ear, O my people, to my law; incline your ears to the*
> *words of my mouth. I will open my mouth in a parable; I will*
> *utter dark sayings of old, which we have heard and known,*
> *and our fathers have told us. We will not hide them from*
> *their children, telling to the generation to come the praises of*
> *the LORD, and His strength and His wonderful works that*
> *He has done. For He established a testimony in Jacob, and*
> *appointed a law in Israel, which He commanded our fathers,*
> *that they should make them known to their children; that the*
> *generation to come might know them, the children who*
> *would be born, that they may arise and declare them to their*
> *children, that they may set their hope in God, and not forget*
> *the works of God, but keep His commandments; and may not*
> *be like their fathers, a stubborn and rebellious generation, a*
> *generation that did not set its heart aright, and whose spirit*
> *was not faithful to God.*
>
> *The children of Ephraim, being armed and carrying*
> *bows, turned back in the day of battle. They did not keep the*
> *covenant of God; they refused to walk in His law, and forgot*
> *His works and His wonders that He had shown them.*
>
> PSALM 78.1-11

This is exactly the scenario for which the leaders of public schools are striving. They make no bones about their purpose, but for one reason or another, Christian parents aren't paying attention. The following two quotes should raise many red flags for Christian parents:

I think the most important factor leading us to a secular society has been the educational factor. Our schools may not teach Johnny to read properly, but the fact that Johnny is in school until he is 16 tends to lead toward the elimination of religious superstition. The average child now acquires a high school education, and this militates against Adam and Eve and all other myths of alleged history. [3]

Our goal is behavioral change. The majority of our youth still hold to the values of their parents, and if we do not recognize this pattern, or we do not re-socialize them to accept change, our society may decay. [4]

In stark contrast to the false education received in the public schools, whereby students are systematically trained in error and unrighteousness, a true education will shape the student's views of people and current events, as well as defining their priorities for living. In other words, they will learn who they are, what their purpose is, whose they are. Dr. Glen Shultz describes the difference between a Christian education and the education received in Public schools.

Schools were established in order to provide support to the biblical values and beliefs of the home. The school was to enable the child to be able to read the Bible and think from a biblical perspective. As schools became state controlled, the

Q. 11 NOTES

1 Milton, John, *Paradise Lost*, (Penguin Classics [1667])

2 Colossians 2.3, 7

3 Blanshard, Paul, *The Humanist* (March-April, 1976), in D.L. Cuddy, "Are Secular Humanists Seeking Our Children's Minds? You Bet," *Commercial Appeal*, August 5, 1986 (Memphis, TN), cited in *Kingdom Education: God's Plan for Educating Future Generations*, Dr. Glen Shultz, (LifeWay Press, 2002), pp.98-99.

4 Goodland, John, "Schooling for the Future" in Roland M. Travis, "Should the Children of God Be Educated in the Temple of Baal?" *Presbyterian Journal*, Feb. 13, 1985, (Ashville, NC: God's World Publications, 1985), cited in *Kingdom Education: God's Plan for Educating Future Generations*, Dr. Glen Shultz, (LifeWay, 2002), p.99

5 Shultz, Dr. Glen, *Kingdom Education: God's Plan for Educating Future Generations*, (LifeWay, 2002), p.96

emphasis changed from supporting the values of the home to instilling the values of the government into the lives of the students. [5]

Christian education instills truth, absolute meaning, and develops unique self-governing individuals. Since public schools neither teach nor believe in absolute truths, they foolishly attempt to promote a "value-free" and "judgment-free" education whereby all ideas are equally accepted with the end goal of a milque-toast lifestyle wherein a person neither stands for anything, nor strives for excellence in his behavior because doing so could result in "hurting someone's feelings." This self-centered, self-serving curriculum of man is opposed by the others-centered, others-serving curriculum of God.

Question 12. Who is responsible for the education of children?

a. The state.
b. Parents.

Children "are a heritage from the LORD," [1] therefore we should "train them up in the way they should go." [2] Moses instructs fathers to "Command your children to be careful to observe all the words of this law." [3] The psalmist Asaph adds

> *[The commandments] Which we have heard and known, and our fathers have told us. We will not hide them from their children, telling to the generation to come the praises of the LORD, and His strength and His wonderful works that He has done. For He established a testimony in Jacob, and appointed a law in Israel, which He commanded our fathers, that they should make them known to their children; that the generation to come might know them, the children who would be born, that they may arise and declare them to their children, that they may set their hope in God, and not forget the works of God, but keep His commandments; and may not be like their fathers, a stubborn and rebellious generation, a*

generation that did not set its heart aright, and whose spirit was not faithful to God. PSALM 78.3-8

Christian education is no more an add-on to our children's worldview than a profession of faith is an "add-on" to one's lifestyle. The total make up of a person includes an on-going Christian education, as well as an all-encompassing worldview. There are no part-time Christians, and there are no part-time Christian students. The more complete our Christian education is, the better equipped we are to carry out Jesus' Great Commission. [4] This is why we must stop sending our children "down to Egypt" to get educated.[5] The prophet Isaiah instructs us that we are not to "strengthen ourselves in the strength of Pharaoh, or to trust in the shadow of Egypt." [6] Isaiah continues to describe the futility in trusting in the knowledge, wisdom and strength of man.

> *Woe to those who go down to Egypt for help, and rely on horses, Who trust in chariots because they are many, and in horsemen because they are very strong, but who do not look to the Holy One of Israel, nor seek the LORD! ...*
> *Now the Egyptians are men, and not God; and their horses are flesh, and not spirit. When the LORD stretches out His hand, Both he who helps will fall, and he who is helped will fall down; they all will perish together.* ISAIAH 31.1, 3

We can't be effective servants for Christ in His Kingdom if we don't see the world as He sees it. This is why we should not subject ourselves or our children to a non-Christian curriculum, even though well-meaning Christian teachers may be teaching it. The reason for this is because it is not concerned with the truth, but rather with error. Unfortunately, a lot of Christians are also apparently not concerned with the truth outside of their homes and churches because they're too busy conforming to the worldview and lifestyles of their non-Christian neighbors (Egypt). God makes no bones about it: the education of our children is the sole responsibility of fathers.

And these words which I command you today shall be in your heart. You shall teach them diligently to your children, and shall talk of them when you sit in your house, when you walk by the way, when you lie down, and when you rise up.

DEUTERONOMY 6.6-7

This does not mean that this responsibility of fathers cannot be delegated to mothers to home school, or to Christian day schools. But on Judgment Day, Jesus is not going to hold mothers, or the Christian day school teachers accountable for the education of our children, but fathers. Our children do not belong to the state. They don't even belong to us. They are on-loan from God to us and we have no biblical choice but to educate them according to His demands! There is no escaping the truth that families, in general, and fathers in particular, are accountable to God for the education of their children.

This also means that in instances where there is no "father," in the home (through death, desertion or divorce) the church "family" should assist the mother in filling this role. In cases where a family cannot afford the tuition to a Christian day school and is not able to Home School, the church must step up to its responsibility. This principle is first brought out in Job where Eliphaz the Temanite accuses Job of "sending widows away empty" [7] and being partial to the wealthy. Regardless of whether Eliphaz was correct in his judgment of Job, his criticism points out the concern that widows are supposed to be looked after. [8] There is no Scriptural support for the idea of having the civil government educate our children, much less indoctrinate them with a false religion.

Just in case you may still be straddling the fence, consider these statistics from our government schools:

- The goal of public (government) schools is to make most of the graduates "wards of the state" by being dependent upon civil government handouts. America is near the bottom in academic performance among industrialized nations. Approximately 40 percent of graduates are functionally illiterate, and of those who go to college, approximately 42 percent have to take remedial courses.

25

- The National Education Association says, "acceptance of homo-sexuality should be the goal for educators."
- Nearly six million children are being given Ritalin or other psychotropic drugs to make them easier to handle.
- Births to unmarried girls, 10 to 15 years old, are up 500 percent since 1968.
- The U.S. Education Department showed that 4.5 million students were victims of sexual misconduct by teachers in the past decade.
- Since 1965 illegal drug use among youth is up 6,000 percent.
- Nationwide there were nearly 1.5 million violent incidents in public schools in the 1999-2000 school year.

To think that we can slip our disobedience by Jesus is to imagine that we don't live in a cause-and-effect world: A world in which Jesus rewards obedience and punishes disobedience. It is also the same as admitting that the Book of Judges makes a mistake by warning us that we will "reap what we sow." [9] Such creative thinking on our part will lead to disastrous consequences. The following words, written approximately 3,500 years ago, describe how all went well for Israel during the obedient days of Joshua, but when the generation that followed Joshua was not careful to instruct their children to live according to God's Word, things became very bad, very quickly. May we all pay particular attention to these inspired words:

> *So the people served the LORD all the days of Joshua, and all the days of the elders who outlived Joshua, who had seen all the great works of the LORD which He had done for Israel. Now Joshua the son of Nun, the servant of the LORD, died when he was one hundred and ten years old. And they buried him within the border of his inheritance at Timnath Heres, in the mountains of Ephraim, on the north side of Mount*

Q. 12 NOTES

1 Psalm 127.3
2 Proverbs 22.6
3 Deuteronomy 32.46
4 Matthew 22.37; 28.18-20
5 Genesis 26.2; Exodus 3.8; 32.7

6 Isaiah 30.2
7 Job 4
8 Acts 2.44-45; 4.34-35; Matthew 23.14; Mark 12.40; Luke 20.47
9 Hosea 8.7

*Gaash. When all that generation had been gathered to their
fathers, another generation arose after them who did not
know the LORD nor the work which He had done for Israel.*

*Then the children of Israel did evil in the sight of the
LORD, and served the Baals; and they forsook the LORD
God of their fathers, who had brought them out of the land of
Egypt; and they followed other gods from among the gods of
the people who were all around them, and they bowed down
to them; and they provoked the LORD to anger. They forsook
the LORD and served Baal and the Ashtoreths. And the
anger of the LORD was hot against Israel. So He delivered
them into the hands of plunderers who despoiled them; and
He sold them into the hands of their enemies all around, so
that they could no longer stand before their enemies.*

JUDGES 2.7-14

Question 13. Where is the best place to educate students?

a. In a structured classroom.
b. Wherever we "sit, walk, lie down, and rise up?" (Deut. 6.7)

As we've seen, parents should be "educating" everywhere, at all times.[1]
To rationalize that we can fulfill our obligation to "train up our children
in the way they should go" by sending them to God-hating government
schools is to go on a fool's errand. It is to break the commandment of
"having no fellowship with the unfruitful works of darkness, but rather
expose them." [2] Have we forgotten Paul's warning that

A little leaven leavens the whole lump.

I CORINTHIANS 5.6; GALATIANS 5.9

Or his counsel to:

*Not be yoked together with unbelievers. For what do
righteousness and wickedness have in common? Or what
fellowship can light have with darkness? What harmony is
there between Christ and Belial? What does a believer have*

*in common with an unbeliever? What agreement is there
between the temple of God and idols? For we are the temple
of the living God. As God has said: "I will live with them and
walk among them, and I will be their God, and they will be
my people."*

*"Therefore come out from them and be separate, says the
Lord. Touch no unclean thing, and I will receive you." I will
be a Father to you, and you will be my sons and daughters,
says the Lord Almighty.*   2 CORINTHIANS 6.11-18

These verses are not instructing us to withdraw from the world, but to refrain from associating with people who live according to a non-Christian worldview. In doing this we will be kept from the temptation to be influenced by non-Christian ways, and we'll also be able to provide a reason to them for why we live the way we do. This does not mean we won't maintain contact with non-Christians (to evangelize), but simply that we won't participate with them in their non-Christian agenda. Instead of having them "leaven" us, we will be "leavening" them. The esteemed 20th century theologian B.B. Warfield writes:

*In all our association with unbelievers, we, as Christian
men, are to furnish the standard, and we are to stand
by our Christian standard, in the smallest particular,
unswervingly.*[3]

Warfield continues:

*The reason, then, why a Christian must not take on himself
the alien yoke of unbelievers is just because it is to him alien;
he is in and of himself, because a believer in Christ and,
therefore, a temple of the living God, a different, a contrary,
an opposite kind of being from the unbeliever; and it is,
therefore, incongruous in the same yoke with an unbeliever,
to seek to live on the same plane, or consent to order his
life or to determine questions of conduct by his standards, in
any degree whatever.*[4]

28

Paul follows this theme by urging us to:

> *Let no one deceive you with empty words, for because of these things the wrath of God comes upon the sons of disobedience. Therefore do not be partakers with them.* EPHESIANS 5.6-7

For those who say, "We have weekly devotionals in our home, plus our children attend youth groups at church, plus their weekly Sunday school class and worship services, so they are being taught 'the truth,'" let's ask them to smell the coffee and tell us if they really believe that three or four hours of biblical instruction each week can contend with 30 hours of non-Christian indoctrination. They may also be asked to respond to the following words from Puritan Pastor Thomas Brooks:

> *How hard is it to keep the commandment of labor among the slothful, or the commandment of diligent among the negligent, or that of liberality among the covetous, or that of humility among the ambitious, or that of love among the malicious, or that of union among the contentious, or that of chastity among the lascivious, or that of righteousness among the unrighteous, or that of faithfulness among the unfaithful, or that of fruitfulness among the unfruitful, or that of thankfulness among the unthankful, or that of faith among the doubtful.* [5]

Question 14. Should teachers get to know the worldview of their students, or should they stick to the curriculum?

a. Stick to the curriculum.
b. Learn the Worldview of the students.

This may be beginning to sound like a broken record, but since the curriculum of the public schools has no way of determining anything

Q. 13 NOTES

1 Deuteronomy 6.6-7
2 Ephesians 5.11

3 Warfield, B.B., *Faith And Life*, (Banner of Truth Trust, 1916, 1974), p.249
4 Warfield, ibid., Faith, p.251
5 Brooks, ibid., Works, p.67

definitive, it is not concerned with the worldviews of its students. The promoters of false education, therefore, have no option but to stick to a strict presentation of the curriculum and leave it up to the students to "connect the dots" as to how to fit the subject matter into their lifestyles, and to figure out how to make heads or tails of it.

On the other hand, Christian educators promote an education based upon the truth and know that the biblical worldview makes more sense than any other worldview. So in the process of forming the minds of their students to love and serve their Creator, they want to know how their students view the world. Knowing this helps them make any needed biblical adjustments and corrections in the student's worldview. Christian teachers also know that their calling is to not merely to teach a trade, but to cultivate the student's mind with biblical ethics so he can incorporate them into whatever vocation he pursues. This includes explaining how to re-think God's thoughts and develop their reasoning for conversations with non-Christians.

Obviously, the first step in this process is to describe what a Christian worldview is and to impress upon the students the vital truth that God's Word is completely sufficient for framing all of their daily decisions, so that they will not only have a cause to study the Bible, but to obey it's instructions! In doing this, they are helping "equip" our children to live-out their faith. (EPHESIANS 4.12)

Question 15. Teachers should pray with and for their students.

a. False.
b. True.

Since Christian teachers view their students as special creatures of God, rather than biological accidents or economic units to support the state, there is every reason to pray for and with their students. We should pray for their salvation, and that they would not only accurately understand what they are being taught, but how to incorporate it into their daily lifestyle. With the knowledge that 70 percent of their Christian friends who go through the public schools will stop going to church when they graduate from high school, [1] we should pray that our children will be a positive influence on them. King Solomon offers us confidence in this regard: "Train a child in the way he should go, and when he is old he will not depart from it." [2] This is a warning as well as a promise, and Solomon's point is that it is very difficult to overcome 30 hours of ungodly "training" each week with two or three hours of Sunday School, youth group and a sermon.

In addition, we should pray about the daily situations and circumstances our children will encounter and that they will not be negatively affected with the worldview of public school students who believe that

- marriage doesn't necessarily mean "one man and one woman"
- extra-marital sex is morally acceptable
- abortion is morally acceptable
- America was founded by religious "pluralists"
- socialism is preferable to capitalism
- the universe and life "just happened"
- the Bible is untrue
- the West—and America, especially—have been guilty of genocidal crimes against every culture we have come in contact with and that these crimes have flowed essentially from its belief in Christianity

If your children are in the public schools, and if this doctrinal list of teaching points isn't troubling enough, perhaps you can convince yourself to withdraw them by asking: "What will your child learn today in public school about how to bring glory and honor to our Lord, Savior and King, Jesus Christ?" By now there should be no doubt that unless the answer is "Nothing," the teacher will be fired immediately if not sooner. (Regardless of what your Christian friends who work in the public schools tell you.) The instruction that *all* public schools are providing is not "value-free" or "neutral." Think about it. Do you know anyone who is unbiased or neutral about *anything*? Just as Christian teachers bias their instruction toward the most holy God, so do public schools require their teachers (even Christian teachers!) to bias their instruction toward sinful man.

Q. 15 NOTES
1 George Barna Research, www.barna.org
2 Proverbs 22.6

Question 16. When it comes to the issue of Christian education

   a. Pastors should approach this in a pragmatic manner by not ad dressing it because it is a divisive issue and they will lose members (or their job!). Besides many churches have members (and including officers) who are affiliated with the public schools and/ or who send their children to the public schools.

   b. Pastors should approach this in a pious manner by obeying God's clear commands and thoroughly explain the sin of sending Christian children to schools that hate God and promote the worship only of false religions. (DEUTERONOMY 6.4-7; ISAIAH 36.9; 2 CORINTHIANS 6.14; MATTHEW 15.14, ETC.) In the process of doing this, the Pastors are providing a testimony to their members that they practice what they preach by trusting-in and relying-upon God's sovereign control of His creation to honor our obedience and curse our disobedience.

It could be argued that the *worst* sin American Christians are committing is not the ineptness in which they approach the abortion holocaust, but their decision to continue to send their children to the God-hating public school system where they are indoctrinated for 12+ years in a non-Christian worldview.

Should we "Exit" our children from public schools? I would hope by now that the answer is a clear, unhesitating and loud, "YES!" This decision, like any decision we make, boils down to whose opinion we trust the most: God's or man's.

There is no biblical excuse for pastors and denomination leaders to justify their decisions based exclusively upon pragmatic reasons (i.e., "I have public school teachers and administrators in my congregation," or "This is a divisive issue that will cost us members if we obey God," etc.). None of us is called to be pragmatic. We are called to be pious, and our decisions need to have a "pious bias" if we expect for God to bless our actions and decisions.

Should not the concern from pastors and denominational leaders be "we are losing favor with God and putting ourselves at risk to receive His wrath by not withdrawing our children (and ourselves as teachers and administrators) from the public schools?!"

While we are quick to admit that "God's Word is truth," we are slow to make our daily decisions conform to His Word. We are thus living as though we have to "help out" our God by making correct decisions that He has not considered! By doing this we are limiting our answers to solutions that are not "true," and solutions which, regardless of the amount of time, effort and good intentions spent implementing them, will be unsuccessful, because they don't conform to God's will. In addition, we are demonstrating to our non-Christian neighbors that Jesus is culturally irrelevant!

Does Jesus not command us in His Lord's prayer to pray that His Father's will "be done on earth as it is in heaven?[2] Then how "on earth" do we expect to carry out that command by implementing "our will" through solutions that are based upon "our intentions, instead of God's intentions? When God tells us to "come now and let us reason together,"[3] He is not suggesting that we match wits with Him, but rather that we re-think His thoughts. David clarifies this process by stating "in Your light we see light."[4] As damaging as it may be to our inflated and arrogant egos, we don't need to think of correct answers to our cultural problems. God already has and they are on the pages of His inerrant Word for everyone to see!

To imagine for one second that our wisdom is on a par with God's is probably the farthest thought from any Christian's mind, yet we continue to approach cultural issues in ways that are identical to non-Christians by only applying our thoughts. Such a reasoning process is perfectly understandable for non-Christians, since they don't believe in God, but we have no excuse for such decision-making. Jesus correctly tells us "If the blind lead the blind, both shall fall into the pit," [5] and our culture, which is being primarily influenced by non-Christians is rapidly moving toward

Instead of wasting time on peripheral issues about whether creationism is taught along with evolution, or attempting to get prayer re-instated, or to eliminate the pro-homosexual curriculum, we should concentrate on the core issue of how disrespectful, and dishonoring it is to our Lord, Savior and King, Jesus Christ to ignore His clear instructions on not being "unequally yoked" with non-Christians. [1]

falling into the pit. Our culture is headed in this direction because the "blind" are not only leading the "blind," but also those of us who have been supernaturally "enlightened" by the Holy Spirit!

Each of us should demand from our church officers a biblical explanation of why all children of church members should not exit the public schools. If this is not forth coming, begin to look for a church that fears God more than it fears man. In other words, we need to become members of a church and denomination that is God-honoring, instead of a man-honoring.

Make no mistake, your attitude regarding public schools is the true determiner of how serious you are about serving in Christ's Kingdom. Admittedly this is a harsh statement and one that contains absolutely no wiggle room. However, in our heart-of-hearts we know this is the case, since we have neither a biblical argument to the contrary, nor a logical or pragmatic one.

Once we decide to get serious about living out our faith by refusing to approach life in a piecemeal and compartmentalized fashion, we will encounter numerous objections from well-intentioned Christian brothers and sisters on our decision to "exit" what are, in effect, the state's churches. These objections can be boiled down into five categories. As will be seen, each represents either a misinterpretation of Scripture or a total ignorance of it.

CATEGORY ONE
Our School is *Different*

Imagined reasons for this objection:

- It is a modern building in the suburbs with computers in every classroom, not a decaying building in the inner city with dog-eared textbooks and a crime problem.
- It has some Christian teachers who don't teach what the curriculum states. (Ha! They would be fired immediately if this were the case.)

Q. 16 NOTES
1 2 Corinthians 6.14
2 Matthew 6.10

3 Isaiah 1.18
4 Psalm 36.9
5 Matthew 15.14

What is not mentioned in either of these reasons is what is being systematically taught day in and day out. An indication that such parents have bought into Satan's myth about there being compartments to life is the thinking that "public schools will prepare our children for 'real life,' while Sunday school prepares them for the religious, private compartment of their life." Perhaps no statistic underscores this "two compartment" mindset on the part of Christian parents better than George Barna's study, which says, "Only three out of ten born-again parents include the salvation of their child in the list of critical parental emphases."[1] Does this mean that Christian parents are not interested in the eternal salvation of their children? Not at all; with their "two compartment" view of life, these parents probably didn't even consider providing a "religious" answer to a "real life" question! Had the question included "education" in a list of possible answers, in all probability the Christian parents would have selected that over their children's salvation. After all, in a "two compartment" world, education prepares you for a good job, and isn't making money what life is all about? (Of course, as your begin to knock down the big bucks, you will want your children to go to church, because that "compartment of life" must not be neglected.) Barna's study, showed only four percent of the respondents identifying prayer as an integral part of parenting. Again, does this indicate that Christian parents don't believe in the power of effective and fervent prayer?"[2] Don't bet the mortgage on it! The respondents were likely considering the range of possible answers to the question from strictly a "real life" compartmentalized viewpoint.

The non-Christian lives according to this compartmentalized mindset (by serving two masters) because he has no choice: Satan has blinded his eyes.[3] Privately, they serve their imagined god, while publicly they serve culture's god (this god manifests itself in several forms: peer pressure, political correctness, and the ever-changing ideological "fads" of the day, just to mention a few of the false idols). This mindset is to be expected from non-Christians because they are living according to the natural inclination of their hearts. We, on the other hand, should live according to the supernatural inclination of our re-born hearts. This is why Christians who live compartmentalized lives are bringing shame to God by trusting more in man's wisdom than in God's.[4] Such brothers and sisters apparently block from their consciousness Jesus' injunction against serving two masters.[5]

We should remind ourselves that our non-Christian neighbors believe that "faith" is "personal and private." That it has nothing to do with "real life." Therefore, when they see us conforming to their worldview, we are enforcing their false belief system! You may ask, "Where did this two-compartment way of looking at life originate?" The answer is, "Satan used the Greek philosopher Plato to popularize the idea." As a non-Christian, Plato couldn't account for the bad things humans do to each other, so he separated the metaphysical (in which he witnessed evil behavior) from the spiritual (in which he imagined only good behavior). To the non-Christian Plato's way of thinking, such a two-compartment view of the world made perfectly practical and pragmatic sense. However, when we conform to this non-Christian view of the world, we place ourselves in an inept and ineffectual mode.

Such an erroneous view of life is countered by the consistent message of Scripture, which explains that it is God's law "that liberates" us to live, work, play and raise our children as we self-govern ourselves according to the ethics of God's Word. [6] When we abandon the explicitly Christian view of life which offers clear answers to cultural issues, all we have left is a clouded alternative view that promises not cultural victory, but merely "less of a cultural defeat" than the social agenda of liberal legislators. Instead of replacing man's view of the world with God's, we have simply replaced non-Christian liberal man's view with non-Christian conservative man's view.

So what do we do? We remind ourselves, and others, of these four pivotal questions.

- God wrote the instructions! Shouldn't we expect to fail if we neglect to live by them?
- Shouldn't we expect to fail if we continue to elect non-Christians to office and continue to send our children to, or to teach in, the ungodly public schools?

CATEGORY ONE NOTES

1 www.barna.org
2 James 5.16
3 2 Corinthians 4.4
4 2 Kings 18.21
5 Luke 16.13
6 Psalm 19.7-11; Matthew 5.17-18; 22.37-40; 2 Peter 2.21

- If we continue to fear our employer, customers, or congregation more than we fear the triune Creator God, and if we continue to live by their rules, instead of by His rules, should we expect anything but failure?
- Shouldn't we expect to be laughed at, ridiculed as a "fringe group" and dismissed as being "culturally irrelevant" when all we do is deal with the various fruit falling from man's sinful tree, (i.e., abortion, gambling and pornography), instead of attacking the root of man's tree (sin) by instituting programs and policies based on God's rules?

> *We must remind ourselves that we have not been called to offer a moralistic conservative alternative to the agenda of liberals, but God's alternative to man's agenda.*

CATEGORY TWO
We Can't Afford Christian Schools, Besides, Our Child is Being "Salt and Light" by Evangelizing Non-Christian Friends.

The money objection may be literally true, or it could be a refusal on the part of parents to lower their standard of living in order to pay for a true education for their children. In the event it is really a money matter, the church should be looked to for scholarship aid. After all, what more worthwhile "missionary activity" could there be than educating our children in the truth? As far as "salt and light" or "carrying out the Great Commission" is concerned, such parents should be encouraged to recognize that their Christian worldview garden not only has TULIPs and FLOWERs growing in it, but also a few non-Christian WEEDs from the non-Christian worldview garden (See "The Christian Worldview Garden" chart in the Third Cut). They may sincerely want their child to be a "missionary" to a few of his friends, but the horrible truth is that it will be the non-Christian environment that is the odds-on favorite to "convert" the Christian student to heathen ways, rather than vice versa. Let's fast-forward past the obvious truth that missionaries receive in-depth training, and a child receives no such training, and go to the negative lessons he or she will learn just by observing how daily events unfold. If he acts in an unruly (non-Christian) manner he will be rewarded by teachers, administrators and non-Christian friends, whereas if he acts in a Christ-honoring manner, he will be disciplined and perhaps even expelled, by teachers and/or administrators, as well as being cast aside by non-Christian students. As for placing your trust in those teachers or administrators who profess to be Christians, you should realize that they know full well they will be fired if they attempt to incorporate biblical ethics into their lesson plans. This means that Christian students see Christian teachers and administrators as placing more confidence in ungodly principles than in godly principles. What kind of testimony is this for our children to be exposed to!

CATEGORY THREE
We Went to Public Schools and We Turned Out OK

"One in ten Christian adults possessing a Christian worldview" doesn't sound "OK" to me. Neither does the fact that only 14 percent of Christians read their Bibles once a month, with 41 percent seldom, if ever, reading it. And for the effect on our children of daily doses of non-Christian dogma, only 12 percent of high school students turn to the Bible for instruction, and only nine percent believe in unchanging moral truth (Nehemiah Institute, www.nehemiahinstitute.com). Then, there is the uncomfortable statistic of seven out of ten high school graduates who have been raised in the church who stop attending church when they go to college. One would have to have a very fertile imagination to believe that any of these results of government education are "OK."

CATEGORY FOUR
What about Socialization and Extra-curricular Activities?

Texas attorney Bruce Shortt, in his excellent book, *The Harsh Truth About Public Schools*, writes:

> *Some Christian parents are a little schizophrenic—they want their children to be Christian and to be like everyone*

else. This is obviously impossible. ...Christians are not
commanded, "Go and be like everyone else." In 2 Corinthians
6:14 and 17 we are asked, "what communion hath light with
darkness?" and are then told to "come out from among them,
and be ye separate ... and touch not the unclean thing..."
Similarly, Psalm 1.1 admonishes us not to walk in the counsel
of the ungodly, stand in the way of sinners, or sit in the seat of
the scornful. So the real question is, to which standards are we
going to socialize our children—to those of Pharaoh's schools
or to those of Christ?

THE HARSH TRUTH ABOUT PUBLIC SCHOOLS,
BRUCE SHORTT, (CHALCEDON FOUNDATION, 2004), P.328

To those who say, "You don't expect us to withdraw from our culture do you?" we can respond by saying, "Tell me exactly which non-Christian behaviors you want your child to conform to?"

As for extra-curricular activities, like athletics, it is becoming more common for home school associations to field teams to play private schools and Christian schools. Several quarterbacks from these small teams have been selected to play for major colleges and have excelled, with one, Tim TeBow of the University of Florida, winning the 2007 Heisman Trophy! So while it is true that the weekly competition may not be as challenging, college and professional scouts are fully capable of judging talent, and your son won't have to be sacrificed to the ungodly instruction of public schools in order to earn a college scholarship.

CATEGORY FIVE
Our Pastor Hasn't Said it is a Problem!

This is a common objection and a sad commentary on the state of many of our churches. With an estimated 85 percent of Christian parents sending their children to the government schools [1] (and with many Christian parents working in them as well) some pastors are hesitant to raise this issue for fear of offending some of their members. However, what they are doing by making this decision only demonstrates that they fear their congregations more than they fear the Lord. This being the case, why would you want to trust your spiritual development to a person who places human wisdom above God's? Long story short, there is no biblical argument for sending our children to God-hating schools.

If your pastor falls in this category, give him the benefit of the doubt and approach him privately and ask for his reasons. If he can't provide a biblical answer (and he won't be able to) or if he hasn't thought this through, but still refuses to repent, then shake the dust off your feet from that moralistic social club and find a Christian church with a Christian pastor. [2]

Question 17. Is it a sin to submit our children to programs and policies of non-Christians, and/or to join with non-Christians in business ventures?

    a. No.
    b. Yes.

Christians who teach or who serve in administrative positions in the public schools should be shown from Scripture how what they are doing is a direct disobedience to Paul's counsel to not be "unequally yoked together with unbelievers." In his words, "What communion has light with darkness? And what accord has Christ with Belial?" [1] We need to recognize that our decisions and actions reflect the God we worship, and in whom we have faith and trust. Since "actions speak louder than words," God is not interested in our words, but only that we live-out what we profess to believe. There is no escaping the truth that government schools

---

CATEGORY FIVE NOTES
1   Shortt, ibid., *Harsh*, p. 21
2   *EXIT Strategy: A Handbook to Exponentially Improve Your Serve for God,* Buddy Hanson, (Hanson Group, 2005), pp.222-228

Q. 17 NOTES
1   Matthew 12.30
2   2 Corinthians 10.4-5
3   Psalm 2.3

promote the worship of any god except the triune God of Scripture. So, by sending our children there, we are, in essence, sending them to Baal,[2] and by working in them we are breaking the first commandment to "have no other gods" [3] before us.

In your wildest dreams can you ever imagine
the Public (Government) Schools teaching the vital principles
discussed in these 17 questions?

Does Your Child's Teacher*

EDUCATE   OR   HALLUCINATE

God's Anti-Virus Protection	Man's Non-Christian Viruses
• God is sovereign (God's Word).	• Man is sovereign (science & technology).
• Truth is absolute & unchanging.	• Truth is "whatever works for me."
• We must conform to God's ethics.	• We establish the ethics.
• Man's problem is sin. We need to be spiritually recreated by God.	• Man's problem is lack of education and a misguided society. Society must be re-created by man (the state).
• The family is God's basic institution.	• The individual, or the state is basic.

* Parent or a Christian day school teacher.

SOURCE: Rushdoony, R.J., *Philosophy of the Christian Curriculum*, (Ross House Books), pp.172-73.

Has the information in this section revealed that you may have been looking at the world through blurred lenses? If so, how does this information help you to change your mantra as you approach each day in Christ's Kingdom? Yes, I said, "mantra," and yes, that usually means something that is chanted, but for our case we're using it as an unspoken mantra, or that "frame of reference" we bring to our daily decision-making that enables us to either accept or dismiss proposals that don't conform to our predisposed way of viewing the world. The upside of having such a mantra, or frame of reference is that we don't have to start from scratch in evaluating each decision, which means it saves us a lot of time. The downside is that if our mantra needs changing, and we don't realize it, then we will, with the best of intentions, make decisions that are not in our best interests.

Both Satan and Jesus have a mantra that they would prefer us to use in our daily decision-making. Take a look at both mantras to decide which one is currently dictating your decisions. The clearer your focus becomes with each area of decision-making, the sharper your decisions will reflect God's will, instead of Satan's.

What's in Your Mantra?

Satan's Version: Salvation & Frustration

"You are losers in the here-and-now, but winners in the hereafter."

"Jesus loves us and came to save us from our sins so that when we die (or are raptured!) we will be freed from the shackles of Satan's dominion upon the earth, and will joyfully spend eternity with fellow believers worshiping the triune God of the Bible. Until that time Jesus' Word encourages us to save as many people as we can and comforts us in our trials on this evil-infested earth by giving us a 'hope to cope' with all that Satan throws at us."

Jesus' Version: Salvation & Occupation

"You can be winners in both the here-and-now, and in the hereafter (by living according to My Word!)."

"Jesus loves those whom the Trinity chose before the foundation of the earth (EPHESIANS 1.4,17; 2.8) and came to earth to perfectly fulfill the Law (JOHN 1.1,14; MATTHEW 5.17; HEBREWS 4.15; 1 JOHN 4.10) and pay our sin debt by dying and overcoming death (JOHN 10.17-18; 1 CORINTHIANS 15.45) and has given us His Word to instruct us in how to live and govern ourselves (PSALM 119.105; JEREMIAH 31.33; JOHN 17.17; COLOSSIANS 3.16; ROMANS 8.9, 14, 16; 2 TIMOTHY 3.16-17) and complete Jesus' victory over Satan (1 JOHN 3.8; 4.4; COLOSSIANS 2.13-15; HEBREWS 2.14) by taking dominion over the earth (GENESIS 1.26-28; 9.1-4; MATTHEW 28.18-20; ROMANS 8.37) and restoring God's will "on earth, as it is in heaven." (MATTHEW 6.10; REVELATION 11.15).

Second Cut

Civil Government

QUESTIONS 18–23

Question 18. What does the separation of church and state mean?

    a. The church shouldn't have anything to do with the state, and the state shouldn't have anything to do with the church. Both should be entirely separate.

    b. God gave each self-governing sphere (individual, family, church, state) particular responsibilities, and neither should usurp any responsibilities of the other.

Contrary to what is being taught in the public schools, our Founders never intended for America to be a secular state. A reading of any of the original state constitutions would quickly prove that America was founded upon biblical laws, not upon a pluralism of religious laws. While America grants the right for citizens to worship any god they may imagine, our laws clearly reflect biblical ethics. Instead of the socialism and Marxism that is reflected in our current democratic form of top-down central government, America was founded as a bottom-up self-governing constitutional republic with four self-governing spheres: individual, family, church and state. Each of these self-governing spheres is assigned specific responsibilities by God, and none should attempt to usurp the responsibilities of the others. The important thing to remember is that

> *It is impossible for any society to be governed by more than one set of ethics.*

Either God's ethics will be accepted, or man's. Either man determines the rewards and punishments of civil behavior, or God does. Like oil and water, there can be no mixture. Sooner or later, we will either be ruled by God's perfect, never-changing, and personally liberating ethics, or we will be ruled by man's imperfect, ever-changing and enslaving ethics.

The different roles and goals of the church and state can be seen in the following chart.

Church & State:
Different Roles, Different Goals

Church
1. Minister of Grace/Excommunication
2. Expose Evil
3. Teach God's Law
4. Funded by God's social tax–the tithe

5. Church courts
6. Welfare

State
1. Minister of Justice/Execution
2. Restrain Evil
3. Enforce God's Law
4. Financed by God's civil tax– the head tax
5. Civil courts
6. Warfare

See: Choose This Day: God's Instructions on How to Select Leaders, Buddy Hanson (Hanson Group, 2003).

Both the church and the state have similarities, as well as explicit differences:

SIMILARITIES between Church & State
1. They are both from God and are "ministers of God" and shall give account of their administrations to God.

2. Both must observe the law and commandments of God and each has specific directions from Scripture to guide them.
3. Both are "fathers" and ought to be honored and obeyed according to the principles in the fifth commandment.
4. Both are appointed for the glory of God and the good of mankind.
5. Both compliment each other.

As far as their DIFFERENCES
1. In their ultimate goal, the Civil Rulers bring about temporal peace; the Church offers salvation and eternal peace.
2. The State executes capitol offenders; the Church excommunicates unrepentant and disobedient members.

Question 19. Should we depend upon the civil government to "legislate" us out of our cultural problems, or should we "self-govern" ourselves out of our cultural problems?

a. Legislate.
b. Self-govern.

Non-Christians, with their self-centered interests, are motivated to amass power and control while bringing honor and esteem to themselves. This was the self-expressed motivation behind the building of the Tower of Babel: "Let us make a name for ourselves." (GENESIS 11.4) At the opposite end of the spectrum, Christians should be motivated to build a name for God and to serve His interests. This is why we read of decentralized governing bodies throughout Scripture. For example, Moses instructs Israel to "Appoint judges and officers in all your gates [cities]," and Joshua "called twelve men ... one from every tribe ..." into leadership roles. (JOSHUA 4.4) Jethro, the priest of Midian, and Moses' father-in-law, advised Moses to:

> ... select from all the people able men, such as fear God, men of truth, hating covetousness; and place such over them to be rulers of thousands, rulers of hundreds, rulers of fifties, and rulers of tens. EXODUS 18.21-22

47

A system of bottom-up self-government results in the personal liberty to live and govern ourselves according to God's ethics, whereas a system of top-down central government results in rules and regulations that contract and reduce our personal liberty because some bureaucrat in some state or federal office thinks we should live like he or she wants us to live.

Question 20. Our civil laws

a. Should be based upon man's opinions and "best guesses," which means sometimes there will be some "gray" areas when the courts administer justice.
b. **Should be based upon God's absolute ethics as revealed on the inerrant pages of the Bible, which means there are only "black and white" areas of right and wrong behavior.**

Recent years have seen Christian lawmakers in particular and all Christians in general discuss cultural issues according to our own thoughts, rather than re-thinking God's thoughts. This is a very bad habit and one that needs to end quickly if we expect to restore a Christian culture. On the one hand we are quick to defend the Bible as God's inerrant Word and as being absolute truth. On the other, we seem to absolutely ignore what it has to say! As a result of such thinking we continue to reap the negative consequences of a morally declining culture. We have gotten ourselves into our current situation by letting non-Christians frame the debates. Without Christian influence, we are doomed to lose every debated issue about culture, because regardless of whether "conservative" non-Christians, or "liberal" non-Christians win, the solutions with which we have to live will be non-Christian.

We must get over the attitude that it is not right to impose our beliefs on others.

Had earlier Christians acted like we have for the last few generations, we would still be enslaving people, sacrificing children, (instead of baptizing them), and rather than having someone over to supper, we likely would be having them for supper. Before Christianity or Judaism taught otherwise, each community's medicine men looked upon sick people as having evil spirits, so why would they want to set up hospitals or medical care to nurse someone back to health who was evil?

In order for us to begin winning the culture battle, we must understand that the issue is not between conservatives and liberals, but between Christians and non-Christians. Since "God's Word is Truth," [1] this makes any proposed solution to culture's problems false, unless it is based upon God's Word. This includes conservative non-Christian solutions! Neither of the current ungodly political parties is going to save us, and until Christians become more committed to God's commands than to a political party's sinful self-interests, we will continue to lose ground in the culture war. When it comes to deciding under which laws a community should live, it must determine which religion those laws represent. You may be tempted to think that the previous sentence is a typo, but it isn't. The truth of the matter is

> *If we continue to stand for tolerance instead of truth, our culture will continue its rapid decline, just as have all other societies throughout history that refused to follow God's directions for living.*

All law is "religious!"

Someone may object, "Wait a minute! Law is law and religion is religion." But when it is remembered a religion is simply a collection of beliefs and values and a society's laws reflect that system of beliefs, it will be seen that law is inescapably religious. For example, should a person's property be taxed? In order to answer that it must be asked: "Who owns it, God or the State?" It's a religious question! So, can you see that if the source of law is man's reason, then man's reason is the god of that society?

Isn't it interesting that the State is doing the very thing it warns might happen if God's principles were brought into their decision-making! While telling us, "You shouldn't legislate morality!" non-Christian legislators are doing that exact thing through their laws.

I've never met a Christian who has imagined that he or she is smarter than God, but far too many of us live as though that's the case, by rarely,

49

if ever, thinking about what the Bible has to say before making our day-to-day decisions.

Somewhere in the recesses of our mind we know that God is smarter than we are and we know that He is in charge because He is the Creator and we are His creatures. It is this pivotal truth that needs moving into the front burner position of our minds. We must be ever conscious that we are operating in His world and that our efforts will fail unless we consistently live by His rules. Piecemeal obedience will not enable us, our communities, our state, or America to be the recipients of God's promised blessings.

What better political platform could there be than the principles in the Ten Commandments that promote:

- respect for those in authority. (5th Commandment, Exodus 20.12)
- the value of life. (6th Commandment, Exodus 20.13)
- the dignity of women and the importance of the family.
- (7th Commandment, Exodus 20.14)
- personal property rights. (8th Commandment, Exodus 20.15)
- being honest in our personal and business relationships.
- (9th Commandment, Exodus 20.16)
- living at peace with our neighbors. (10th Commandment, Exodus 20.17)

This means whenever a society changes its law, it also changes its god! The reason this is so is because there can be no tolerance in a law-system for another religion. Their subjective standards, which allow their followers to act pretty much as they believe, cannot stand up to the triune God's objective standards. Followers of false religions prefer to imagine they are, in essence, their own god, determining good and evil. They only have to read to the third chapter in Genesis to see that the triune God of the Bible severely judges such an attitude. [2]

As Elijah states, "If the Lord is God, follow Him; but if Baal, follow Him." [3]

Q. 20 NOTES   **2** Genesis 3.15
1 Psalm 119.160   **3** 1 Kings 18.21

Question 21. Our elected representatives should govern as

   a. Politicians.
   b. Statesmen.

Setting out to find a statesman in office would be akin to hunting for that proverbial needle in the haystack. There doubtless are a few statesmen in all levels of civil government, across the country, but they are rare birds. Once more, this only serves as a reminder of how important a Christian worldview is, because we are talking about elected representatives, which means that when we begin to point the finger of blame for the sad state of representatives, we are ultimately pointing at ourselves! As the prophet Hosea said approximately 2,700 years ago, "They sow the wind and reap the whirlwind." (HOSEA 8.7) We are, indeed "reaping what we sow," and the only way to correct this situation is to identify Christian candidates who have a developed Christian worldview, and to support them!

The basic difference between a politician and a statesman is that the politician legislates according what it takes to stay in office, while the statesman legislates according to what is the biblically right thing to do. The adage, "Politics makes strange bedfellows," speaks volumes. Politician "A" may have a long record of disliking Politician "B," but if Politician "A" believes that supporting Politician "B's" legislation will help him get re-elected, then Politician "A" will do whatever he can to see that Politician "B's" bill is passed. Such a scenario, of course, would not cross the mind of a statesman.

A statesman fears God, not the voters and knows that if God wants him to remain in office, he will, and if He doesn't, he won't. May we all pray that we can encourage statesmen to run for civil office, both as legislators and judges.

Question 22. When we vote

   a. Do we vote for the "lesser of two evils?" Or
   b. Do we vote to "overcome evil with good?" (ROMANS 12.21)

In regards to voting, it matters little whether the candidate is a Democrat, Republican or an Independent. Neither does the person's chances of winning matter. The only thing that matters is whether our actions (and their platform) conforms to Biblical ethics. As creatures, we often act as if we are mini-Creators (who can bring about specific results at a specific time), rather than acting as obedient creatures, resting in the assurance that our Creator will bring about His perfect results in His perfect timing.

> *Voting, then, is not about winners and losers, but about obeying God. In short, our choice is to vote according to God's will and be blessed, or vote according to our will and be cursed.*

We don't have to read very far in Scripture to find that there is not a one-to-one correspondence between obedience and blessings. The blessings that will flow from today's obedience may not happen today...they may be down the road, but they will come in God's perfect timing.

If we vote for the "lesser of two evils," we are still voting for evil and there is no way to justify that from Scripture. Indeed, we are acting as though this is the best we can do, which means we have completely dismissed the truth that God is sovereignly ruling over His creation. It is not by the people, but by God that our civil rulers reign.

> *By Me kings reign, and rulers decree justice. By me princes rule, and nobles, all the judges of the earth.*
>
> PROVERBS 8.15-6

> *For there is no authority except from God, and the authorities that exist are appointed by God. Therefore whoever resists the authority resists the ordinance of God, and those who resist will bring judgment on themselves.* ROMANS 13.1-2

> *Let us not forget that evil is a bad thing! Solomon tells us Do they not go astray who devise evil? But mercy and truth belong to those who devise good.* PROVERBS 14.22

The apostle Paul adds

> *But if you do evil, be afraid.*   ROMANS 13.4

King David tells us

> *All the paths of the LORD are mercy and truth, to such as keep His covenant and His testimonies.*   PSALM 24.10

All of God's paths are "mercy and truth." None of them are second best attempts at serving Him by choosing the "lesser" of two evils. May we all repeat this vital truth to ourselves until we "get it:"

> **All of God's paths are "mercy and truth."**

This means that if we vote for Christians we will be successful, but it may not be readily apparent. It took 120+ years for God to make it obvious to the world that Noah's actions were successful, but Noah knew that he was a success each step of the way because he was obeying God. So, even though we may be greatly tempted to vote for "the lesser of two evils" instead of the Christian candidate, as Christians we really have no option but to vote for the Christian candidate, and if one is not on the ballot, to either write-in someone, or not vote. Before we conclude pragmatically, that we will "waste" our vote by voting for a Christian who doesn't appear to have a chance of winning, we should remind ourselves that we haven't been called into Christ's Kingdom to think in exclusively pragmatic terms, we did that before becoming a Christian. Now we are supposed to think exclusively in theological terms and when we do so we will realize that it is not possible to "waste" our vote by obeying God! Perhaps we need reminding that God blesses our obedience and curses our disobedience!

> *No temptation has overtaken you except such as is common to man; but God is faithful, who will not allow you to be tempted beyond what you are able, but with the temptation will also make the way of escape, that you may be able to bear it.*
> 1 CORINTHIANS 10.13

Question 23. Which economic policies do you favor?

    a. Those which promote the socialistic "heavy hand" of civil government?

    b. Those which promote biblical capitalistic principles of self-government?

I started not to include this question because to answer it adequately would require a very detailed exposition. However, the question, itself, is symbolic of the critical necessity to re-think God's thoughts, and it illustrates, probably as no other question, just how much our thinking has been infected with non-Christian viruses. So, instead of answering it, I will list some "considers" about it in order to highlight how much we are pulled in various directions by the strings of the non-Christian agenda.

- Consider that the total of our taxes takes upwards of 45 percent of our gross income. Taxes that go toward paying for the many and various social programs that the Bible says should be funded by individuals, families and churches.
- Consider that God asks for only 10 percent of our net income, [1] plus whatever amount of "offerings" we decide to contribute. [2]
- Consider how much personal liberty we would have if we obeyed God's commands to self-govern ourselves instead of looking to the civil government to fulfill our responsibilities. If we only paid the civil government to protect us from invasion and keep our communities crime free, we would have upwards of 30 percent more take home pay.
- Consider that the earth is the Lord's and not the State's and therefore property tax is unbiblical. [3] The biblical record is clear: whenever a society disregards God's sovereign claim as Lord of the earth, it is "cursed by Him and sold into bondage." [4]
- Consider that when the civil government of America was established, it was a constitutional republic, instead of a democracy (which all of the founders held in low esteem). The Word "democracy" does not appear in the Declaration of Independence, the

United States Constitution, or the Bill or Rights. Article IV, Section 4 of the U.S. Constitution says, "each state shall maintain a republican form of government." This truth is reflected in the Pledge of Allegiance, wherein we state, "to the republic for which it stands." (not "to the democracy!")

Recognizing the drastic differences in a country that was governed by absolute principles (a representative republic) and one that reinterpreted the meaning of its laws according to the latest opinion poll (a democracy), the writers of the Constitution were careful to point out that our laws were based upon biblical ethics. Noah Webster adds, "Our citizens should early understand that the genuine source of correct republican principles is the Bible, particularly the New Testament, or the Christian religion." [5] Alexander Hamilton, demonstrating his understanding of the fallen nature of man [6] writes: "Because the passions of men will not conform to the dictates of reason and justice without constraint ..."[7] The "Father of the U.S. Constitution," James Madison writes in the 10th essay of The Federalist Papers, "...democracies have ever been spectacles of turbulence and contention; have ever been found incompatible with personal security or the rights of property; and have in general been as short in their lives as they have been violent in their deaths." The second President of the United States, John Adams, observes, "Democracy never lasts long. It soon wastes, exhausts, and murders itself." [8] At a time in which America was still operating under a collective Christian worldview, Department Training Manual No. 2000-25, published in 1928, defines democracy in this way:

A government of the masses. Authority derived through mass meeting or any other form of "direct" expression. Results in mobocracy [mob rule]. Attitude toward property is communistic—negating property rights. Attitude toward law is that the will of the majority shall regulate, whether it be based upon deliberation or governed by passion, prejudice, and impulse, without restraint or regard to consequences. Results in...anarchy.

- Consider that wives weren't allowed to vote, because that was seen as diminishing the husband's role as "head of the household." [9] This principle is one of a representative form of self-government, not a democracy, and since as has been pointed out, America was founded as a constitutional republic, women relied on their husbands to "represent them" in civil matters. It should also be pointed out, that this was not anti-women, since if a woman was not married, but owned property, she was allowed to vote. In the 1820s, as the humanistic ideas of the Enlightenment began to replace biblical ideas, and our constitutional republic was beginning to be replaced by a democracy, women were given the carte blanch right to vote with the ratification of the 19th Amendment in 1920, and the authority of the family structure began to disintegrate.
- Consider that only property owners could vote. The reason behind this was not to discriminate against people who didn't own property, but rather to encourage them to obtain property so they could vote. This simply reflects the Christian capitalistic worldview of America's founders, in contrast to today's socialism that deludes personal initiative and promotes dependence upon the civil government to provide various economic handouts. [10]
- Consider that it was not until after The War of Northern Aggression that the local civil government was replaced in importance by the state governments, which were eventually replaced in importance by the federal government. We need to begin turning this cart around so that the term "government" is not exclusively

Q. 23 NOTES

1 Leviticus 27.30-33; also a second tithe, the "festival tithe," Deuteronomy 14.22-27 for families to "rejoice before the Lord;" a third tithe was required every third year to be shared with foreigners in common feasting and rejoicing before the Lord. Deuteronomy 14.28f. See *Tithing & Dominion*, Edward Powell and Rousas John Rushdoony, (Ross House Books, 1979), pp.2-4
2 Deuteronomy 16.10-11; Exodus 36.7; Leviticus 22.21

3 Exodus 9.29; Deuteronomy 10.14; Psalm 24.1; 1 Corinthians 10.26
4 1 Samuel 8; Malachi 3.8-10
5 Webster, Noah, *History of the United States*, (Durrie & Peck, 1832), p.6
6 Genesis 6.5; 8.21; Jeremiah 17.9; Proverbs 21.2; 2 Timothy 3.13
7 *The Federalist* #15, p.180
8 *The Works of John Adams*, Vol. VI, (Little and Brown, 1851), p.484
9 Ephesians 5.22-33
10 2 Thessalonians 3.10

associated with civil government, but that the other three spheres of "government", the Individual, Family and Church are also given their due and that their God-given responsibilities are not usurped by any of the other self-governing spheres.
- Consider that all of the previous "considers" point to capitalism as the biblical form of self-government, not socialism.

Question 24. Do you see the role of civil government as:

a. Providing a wide array of social programs, including education?
b. Defending us against attack and keeping our communities safe for us to live, work, play and raise our families the way we want?

According to God's divine division of labor, we should govern ourselves according to four self-governing spheres: Individual, family, church and state, with none of the spheres usurping any responsibilities of the other spheres. All of the social services for which we are so heavily taxed today should be provided through these spheres, with the State's only responsibilities being to protect us from invasion, and keep our communities safe from criminals so we can live, work, play and raise our families in the way we want without civil government interference. [1]

Living in conformity to, God's laws, produces personal liberty. However, the non-Christian State doesn't want us to be self-governing, because it views itself as god with society being in lock-step with its decrees. The Church, meanwhile, is looked upon as merely a "department of state." Virginia Pastor Paul Michael Raymond provides this description:

> *The tendency of the state is to see itself as the center of the social order, rather than as an administrator of justice. When that happens, the state sees its purpose as messianic, saving its citizens from some sinister force, manipulating economic forces, and restricting liberty in the name of safety and the greater good. When the state wants to be man's savior, it first moves to become his lord.* [2]

As in all areas of life, the ultimate question is "Who is sovereign … man or God?"

- Non-Christians say *"**Man** is the measure of all things,"* while Christians say, *"**God** is the measure of all things."*
- Non-Christians say, "The *voice of the people* is the voice of God," while Christians say, "The *voice of God should be* the voice of the people."

When sovereignty is located in the state and not Christ four possible scenarios arise:

1. Natural reason becomes sovereign, (instead of the supernatural reasoning of re-thinking God's thoughts). Or
2. The strongest or most powerful become sovereign (i.e., the elite). Or
3. The collective voice of the people becomes sovereign. Or
4. He who has the most bullets becomes sovereign.

Question 25. We should "Render to Caesar"

a. Everything he asks, because Jesus says so.
b. Only the things that are Caesar's, because Jesus says so.

It should be clear by now that Christianity does not promote "blind obedience" to any of its doctrines. We only have to call the mind the Hebrew midwives who disobeyed the edict of Egypt's King to kill all new born males, [1] or Daniel, Shadrach, Meshac, and Abed-Nego who refused King Nebuchadnezzar's decree to worship idols, [2] or the apostles who refused obey the High Priest's injunction to stop preaching the gospel. [3] Civil Rulers govern according to their worldview, and if that view happens to be non-Christian, their policies and legal decisions will promote a false religion. There is no mention in Scripture about civil government

---

Q. 24 NOTES
1 1 Samuel 13.1-14; 2 Chronicles 26.1-5, 16-18
2 Paul Michael Raymond pastors The Reformed Bible Church in Appomattox, VA

being pluralistic in its religion. Indeed, the first commandment says we are to have "no other gods before us." [4]

Therefore in *submitting* to civil rulers who are enforcing God's rules, we should also resist those who are enforcing man's rules. As long as civil rulers enforce God's rules, instead of making up rules (laws) of their own, citizens have no option but to obey them. What this means is that in order to properly function as God's ministers, civil rulers should be familiar with and study God's Word so they can carry out His will for their citizenry (promoting peace and keeping their community safe). In the words of Samuel: "He that rules over men must be just, ruling in the fear of God." [5] The 17th century Scottish Presbyterian theologian, Samuel Rutherford writes that tyranny exists when the civil governor "replaces God's laws with his own. ...since tyranny is Satanic, not to resist it is to resist God, or expressing this in positive terms, to resist tyranny is to honor God. Secondly, since the obligation of self-defense is given by God, to give up that right is sin. Thirdly, since the king is granted power conditionally, it follows that the people have the power to withdraw their sanction if the conditions are not fulfilled. The king or political authority or civil magistrate is a fiduciary figure—that is, he holds his authority in trust ....[6]

Question 26. Should Christians be involved in civil government?

    a. No, all politicians are crooks, and we should not dirty our hands in that field.

    b. Yes, a Christian can bring honor and glory to God in all areas of life, and since God has given only one ethical code by which to live, Christian statesmen can help ensure that only biblical legislation takes place.

Instead of living and governing ourselves according to the bottom–up system of God-appointed self-governing spheres of the: Individual, fam-

---

Q. 25 NOTES
1 Exodus 1.15-17
2 Daniel 3.17-18
3 Acts 5.29
4 Exodus 20.3

5 2 Samuel 23.3
6 Jordan, James B., *The Journal of Christian Reconstruction*, Vol. V, No. 2, "Rutherford," pp.67-68, quoting *Lex Rex*, pp.34-35, 69, 145.

ily, church and state, we have succumbed to the idol of top-down state government. In the process we have deserted the God-ordained system that introduced to the world the most amount of personal liberty ever known.

- We have gradually given up our property rights to fund a system of public education that hates God;
- our family rights and justice in the courts have been lost because we have refused to base our judicial decisions on the absolute ethics of God's Word; and
- we've forfeited our ecclesiastical rights to preach the whole counsel of God because instead of incorporating biblical ethics into our worldview and lifestyle, we've incorporated our churches to the state.

Those who insist that Christians should have nothing to do with political offices should be reminded of the following five points:

- God invented civil government. Romans 13, instructs "The powers that be are ordained of God," and Paul goes on to say that civil rulers are called "Ministers of God." ROMANS 13; 1 PETER 2.13-14; PROVERBS 16.12; PSALM 119.46-47; 82.1-2
- God commands that we obey Civil Rulers. ROMANS 13.1-3
- Civil Rulers are commanded to rule on God's terms. PSALM 2.10FF
- It should be recalled that Moses, Gideon, Barak, Samson, Jephthah, David and Samuel were all involved in civil government (and were complimented for being so involved in Hebrews 11.32).
- Paul echoes the importance of political involvement by requesting we pray "first of all" for civil rulers. 1 TIMOTHY 2.1-2

Has the information in this section revealed that you may have been looking at the world through blurred lenses? If so, how does this information help you to change your mantra as you approach each day in Christ's Kingdom? Yes, I said, "mantra," and yes, that usually means something that is chanted, but for our case we're using it as an unspoken mantra, or that "frame of reference" we bring to our daily decision-making that enables us to either accept or dismiss proposals that don't conform to our predisposed way of viewing the world. The upside of having such a mantra, or frame of reference is that we don't have to start from scratch in evaluating each decision, which means it saves us a lot of time. The downside is that if our mantra needs changing, and we don't realize it, then we will, with the best of intentions, make decisions that are not in our best interests.

Both Satan and Jesus have a mantra that they would prefer us to use in our daily decision-making. Take a look at both mantras to decide which one is currently dictating your decisions. The clearer your focus becomes with each area of decision-making, the sharper your decisions will reflect God's will, instead of Satan's.

What's in Your Mantra?

Satan's Version: Salvation & Frustration

"You are losers in the here-and-now, but winners in the hereafter."

"Jesus loves us and came to save us from our sins so that when we die (or are raptured!) we will be freed from the shackles of Satan's dominion upon the earth, and will joyfully spend eternity with fellow believers worshiping the triune God of the Bible. Until that time Jesus' Word encourages us to save as many people as we can and comforts us in our trials on this evil-infested earth by giving us a 'hope to cope' with all that Satan throws at us."

Jesus' Version: Salvation & Occupation

"You can be winners in both the here-and-now, and in the hereafter (by living according to My Word!)."

"Jesus loves those whom the Trinity chose before the foundation of the earth (EPHESIANS 1.4,17; 2.8) and came to earth to perfectly fulfill the Law (JOHN 1.1,14; MATTHEW 5.17; HEBREWS 4.15; 1 JOHN 4.10) and pay our sin debt by dying and overcoming death (JOHN 10.17-18; 1 CORINTHIANS 15.45) and has given us His Word to instruct us in how to live and govern ourselves (PSALM 119.105; JEREMIAH 31.33; JOHN 17.17; COLOSSIANS 3.16; ROMANS 8.9, 14, 16; 2 TIMOTHY 3.16-17) and complete Jesus' victory over Satan (1 JOHN 3.8; 4.4; COLOSSIANS 2.13-15; HEBREWS 2.14) by taking dominion over the earth (GENESIS 1.26-28; 9.1-4; MATTHEW 28.18-20; ROMANS 8.37) and restoring God's will "on earth, as it is in heaven." (MATTHEW 6.10; REVELATION 11.15).

Third Cut

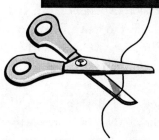

Worldview & Lifestyle

QUESTIONS 27–44

Question 27. What does having a Christian worldview mean to you?

a. It helps me to know the differences between how Christians and non-Christians view the world.

b. It helps me to know the descriptions of the differences between a Christian and non-Christian worldview, and helps me know God's prescriptions for how to deal with the various cultural issues.

Your first worldview most likely was gradually formed during your years in the public schools, as you learned from peer pressure which types of behaviors were "in," and which types were "out." At some point along the way you made a profession of faith and hopefully began to develop a "new" worldview. Take a trip down memory lane and recall what type of effect your profession of faith had on your "old" worldview. Obviously, you immediately eliminated some behaviors, and set goals to eliminate others, but did your profession of faith lead to substantial or superficial changes in your old (non-Christian) worldview? Or, did you basically keep the overall framework for how you had always approached situations and circumstances and merely "add" some Christian elements such as:

- Cleaning up your language.
- Not seeking revenge.
- Looking for ways to serve others.

As you look back to your conversion experience, can you unequivocally state that you made a concerted effort to "put off" your old worldview framework and "put on" your new Christian worldview, [1] thereby viewing the world in an entirely different manner than you did as a non-Christian? If you did, congratulate yourself, because this is a very difficult thing to do. Indeed, unless you have someone discipling you along the way, it is a rare accomplishment. Research shows that, only five percent of adult Christians admit to having a Christian worldview. Undoubtedly, the main reason for this is that churches rarely spend any time in showing us how to live as Christians by incorporating the biblical truths we profess to believe into our daily decision-making. To prove the point, when was the last time you heard a series of sermons on this all-important topic of seeing the world with entirely new eyes?

While there are a few people who like to live on the edge, and are always seeking to do new things in new ways, most of us prefer to live in a rut. This is not to say that the "rut" is necessarily bad, but rather it is composed of a daily routine with which we have become comfortable. Our daily "rut" includes hanging out with the familiar people, going to familiar places, and thinking familiar thoughts. Therefore, for many of us, change is not a pleasant thought. So, the older we are when we become Christians, the more entrenched we are in our rut, and while there are some obvious habits we quickly replace, there are others that we tend to procrastinate over as if to say, "I'll get around to dealing with that sin later."

This all-too-common attitude results in our Christian worldview being blurred by some old familiar thought and decision-making patterns, and unless we have a discipler to give us a few much needed spiritual slaps in the face, our new walk with God is likely to resemble a child who walks along the roadway with one foot on the curb and the other one on the street. This may be an enjoyable temporary experience for the child, but for adults attempting to live in this manner, it's a very up and down and uncomfortable experience.

The most common way Christians are introduced to the differences between the Christian and non-Christian way of viewing events and circumstances is through a book, or by attending a worldview seminar. While there are some writers and organizations who are doing an excellent job of describing the differences between how a Christian and non-Christian should view and live in the world, it is rare to find any writer or organization who also provides God's prescriptions for how to deal with the various cultural issues. Think about how confused your favorite football team would be on game day if during the week their coaches only told them of the different plays that their upcoming opponent would run, but didn't provide instructions on how to defend them!

The Need for a Christian Worldview [2]

Woe to those who call evil good and good evil, who put darkness for light and light for darkness, who put bitter for sweet and sweet for bitter. ISAIAH 5.20

The people who know their God will display strength and take action.
DANIEL 11.32

If we were to use the analogy of gardens to represent worldviews, the Christian Worldview Garden would have a theological TULIP and practical-applications FLOWERS, and the non-Christian Worldview Garden would have WEEDS. [3] In the following chart, notice that there are no Scripture references in man's worldview, since non-redeemed sinners have no desire to live by any rules except what their fallen imaginations can create. A quick

Since, for one reason or another, today's church doesn't emphasize discipling, each of us is pretty much on our own in working out our worldviews and that is why it has been so easy for non-Christians to pull our strings without us even being aware of it!

65

The Christian Worldview Garden*

FLOWER

From Him, through Him and to Him are all things. ROMANS 11.36
Lean not on your own understanding. PROVERBS 3.5
Obedience brings blessings. LEVITICUS 26; DEUTERONOMY 28
Word of God is true. PSALM 119.160
Exhibit humility. MATTHEW 23.12
Repent. EZEKIEL 14.6
Saved to succeed, not secede.

TULIP

Total Depravity or Total Inability Romans 5.12; Genesis 6.5; Jeremiah 17.9
Unconditional Election Psalm 33.12; Ephesians 1.4; Romans 9.11-13
Limited Atonement Matthew 1.21; 2 Corinthians 5.21; 1 Peter 3.18
Irresistible Grace 1 Corinthians 2.10-14; Titus 3.5; Ezekiel 36.26-27
Perseverance of the Saints Isaiah 43.1-3; John 6.35-40; Romans 8.35-39

The non-Christian Worldview Garden

WEEDS

Word of man
Envy
Evil thoughts, actions
Do to others before they do to you
Selfishness

* See *FLOWERS For Your Christian Worldview Garden*, Buddy Hanson, (Hanson Group)

glance at these three acronyms will reveal that we need to incorporate the ethics of TULIP and FLOWERS into our lifestyle. But, as it is with every garden, we all have a couple of the ethics of the WEEDS acronym that have sprouted in the midst of our worldview. If not repented of, these WEEDS will stunt the growth of our TULIP and FLOWERS ethics. The only effective way to pull up these WEEDS is to make certain we can attach a biblical ethic to our daily decisions. If we can, we will have a glorious garden for our non-Christian neighbors to observe. If we can't, we should refrain from deciding on a particular action, regardless of whether it pertains to our home, church or vocation.

By building our house upon the words of Christ and faithfully acting upon them, we have a sure and solid foundation upon which to base our life. Paul writes, "No one can lay any foundation other than the one already laid, which is Jesus Christ." [4] This foundation can't be built by just hearing His words. It is critical that we incorporate Christ's Words into our lifestyle. To attempt to base our life upon anything else is to build our house on sand, and we all know that flowers don't grow in the sand.

Being the recipient of a Christian worldview should rank second in importance only to our salvation, because we are not only a member of Christ's Kingdom and God's family, but, thanks to the Holy Spirit's writing of God's law on our heart [5] we now know how to live in a manner that is pleasing to our Lord, Savior and King! Often we hear someone say, "With the vast majority of Americans professing to be Christians, why is our culture continuing to unravel?" One possible key to the answer is the response to a question in George Barna's "The 12 Most Significant Religious Findings from 2006," which reveals that only 15 percent of church members rank their relationship with God as their top priority! [6] If this low percentage shocks you, you're not alone, because another response in the research reveals that pastors thought the percentage would be 70 percent.

This raises an obvious and an uncomfortable question: "Are approximately eight out of ten people who profess to be Christians, not really Christians?" Since only God knows the heart, the only indicator of whether a person is truly a Christian is whether their lifestyle bears the "fruit" of their profession. [7] Please give careful consideration the following questions about your lifestyle:

- Does your daily behavior "bear fruit to God and eternal life," or does it "bear fruit to man and to eternal death?" [8]
- Where does bringing "honor" to God rank in your worldview and lifestyle? [9]
- Are you living as though God is not really concerned about how He instructs you to live, or are you living according to His "narrow ways?" [10]

- Are you neglecting to prepare yourself to live according to His Word, as was the case with the "foolish virgins?" [11] And finally,
- Does your lifestyle reflect such a nonchalant attitude that Jesus will say to you on Judgment Day:

Not everyone who says to Me, "Lord, Lord," shall enter the kingdom of heaven, but he who does the will of My Father in heaven. Many will say to Me in that day, "Lord, Lord, have we not prophesied in Your name, cast out demons in Your name, and done many wonders in Your name?" And then I will declare to them, "I never knew you; depart from Me, you who practice lawlessness!" MATTHEW 7.21-23

May none of us live in such a manner that Jesus will have to ask us this question! Instead, may we not only understand the distinctive differences between a Christian and non-Christian worldview, but also understand God's prescriptions for how to deal with the various cultural issues and live-out those prescriptions by presenting a godly antithesis to the non-Christian cultural agenda.

Question 28. In order to have a satisfying lifestyle

a. We can depend upon our self-sufficiency, personal initiative, education and the practical application of our knowledge to an ever-changing value standard of relative ethics.

Q. 27 NOTES
1   Colossians 3.9-10
2   This discussion is taken from *EXIT Strategy: A Handbook to Exponentially Improve Your Service for God*, Buddy Hanson, (Hanson Group, 2005), Chapter Four
3   Since this discussion centers on one's lifestyle (teleological) rather than the doctrine (theology) behind it, the reader is invited to see *Choose This Day: God's Instructions On How To Select Leaders*, (Hanson Group, 2003), p. 25 for a brief comparison between Calvinism and Arminianism

4   1 Corinthians 3.11
5   Jeremiah 31.33
6   The Barna Group, www.barna.org
7   John 15
8   Romans 7.4-5
9   Malachi 1.6
10   Luke 13.25
11   Matthew 25.11

b. **We can depend upon God's Word to sufficiently provide us with all the wisdom needed to live and govern ourselves successfully in accordance with an absolute and unchanging value standard.**

We say that the Bible is the inspired "Word of God" and that it is "profitable" for giving us daily instructions on how to live and govern ourselves, so that we may be "thoroughly equipped for every good work."[1] The question is, "Do we really believe it by applying His instructions to our daily lifestyle?" [2] Jesus tells us that the only way to prove to ourselves that we are truly Christians is if we "abide in His Word." [3] The apostle John puts it this way:

Now by this we know that we know Him, if we keep His commandments. He who says, "I know Him," and does not keep His commandments, is a liar, and the truth is not in him. But whoever keeps His word, truly the love of God is perfected in him. By this we know that we are in Him.

1 JOHN 2.3-5

Not only is there no wiggle room in John's divine directive; a person with a spiritually re-born heart will not be looking for any wiggle room. He knows that "without holiness no one will see the Lord," [4] and he also remembers how dissatisfied he was with his former worldview and lifestyle wherein he was looking in all the wrong places for answers, until the Holy Spirit mercifully changed his heart. As the prophet Isaiah puts it,

But the wicked are like the troubled sea, when it cannot rest, whose waters cast up mire and dirt.   ISAIAH 57.20

As a result of our supernatural heart transplant, our primary concern as each day begins is how to extend Christ's Kingdom by bringing glory and honor to God in the various situations and circumstances in which

---

Q. 28 NOTES
1 2 Timothy 3.16-17   2 John 14.15
3 John 8.31   4 Hebrews 12.14

he will find himself during the day. Jehovah's rebuke to ancient Israel applies equally to 21st Century Americans:

> *Why do you spend money for what is not bread, and your*
> *wages for what does not satisfy? Listen carefully to Me, and*
> *eat what is good, and let your soul delight itself in abundance.*
> ISAIAH 55.2

Our former lifestyle proved beyond doubt that our rules didn't work, and that our wisdom was insufficient to bring about a satisfying lifestyle. This is why we are continuing to "put off" our former foolish ways and "put on" God's perfect instructions for how to live and govern ourselves.

Question 29. When it comes to one's worldview and lifestyle:

   a.   Are there two ethical value standards: a "religious" one to be used in our homes and churches, and a "real life" one to be used in our vocations and/or with non-Christians?
   b.   **Is there only one absolute and unchanging ethical standard for all areas of our life and for all the situations and circumstances in which we may find ourselves?**

To have a divided heart is to compartmentalize our lives into secular and sacred categories. According to this erroneous mindset, when it comes time for the sacred part of our life we study the Bible, go to church, pray, go on a short-term missionary trip, etc. All the other areas of our life are secular and relate to the "real world," where we live by our rules. This is a dichotomy that is held by many of our Christian brothers and sisters, yet the idea comes from Plato and Greek philosophy and not from Jesus and Christianity.

Jeremiah's remarks to Ezekiel for the exiles in Jerusalem and Judah six hundred years before the birth of Christ still ring true today for many in the Church.

> *They sit before you as My people, and they hear your words,*
> *but they do not do them; for with their mouth they show much*
> *love, but their hearts pursue their own gain.* EZEKIEL 33.31

Our daily petition to Jesus should echo that of David:

Give me understanding and I shall keep Your law; indeed, I
shall observe it with my whole heart.   PSALM 119.34

It is only with God's help that we can transform ourselves from being a self-righteous, moralistic, goody two-shoes conservative citizen, to being an others-centered servant in Christ's Kingdom. To approach life as though it is made up of two distinct realms: "religion," and "real life," is to live according to a make believe worldview and lifestyle. Life is unified by applying God's ethics to all of our situations and circumstances, and not just to church related busyness. Paul admonishes us, "Whether you eat or drink, or whatever you do, do all to the glory of God." [1] There is no greater encouragement of this myth of sacred and secular realms of life than Christian parents who send their children to public schools. Such an action fosters in the minds of these students that the sacred (Church instruction) portion of our life represents what could be characterized as a "Two Percent Solution" for our culture, while the secular (non-Christian God-hating public school instruction) represents an "Eighteen Percent Solution."*

We must make no mistake about God being in absolute control of His creation:

O LORD, I know the way of man is not in himself; it is not
in man who walks to direct his own steps.

                                                JEREMIAH 10.23

The steps of a good man are ordered by the LORD, and He
delights in his way.   PSALM 37.23

For of Him and through Him and to Him are all things, to
whom be glory forever. Amen.   ROMANS 11.36

---

* *Three hours a week in church-related activities (worship service, Sunday School, Youth Group) amounts to two percent of a person's time during the 168 hour week. Six hours a day, five days a week amounts to 30 hours of a person's time during the 168 hour week, or eighteen percent.*

A 2,500 year old object lesson is provided for us by God in describing the victory He enabled Israel's evil King Ahab to have over the superior forces of Syria. Elijah tells King Ahab:

Thus says the LORD: 'Because the Syrians have said, "The LORD is God of the hills, but He is not God of the valleys," therefore I will deliver all this great multitude into your hand, and you shall know that I am the LORD.'
1 KINGS 20.28

Just as our lifestyles should not be divided between two separate and distinct ethical realms, neither should our hearts be "divided." [2] A divided heart, if un-repented of, will eventually lead to Jesus' not even hearing our prayers.[3] The reason for this is that our life is a process through which we are becoming either holier, or un-holier. There is no neutral gear for our heart: There is only forward (toward God) or backward (away from God). From the time we are born to the time we die we are either conforming our actions to God's will or to Satan's will, "for out of our heart spring the issues of life." [4]

But the path of the just is like the shining sun, that shines ever brighter into the perfect day. The way of the wicked is like darkness; they do not know what makes them stumble.
PROVERBS 4.18-19

David recognizes this truth, and in his pursuit toward a holier life sang,

I will praise You, O LORD, with my whole heart.
PSALM 9.1

May we foster the following attitude in our heart:

I wait for the LORD, my soul waits, and in His Word I do hope. My soul waits for the LORD more than those who watch for the morning...
PSALM 130.5-6

Possible reasons for a person's lackadaisical attitude toward serving Christ with all his heart, soul, and mind [5] could be that he has been taught something that is not true, or simply that he believes his salvation is the end, instead of the beginning of his Christian life. Perhaps he doesn't realize that one's salvation begins a process by which he will be equipped and prepared to restore God's creation to its pre-Fall splendor.

The outworking of God's plan is gradual because it comes about as a result of our obedience, not by means of an instantaneous, supernatural event. God's creation is orderly, not chaotic. When consequences B, D and F happen it is because events A, C and E have happened. There is no Scriptural support for consequence F to occur immediately after event A. [6]

It should be remembered that the Christian Church in the first century began very small in number, estimated to have no more than 120 members. This makes Jesus' Parable of the Mustard Seed come into sharp focus:

> *The kingdom of heaven is like a mustard seed, which a man took and sowed in his field, which indeed is the least of all the seeds; but when it is grown it is greater than the herbs and becomes a tree, so that the birds of the air come and nest in its branches.* MATTHEW 13.31-32

Jesus' Parable of the Leaven also presents a description of a gradual development of His Kingdom:

> *The kingdom of heaven is like leaven, which a woman took and hid in three measures of meal till it was all leavened.*
> MATTHEW 13.33

More than 700 years before the birth of Jesus, Isaiah, in speaking of the "last days,"* proclaims how a small remnant of Christians will mushroom over the entire earth.

---

* *The "last days" are all the days between Jesus' time on earth and His return.*

73

A little one shall become a thousand, and a small one a strong nation: I the LORD will hasten it in its time.

ISAIAH 60.22

We need to be careful that our calling from God for whole-hearted obedience is not followed by a half-hearted commitment on our part. A theme that is woven throughout Scripture is man's attempt to "help God out" by adding some of our wisdom to His. Whether it be marrying non-Christians, [7] worshiping God inways that He has not instructed, [8] adding non-Christian beliefs to God's instructions,[9] hating our enemy, [10] voting for the "lesser of two evils," or in refusing to deny ourselves, [11] Scripture makes it abundantly clear that such follies will not only be unsuccessful, but that we will suffer grave consequences.

Do not add to His words, lest he rebuke you and you be found a liar. PROVERBS 30.6

Another reason we may not be serving (and therefore loving) Christ with all of our heart, soul and mind is that we don't understand that God does not exist for us, but we exist for Him. This is an important distinction. If the sole purpose of salvation were merely to escape eternal punishment, that would be a huge blessing and something for which we could praise God. However, Scripture shows that our salvation includes restoring creation to its pre-Fall splendor. How else can it be explained that God gave us His inerrant Word? Surely we wouldn't need it if nothing were expected from us other than living throughout eternity with God and all the saved saints! With this divinely-ordained mission in mind we should constantly and consistently walk according to His law. (For an additional discussion, see the answer to Question 28.) [12]

Q. 29 NOTES
1 1 Corinthians 10.31
2 Hosea 10.2
3 Isaiah 1.11-15
4 Proverbs 4.23
5 Matthew 22.37

6 Zechariah 4.10;
Mark 4.28
7 Genesis 6.1ff; Joshua
23.10-13; 1 Samuel 14.13
8 Exodus 32; Leviticus
10; Numbers 25
9 Galatians 1

10 Matthew 5.43-46
11 Luke 9.23
12 *What's Scripture Got
To Do With It?* Buddy
Hanson, (Hanson Group,
2005), pp. 73-76

Question 30. Is your worldview and lifestyle based upon:

a. The 2nd Table of God's Law: Commandments 5-10 (honor those in authority, don't kill, cheat, steal, lie or be jealous)?

b. Upon both the 2nd Table and the 1st Table of God's Law: Commandments 1-4 (worship only the one true God of the Bible, don't make idols, or misuse the name of the Lord, and to keep the Lord's Day holy)?

The Ten Commandments provide a skeletal framework for every biblical principle. The 20th Century British evangelist Arthur Pink recognized this truth by remarking "The Bible is a commentary on the Ten Commandments." His point is that the remainder of the Bible merely adds "meat" to the skeletal bones of these ten laws. Therefore, if we're serious about our profession of faith, it is absolutely essential that we have a solid understanding of the Ten Commandments so that we can incorporate their principles into our daily duties and be consistent servants for Christ in His Kingdom.

The importance of basing the 2nd Table (our relationship to each other; Commandments 5-10) on the 1st Table (our relationship to God; Commandments 1-4) is because this is the principle that separates a person from being a morally upright, law-abiding, conservative citizen, from a Christian. The conservative will say, "I don't believe we should kill people," but has no way to absolutely refute the liberal who says, "babies in the womb are not 'people.'" Of course, neither can the liberal absolutely refute the conservative's beliefs. Both can work to get more votes to support their various positions, but in the end, both know that while they may win the popular vote today, they could well lose it tomorrow. The danger is that the losing side will not be satisfied with the voice of the people and attempt to gain victory through violence and intimidation, rather than the ballot box. Only God's Word prevents this kind of behavior, because God's Word is unassailable. God is the Creator and we are mere creatures. God is also the inventor of all knowledge and we only know "in part and we therefore prophesy in part." (1 CORINTHIANS 13.9-12) The only way to reconcile opposing points of view is to compare them with God's counsel and to abide by what He says in context.

75

Question 31. When God tells us to "walk in all the ways that I have commanded you, so that it may be well with you," (JEREMIAH 7.23) what does this verse mean to you?

    a. God made a mistake, He really didn't mean it, and we won't be punished if we only make an effort to obey those parts of the Bible that conform to our current worldview and lifestyle. After all, nobody is perfect!

    b. Even though we are imperfect and will never be able to obey God perfectly, we should strive to do that because God never makes mistakes and means what He says. So we should put forth our best effort, knowing that we will blessed if we obey God, and cursed if we disobey Him.

There is only one way for us to "please Him in all respects" and that is by "walking in all the ways God has commanded us." [1] As imperfect and sinful creatures we will never be able to perfectly obey God, but our lack of perfection, does not mean that we are incapable of walking in "all of His ways." Who would not agree that walking in all of God's ways imperfectly (even though we may be uncomfortable in some of them) beats selectively choosing to walk only in some of His ways (those in which we feel the most comfortable)! As sports writers like to say after an underdog upsets a highly favored opponent: "That's why they play the game." Life is not a "game," and each of us faces particularly challenging issues, but that doesn't mean we should forfeit ourselves to various challenges without giving our best efforts. After all, who knows what major blessings (victories) God is waiting to grant to us through our obedience to Him in all of our ways! Jehovah speaks the following encouraging words through the prophet Jeremiah:

> *Walk in all the ways that I have commanded you, that it may be well with you."*   JEREMIAH 7.23

Determining to walk in all of God's ways does not mean everyone should attempt to be a pastor, or a Bible teacher; it means that we should not be selective in our obedience to the all-encompassing principles contained in the Ten Commandments. [2] For example, do we ever wonder how we can say, "God's Word is true," then send our children to schools that teach lies all day? Or, do we wonder why Christians who teach in such God-hating schools say they are doing so to be "salt and light," when they know that to associate themselves with non-Christians in a business relationship is to refuse to heed Paul's injunction to not be "unequally yoked together with unbelievers?" [3]

We lament our cultural decline, yet God promises to establish a holy culture if we will "keep the commandments of the LORD our God and walk in His ways." [4] In spite of our disgust and discouragement at the times in which we live and the unpleasant ways in which they affect our life, we prefer to limit our obedience by being selective in the ways and to the extent that we obey God. Jeremiah speaks to a similar attitude when he foretells the coming destruction of the Southern Kingdom of Judah:

> *Ask for the old paths, where the good way is, and walk in it;*
> *then you will find rest for your souls. But they said, "We will*
> *not walk in it."* **JEREMIAH 6.16**

In a similar manner Paul counseled the Christians in Philippi:

> *Only conduct yourselves in a manner worthy of the gospel of*
> *Christ; so that whether I come and see you or remain absent,*
> *I may hear of you that you are standing firm in one spirit,*
> *with one mind striving together for the faith of the gospel;*
> *in no way alarmed by your opponents, which is a sign of*
> *destruction for them, but of salvation for you, and that too,*
> *from God. For to you it has been granted for Christ's sake, not*
> *only to believe in Him, but also to suffer for His sake.*
> **PHILIPPIANS 1.27-29**

A decade earlier, Paul's message in Rome had been the same:

> *I urge you therefore, brothers, by the mercies of God, to present*
> *your bodies a living and holy sacrifice, acceptable to God,*
> *which is your spiritual service of worship.* **ROMANS 12.1**

As people who have been called out of the dark and vain imaginings of our fallen mind, so that we can re-think our Creator-God's thoughts and follow His will, we have much for which we can be thankful. First and foremost, we should be especially grateful for the guidance by the Holy Spirit into a correct understanding of who we are, what we are supposed to be doing and what our purpose is. As each of us strives to be more consistent in our obedience, our knowledge of Scripture will grow.

Knowing that God is sovereignly controlling all aspects of His creation, should give us the peace of mind and the confidence that nothing outside of His ultimate purposes will be accomplished. Christ's plan is for us to follow Him, not wander from Him. Solomon states, "A man who wanders from the way of understanding will rest in the assembly of the dead." [5] This statement emphasizes that there is no room in Christianity for split allegiances. Either we are for Jesus, or we are against Him. If we profess to be followers of Christ but still have our eyes on the glitter of the world, we should not be surprised if this glitter becomes a glare that blinds us to the demands of Scripture.

But if your eye be bad, your whole body will be full of darkness. If therefore, the light that is in you is darkness, how great is the darkness! MATTHEW 6.23

> Jesus is well aware that we are "works in progress," and He accepts that. What He refuses to accept is our attitude of intentionally compromising His instructions to suit our will and our agenda.

Jesus is not talking here of the inconsistent level of obedience we all have. While we strive to consistently obey Him, we know that for the remainder of our lives we will be going through a process of "weeding out" the remnants of our former sin nature, and this is going to result in our being better servants of Him on some days than we are on other days.

After all, we have been given the mission of bringing about His will on earth as it is in heaven! [6] He did not call us to join Him in a joint venture where both of us decide on what is to be done. He's holding all of the cards and makes all of the decisions, and He demands and commands that we do things His way. [7] Whether it is our intention or not, our attitude of being selective in the areas of obedience is the same as saying, "We're in control and are perfectly capable of calling the shots of everyday decisions." Such an attitude sees God as a Supernatural Rescuer whom we are holding in reserve for times when we are in serious trouble, as if we were co-equal partners, instead of correctly viewing our situation as divinely called employees whose task is to serve our Supernatural Employer. In the Old Testament, Jehovah makes the case for obedience perfectly clear:

> *Therefore you shall observe all My statutes and all My judgments, and perform them: I am the LORD.*
>
> LEVITICUS 19.37
> ALSO LEVITICUS 20.8; NUMBERS 15.40;
> DEUTERONOMY 4.2, 33; 10.12; 11.8, 22, 32; 28.1;32.46;
> JOSHUA 22.5; 23.6; LUKE 11.28

In the New Testament Jesus reinforces the same message:

> *No one can serve two masters; for either he will hate the one and love the other, or else he will be loyal to the one and despise the other. You cannot serve God and [man].*
>
> MATTHEW 6.24

We must remember "all our ways are before Him." [8]

> *Whoever therefore breaks one of the least of these commandments and teaches men so, shall be called least in the kingdom of heaven; but whoever does and teaches them, he shall be called great in the kingdom of heaven.*
>
> MATTHEW 5.19

Paul quotes Moses to drive home this crucial point:

> *Cursed is everyone who does not continue in all things which are written in the book of the law, to do them.*
>
> GALATIANS 3.10; DEUTERONOMY 27.26

Jeremiah also paints a sobering picture of what could happen to a disobedient and unrepentant people:

> *"Do you not fear Me?" says the LORD. "Will you not tremble at My presence, Who have placed the sand as the bound of the sea, by a perpetual decree, that it cannot pass beyond it? And though its waves toss to and fro, yet they cannot prevail; though they roar, yet they cannot pass over it. But this people has a defiant and rebellious heart; they have revolted and departed. They do not say in their heart, "Let us now fear the LORD our God, Who gives rain, both the former and the latter, in its season. He reserves for us the appointed weeks of the harvest."*
>
> *Your iniquities have turned these things away, and your sins have withheld good from you. "For among My people are found wicked men; they lie in wait as one who sets snares; - they set a trap; they catch men. As a cage is full of birds, so their houses are full of deceit. Therefore they have become great and grown rich. They have grown fat, they are sleek; yes, they surpass the deeds of the wicked; they do not plead the cause, the cause of the fatherless; yet they prosper, and the right of the needy they do not defend. Shall I not punish them for these things?" says the LORD. "Shall I not avenge Myself on such a nation as this?'*
>
> *"An astonishing and horrible thing has been committed in the land: The prophets prophesy falsely, and the priests rule by their own power; And My people love to have it so. But what will you do in the end?*　　　JEREMIAH 5.22-31

No matter how fortunate we are to be constantly exposed to biblical preaching and Christian friends, if there is no real commitment on our part to persevere in the faith, and to live for God and be diligent in our prayer life, we will sooner or later find ourselves "wandering out of the way of understanding." The only way to prevent this from happening is to be careful that we are always

*Giving all diligence, add to your faith virtue, to virtue
knowledge, to knowledge self-control, to self-control
perseverance, to perseverance godliness, to godliness brotherly
kindness, and to brotherly kindness love. For if these things
are yours and abound, you will be neither barren nor
unfruitful in the knowledge of our Lord Jesus Christ. For
he who lacks these things is shortsighted, even to blindness,
and has forgotten that he was cleansed from his old sins.*

2 PETER 1.5-9

There are two main rationalisms used by Christians to keep from presenting a powerful testimony to those with whom we come in contact. First, we try to explain away certain biblical ethics that do not conform to our own selfish desires about how we should live. "God's Word is certainly true," we say, "but, when God made this statement, it applied exclusively to particular people and particular events and circumstances that no longer apply."

A second rationalism that is used to avoid submitting our life to God's rules is to say, "God's Word is true and has been preserved through the ages without error, but it only applies to 'church-related activities.' (i.e., God's counsel is valuable in 'personal matters of morality' inside our homes or inside the church, but as far as how to conduct one's daily activities outside our homes and churches, or to establish laws by which to live, or to incorporate God's ethics in our vocations, God's Word is 'out-of-bounds' and inapplicable.)" What is really meant by such statements is that we are smarter than God when it comes to matters of "real life."

Whenever we are tempted to use either of these rationalizations we should remember that there are no "buts" to obeying God's Word. His Word is true, period. Christians who fall prey to such rationalisms live as though God's Word is potent enough to call them out of spiritual darkness and save them, yet not practical enough to guide them in their daily activities. This type of attitude only reflects a lack of trust in the sufficiency of God's Word. In fact, so much does such a professing Christian distrust God's ability to "provide for him," that he only turns one seventh of his life (Sunday) over to Him, while trusting the remaining six sevenths to man's thoughts, ideas and laws. We should point out to these

81

brothers and sisters that God's Word is entirely sufficient for all of one's spiritual needs, it provides all the ethics necessary for holy living, and it needs none of our wisdom to be added to it. [9] Jesus says that He teaches "all things that I heard from My Father." [10] The apostles also were faithful to teach God's whole counsel. As Paul states, he "kept nothing back that was profitable." [11] These statements mean that we have all the information necessary in order to live and govern ourselves in a holy manner. [12]

Question 32. I believe that

    a. God exists for us.

    b. We exist for God.

In sports, coaching staffs spend a lot of time studying their opponents in an effort to identify their "tendencies:" the plays their opponents have a tendency to run in certain situations. Then, when those situations arise, the coaches will call for a defensive alignment that is designed to counter that play. This is a principle we should apply to our worldview and lifestyle. Humans are humans. Even though we have a lot more technical savvy than our predecessors, we still have the same sinful tendencies, and one of the ways they manifest themselves is in our forgetfulness of God's guiding hand in our daily situations and circumstances. The following list highlights some common tendencies we have in forgetting the great advantages and benefits of being a member of Christ's kingdom:

Q. 31 NOTES

1 Deuteronomy 5.32
2 For a comprehensive study of the practical applications of the Ten Commandments, see *God's Ten Words: Practical Applications from the Ten Commandments*, Buddy Hanson, (Hanson Group, 2002)
3 2 Corinthians 6.14
4 Deuteronomy 28.9
5 Proverbs 21.16
6 Matthew 6.10

7 2 Corinthians 11.2; Exodus 20.5
8 Psalm 119.168
9 2 Timothy 3.15-17; Revelation 22.18-19; Galatians 1.8-9; 2 Thessalonians 2.2
10 John 15.15
11 Acts 20.20,27
12 This portion is excerpted from *EXIT Strategy: A Handbook to Exponentially Improve Your Service for God*, Buddy Hanson, (Hanson Group, 2005), pp.103-110

- Forgetting God's daily blessings and providential care for us.
- Forgetting that He has enabled us to be the only people on the face of the earth to correctly understand the truth, and choosing to "conform" ourselves to the untruths of our non-Christian neighbors (i.e. setting up the false dichotomy of "sacred" and "secular" areas of life).
- Forgetting that there are lessons in everything that happens to us[1] and complaining about His chastening of us instead of looking for valuable lessons through which to improve our behavior.
- Forgetting our reference point in all of our situations and circumstances (God), thereby making man (i.e. peer pressure, popular opinion, etc.) our reference point.
- Forgetting that God's ethics apply throughout His creation, not just inside our homes and churches.
- Forgetting that "The wicked shall be turned into hell, and all the nations that forget God." [2]

Forgetfulness of God's daily blessings, if not repented of, can result very serious and unpleasant consequences. Ezekiel tells us that those who "cast away the knowledge of God" will themselves be cast away from His presence. [3] The 17th Century British Nonconformist Pastor Matthew Henry comments: "…the paths of all who forget God; and the hope of the hypocrite shall perish." [4] Henry adds,

Forgetfulness of God is at the bottom of men's hypocrisy, and of the vain hopes with which they flatter and deceive themselves in their hypocrisy. Men would not be hypocrites if they did not forget that the God with whom they have to do searches the heart and requires truth there, that He is a Spirit and has His eye on our spirits; and hypocrites would have no hope if they did not forget that God is righteous, and will not be mocked. [5]

Seventeenth century Parliamentarian Sir William Lord Russell provides this timeless advice to his son. We would all be the better if we would heed it:

*Fail not, what employment soever you have, every night,
as in the presence of God and His holy angels, to pass an
inquisition on your soul, what ill it has done, what good it
has left undone; what slips, what fall, it has had that day;
what temptations have prevailed upon it, and by what
means or after what manner. Ransack every corner of your
dark heart; and let not the least peccadillo, or kindness to a
sin, lurk there; but bring it forth, bewail it, protest against,
detest it, and scourge it by a severe sorrow. Thus, each day's
breach between God and your soul being made up, with
more quiet and sweet hope you may dispose yourself to rest.
Certainly at last this inquisition, if steadily pursued, will
vanquish all customary sins, whatever they may be. I speak it
upon this reason, because I presume you will not have the face
to appear before God every night confessing the same offense;
and you will forbear it, lest you may seem to mock God, or
despise him, which is dreadful but to imagine.* [6]

Question 33. Who's "running the show?" Who's in charge of planet earth?

    a. Satan.

    b. Jesus.

If the earth is Satan's domain, and heaven is God's domain, then there is really nothing we can do to stem the Satanic Tsunami that is sweeping across our culture. To have such a view is to see the world through man's eyes, not God's. It is to live according to our rules, not God's.

The "Humanist Manifesto III, states, "The knowledge of the world is derived by observation, experimentation, and rational analysis." In opposition to this the prophet Habakkuk and the apostle Paul tell us "the

Q. 32 NOTES

1   Romans 8.28
2   Psalm 9.17
3   Ezekiel 23.35
4   Job 8.13
5   Henry, *ibid.*, Volume III, p.51

6   Flavel, John, *Keeping The Heart*, (Soli Deo Gloria, 1662, 1998), p. ix; portions of this answer are excerpts from *What's Scripture Got to Do With It?* Buddy Hanson, (Hanson Group, 2005), pp.84-85

just shall live by faith." 1 Paul also says that we should "walk by faith, not by sight." 2

In our day there are two camps of Christians (!) who approach life from opposite directions. One camp views their daily situations and circumstances by sight, and the other by faith. The camp that comes by sight sees a storm, a draught, or a war, then remembers God using a similar event in Scripture to bring judgment upon a community, or nation. So they conclude, "This is a sign that 'the end' is near." Obviously, if a person believes "the end is near," he is presupposing that Satan is going to win in history, and is therefore not going to be very concerned about attempting to improve the current cultural situation. They may know a lot about what God's Word says, but they approach God's Word as being something that's meant to be turned to in times of trouble to COMFORT them from cares and concerns and to REASSURE them that once they get to heaven everything is going to be hunky dory.

Since their focus is primarily on the "hereafter," instead of the "here-and-now" and the "hereafter," they view the truths of the Bible as being something to internalize, rather than to externalize. So when it comes to the situations and circumstances they face as they go through life, their reaction is to place more trust in what they see, than in what God says.

In contrast to this camp of Christians who live by "sight," the other camp of Christians approaches life by faith and notices that from cover-to-cover God's Word tells us that if we live according to His rules we will be rewarded, and if we live according to our rules, we will be punished.[3] The people in this camp don't approach the Bible as being simply a descriptive brochure about our eternal destination, but as a travel guide that tells us how to live and govern ourselves on our way to heaven.

To view life by "sight" is to approach it with a "death wish," (because that's the only way things are going to get better), instead of with a "life wish" (to redeem the earth according to biblical ethics). Many of our brothers and sisters in the "sight" camp will acknowledge that our disobedience, (our evil and sinful actions) are the root causes for storms and wars, but they are not willing to complete the loop in their logic.

> If our "bad actions" cause God to discipline us, why can't our "good actions" cause Him to bless us?

85

Not too long ago there was a commercial on TV that had a husband and wife walking through a large department store. When they passed the washers and dryers the wife didn't just "see" the washers and dryers. What she "saw" was her daughter sitting beside the dryer hugging her teddy bear that was clean, warm and fluffy because she just got it out of the dryer. Next, the couple passed the outdoor furniture section. Again, the wife didn't just "see" the patio furniture, but rather she saw her daughter surrounded by a group of friends at her birthday party. This commercial hit home with me because too many of our brothers and sisters are only "seeing" washers and dryers and outdoor furniture. They are not "seeing" how they can be used. When you see a Bible, you see God's Word, but it's not just God's Word, as wonderful as that is. It is also our Owner's Manual; our Instruction Book for life. Now there's a big difference between this Owner's Manual and the manuals that come with our cars and computers. This one makes sense!

In order to be effective servants of Christ's Kingdom, we must "see" the world as He sees it, and the first eye-opening revelation every Christian should have is that Jesus is alive and well on planet earth. Indeed, He is in complete control of His creation and nothing happens of which He is not aware. This truth should be the cornerstone of our worldview, because if Satan were the "God of this world," the only thing left for Christians would be to punt. This would mean Jesus was unsuccessful in His earthly mission to defeat Satan and would also mean that His mission for us to "subdue and rule over creation" has been overturned.

Fortunately, Jesus was successful in His earthly mission. In Paul's words, God "delivered us from the domain of darkness and transferred us to the Kingdom of His beloved Son…" While on earth, Jesus assured Christians, "the gates of Hades will not prevail against (the work of the Church)." [4] So thorough was Christ's victory over Satan that all we have to do is this: "Submit to God, resist the devil [and] he will flee…" [5] This may sound very different from what is taught in many Christian books and from some pulpits, but this is what God's Word says.

Jesus currently sits at the right hand of God the Father where He has "all authority" in heaven and earth. Again, this may not "fit" with what many in today's church are teaching, but this is what God's Word says.

So to stay on the sidelines of life and not advocate and promote God's principles, is to live as if God's Word is meaningless for day-to-day activities, and to imply that man's will is superior to God's.

The thought of being called by God to transform not only our lives, but our culture and even the entire world is very imposing. If we only focus on what God has promised, we're likely to be overwhelmed by its seeming improbability. However, by focusing on the Promiser, we can restore our confidence and assurance in what's promised.

Whatever else we do, we should not forget that Jesus is going to win, with or without us. He doesn't need America to bring about His will on earth, but He has given us the opportunity to take the lead in discipling the nations. Yet if we fail to repent and turn our focus to serving His will instead of our own He could very easily raise up some other generation, or some other country to accomplish His purposes.

May we not give such a horrible legacy to our children and grandchildren. May we repent of our self-serving, indolent behavior and return to living our whole life in conformity with God's Word. By dedicating ourselves to living according to His rules we can expect untold blessings for ourselves, our children and their children. May we so live! [7]

> Just as Noah looked not to his immediate circumstances, but to God's Word, so should we focus our thoughts not upon our immediate circumstances, but upon God's controlling hand over all circumstances. As the Lord said to Abraham, "Why did Sarah laugh ...Is anything too difficult for the Lord?" [6]

Q. 33 NOTES

1 Habakkuk 2.4; Romans 1.17; Hebrews 10.38

2 2 Corinthians 5.7

3 Leviticus 26; Deuteronomy 28

4 Matthew 16.18

5 James 4.7

6 Genesis 18.14

7 Portions of this answer are excepts from *EXIT Strategy*, p.115

Question 34. As Christians do we have a

a. Hope to cope? Or a
b. Hope to conquer?

What does it mean to you to be a member of Christ's Kingdom? In sports, coaches have two major motivational talks. If they are coaching a storied program with numerous championships and all star players, they will remind their players of the great tradition their team has and often talk about past teams and individual players who overcame great obstacles to build their winning tradition and how the current team should want to do everything it can to carry on their winning ways. It's not unusual for coaches in such situations to invite former players to give a pep talk before a particularly big game.

On the other hand, if the coach has a team that doesn't have an illustrious past, they will emphasize that this team can begin such a tradition. A tradition that they can one day point out to their children that they were one of the players responsible for turning the program around and helping the program achieve greatness. These talks serve as great motivators because everybody wants to be part of something special.

As a Christian, and therefore a member of God's family, you are part of the most storied and gloried "family" on the face of the earth. No other family has achieved more victories, or overcome such great obstacles and no other family will achieve the greatest victory on earth, which will be bringing about God the Father's will. [1]

> Perhaps it's time for a halftime locker room talk to remind ourselves exactly who we are, who came before us, and what they have accomplished.

Yet, instead of confidently striving for holiness in our daily decisions and actions, as we steadily advance toward this grand goal, too many of us seem content to strive for spirituality, whereby we turn our beliefs inward as if the only reason the Bible was given to us was to enable us to "cope" with an unbeatable agenda of non-Christians.

As you remind yourself of the dedication and diligence of these teammates of the past had and the remarkable victories they were enabled to achieve for Christ's Kingdom, also remind yourself that you have the same "Coach" they did, and His "play calling" is just as sharp today as it was when they walked on the earth. If you are facing some tough circumstances, remember the circumstances they faced and the odds that appeared to be humanly impossible to overcome. Then remember that the first order of duty for a Christian is not to walk exclusively by "sight," but by "faith" [2] in our triune God's controlling hand of history. Have you ever comforted someone with the statement: "Faith is the substance of things hoped for, the evidence of things not seen?" [3] If so, now's the time to demonstrate to your non-Christian neighbors that you believe what you say by showing them with your worldview and lifestyle that "what they see with their natural eyes," is not all that they can get. That once they repent and turn their lives over to Jesus, they will be the recipients of God's supernatural assistance to guide and direct their daily actions.

Nine Noble Noisemakers For Christ's Kingdom

- **Noah** worked diligently for more than 120 years to build an ark to save his family against a natural event that had never happened. (GENESIS 6.8-22; HEBREWS 11.7)
- **Abraham** left his home, family and friends to go to a place he knew not. (GENESIS 12.1-4; HEBREWS 11.8)
- **Moses** refused to be called the son of Pharaoh's daughter, choosing rather to suffer affliction with the people of God than to enjoy the passing pleasures of sin, esteeming the reproach of Christ greater riches than the treasures in Egypt, for he looked to the reward. (HEBREWS 11.24-26)
- **Gideon** reduced his army from 32,000 to 300 then attacked and defeated the huge Midianite army. (JUDGES 6.11; 7.1-25)
- **David** said to Goliath, "You come to me with a sword, with a spear, and with a javelin. But I come to you in the name of the LORD of hosts, the God of the armies of Israel, whom you have defied." (1 SAMUEL 17.45)
- **Shadrach, Meshach, and Abed-Nego** said to the king, "O Nebuchadneaaar, we have no need to answer you in this matter. ...Our God whom we serve is able to deliver us from the burning fiery furnace, and He will deliver us from your hand, O king. But if not, let it be known to you, O king, that we do not serve your gods, nor will we worship the gold image which you have set up." (DANIEL 3.16-18)
- **Mordecai** admonished his cousin Esther, "Yet who knows whether you have come to the kingdom for such a time as this?" (ESTHER 4.14)

Make Some "Noise" for Christ's Kingdom T-O-D-A-Y!

Once a person submits his life to Jesus he will find that he will begin making some divinely-inspired "noise" for Christ's Kingdom. The previous "Nine Noble Noisemakers" remind us of what God can accomplish through our faithful, consistent and persistent obedience to His perfect counsel on how to live, raise our families and govern ourselves.

Our "halftime intermission" is up and the question is: "How are you going to approach the "field of play," (our culture) which is dominated by a collective non-Christian worldview?" Are you going to uphold our gloried and storied tradition by living with the same boldness and un-flinching confidence as those who have gone before us, such as: Noah, Abraham, Moses, Gideon, David, Shadrach, Meshach, Abed-Nego and Mordecai? You have no excuse not to, because just as they were enabled to accomplish great victories over seemingly overwhelming odds, so will we be enabled to be victorious. "And just how may I be so confident of that?" you may ask. My reply is that Jehovah promised it literally from the "get-go" with these encouraging words:

> *I will put enmity between you (Satan) and the woman, and*
> *between your seed and her Seed; He (Jesus) will bruise you on*
> *the head, and you shall bruise His heel.*　　GENESIS 3.15

These words transcribed by Moses sound like we are called to do a lot more than "cope." And, if you prefer some encouraging words from the New Testament, how about these:

> *The God of peace will crush Satan under your feet shortly.*
> 　　　　　　　　　　　　　　　　　ROMANS 16.20

The apostle Paul doesn't sound like his goal and the goal of fellow Christians is to merely "cope" with whatever non-Christians throw our way.

> *Peter, on this rock I will build My church, and the gates of*
> *Hades shall not prevail against it.*　　MATTHEW 16.18

Do these words by Jesus indicate that His church is too wimpishly "cope" with Satan's attacks?

Now, therefore, you are no longer strangers and foreigners,
but fellow citizens with the saints and members of the
household of God, having been built on the foundation of
the apostles and prophets, Jesus Christ Himself being the
chief cornerstone, in whom the whole building, being fitted
together. Grows into a holy temple in the Lord, in whom you
also are being built together for a dwelling place of God in the
Spirit.   EPHESIANS 2.19-22

Does the church, as it has been and continues to be divinely assembled by Jesus, sound like it is being "fitted together" to merely whine, complain and "cope" about how bad the culture is becoming, because Jesus is clueless about how to lead us out of this cultural mess? Or do these verses sound like Jesus, as our "chief cornerstone," is recruiting an all-earth championship team ... a "world-beater," if you will?

All authority has been given to Me in heaven and on earth.
Go therefore and make disciples of all the nations, baptizing
them in the name of the Father and of the Son and of the
Holy Spirit, teaching them to observe all things that I have
commanded you; and lo, I am with you always, even to
the end of the age.   MATTHEW 28.18-20

Should the fact that Jesus (not Satan) has "all authority" on earth, cause anyone to believe that Christians are called to be historical winners, and not historical losers who cannot do anything more than "cope" at the non-Christian cultural agenda? Where's the Scriptural support for being called into Christ's Kingdom to merely "grin and bear" the consequences of the non-Christian cultural agenda?

The kingdoms of this world have become the kingdoms of our
Lord and of His Christ, and He shall reign forever and ever!
                                                     REVELATION 11.15

Do I even have to ask if this verse sounds like our ultimate goal should merely be culturally irrelevant people who can only "cope" with cultural events? I certainly wouldn't have to ask it to our forefathers, whose motto during the American Revolution was, "No King but King Jesus!" It should be understood that "Cope" is a philosophical concept, and that God didn't call us to be philosophers, but to be doers, and victorious doers at that.

No matter how deliberately and diligently non-Christians work to bring down God and establish their ways, they are under the complete control of their Creator and their actions will be used to help achieve God's eternally perfect plans for the earth.

> *For I am persuaded that neither death nor life, nor angels nor principalities nor powers, nor things present nor things to come, nor height nor depth, nor any other created thing, shall be able to separate us from the love of God which is in Christ Jesus our Lord.* ROMANS 8.38-39

> *And Jesus came and spoke to them, saying, "All authority has been given to Me in heaven and on earth. Go therefore and make disciples of all the nations, baptizing them in the name of the Father and of the Son and of the Holy Spirit, teaching them to observe all things that I have commanded you; and lo, I am with you always, even to the end of the age."* MATTHEW 28.18-20

Where in this verse does Jesus include the bland concept of "coping?"

- Could it be that these "copers" have forgotten Jesus' promises that Christians will "inherit the earth?" [4] Perhaps.
- Could it be that they have forgotten that "The King's heart is in the hand of the LORD, and like the rivers of water; He turns it wherever He wishes?" [5] Perhaps.
- Could it be that they have forgotten the apostle Paul's rhetorical question: "If God be for us, who can be against us?" [6] Perhaps.

The best antidote to such blasphemously pessimistic thinking is to open the Bible and let God straighten out our muddled thinking. By studying God's Word, we destroy non-Christian viruses that have sneaked into our worldview and lifestyle. It also helps us to keep His victorious promises fresh in our mind. God's promises help us to distance ourselves from the hallucinatory hopes and incoherent imaginations of non-Christians.

The next time you're looking for something to study in your Daily Spiritual Practice, check your concordance for the words, "walk, walks, and walking." That will keep you busy for a few days. On the other hand, if you don't have much time for Daily Spiritual Practice, check your concordance for the words "analyzing, contemplating, coping, hanging-on, and nail-biting," because you will be able to handle them in no time flat.

In his "Thesis on Feurback," Karl Marx writes, "The philosophers only interpreted the world differently, the point is to change it." [7] Did you get that? Marx is saying, philosopher A says that he thinks we should live this way, and philosopher B says he thinks we should live that way, but we should be doing, not talking, because the point is to change the world, not talk about it.

Think about this for a few seconds. Non-Christians, who not only don't have the truth, but don't believe that it exists, and who have never had a civilization sustain itself based upon their self-centered and ungodly ethics, believe that they can change the world for the better. How they define "better," when they have no absolute standard for the meaning of words, is a topic for another time, but for now let's contrast the optimism of a group that has no definitive basis for being optimistic, (indeed, no definitive basis for anything) with the pessimism of a group (us!) who have no definitive basis for being pessimistic! Do we really want to follow a group of people who don't know how they got here; what their purpose is, or where they're going?!

Nothing is more valuable to God than His own Word. Even we, as sinful creatures place a priority on our words, because from them our reputation is established. If our words are true, we have an honest reputation and will be respected, but if our words are false, there is no reason for anyone to respect us, because they will never know if what we are saying is sincere or insincere. This reality is poignantly presented by William Shakespeare in his classic play "Othello," when Cassio cries out to Iago,

Reputation, reputation, reputation! O, I have lost my reputation! I have lost the immortal part of myself, and what remains is bestial. My reputation, Iago, my reputation! [8]

We are commanded to live by God's rules, instead of ours. Even though God's reputation doesn't rise and fall based upon our obedience to His Word, our reputation does! If we are serious about our profession of faith, we will not attempt to hide our disobedience from God in order to "follow the dictates of our heart," [9] by walking in the stubbornness of our imagination. As Jehovah proclaims through the prophet Isaiah: "Woe to the rebellious children who take counsel, but not of Me, and who devise plans, but not of My Spirit."[10] The famous early American inventor and statesman, Benjamin Franklin showed that the situation was not much different in his day, by proclaiming: "How many observe Christ's birthday! How few, his precepts! O! tis easier to keep Holidays than Commandments."

> The question that is staring at each of us in the mirror is: "Am I 'working out' my mission in Christ's Kingdom with 'fear and trembling?'" [11]

May we all step forth from our homes today with the confident attitude of upholding our gloried and storied tradition by "making some sanctified noise" for Christ's Kingdom!

Question 35. It is said that a "text without a context is a pretext," and so is a "worldview and lifestyle without a biblical reference point, pointless." This is why we should always ask before making any decision, or addressing any cultural issue:

> What does the Law of God say about it?

Q. 34 NOTES

1 Matthew 6.10
2 2 Corinthians 5.7
3 Hebrews 11.1
4 Matthew 5.5
5 Proverbs 21.1

6 Romans 8.31
7 *The German Ideology*, "Thesis on Feurbach," Karl Marx & Friedrich Engels (International Publishing, 1947, 1960), p. 199

8 Othello, Act 2, Scene 3, William Shakespeare
9 Deuteronomy 29.19
10 Isaiah 30.1
11 Philippians 2.12

a. Is the context of my decision-making man's word?

b. Is the context of my decision-making God's Word?

These nine words form a boundary between a non-Christian worldview and a Christian worldview. Non-Christians are constantly searching for new ideas because their "old ideas" don't work. "How lucky can those Christians get!" they must wonder. "Throughout history their ideas have proven successful and ours have proven disastrous. Isn't it about time for the law of percentages to kick-in?! Oh, I know what we can do, since our fixed standard of ethics hasn't worked, let's adopt 'evolving standards.' Let's have one group of citizens propose one set of ethics (a thesis), and have another group of citizens propose another set of ethics (an anti-thesis), then mix them together and come up with a synthesis of behavior. This way everyone comes away with something and we can build a consensus."

This approach in formulating a worldview is perfectly practical, pragmatic, logical and natural for non-Christians, since they cannot discern God's perfect Life Plan. But for us, a cafeteria-style of obedience where we pick and choose different elements of God's Word to obey depending upon how easily they enable us to "build coalitions" with our non-Christian neighbors, is completely unacceptable, because we are commanded to follow God with our "whole heart,"[1] not a "partial heart." In the words of the prophet Elijah

How long will you falter between two opinions? If the LORD is God, follow him; but if Baal, follow him.

1 KINGS 18.21

None of this is to imply that non-Christians are stupid. They want meaning in their lives, just as much as we do, but without the supernatural help of the Holy Spirit, they have no way to arrive at the correct answers for life's issues. Still, they recognize that the collective worldview of a society should transform culture. Karl Marx and Friedrich Engels write, "[We] have a world to win …working men of all countries unite!"[2] Yet for all of the passion that non-Christians have for improving the world, we don't seem to be able to connect the Spiritual Dot about our

95

responsibility to redeem the world. Where's our passion?! It appears that we are happy to just watch civilization go down the tubes. However, Scripture doesn't teach anything close to such a pessimistic and defeatist scenario. To the contrary, it teaches that particular civilizations have and will "go down the tubes," because they have not and are not implementing biblical ethics into their daily decision-making. But while particular civilizations are destroyed, it does not mean that Satan defeats Jesus in history (especially when Jesus came to "defeat the works of the devil" [3] and since Jesus tells us that His earthly mission to do that and to redeem us "was finished." [4]

God's eternally perfect plan of Christianizing the world, is still proceeding according to His eternally perfect timetable. As Christians, we are enabled by the Holy Spirit to present a holy testimony in our daily walk, as we obediently carry out our service in Christ's Kingdom. We "know the commandments," [5] and we also know that God's Word has been given to us, not merely for us to believe in it, but to live by. It is not given to us so that we can fill our minds with interesting thoughts, but so that we can fill our lives with holy behavior.

As you therefore have received Christ Jesus the Lord, so walk in Him, rooted and built up in Him and established in the faith, as you have been taught, abounding in it with thanksgiving. COLOSSIANS 2.6-7

This means that the testimony we should be presenting to our non-Christian neighbors should be marked by our being "steadfast, immovable, always abounding in the work of the Lord, knowing that our labor is not in vain in the Lord." [6]

Q. 35 NOTES

1   Psalm 119.2, 10, 34, 69; Jeremiah 3.10; 24.7; Mark 12.33

2   Max Eastman, *Capital, The Communist Manifesto, and other writings of Karl Marx,* (Carlton House, 1932), p. 355

3   1 John 3.8

4   John 19.30

5   1 Thessalonians 4.1

6   1 Corinthians 15.58

OBJECTION 1: "The Jewish church was a theocracy." or "Israel, as a nation, is a type of the church of Christ, which means that any civil laws that applied to Israel are today applied to the church."

By definition a theocracy is a community that establishes its laws according to the laws of God. Theologian James B. Jordan turns this objection back on those who raise it: "It has been contended that today we are not living in a 'theocracy,' but are living under 'pluralism.' What does this mean? Surely every Christian desires Christ to be king in some sense, and thus in some sense desires a 'theocracy.' Moreover, even if we are not living today in a theocracy, is this not just the issue at stake? To argue that our present government is pagan is simply to admit the need for a Christian theocracy. Theocracy, after all, means 'the rule of God' or 'the authority of God.'" [1] Those who deny the authority of God's laws toward their culture because "the Jews lived under a theocracy and therefore cannot be an example to us," should understand that when they pick up one end of that stick, they pick up both ends.

> To dismiss God's civil advice to the Old Testament kings is to also dismiss His personal advice, since it is one and the same code of conduct!

If taken to its logical conclusion, this type of thinking would nullify the lessons of the entire Old Testament! In His Sermon on the Mount, where Jesus validated the Decalogue and the Old Testament Case Laws, He says:

> *You have heard that it was said to those of old, "You shall not murder, and whoever murders will be in danger of the judgment [and] I say to you that whoever is angry with his brother without a cause shall be in danger of the judgment.*
> **MATTHEW 5.21-22**

Notice that Jesus mentions the word judgment twice. This clearly shows it is not only wrong to do certain actions, but that judgment (punishment) should be the expected result of our disobedience. The apostle Paul also helps answer this objection by stating: "Now all these things

97

happened to them for examples..." [2] Elsewhere he gives the following familiar advice about the applicability of the Old Testament:

> *All Scripture is given by inspiration of God, and is profitable*
> *for doctrine, for reproof, for correction, for instruction*
> *in righteousness, that the man of God may be complete,*
> *thoroughly equipped for every good work.*
>
> 2 TIMOTHY 3.16-17 [3]

OBJECTION 2: "The Law has been replaced by grace."

The esteemed 19th Century Pastor Robert L. Dabney points out that such an objection is very dishonoring to Jesus.

> *For the Decalogue is as much Christ's law as the Sermon on*
> *the mount. He was the authoritative agent for giving both.*
> *For it was "with the angel which spoke unto him in Mount*
> *Sinai," [Christ, Acts 7.38] that Moses "received these lively*
> *oracles to give to us." Second: It would be dishonorable to a*
> *perfect God to suppose that He would reveal to His chosen*
> *people, as a rule of righteousness, a law which allowed some*
> *sin. Third: God forbade that the law should receive addition.*
> *[Deuteronomy 4.2; 12.32] Fourth: Christ honored this*
> *law, declared it everlasting and unchangeable, and said that*
> *He came not to destroy, but to fulfill it. Fifth: Christ says*
> *that on His abridgments of this law hang all the law and the*
> *prophets. And last: St. Paul, having resolved the precepts of*
> *this Decalogue into the one principle of love [Romans 13.9],*
> *verse 10th says, "Love is the fulfilling of the law." This*
> *is said by this minister of the new dispensation. And both*
> *the Old and New testaments assert the perfection of this Old*

OBJECTION 1 NOTES

1 Jordan, James B., *The Journal of Christian Reconstruction*, Vol. V, No. 2, "Calvinism and the 'Judicial Law of Moses,'" (Chalcedon, 1979), Gary North, ed.

2 1 Corinthians 10.6-11

3 This objection is excerpted from *The Christian Civil Ruler's Handbook*, Buddy Hanson, (Hanson Group, 2004), pp.57-58

Testament law ...It cannot be abrogated or relaxed, because it is as immutable as He. [1]

The law of the Lord is perfect, restoring the soul; the testimony of the Lord is sure, making wise the simple.　　PSALM 19.7

So then, the Law is holy, and the commandment is holy and righteous and good.　　ROMANS 7.12

The following Scriptures show that God's entire Word has always applied to the entire world:

- In John 14.15 **Jesus** teaches that if we love Him we will "keep His commandments." [Which commandments is Jesus referring to, if not all of them?]
- **The City of Sodom and Gomorrah** was not a "Christian" city, yet it was destroyed for breaking God's law: "Now the men of Sodom were wicked exceedingly and sinners against God." [2] Why were they so punished if the law was only intended for Israel?
- **Jonah** preached to the non-Israelite city of Ninevah because of its national sins. [3] Why did God demand that they repent since they were not a Christian city?
- **Strangers** outside the covenant community of Israel were obliged to obey God's commands: "There shall be one standard for you, it shall be for the stranger as well as the native, for I am the Lord your God." [4]
- **A Psalmist** proclaims to the Kings and judges of the earth [not just to Israel] to: "take warning…and worship the Lord with reverence …" and to do "homage to the Son." [5]
- **John the Baptist** used Old Testament commands to accuse Herod—an Idumen, not a Christian—of adultery. [6]
- **Jesus** tells His disciples that persecution will give them an opportunity to speak "before governors and Kings … as a testimony to them and to the Gentiles." [7]
- **John the Baptist** [8] gave instructions to tax collectors and to soldiers based upon the 6th, 9th and 10th Commandments, rather than upon some neutral law.

- **The apostle Paul** lists the Ten Commandments as still being applicable. [9] Since the Ten Commandments sum up all of God's moral commands, would not this indicate that we should still be obliged to obey all of them? [10]

Question 36: Which statement correctly describes the Christian attitude?

a. We should keep in our place and not impose our religion on others.

b. We should "boldly" and "confidently" live by God's ethics at all times and in all places.

It would be difficult to tell from the worldview and lifestyle of most 21st Century Americans, but according to King Solomon, "The righteous are bold as a lion." [1] Solomon's father, King David, declares, "I will not be afraid of ten thousands of people who have set themselves against me all around." [2] David adds, "The LORD is my light and my salvation; whom shall I fear? The LORD is the strength of my life; of whom shall I be afraid? ... Though an army may encamp against me, my heart shall not fear; though war may rise against me, in this I will be confident." [3]

You may say, "Alright Hanson, the Bible says that, and God's Word is true, therefore I know that that should be my attitude, but I'm a long way from there right now." My response to that is, "No problem!" The "problem" is in not recognizing how far our current attitude may be from where it ought to be. Because, like any other issue, if we don't recognize that we have a problem, we are not going to be motivated to do anything about it. My purpose is to point out, or to remind you, as the case may be, what kind of attitude a Christian should have.

OBJECTION 2 NOTES

1 Dabney, Robert L., *Discussions*, Vol. One, (Banner of Truth Trust), p.357
2 Genesis 13.13
3 Jonah 1.1

4 Leviticus 24.22
5 Psalm 2.12
6 Mark 6.18; Leviticus 18.16; 20.21
7 Matthew 10.18
8 Luke 3.13-14

9 Romans 13.9-10
10 Hanson, Buddy, *God's Ten Words:Practical Applications from the Ten Commandments*, (Hanson Group, 2002). P. 195

If you're not really a Christian; if you are merely a good, morally upstanding, law-abiding conservative, you will have one of two reactions to this: Either you will say, "Hanson, you're a fanatic," and dismiss God's required attitude, or you will say to yourself, "Man, I never realized exactly what a Christian attitude is. I need to get serious about my profession of faith, repent, and get with God's program." This is the beauty of God's Word! We may be studying the Bible about a particular topic, when BAM! Some truth leaps from the pages and hits us between the eyes and we realize that we need to repent and correct our course.

The Holy Spirit won't let us do otherwise, because by the very definition of being a Christian, we love God and want to please Him by living according to His will, not ours. Someone may say, "That sounds good, but where should I begin in my Bible study?" I could provide a long answer to that, but the bottom line answer is: "It doesn't matter." Just read a portion of God's Word every day, then stop and think about what it is saying, and how you can incorporate it into your worldview and lifestyle. Don't concern yourself about reading a chapter a day, or beginning a structured program to read through the Bible in a year, because if you do that, your goal will be to complete the program, instead of understand what God's Word is saying to you.

It's not how much you know about God's Word that's important, but how important God's Word is to your worldview and lifestyle.

We could probably fill a room with people who have doctorates in theology, but who are clueless about how to incorporate their knowledge into their worldview and lifestyle. Oh, they could give you chapter and verse on any topic about which you may inquire, but God doesn't want us to merely be able to *converse* about His Word, but to *disperse* it by taking it with us as we *traverse* the non-Christian cultural landscape and reverse the current ungodly cultural agenda so that it reflects the biblical ethics upon which our country was founded. The following words from the prophet Isaiah, written approximately 3,000 years ago to his Jewish neighbors in Babylonian exile, sound as though he is describing 21st century America:

Therefore justice is far from us, nor does righteousness
overtake us; we look for light, but there is darkness! For
brightness, but we walk in blackness! We grope for the wall
like the blind, and we grope as if we had no eyes; we stumble
at noonday as at twilight; we are as dead men in desolate
places. We all growl like bears, and moan sadly like doves;
we look for justice, but there is none; for salvation, but it is
far from us. For our transgressions are multiplied before You,
and our sins testify against us; for our transgressions are with
us, and as for our iniquities, we know them: in transgressing
and lying against the LORD, and departing from our God,
speaking oppression and revolt, conceiving and uttering
from the heart words of falsehood. Justice is turned back, and
righteousness stands afar off; for truth is fallen in the street,
and equity cannot enter. So truth fails, and he who departs
from evil makes himself a prey.   ISAIAH 59.9-15

Does anyone dispute that our courts are in disrepute, or that "righteousness stands afar off" with our civil rulers, and that the non-Christians have so thoroughly captured every influential cultural institution that "he who departs from evil makes himself a prey?" Truly, we have been flooded with non-Christian ideas in our schools, the news media, the entertainment sector and the civil government. Yet listen to the divine comfort Isaiah provides:

When the enemy comes in like a flood, the Spirit of the LORD
will lift up a standard against him.   ISAIAH 59.19

Certainly, there is no room for whining and complaining on the part of Christians, because our omnipotent, omniscient, and omnipresent Lord, Savior and King, Jesus Christ, is in complete control of His creation and gives us His Word that He will take care of the bad guys through our faithful obedience. Pessimism, intimidation and cowardice should have no part in the everyday attitude of Christians. Daniel, who knew more than a little about being mistreated, proclaims: "The people who know their God shall be strong, and carry out great exploits." [4] This is a good place to ask where Daniel got his courage to stand up to King Nebuchadnezzar?[5] Or, for that matter, what enabled Moses to tell the powerful Pharaoh, "Thus says the LORD God of Israel: 'Let My people go…"[6] Or, for David to stand against the giant Goliath?[7] Or, for the apostle Paul to boldly present gospel to King Agrippa?[8]

The answer is the provided by Isaiah and applies to each of us:

He gives power to the weak, and to those who have no might He increases strength. Even the youths shall faint and be weary, and the young men shall utterly fall, but those who wait on the LORD shall renew their strength; they shall mount up with wings like eagles, they shall run and not be weary, they shall walk and not faint. ISAIAH 40.29-31

There should be no doubt but that our courage to stand for Jesus in all situations and circumstances is provided by Jesus, Himself. In case you need a statement that puts it clearer than "those who wait on the LORD shall renew their strength …they shall walk and not faint," you can refer to the following divinely inspired words that Jehovah gave to the prophet Isaiah:

Fear not, for I am with you; be not dismayed, for I am your God. I will strengthen you, yes, I will help you, I will uphold you with My righteous right hand. ISAIAH 41.10

Non-Christians are limited by the natural, what they can see, touch, feel, smell, and taste. We, on the other hand, are guided by supernatural wisdom. Christianity proves the old adage, that there is "more than meets the eye." An excellent example of this occurred approximately 2,500 years ago when the King of Syria was making war against Israel. The prophet Elisha's servant awakened one morning to see the King's army had surrounded them during the night.

Alas, my master! What shall we do?" he asked the prophet, and Elisha answered, "Do not fear, for those who are with us are more than those who are with them."

*And Elisha prayed, and said, "LORD, I pray, open his eyes
that he may see." Then the LORD opened the eyes of the
young man, and he saw. And behold, the mountain was full
of horses and chariots of fire all around Elisha. So when the
Syrians came down to him, Elisha prayed to the LORD,
and said, "Strike this people, I pray, with blindness." And he
struck them with blindness according to the word of Elisha.*

2 KINGS 6.15-18

This historical object lesson is a positive example of why we should "walk by faith, not by sight." [9] Another memorable positive example of walking by faith is when Moses, "By faith forsook Egypt, not fearing the wrath of the king; for he endured as seeing Him who is invisible. [10]

For those who find it too tempting to "walk by sight," God is gracious enough to provide numerous examples of the negative consequences that will be the result of that. One of the most well-known is when Lot saw the beautiful plain of Jordan and requested to Abraham that he be given that portion for his clan.

*And Lot lifted his eyes and saw all the plain of Jordan, that it
was well watered everywhere (before the LORD destroyed
Sodom and Gomorrah) like the garden of the LORD, like the
land of Egypt as you go toward Zoar.* GENESIS 13.10

Notice the verse includes the statement: "before the LORD destroyed Sodom and Gomorrah." As Lot discovered, "All that glitters isn't gold." The next familiar example proving that we should not exclusively trust in appearances is when the twelve spies brought back their report to Moses concerning the Promised Land.

*There we saw the giants (the descendants of Anak came from
the giants); and we were like grasshoppers in our own sight,
and so we were in their sight."* NUMBERS 13.33

A familiar New Testament example is when Peter saw Jesus walking on the sea, and Peter impetuously exclaimed, "Lord, if it is You, command me to come to You on the water." [11] However, Peter discovered that walking on water was not as easy as it appeared.

> *But when he saw that the wind was boisterous, he was afraid; and beginning to sink he cried out, saying, "Lord, save me!"*
> MATTHEW 14.30

The "New Testament Isaiah," the apostle Paul, provides a summarizing statement: "If God is for us, who can be against us? He who did not spare His own Son, but delivered Him up for us all, how shall He not with Him also freely give us all things? …we are more than conquerors through Him who loved us." [12]

Question 37. Which group of people controls history?

a. Non-Christians.
b. Christians.

When it is understood that it is the church, and not non-Christians, who controls history through both our obedience and disobedience, our challenge is what kind of America do we want our children to inherit: a monotheistic republic that is modeled upon exclusive obedience to biblical truths, or a politically correct, pluralistic non-Christian democratic tyranny that views all religions as equally irrelevant to "real life" issues? In the midst of our current cultural decline, 21st Century America is not too different from the Northern Kingdom of 2,700 years ago, when Jehovah proclaimed to the tribe of Ephraim: "I have written for him the great things of my law, but they were considered a strange thing." [1] One only has to scan the episodes of the disobedient cultures and civilizations described on the pages of the Old Testament to recognize how seriously God takes His Word and how much He hates those who "consider it a

Q. 36 NOTES

1 Proverbs 28.1	5 Daniel 6.10	9 2 Corinthians 5.7
2 Psalm 3.6	6 Exodus 5.1	10 Hebrews 11.27
3 Psalm 27.1, 3	7 1 Samuel 17.45	11 Matthew 14.28
4 Daniel 11.32	8 Acts 26	12 Romans 8.31-37

strange thing." As the 20th Century British Anglican author, C.S. Lewis notes, "To walk out of God's will is to walk into nowhere." [2]

Asaph's psalm appealing to Israel to repent is perfectly applicable for modern America. May we prayerfully listen to and hearken to these words from Jehovah as recorded by Asaph:

> *Hear, O My people, and I will admonish you! O Israel, if you will listen to Me! There shall be no foreign god among you; nor shall you worship any foreign god. I am the LORD your God, Who brought you out of the land of Egypt; open your mouth wide, and I will fill it.*
>
> *But My people would not heed My voice, and Israel would have none of Me. So I gave them over to their own stubborn heart, to walk in their own counsels. Oh, that my people would listen to Me, that Israel would walk in My ways! I would soon subdue their enemies, and turn My hand against their adversaries. The haters of the LORD would pretend submission to Him, but their fate would endure forever. He would have fed them also with the finest of wheat; and with honey from the rock I would have satisfied you.*
>
> PSALM 81.8-16

According to the apostle Paul, the solution for defeating the agenda of non-Christians is to "bring every thought into captivity to the obedience of Christ." While this godly "solution" to our cultural issues is very simple, each of us knows that it is not easy, since we all involved in the on-going battle of "putting off" our old ungodly habits, and "putting on" new holy habits. [3]

> *For though we walk in the flesh, we do not war according to the flesh. For the weapons of our warfare are not carnal but mighty in God for pulling down strongholds, casting down*

Q. 37 NOTES
1 Hosea 8.12
2 Lewis, C.S., *"Till We Have Faces"* (Fount, 1956, 1978)
3 Colossians 3.9-10

arguments and every high thing that exalts itself against the knowledge of God, bringing every thought into captivity to the obedience of Christ, and being ready to punish all disobedience when your obedience is fulfilled.

2 CORINTHIANS 10.3-6

Question 38. Are the times in which we are living "normal," or "abnormal?"

   a. Normal.
   b. Abnormal.

With nine out of ten adult Christians not having a developed Christian worldview, many of our brothers and sisters are unable to have a correct "discernment" of the cultural issues that face us and may conclude that "things aren't what I would like for them to be, but I guess that's just the normal way things are, so I'll suck it up and do the best I can and pray for Jesus to come quickly and rescue me from this sinful world!"

Some of you may be thinking, "Where does faith come in for a person who thinks this way?" In other words, "What good is the Bible for our everyday life?" Their answer would be, "Our Christian faith is very good

Are we living in a *BIverse,* or a *UNIverse?*

Private Ethics
(Religious Life)

Public Ethics
(Real Life)

BIcycle, BIverse

ALL The Word
For ALL of Life

UNIcycle UNIverse

and beneficial inside our homes and churches, in the 'religious' realm of life, but we're on our own in the 'real world' portion of life."

In dealing with this attitude the best thing we can do is remind ourselves that God created a *uni*verse, not a *bi*verse. As we discussed in a previous answer, there is no such thing as "religious" and "real life" compartments of life. God created everything, and proclaimed it "good," (GENESIS 1.10) therefore every area of life is "religious." The illustration on the previous page demonstrates this.

Many Christians go through life as though they were riding a worldview bicycle. They carry two sets of ethics everywhere they to. When they are inside their homes and churches, they use their "religious life" (or private) ethics, (the rear wheel), and when they are outside (in the "real world") they use their "real life" (or public) ethics (the front wheel). Christians with this worldview approach life as "role players" who go way beyond the church and state debate to the separation of God from culture! The "religious" wheel is at the rear of the bicycle because that is the wheel that Dee Ciple uses to apply the religious brakes whenever he decides that a certain behavior is becoming too ungodly. In the meantime he "rides" through life making certain to keep his public and private ethics separate, as though he is merely a Christian role player who is living among a bunch of non-Christians. The illustration on the right shows a unicycle to demonstrate that we are not "role players," living in a divided universe, but "whole players," living in a unified universe! ALL of God's Word applies to ALL areas and aspects of our worldview and lifestyle at ALL times! So, instead of having two sets of ethics that we interchange depending upon the "role" we are currently in, we have one set of ethics that we apply everywhere, since God created a universe and not a biverse. In other words, it's not a bicycle that we should be riding, but a unicycle!

Question 39. God's Word is:

a. Something soothing for our troubled mind.
b. A lamp to our feet.

But you must continue in the things which you have learned and have been assured of, knowing from whom you have

learned them, and that from childhood you have known
the Holy Scriptures, which are able to make you wise for
salvation through faith which is in Christ Jesus. All Scripture
is given by inspiration of God, and is profitable for doctrine,
for reproof, for correction, for instruction in righteousness,
that the man of God may be complete, thoroughly equipped for
every good work.   2 TIMOTHY 3.14-17

The Bible should be our most prized physical possession because it is God's instruction manual for living, and everything we do should be viewed "through the spectacles of Scripture." [1] Jesus instructs, "Man does not live on bread alone, but on every word that comes from the mouth of God." [2] We all readily agree that God's Word is true; [3] and that it "equips us for every good work," [4] is a "lamp to our feet and a light to our path," [5] and will not return to God without "accomplishing its purpose." [6]

When Jesus became the Word in fleshly form He taught, "I am the way, the truth, and the life. No one comes to the Father except through Me." [7] In explaining the Helper He would send to all Christians upon His resurrection, Jesus describes the Holy Spirit's work as "guiding us into all truth." [8] This is what Asaph means when he writes, "You will guide me with Your counsel." [9]

Seventeenth Century English Pastor Richard Alleine advises,

The faithful Christian will not lean to his own understand-
ing. He is fearful to walk in his own counsels. He knows that
it is not in man who walks to direct his own steps, but withal
he knows he has a better guide. [10]

This means that we should "set our face like a flint" as we conform our daily routines to Biblical ethics, being confident that "the Lord God will help us" and "no one will be able to condemn us" as long as we stay true to the principles in His Word. [11] Since the Holy Trinity created all things, all things are understandable only in terms of the triune God, the only way for any of us to be part of the "solution" to our culture's problems is for us to live according to His rules and to base our "solutions" upon His revealed Word. As Christians, we should readily agree that since we are living in God's creation, the only way we can hope to be

109

successful in carrying out our duties is that we do so in accordance to His revealed law.

> Christians have the most valuable "self-help" book ever written. It promises to make us wiser than any non-Christian and, if followed, to make our wisdom so apparent that non-Christians will come to us praising our actions and inquiring about our God.

• So why aren't we using the Bible's perfect counsel in making our daily decisions?

• Why do we proclaim that the Bible is the very Word of God, is without error, is applicable to all people at all times, and "thoroughly equips us for every good work," and then neglect to apply what it teaches to our everyday situations and circumstances? [12]

• Why do we insist on living as though God's Word is not "a lamp to our feet and a light for our path?" [13]

Could it be that we have been "spoiled through philosophy and vain deceit, after the tradition of men, after the rudiments of the world, and not after Christ?" [14] If so, how did it come about that we lost our trust in God to the extent that we not only fail to consider His wisdom in our day-to-day decisions, but are even ashamed [15] to give as a reason for making a particular decision that we are Christians and are simply following His decrees? [16]

Possibly the chief culprit in fostering this ungodly pietistic attitude of worshiping a god who is culturally impotent is that too many of us send our children to God-opposed public schools, where instead of being systematically and thoroughly trained in how to apply Biblical ethics to their lifestyle, they are indoctrinated with the blasphemous idea that one god is just as good as another, and that they should be good citizens and follow the dictates of the State. Instead of learning that they will be "blessed if they take to heart what is written in it," [17] they learn that they will be expelled from school, and later that they may be passed over for a deserved promotion or even fired, for publicly elevating God's thoughts above man's.

Instead of being taught to value "everything a loss compared to the surpassing greatness of knowing Christ Jesus as our Lord," [18] we are encouraged to keep our religious beliefs to ourselves for fear of losing worldly esteem. As we continue to compartmentalize our beliefs we wonder why our culture continues to disintegrate. After all, we contribute to a few charities, give (a little) to our churches, perform volunteer work, and are involved in "improving" the public school curriculum, but the only thing that seems to be happening is that we are becoming physically exhausted while our culture continues its downward spiral.

Whether we realize it or not, our refusal to repent and live according to God's perfect instructions is an attempt to become our own source of truth and wisdom. It is to "love darkness rather than light, for everyone practicing evil hates the light." [19] Paul explains, "The sinful mind is hostile to God. It does not submit to God's law, nor can it do so." [20] We should also remember that we have an obligation to God's law: not as a way to salvation, since we are justified by faith, but as a way of life. In other words, we have not been saved to follow the ethics of other gods. Our exclusive Calling is to do and bring about "His will on earth," [21] and the only way to achieve this is to obey His law, since that describes the manner in which He calls us to live. We should not only strive to not commit adultery, murder, steal, covet, or to break any of God's other laws, but we should also "delight" in doing and proclaiming God's will.[22] God's law was given to us for the enrichment of our lives. In essence, God's law:

1. Provides God's unchanging moral standard. (PSALM 119.9-12; DEUTERONOMY 28.2-7, 15-19)
2. Points us to Christ, since it is obvious that we can't perfectly keep the law. (GALATIANS 3.24; ROMANS 7.7-16)

Q. 39 NOTES

1 Calvin, John, *Institutes of the Christian Religion*, Vol. I, (Westminster, 1960), p.70
2 Matthew 4.4
3 Psalm 119.160; John 17.17
4 2 Timothy 3.16-17
5 Psalm 119.105
6 Isaiah 55.10-11
7 John 14.6
8 John 16.13
9 Psalm 73.24
10 Alleine, Richard, *The World Conquered by the Faithful Christian*, (Soli Deo Gloria, 1668, 1995), p.87
11 Isaiah 50.7-9
12 2 Timothy 3.16-17
13 Psalm 119.105
14 Colossians 2.8
15 Romans 1.16
16 Psalm 25.1-3
17 Revelation 1.3
18 Philippians 3.8
19 John 3.19-20
20 Romans 8.5-8
21 Matthew 6.10
22 Psalm 119.92; Romans 7.22

3. Testifies to the nations of their need to repent. (DEUTERONOMY 5.5-8; ISAIAH 42.6-7; DEUTERONOMY 26.18-19)
4. Instructs us how to live and relate to each other. (2 TIMOTHY 3.16-17; 2 PETER 1.3-4; JOSHUA 1.7-8)

David could well have been meditating on these four uses of God's law when he wrote these lines:

> *The law of the LORD is perfect, reviving the soul. The statutes of the LORD are trustworthy, making wise the simple. The precepts of the LORD are right, giving joy to the heart. The commandments of the LORD are radiant, giving light to the eyes.*
> *The fear of the LORD is pure, enduring forever. The ordinances of the LORD are sure and altogether righteous. They are more precious than gold ...they are sweeter than honey. By them is Your servant warned; in keeping them is great reward.* PSALM 19.7-11

Question 40. How do we "enlarge the place of Christ's tent?" ISAIAH 54.2

a. Be seeker-friendly and water down God's Word so that we won't offend non-Christians by using words such as "sin," and "hell."
b. **Teach the whole counsel of God's Word and trust in God's sovereign control to bless the preaching of His Word.**

When political parties talk of having a "Big Tent," they mean that they are watering down the principles of their party in order to attract voters with a variety of ethical beliefs. So, as the political tent gets "bigger," the relevance and the integrity of the party's platform becomes "smaller." However, when the prophet Isaiah urged his neighbors in Judah and Jerusalem to "enlarge the place of their tent" so that their "descendants will inherit the nations," [1] he was not talking about watering down Jehovah's instructions on how to live, but rather to strictly observe them. The same principle holds true for us. The more closely we consistently follow God's instructions, the "bigger" Christ's tent (Kingdom) will become. [2]

The two critical elements for carrying out our calling are:
- A dependence upon the whole counsel of God, and
- An accurate understanding of history.

When we depend upon God's Word to be our ever-present counselor we will not only be careful to defend the Christian worldview, but to depend upon it. Our focus wont' be on looking for the next non-Christian victim to "blow away with our supernatural wisdom, because, after all, what accomplishment is that?

- As recipients of the Holy Spirit's supernatural heart transplant, we know the truth, while non-Christians don't even know if "truth" exists.
- We know who we are, where we came from, what we're supposed to do, and how to do it. Non-Christians don't have a clue!

Would an NFL team blow away a high school team? Of course, but what would be impressive about it? God didn't call us into Christ's Kingdom to only win debates. He called us to win the culture. We win the culture by demonstrating through our daily actions that the Christian worldview and lifestyle is great. Non-Christians know their worldview and lifestyle is not what it should be, but they think that they can improve it, and maybe even make it great. That's why they are constantly re-discovering old philosophies and worshipping different gods. They want to be great. They want to be winners, but they can point to not one civilization that has ever sustained itself on non-Christian ethics. They've tried them all, and they know they've tried them all, but unlike Christians, they're not giving up. Instead of concluding, "We've tried everything and nothing has worked, they say, "We're going to try this philosophy of living again, because the last time it was tried, the wrong people were leading it, and the circumstances were different, but now we have the right people and the right circumstances. All that can be said about such blind and misguided optimism is "Mercy!" This brings us back to the second critical element for carrying out our calling: An accurate understanding of history. Non-Christians are so messed up that even if they could point to some past civilization that sustained itself on ungodly ethics, they couldn't acknowledge it, because they don't believe in absolutes, and therefore don't believe in history!

We, on the other hand, do believe in absolutes, therefore we also believe in history and history is chocked full of civilizations that have sustained themselves on biblical ethics.

God's Word works, and man's word fails

There's no other way to slice and dice it. And this is why we should approach each day of our life confident because we know that God not man, is pulling culture's strings. So, the question is not "What are you going to do after you win the debate?" but "How are you going to live after you win the debate!" and the answer should be: "I'm going to live for God's glory by incorporating His perfect counsel into all of my decisions in all of my situations and circumstances!" As we begin each day of service in Christ's Kingdom, our petitions to Jesus should not only include heartfelt thanks for being "delivered from the power of darkness and into Christ's Kingdom," [3] but should also include a request that our decisions and actions of the day will enable us to be "counted worthy of our most privileged calling," by conforming them to His will and "pleasure." [4] This is the only way that "His name will be glorified" in us and "we in Him." [5]

As we recall that we have been raised:

- from the depths of despair,
- from the uncertainty of our ultimate purpose,
- from the inability to distinguish facts from fiction,
- from false opinions to true obligations,
- from obscure reasons for living to obvious and meaningful obligations and invaluable privileges of serving as a member of Christ's Kingdom,

we should be humbled and energized to take ground for Christ's Kingdom as we go about our daily duties. Our approach to a new day is a far cry from non-Christians who approach each day in terms of "What's in it for me," and set each day's priorities to bring attention to themselves so that they, and not God, will receive the honor.

114

All of this also clarifies why no situation or circumstance should shake us from   the confidence in God's absolute promises to bless us when we base our daily decisions upon His counsel. We know, beyond doubt, He has not only prepared us for the situations and circumstances we will face today, [6] but that He has placed us in them! Therefore, our labor in His service "will not be in vain" [7] as long as we are obedient to His revealed counsel. Since we have been rescued from our sinful ways, we should have no higher consideration than to present a holy testimony in all we say and do. [8] Paul describes this as "abounding," or being plentiful with our obedience.

> *And this I pray, that your love may abound still more and more in knowledge and all discernment, that you may approve the things that are excellent, that you may be sincere and without offense till the day of Christ.*
>
> PHILIPPIANS 1.9-10

> *But as you abound in everything—in faith, in speech, in knowledge, in all diligence, and in your love for us—see that you abound in this grace also.* 2 CORINTHIANS 8.7

> *Finally then, brethren, we urge and exhort in the Lord Jesus that you should abound more and more, just as you received from us how you ought to walk and to please God.*
>
> 1 THESSALONIANS 4.1

Our goal at the start of each day should be to live like Christians by ordering our steps according to God's Word, [9] by "being fruitful in every good work, and increasing in the knowledge of God," [10] so at the end of the day we will "not be ashamed" when we look into His commandments. [11]

Since we know that we enter a spiritual war zone with the first step outside of our home, we should pray that we do not become "futile in our thoughts" [12] but rather that our thoughts be inclined to obey God with every decision, [13] and that our obedience will result in "the Word of the Lord running swiftly" throughout the earth so "that we may be delivered from unreasonable and wicked men," [14] and that "their house will be destroyed, but the tent of the upright will flourish." [15]

Paul's divine instructions on how to approach each day's duties include being patient and forgiving toward others, by humbly putting God's interests above our interests. [16] Personal interests, pride and revenge are character traits that are common to every non-Christian, and are traits that we are to put off as we put on our new person and "walk worthy of the vocation to which we are called." [17]

If our profession of faith in Christ is worth anything, it is worth everything. After all, it is our calling to bring credit, not discredit to God and to His Word. As Matthew Henry states, "A man may sleep and go to hell; but he who will go to heaven must look about him and be diligent." This means that we must "earnestly contend for the faith," [18] rather than corrupt it by accommodating it to the ideas of non-Christians. By being "diligent to make our calling and election sure," [19] we "glorify our Father" by conducting ourselves in this manner. [20]

Our obedient decisions and actions will create a visible separation from those who "talk" a good game, because sooner or later their actions will reveal their real priorities and the truth that their heart is "far from God." [21] A perfect example of this is when the Pharisees accused Jesus of being "a drunk and a friend of tax collectors and sinners," His reply was "Wisdom is justified by her children." [22] By "children," Jesus meant that His actions on earth would prove His wisdom. May the "wisdom" that is reflected in our daily decision-making be God's perfect wisdom, not man's errant wisdom. Otherwise our faithfulness will be no more substantial than "a morning cloud, which like the early dew goes away."[23]

Q. 41 NOTES

1	Isaiah 54.1-2	10 Colossians 1.107.6;	16 Ephesians 4.2-3;
2	Matthew 13.31-33	Isaiah 29.13	Philippians 2.3-4
3	Colossians 1.134	11 Psalm 119.6	17 Ephesians 4.1
2	Thessalonians 1.11	12 Romans 1.21	18 Jude 3
5	2 Thessalonians 1.12	13 Proverbs 21.2;	19 2 Peter 1.10
6	Isaiah 5.4	Colossians 1.9; 2 Thessa-	20 John 15.8
7	Philippians 2.16	lonians 3.4	21 Matthew 15.8; Mark
8	Romans 6.2	14 2 Thessalonians 3.1-2	22 Matthew 11.19
9	Philippians 1.27	15 Proverbs 14.11	23 Hosea 6.4

Question 41. Our duty as Christians:

a. Rely-upon and trust-in the advice of others when they tell us that we are supposed to live and interpret the Bible within the framework of current events.

b. Trust-in and rely-upon God's Word to guide and direct our daily actions.

In the Lord's prayer, "Your will be done," [1] comes before "Give us this day our daily bread," [2] which should remind us of the necessity to trust in God's Word to guide and direct our lives. The renowned 20th century British Bible teacher, Arthur Pink, writes:

> *Our actions must be regulated by the Word of God if our souls are to be nourished and strengthened. That was one of the outstanding lessons taught Israel in the wilderness: their food and refreshment could only be obtained so long as they traveled in the path of obedience.* [3]

Think about what your answer would be to a new Christian's question of "How should I live, now that I am a Christian?" It might be a helpful exercise to write out your answer, then go back and add Scripture verses to back-up your description. This will prove helpful in two ways: first, the new Christian will probably ask where parts of your description are found in the Bible, and second, it will let you know if any of the parts of the description you are providing are your opinion of how a Christian should live, or whether they are, in fact, God's opinion. After all, your new Christian friend is not really asking for your opinion, but God's opinion. Hopefully, the description you provide will include the importance of our role as servants in Christ's Kingdom. The reason this idea is so important is that, by definition, servants obey their masters, which means that anyone who refuses to obey Jesus' commands has to question whether they are truly Christians.

This by no means implies that a Christian will perfectly obey God's Word. If anyone was capable of that there would have been no reason for Jesus to come to earth to fulfill that obligation. Instead, it means that

117

each day we give our best effort toward that, knowing that we will fall short, but that we will get up the next day hoping to improve the consistency of our obedience and continue this process for the rest of our time on earth. Legendary college basketball Coach John Wooden used to tell his UCLA Bruins, "Doing the best you are capable of doing is victory in itself, and less than that is defeat." Wooden's advice to athletes also applies to Christians as we approach each day of service in Christ's Kingdom. UCLA's ten National Championships under Wooden didn't just happen because he knew the right words to say. They prepared to win by being in top physical condition and being humble enough to execute their plays the way their Coach demanded, instead of free-lancing and doing things their way. The same holds true for Christians. We may say that we're going to give our best efforts at consistently obeying God's Word, but if we don't put in the time and effort to read and think through the various biblical ethics, how can we expect to carry them out during the day ahead? No matter whether a person is young or old in the faith, he needs a disciple; someone he can pray with and ask questions about portions of Scripture with which he is unclear. Jesus did His part by giving His all for us, and now it's our turn. We must be willing to give our all for Him on a daily basis. Coach Bob Knight has won more games than any coach in basketball, and he states: "Everybody's got the will to win, but few people have the will to prepare to win." Coach Knight's words could easily be changed to say, "Every Christian has the will to go to heaven, but few Christians have the will to prepare for heaven." How is it with you? Could your Christian testimony be accused of merely saying the right words, or could it be said of you that you practice what you preach?

Israel was taken into Assyrian captivity because while they proclaimed to "fear the LORD," they practiced the "rituals of the nations from among whom they were carried away." [4] Today, we like to refer to the stirring words of Joshua: "But as for me and my house, we will serve the Lord." [5] However, in light of the widespread apathy among so many Christians, before we are too quick to apply Joshua's statement to our family, perhaps we must ask ourselves if our worldview and lifestyle demonstrate that we are really willing to "serve the Lord." Otherwise, we may be repeating the 2,600 year old mistake of Israel and be inviting God's wrath. Paul describes those who "profess to know God, but in works they deny Him" as being "abominable, disobedient, and disqualified for every good work." [6]

He adds

> *Be an example to the believers in word, in conduct, in love, in spirit, in faith, in purity.*   1 TIMOTHY 4.12

In other words, we should "Consider our ways!" [7] even if obeying God will probably lead to persecutions. Jesus tells us that "A servant is not greater than his master. If they persecuted Me, they will also persecute you." [8] This is why "We must be prepared for the frowns of Providence." [9] But, the good news is that even though "No chastening seems to be joyful for the present, but painful: nevertheless, afterward it yields the peaceable fruit of righteousness to those who have been trained by it." [10] What a great promise! Reminding ourselves that nothing happens by chance in Jesus' Kingdom, should keep us from complaining and/or asking "Why?" when we go through various trials. To do so is the same as saying that Jesus doesn't know what is happening on earth, and it also overlooks the truth that the root cause behind any trial we experience is us! A notable of example of this is when the priest Eli learned that his two spoiled and unruly children had been killed, he knew that they had received the judgment they deserved, and replied: "It is the LORD. Let Him do what seems good to Him." [11]

David perfectly expresses what our attitude should be in his magisterial psalm regarding God's law.

> *I know, O LORD, that Your judgments are right, and that in faithfulness You have afflicted me.*   PSALM 119.75

In one way or another, we have gotten off the track of consistent biblical obedience and Jesus is using whatever means we require to get our attention focused back on His Word. May we all lay hold of God's most merciful "afterward," as Paul proclaims in regards to our suffering yielding "the peaceable fruit of righteousness." And, may we strive to live such a consistent life of obedience, that Jesus will have no reason to bring hardships on us in order to get our thoughts re-focused.

It goes without saying that Satan has a vested interest in keeping us from carrying out our commanded duties from God. A lot can be learned about his strategy by reviewing his temptation of Jesus in the wilderness. Since this was his best opportunity we can expect that he gave it his best shot and will use the same three-part strategy against us. Satan's 3-D Strategy is aimed at discouraging our

- Dependence on God, our
- Desire for the Word of God, and our
- Duty to carry out our calling.

As Christians, we are set apart from everyone else by God's revealed truth, and the Holy Spirit, who enables us to correctly understand it. Satan cannot do anything about the Holy Spirit, so he focuses his attacks upon discrediting our reliance upon God's Word, for it is there that we learn to:

- Depend upon and rest in God's providence.
- Desire the "pure milk of the Word that we may grow thereby." [12] And
- Clarify our duty to live out our faith.

Obviously, if Satan can be successful in building a wedge in any of these three areas, he will at least frustrate our lives by distracting us from the duty we have at hand of carrying out God's will. Satan began his temptation of Jesus by stating, "If you are the Son of God, command these stones to become bread." [13]

But Jesus answered, "It is written, 'Man shall not live by bread alone, but by every word that proceeds from the mouth of God.'" [14] Satan knows full well that each of us cannot be defeated if we maintain a faithful dependence upon God (the first "D"), so he plays to our ego by hinting that we can accomplish our calling in our own wisdom and abilities, instead of relying completely upon God's Word. There is no doubt that Jesus could have turned the rocks into bread, and after fasting for forty days he may have been tempted to do so. However, He reminded Himself that He came to do His father's will, [15] and stated that to Satan in verse four. Calvin notes how Christ uses Scripture as His shield:

For this is the true way of fighting, if we wish to make ourselves sure of the victory. [16]

Paul refers to God's Word as the "sword of the Spirit," [17] and we should never underestimate its power to provide perfect wisdom and understanding in the various situations and circumstances that confront us. We will only find comfort as we rest in the doctrine and decrees of God's revealed truths.

Satan's second "D" is designed to diminish our desire for God's Word. As he said to Eve, "Has God indeed said?" [18] The less we rely on God's Word, the more we will rely on our own resources, and Satan knows that convincing us to do this will knock us off our intended course (which is completing Jesus' victory over him and his legions!). It is very tempting to abandon our roles as creatures, where we carry out God's will, and act as though we were the Creator by attempting to directly control the outcome of events. As long as we trust in God's promises we have a sure and certain hope that "all things will work together for good," [19] but once we leave the parameters of His Word and depend upon our own resources, we have no certain assurance for success. Indeed, history attests that the only assured result of our own efforts is failure.

The final "D" of Satan's strategy is to deflect us from our duty of Christianizing the world. [20] By convincing us that "getting people saved" is the end, rather than the beginning of the Christian walk, Satan hopes to delay the final outcome that he and his legions so dread. In Jesus' Parable of the Unjust Steward we are told, "The sons of this world are more shrewd in their generation than the sons of light." [21] Satan and his army of supernatural demons are well aware of their impending ultimate defeat and know full well that the only strategy they have is to entice us to "conform to the world," rather than giving us unobstructed access to conforming the world to God's standard. [22] While their thinking is flawed (since there is nothing they can do to "slow down" God's ultimate victory) their plan is still effective in revealing which community of Christians will take the lead in restoring the earth to God's will. [23]

James tells us that the "demons believe—and tremble!" [24] Yet their belief is intellectual and not saving; and it is not accompanied by the "fruit of the Spirit," [25] nor a change in their lifestyle, nor a peace with God. [26] True faith is believing "with all our heart," [27] and is not marked by knowledge, alone, but by love. They "tremble" not out of respect, but from hatred. Through the ages they have witnessed God protecting Christians from their snares and temptations, and they are aware of the upcoming Judgment Day. They hate it that they can neither resist Christ's authority, nor run from His reach. They know God, but only as a Judge, not a Father; an enemy, not a friend. [28] This is brought out in the episode in which Jesus heals a couple of demons and the demons ask, "Have You come here to torment us before the time (Judgment Day)?" [29]

The apostle Paul has some good news for us with respect to how Satan's power over us has been defeated by Christ's innocent death on the cross:

> *Since the children have flesh and blood, He too shared in their*
> *humanity so that by His death He might destroy him who*
> *holds the power of death—that is, the devil—and free those*
> *who all their lives were held in slavery by their fear of death.*
> HEBREWS 2.14-15

What these verses mean is that Satan is a defeated foe, but that his defeat applies only to those who by faith accept Jesus Christ as their Lord, Savior and King. For everyone else, he is still an all-powerful adversary. John contrasts the lifestyle of the non-Christian with that of the Christian:

> *He who does what is sinful is of the devil, because the devil*
> *has been sinning from the beginning. The reason the Son of*
> *God appeared was to destroy the devil's work. No one who is*
> *born of God will continue to sin, because God's seed remains*
> *in him; he cannot go on sinning, because he has been born of*
> *God. This is how we know who the children of God are and*
> *who the children of the devil are: Anyone who does not do*
> *what is right is not a child of God; neither is anyone who does*
> *not love his brother.* 1 JOHN 3.8-10

According to the divinely-inspired words of the apostle John, Christians have no reason to let the fear of Satan keep us from living a confident and triumphant life for God. However, we should not consider Satan as being completely out of our way. He is still a very significant opponent. He has lost the war, but he can still defeat us in some costly battles if we don't remain on our spiritual toes. As Jesus taught His disciples,

> *Every kingdom divided against itself will be ruined, and*
> *every city or house divided will not stand ... How can anyone*
> *enter a strong man's house and carry off his possessions unless*
> *he first ties up the strong man?* MATTHEW 12.25,29

So all we have to do to defeat Satan is to not let him get the best of us. By stepping out in obedient faith, we will be able to exclaim with the seventy-two disciples, "even the demons submit to us in Your name." [30] Jesus' comforting reply to them (and us) is, "I saw Satan fall like lightning from heaven." (v.18) What all of this means is that Satan will not be driven back by an instantaneous supernatural act of God, but rather by our steady and consistent obedience to God's commands and a faithful acceptance of God's promises.

Q. 41 NOTES
1   Matthew 6.10
2   Matthew 6.11
3   Numbers 9.18-23, Pink, A.W., *Elijah*, (Banner of Truth Trust, 1976), p. 60
4   2 Kings 17.33
5   Joshua 24.15
6   Titus 1.16
7   Haggai 1.5
8   John 15.20
9   Pink, ibid., *Elijah*, p.79
10 Hebrews 12.11
11 1 Samuel 3.18
12 1 Peter 2.2
13 Matthew 4.3
14 Matthew 4.4,7,10
15 John 6.38
16 *Calvin's Commentaries, Vol. XVI*, (Baker Books, 1981), p.214
17 Ephesians 6.16-17
18 Genesis 3.1
19 Romans 8.28
20 Matthew 28.18-20
21 Luke 16.8
22 Romans 12.2
23 Genesis 1.28; 9.1-4; Matthew 28.18-20; 1 Corinthians 15.25; etc.
24 James 2.19
25 Galatians 5.22-26
26 Romans 5.1; Ephesians 3.12
27 Acts 8.37
28 Matthew 25.41; 2 Peter 2.4
29 Matthew 8.29
30 Luke 10.18

Question 42. Are we

    a. Armed with God's perfect counsel and not dangerous, or

    b. Dangerous, because we have the potential of changing our culture with God's ethics, but don't know how to go about it because many pastors have done a poor job of teaching us?

While non-Christians are "armed," with their explicit ideology for changing the world, they are "not dangerous," because none of their plans, strategies or tactics are founded on the truth. On the other hand, we are "dangerous," in that we have access to God's perfect plan to restore the earth to God's will, but sadly too many of us are currently not "armed" with His plan, because of the erroneous teaching that God doesn't have a plan to redeem the earth.

King David, however, contradicts this blasphemous teaching by telling us "The battle is the Lord's," [1] and it is God who is "directing all things after the counsel of His own will." [2] Paul, known by some as the "New Testament Isaiah," reassures us that our "labor is not in vain in the Lord," [3] and perhaps his basis for writing this is the statement of Jehovah that was recorded by Isaiah:

> *For I will contend with them that contend with you, and I will save your children.*   Isaiah 49.24-26

Each of us can rejoice that the task ahead of us is never as great as the power behind us. The key is in fighting the culture war on God's terms, and not on the terms of our enemies. Since they have no god but themselves, they see themselves as being completely responsible for bringing about the results for which they seek. We, on the other hand, have not been called into the "results" business, but the "obedience" business. "We must not identify our cause with God's cause; our methods with God's methods; or our hopes with God's purposes." [4] Once we realize that we, in and of ourselves, are not "sufficient" to bring about God's will on earth, we should joyfully recognize that we have taken the first positive step toward successfully carrying out our calling to expand Christ's kingdom. The reason for this is that God is completely sufficient! Our commanded duty is very simple, though not easy. God requires that we "trust and obey" [5] His revealed instructions on how to live and govern ourselves.

When we become Christians we are commanded to repent from our former worldview and lifestyle, but that does not mean that we are on our own to invent what we imagine is an acceptable lifestyle. The Jews were cast aside by Jehovah and He turned to the Gentiles because they refused to commit themselves to the gospel. Instead, they sought to establish their own righteousness by establishing numerous laws in their Talmud, and it was the man-inspired Talmud, not the God-inspired Old Testament that the Priests memorized and taught. Are we not attempting the same thing today by approaching our cultural issues from our perspective instead of analyzing them from God's perspective?

Neither does it mean that we are to mentally assent to the truths of Scripture without having any inclination of incorporating them into our world and life view. Jesus expects us to commit our complete lifestyle to following His perfect ethical standard of behavior. The apostle John records these words that should prove more than a little alarming to those who are going through life according to their own drumbeat:

> *Remember therefore from where you have fallen; repent*
> *and do the first works, or else I will come to you quickly and*
> *remove your lamp stand from its place unless you repent.*
> **REVELATION 2.5**

The old bumper sticker: "God said it. I believe it, and that settles it," needs to have one line added to it, so that it reads:

> God said it. I believe it, and am going to
> do something about it. And that settles it!

While it is impossible for us to "put" Jesus into others, we can let them see Jesus in us, by presenting to them a daily antithesis (and a biblical antidote) for the current non-Christian cultural agenda, and God promises that if we will do that, He will bless our obedience by motivating them to ask us why we live the way we do and receive the blessings that we do.[6]

- How can we love God with all our heart, soul and mind unless we give all of our effort? (Matthew 23.37; 1 Corinthians 10.31)
- No matter what we are doing, we should strive to excel in it:

Whatever your hand finds to do, do it with your might; for there is no work or device or knowledge or wisdom in the grave where you are going. ECCLESIASTES 9.10

Question 43. Is your daily testimony (lifestyle)

a About the same as the lifestyle of your non-Christian neighbors?
b. Significantly different than that of your non-Christian neighbors?

For the past century and a half non-Christians have gradually captured the collective cultural agenda and gained control of schools, the media and civil government.

In the midst of our collective non-Christian culture, how should we deal with everyday issues in the way God commands in order to present a Christian testimony and antithesis to our non-Christian neighbors?

As Christians, our worldview and lifestyle should be very different, if not completely different than our non-Christian neighbors. Sadly, many of us would have to say that while we by no means believe the same

---

Q. 42 NOTES

1 1 Samuel 17.47
2 Ephesians 1.11
3 1 Corinthians 15.58
4 Alderson, Dr. Richard, *No Holiness, No Heaven!*, (Banner of Truth Trust, 1986), p. 13
5 Psalm 37.5
6 Deuteronomy 4.5-9

things that non-Christians believe, our lifestyles present no discernable difference when compared to the lifestyles of non-Christians. So let's ask ourselves a tough question:

> *If we really don't believe what they believe, why do we live like they live?*

Now, if you're waiting for me to answer this question, stop waiting, because I don't have one. I'm just asking. But surely we don't go through our daily duties without thinking. We've got to be thinking something! It's impossible to do anything without thinking anything. The next time you're in the grocery store, try buying something without thinking about why you're buying it. Maybe you're out of the product, or maybe you've never tried it and feel adventurous and want to see if you will like it. Whatever your reason may be for purchasing a particular product, you know that nothing just happens to find its way into your grocery cart.

You put it there, and you put it there for a reason.

Once we agree that every decision we make is based upon some thought, we should ask ourselves "What am I thinking when I make my daily decisions?" As fast-paced as our lifestyles are, we obviously don't have time to step back from every decision we make to do some analytical thinking, but this doesn't mean that our decisions aren't made within an overall framework of what we believe is the best thing to do. So if our daily decisions are out of sync with what we say that we believe, then we need to make some major adjustments in the overall mindset under which we are living. The term you are more familiar with for "overall mindset" is "worldview." If you have a developed Christian worldview your daily decisions will be made in the framework of bringing glory and honor to God in everything you think, say and do. This is not to say that you won't make some bad decisions, because no one is perfect, but generally speaking your decisions and your lifestyle will be distinctively different from your non-Christian neighbors because their overall mindset (worldview) is to bring glory and honor to themselves.

This is not complicated. Either our daily decisions demonstrate that God is our friend, or they will demonstrate that He is our enemy. Either they demonstrate that we are a slave to Jesus by imaging Him, or a slave to Satan by imaging him. It's Bottom Line Theology:[1] None of us can serve "two masters,"[2] which means that our "master" is whomever's ethics our decisions reflect.

To say that God's Word is true, yet live as though Satan's word is true is to live a lifestyle that impresses neither God, nor our non-Christian neighbors. They will look upon us as simple minded knuckleheads who don't even have the courage of our convictions, and as a consequence they will have no motivation to worship our God, because we are demonstrating to them that He is clueless as far as providing counsel on how to live and govern ourselves. Another ungodly trait we are demonstrating in our daily testimony is that Jesus is impotent to bring about positive changes in the culture! How unattractive must this be for our non-Christian neighbors!

God's Word is not only true, but its serious. The apostle John tells us that Jesus "became the Word and dwelt among us."[3] Jesus is not only our Savior, but He is our Lord (Boss) and King, meaning that our civil rulers (legislators and judges) should conform their laws to His Word, because ONLY His Word is true. King David writes, it is through "God's precepts that he gains understanding," and that he "hates every false way."[4] Jesus also uses the word "hate" to emphasize what it takes to be His follower.

> *If anyone comes to Me and does not hate his father and mother, wife and children, brothers and sisters, yes, and his own life also, he cannot be My disciple. ... So likewise, whoever of you does not forsake all that he has cannot be My disciple.* LUKE 14.26, 33

Just in case His disciples still didn't "get it," Jesus explains

> *If anyone desires to come after Me, let him deny himself, and take up his cross, and follow Me. For whoever desires to save his life will lose it, but whoever loses his life for My sake will find it.* MATTHEW 16.24-25

Wow! Hate our parents, children, brothers and sisters, even our own life, and deny ourselves and forsake all that we have! Notice that Jesus doesn't say that we will have to do these things in order to follow Him, but be willing to do them, if necessary. In other words, He is demanding that He has first place in our hearts.

But considering all that Jesus has done for us (including giving His life!) is what He is demanding from us unreasonable? If your answer is "Yes," then you have just invented a false religion.

Obviously, before anyone would be motivated to give themselves completely to Jesus by putting Him first in their daily agenda, thoughts and decision-making, they would first have to know who they are and who Jesus is, and what He has done for them. As you read through the "Who, What, When, Where, Why & How" chart, you should be reminded how squared away you are as a Christian and how clueless you were when you were a non-Christian.

Six Questions

QUESTION	CHRISTIAN	NON-CHRISTIAN
Who?	Creature of God	No Idea
What?	Undeserving Ambassador of God who has been called out of darkness and into light" through God's merciful grace.	No Idea
When?	God will bless our obedience in His perfect timing to a "thousand generations."	No Idea
Where?	We're living in God's creation on our way to Heaven, encouraging those on their way to Hell to repent and join us.	No Idea
Why?	Carry out God's will on earth so that the earth will be full of the knowledge of the LORD as the waters cover the sea.	No Idea
How?	Present a godly lifestyle (testimony) for our non-Christian neighbors to observe, share the Gospel, and teach God's principles for living to our families and others.	No Idea

In describing the difference between a "true" and a "false" faith, David presents the best antidote for an ungodly worldview and lifestyle by adding that "God's word is a lamp to his feet and a light to his path." [5] Once again we are reminded that Christianity is a "doing" as well as a "thinking" religion, and not exclusively a "thinking" one. Yes, "reasoning" is important, as Jehovah invites us to "come and reason" with Him, [6] but His meaning is that we first "reason," or think, His thoughts, then we incorporate them into our daily decision-making so that we "walk our talk" and provide a living antithesis to the ungodly worldview and lifestyles of those around us.

Question 44. Do we live in an orderly, cause-and-effect universe, or in a universe where events happen randomly?

    a.   A random universe.
    b.   An orderly universe.

To say that there is no rhyme, or reason to the events that take place is to conclude that God lies to us in Leviticus 26 and Deuteronomy 28, where He states: we will be blessed if we obey Him, and disciplined if we disobey Him. Since we live in an orderly universe, how could it be possible for Satan to be "alive and well on planet earth?" All we have to do is obey God and in God's perfect timing, Satan's defeat will be completed. So, when we see bad events happening we shouldn't give Satan the credit for being in charge of the earth, but rather give man the blame for being disobedient to God's rules. The psalmist Asaph records these words from Jehovah:

> *Oh, that My people would listen to Me, that Israel would walk in My ways! I would soon subdue their enemies, and turn My hand against their adversaries.*   PSALM 81.13-1

Q. 43 NOTES

1 See *Bottom Line Theology: A Bible Study Feast for those who only have Time for a Sandwich*, Buddy Hanson, (Hanson Group)
2 Luke 16.13
3 John 1.1-14
4 Psalm 119.104
5 Psalm 119.105
6 Isaiah 1.18

That sounds like cause-and-effect to me: Jehovah says, "If Israel will obey Me, I will turn My hand against their enemies." The apostle Peter certainly thought we live in an orderly universe. In the first recorded sermon in Scripture, he says, "Repent, and let everyone of you be baptized …" [1] If events are random, we have no expectation of turning them around. But if, as the Bible states, they are the results of our actions (either obedient or disobedient), then we can repent by turning from our disobedient worldview and lifestyle with the assurance that we will receive God's blessings. (If this were not the case, why would the Bible teach us to repent?) [2]

As will be discussed in Replacement String 1, living in a cause-and-effect world means that we can place our trust in what Jesus accomplished on Calvary, instead of trusting in an imagined rescue mission by a heavenly cavalry to remove us from our earthly calling. Jesus called us into His Kingdom to boldly be the "light of the world," not to timidly "put it under a basket" while awaiting Him to do what He has commanded us to do! [3]

Q. 44 NOTES
1   Acts 2
2   Ezekiel 14.6; Zechariah 1.4; 1 Peter 3.11
3   Matthew 5.14-16

Refocusing Your Worldview

Has the information in this section revealed that you may have been looking at the world through blurred lenses? If so, how does this information help you to change your mantra as you approach each day in Christ's Kingdom? Yes, I said, "mantra," and yes, that usually means something that is chanted, but for our case we're using it as an unspoken mantra, or that "frame of reference" we bring to our daily decision-making that enables us to either accept or dismiss proposals that don't conform to our predisposed way of viewing the world. The upside of having such a mantra, or frame of reference is that we don't have to start from scratch in evaluating each decision, which means it saves us a lot of time. The downside is that if our mantra needs changing, and we don't realize it, then we will, with the best of intentions, make decisions that are not in our best interests.

Both Satan and Jesus have a mantra that they would prefer us to use in our daily decision-making. Take a look at both mantras to decide which one is currently dictating your decisions. The clearer your focus becomes with each area of decision-making, the sharper your decisions will reflect God's will, instead of Satan's.

What's in Your Mantra?

Satan's Version: Salvation & Frustration

"You are losers in the here-and-now, but winners in the hereafter."

"Jesus loves us and came to save us from our sins so that when we die (or are raptured!) we will be freed from the shackles of Satan's dominion upon the earth, and will joyfully spend eternity with fellow believers worshiping the triune God of the Bible. Until that time Jesus' Word encourages us to save as many people as we can and comforts us in our trials on this evil-infested earth by giving us a 'hope to cope' with all that Satan throws at us."

Jesus' Version: Salvation & Occupation

"You can be winners in both the here-and-now, and in the hereafter (by living according to My Word!)."

"Jesus loves those whom the Trinity chose before the foundation of the earth (EPHESIANS 1.4,17; 2.8) and came to earth to perfectly fulfill the Law (JOHN 1.1,14; MATTHEW 5.17; HEBREWS 4.15; 1 JOHN 4.10) and pay our sin debt by dying and overcoming death (JOHN 10.17-18; 1 CORINTHIANS 15.45) and has given us His Word to instruct us in how to live and govern ourselves (PSALM 119.105; JEREMIAH 31.33; JOHN 17.17; COLOSSIANS 3.16; ROMANS 8.9, 14, 16; 2 TIMOTHY 3.16-17) and complete Jesus' victory over Satan (1 JOHN 3.8; 4.4; COLOSSIANS 2.13-15; HEBREWS 2.14) by taking dominion over the earth (GENESIS 1.26-28; 9.1-4; MATTHEW 28.18-20; ROMANS 8.37) and restoring God's will "on earth, as it is in heaven." (MATTHEW 6.10; REVELATION 11.15).

Fourth Cut

Decision-Making

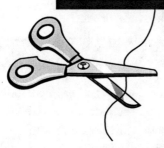

QUESTIONS 45 – 50

Question 45. Is it possible for us to make correct decisions by depending upon our own wisdom and common sense?

a. Yes, after all, God has given us a brain and the ability to communicate.

b. **No, because Adam and Eve's disobedience impaired our ability to reason correctly. This is why we need to filter all of our decisions through a gird of biblical ethics. Thinking God's thoughts after Him is the only way we can be confident that we will arrive at correct decisions.**

Many Christians would probably question the contention that in this highly technological age, we are incapable of making the correct ethical decisions, unless we filter them through a grid of biblical ethics: in other words, unless we re-think God's thoughts. The issue, however is not that we have a learning deficiency, but that we have an ethical deficiency. Adam and Eve's "Fall" has made it impossible for us to make correct decisions. Whether we like to admit it or not, the truth is that each of us is a born sinner. As Eliphaz says to Job: "Man is born to trouble, as the sparks fly upward." [1]

Imagine that you are holding a theological coin that has "God's Word is truth" inscribed on one side. Each of us would be quick to agree with that. However, we may not be so quick to agree with the flip side of the coin, because the only inscription it could have in order to be in agreement with the other side is "Man's word is false." Somehow, this statement doesn't have the ring to it that "God's Word is truth," but we can't have one side of the coin without the other.

> ## God's Word is truth/man's word is false.

What this means is that all decisions, whether in the home, on the job, in the halls of our legislatures, on the judicial benches, in the classroom, or wherever decisions are made…if they don't conform to biblical ethics, they are, by our own definition, FALSE, and we shouldn't expect them to work, regardless of how much money, time, effort or good intentions we devote to them! But why is it that God's Word is true, and man's word is false? Early in Genesis we read:

> *Then the LORD saw that the wickedness of man was great*
> *in the earth, and that every intent of the thoughts of his heart*
> *was only evil continually."* GENESIS 6.5

As soon as Noah and his family stepped out of the ark, we see these words:

> *The LORD said, "I will never again curse the ground for*
> *man's sake, although the imagination of man's heart is evil*
> *from his youth."* GENESIS 8.21

Approximately 1,500 years later, the prophet Jeremiah writes, "The heart is deceitful above all things, and desperately wicked; who can understand it?" [2] And 600 hundred years after that Jesus makes the familiar statement: "For out of the heart proceed evil thoughts, murders, adulteries, fornications, thefts, false witness, blasphemies." [3]

I could go on, but the point is that Adam and Eve's disobedience, their desire to be their own gods and live by their rules, instead of living by God's rules, has caused each of us to be born sinners with rebellious natures. Indeed, natures that don't merely dislike God, but hate Him. To quote King Solomon:

> *God made man upright, but they have sought out many*
> *schemes.*   ECCLESIASTES 7.29

Want to try another coin? How about inscribing "ONLY God's Word Works" on one side. Sounds pretty good, doesn't it? Once again the flip side is damaging to our ego, because it can only read: "Man's Word ONLY Fails." Take your choice:

God's Word is TRUTH/ Man's Word is FALSE
Or
ONLY God's Word Works/Man's Word ONLY Fails.

Either theological coin brings home the necessity of not attempting to make our daily decisions based upon our own wisdom, intelligence and/or common sense. To attempt to do so is to imitate Adam and Eve by seeing ourselves as "gods."

David tells us, "The fool has said in his heart, 'There is no God,'"[4] and by viewing the world through our eyes, we are, in effect, saying the same thing (Not that we are saying there is "no God." We wouldn't dare say that, but through our lifestyle we are saying something just as bad: that there is no God directing and controlling the daily events and circumstances in His creation!). I doubt very seriously if any Christian thinks of himself as being as smart as God, but do we live as though we are gods?

---

45 NOTES
1   Job 5.7
2   Jeremiah 17.9
3   Matthew 15.19
4   Psalm 14.1; 53.1

By refusing to think God's thoughts after Him, and by not incorporating them into our lifestyle, we are allowing non-Christians (who do view themselves as gods) to do our thinking for us. As mentioned, it has been estimated that only 12% of professing Christians read a portion of their Bible once a month, with 45% seldom, if ever, reading it. This means that we are trading God's perfect wisdom for man's imperfect wisdom, then complaining about how bad things are becoming! So, while we may not directly see ourselves as "gods," we must be careful that our lifestyles don't betray us. On Judgment Day Jesus isn't going to ask whether we "saw" ourselves as gods, but whether we "lived" as though we were gods.

Question 46. What is your opinion regarding God's Word?

    a. I have respect for it.
    b. I have a reverential fear of it.

This question may sound a little confusing, because every Christian respects God's Word, but since so few of us are making a valiant effort to "exit" God's truths from our homes and churches and into our daily decisions, could the reason for that be that we don't reverently fear the consequences for not doing so? Indeed, could it not be stated that we are "reaping the consequences we deserve by refusing to apply His truths to our current cultural conditions?! Could it be that in too many instances, we hesitate to take a stand for biblical ethics because we are afraid of the reaction from non-Christians (including Christians who don't have a developed Christian worldview!)? Such "fear," however, is greatly misplaced, for it is our Creator whom we must surely fear, instead of man. As the Paul writes

> *What then shall we say to these things? If God is for us, who can be against us?*   ROMANS 8.31

The 17th Century Puritan Pastor, Thomas Manton, puts this in proper perspective by writing, "The heart is never right until we are brought to fear a commandment more than any inconvenience whatsoever." To this pithy advice we should all give a hearty "Amen!"

The first step, then, in developing a reverential fear of God's Word is to change the mindset of our worldview from Me-Think, to Re-Think. We should recognize that if our thoughts do not reflect God's thoughts, we're not living a godly lifestyle and are not demonstrating a Christian worldview to our non-Christian neighbors. As will be discussed, it is our commanded duty to demonstrate to those who cross our paths that Christianity is not merely a "harmless delusion," [1] that can be lumped together with the other religions of the world, but rather is the only correct conclusion regarding how to live and govern ourselves. Instead of being "cheated by the philosophy and empty deceit, according to the tradition of men,"[2] we are to "cast down arguments and every high thing that exalts itself against the knowledge of God, bringing every thought captive to the obedience of Christ." [3]

We should recognize that there is a huge difference between making a mental assent to the truths of the Bible and a making a dedicated consent to them. Did not the disciple James tell first century Christians: "You believe that there is one God. You do well. Even the demons believe—and tremble!" [4] The point James is making is that we are not called into Christ's Kingdom to merely "know the truth," and then live the remainder of our life with a "dead orthodoxy," [5] but rather to "know the truth" so we can be "set free" from our former sinful and erroneous ways to follow Jesus' living orthodoxy , [6] thereby bringing "honor," instead of dishonor to God. [7] The critical importance of living according to God's law is found in the remark by King Solomon: "Those who forsake the law praise the wicked, but such as keep the law, contend with them." [8]

Q. 46 NOTES

1   J. Gresham Machen, *What Is Christianity?* (Eerdmans, 1951), p.162
2   Colossians 2.8
3   2 Corinthians 10.5
4   James 2.19

5   2 Timothy 3.5
6   John 8.32; Matthew 4.19
7   1 Peter 4.11
8   Proverbs 28.4

The Authenticity of the Word of God

With all the emphasis that Scripture places on being careful to live according to God's Word this is a good place for a brief overview of why we believe that the Word of God is without error. Baptist Pastor Ed Wallen provides this explanation in one of his weekly e-newsletters.

Let us call three witnesses to authenticate that the Bible is the Word of God. **First**, the human writers of the Bible give testimony. Forty, or more, men wrote Scripture as God worked in them over a span of about1600 years. Many of these men never personally met, yet did not contradict each other in their writing. Some were highly educated, but for the most part they were common men without formal education. Some lived in palaces; some lived in fields with their sheep. They were kings, advisors to kings, fishermen, farmers, shepherds, a tax collector, and Paul a Jewish theologian. One thing they had in common – they all claimed to be writing the Word of God. Several thousand (3,808) times in the Bible you will read a claim that the writer was writing the Word of God and later writers often referred to and quoted earlier writings as the Word of God. For example, in the New Testament you will find no less than 320 direct quotes from the Old Testament. (Some examples; Rom. 15:4; 2 Peter 1:21; Heb 1:1; Ja. 4:5).

The **Second** witness is the Lord Jesus Christ Himself. Jesus claimed to be the theme of all Scriptures, (John 5:39). He also declared that He had come to fulfill all Scripture, (Matt. 5:17). He talked about the cross as being previously predicted (Matt. 26:24). He further declared that "Scripture cannot be broken" (Luke 16:17; 18:31). The 22nd Psalm graphically described the suffering and death of Christ on the Cross. Jesus further gave validity to the authority of the accounts of the Old Testament, such as the Creation story (Matt: 19:4, 5); the story of Cain and Abel (Lk. 11:51); the Genesis flood (Matt. 24:37- 38). There are many more instances where Jesus validated the Old Testament to be the Word of God.

The last witness is the Holy Spirit. In order to believe the Bible to be the Word of God, the Holy Spirit will have to give witness to the heart. Believing the Bible to be the inspired Word of God is not the result of intellectual pursuits of knowledge. You will not believe the Bible unless the Holy Spirit works in your heart and mind giving witness to that truth. You must believe the Bible is true because the Bible says it is true. That may be circular reasoning, but it is wise reasoning. If you don't believe the Bible, you are not going to believe the Bible when it says that it is the Word of God. However, if you are going to walk with The Lord, you must agree with Him that the Bible is His Word. "Heaven and earth will pass away, but My words will not pass away" (Mark 13:31). 24

www.biblestudyfoundation.org, P.O. Box 1703 Alabaster, AL 35007
bsf@biblestudyfoundation.org, "Think Scripturally," Ed Wallen, August 14, 2006.

Question 47. What is the "Chief Influencer" of your daily decisions?

   a. What's in it for me?
   b. What's in it for God?

When you begin your decision-making process, should your primary interest be on your thoughts, or upon God's thoughts? This primary interest, or "Chief Influencer," must be identified before you can hope to develop an explicitly Christian approach to decision-making. For non-Christians, the answer is "What's in it for me?" but for Christians the chief concern should be, "What's in it for God," or more specifically "What's in it for Christ's Kingdom?" It is precisely at this point, however, that a "chief influencer" rears its head from the shadows of our mind:

What impact, if any, do we believe our decisions will have
on the future direction of our culture?

For example, if we believe that our obedience will result in an improved culture, we will make one set of decisions, but if we believe that our daily decisions won't positively affect the future, then we will likely operate by another set of decisions. Obviously, if we believe that God created a cause-and-effect universe, instead of one in which He randomly and unpredictably brings blessings and/or curses, (and even supernaturally beams us up from our responsibilities!) we will be moved to conform our decisions and actions according to biblical ethics, because we believe that, in God's eternally perfect timing, we will receive blessings. In addition, we know that if we fail to conform our daily decisions to Scripture, we can expect for God to bring curses upon us and our children and grandchildren.

On the other hand, if we see a disconnect between God's Word, our current cultural situation and the future, we will attempt to fulfill our "religious" obligations by participating in short-term missions to build churches and schools, spend weekends with prison ministries, volunteering with various charities, and so forth. Even though such activities are to be applauded, what would be missing from the Christian walk of such an individual would be any plan to confront the various non-Christian issues that are driving our culture. In other words, without a clearly defined idea of what God has called us to do, our decision-making will very likely take on a life of its own, becoming an end in itself. This approach to decision-making can result in confining God's truths to the inside our homes and churches, as we become, in effect, cautious caretakers of Christ's Kingdom instead of bold biblical risk-takers to expand it.

Why Did the Chicken Cross the Road?

Another factor to consider in our decision-making is that we don't make decisions in a vacuum. Decisions are tied to a "cause," that motivates us to take action. To cite the classic question of why the chicken crossed the road, the answer is not that he simply wanted to get to the "other side," because that, in itself is not a "cause" that would motivate such an action. However, if the chicken happens to be a rooster and there are a lot of hens on the other side of the road, then we may have uncovered the cause for why the chicken decided to cross the road!

This brings us back to our view of the future. Currently, the overwhelming majority of Christians believe that Satan is alive and well on planet earth and that there is nothing we can do to bring about positive changes in our culture. As a result many of us refuse to apply the biblical truths we profess to hold so dearly to our everyday situations and circumstances. If we only looked at the consequences of the behavior from this large group of Christians, we would be tempted to call them lazy, lethargic and apathetic. However, when we look behind the consequences of their decisions to the cause that is motivating their action, we may not be so fast to write them off as simply well-meaning moralistic people who may not, in fact, be true Christians.

Instead, we should explain to them how their worldview and lifestyle is contrary to the consistent teaching of Scripture. Consider, for example, our being identified by Paul as being "more than conquerors in Christ." [1] Why would Paul call us "conquerors" if the Christian lifestyle was nothing more than meeting, eating, and retreating from cultural issues? As the following chart points out, with all of the blessings we have, "Who needs pessimism?!"

With These Blessings, Who Needs Pessimism?!

- He chose us from before the foundation of the world, [2]
- Makes us "alive" at His appointed time, [3]
- Reconciles us to God, [4] and then
- "seals" our redemption by the Holy Spirit, [5] who also
- Guides us into the truth, [6] and enables us to
- Have access to His "throne of grace" 24 hours a day, seven days a week.[7]
- He Writes His law on our heart [8] and
- Sent His Son "who loved us and gave Himself for us," [9] then He
- Created us for "good works," [10] even to be
- "More than conquerors" through Him who loves us, [11] which means that we are able to
- "Knock down" Satan's strongholds, [12] as we
- "Disciple the nations," [13] making the
- "kingdoms of this world, the kingdoms of our Lord and of His Christ." [14]

In the midst of this optimism, we should be careful to walk in a manner that is true to our profession of faith in Jesus and that will bring glory and honor to God in all we think, say and do. The following "Be Careful How You Walk" chart lists sixteen steps listed by the apostle Paul in his letter to the Ephesians. Each of us should be walking in this manner.

How are you doing in your daily Christian walk?

Let's go back to the chicken and his road crossing. If we only focus on the consequence of the chicken's decision, which was to find himself on

Q. 47 NOTES

1	Romans 8.37	8	Jeremiah 31.33
2	Ephesians 1.4	9	Galatians 2.20
3	Ephesians 2.1	10	Ephesians 2.10
4	Ephesians 2.11-13	11	Romans 8.37
5	Ephesians 4.30	12	Matthew 16.18
6	John 16.13; Galatians 4.6; Ephesians 1.13; 1 John 4.13; 5.6	13	Matthew 28.18-20
		14	Revelation 11.15
7	Ephesians 3.12		

Be Careful How You Walk
EPHESIANS 4.17–5.21

STEP 1	Walk no longer as we once walked. 4.17
STEP 2	Put off our old self. 4.22
STEP 3	Renew our mind. 4.23
STEP 4	Speak the truth. 4.25
STEP 5	Be angry, but don't sin. 4.26
STEP 6	Do not steal. 4.28
STEP 7	Speak only wholesome words. 4. 29
STEP 8	Be kind and forgiving toward others. 4.32
STEP 9	Be imitators of God; walking in love. 5.1-2
STEP 10	Do not let immorality or greed be named among you. 5.3-7
STEP 11	Walk as children of light; finding out what is acceptable to the Lord. 5.8-10
STEP 12	Do not participate in the deeds of darkness, but expose them. 5.11-13
STEP 13	Redeem the time, because the days are evil. 5.16
STEP 14	Understand what the will of the Lord is. 5.17
STEP 15	Give thanks always to God. 5.20
STEP 16	Submit to one another in the fear of God. 5.21

the other side of the road, we are tempted to say that just "getting there" was his only motivation. But, as we have seen, to conclude that would be to make an error in judgment, because we would not have considered the "cause" behind his decision.

Since most 21st Century Christians don't believe that applying biblical truths to their everyday decisions will produce positive results, they look for church-related "busyness" activities to fill their need of "doing something" for Christ's Kingdom. The reason for this is that even Christians who don't have a developed Christian worldview know that they have been called into Christ's Kingdom to do something. But since they have ruled out the possibility of their decisions having a positive impact on culture, they erect a wall between "religious life," and "real life." Instead of filtering all of their decisions through a colander of biblical ethics, they only do that with "religious" decisions, and make their everyday decisions in the same fashion as non-Christians. So, without intending to, they are aiding and abetting Satan by living like non-Christians, while professing to be Christians! Satan, of course, could care less about what we profess to believe. His concern is that we don't live up to what we say we believe. As long as we image him with our decision-making, we are no threat to his efforts.

We see, then, that in both of these examples, Christians are attempting to make the best decisions they can. The difference is that one group's decisions are analyzed and designed to positively impact the future through their obedience, while the other group doesn't have a "visionary hope" of the future and consequently focuses their decisions on keeping busy in the present by attempting to earn points with God through "religious" activities while hoping that their "future" will manifest itself quickly in the return of Christ.

Question 48. What's the Context of Your Worldview?

a. It's pretty much the ethics of commandments 5-10: Honor those in authority, don't murder, cheat, steal, lie or covet.

b. **It is a combination of all Ten Commandments, plus the application of the Case Laws that follow them, whereby Moses tells us how to live and govern ourselves.**

When it comes to quoting a particular portion of Scripture, I think it's safe to say that we're pretty careful to make certain that we don't cite it "out of context," and are also quick to inform someone else, if they are using a passage out of context. However

> *When was the last time you checked your worldview and lifestyle to see if it is "in context" with the Scripture. Think about it. As Christians, aren't we supposed to conform our worldview and lifestyle to Scripture, and not to "the world?"* [1]

As you are thinking about your answer, let me throw this into the hopper: Do you view the situations and circumstances facing you today in the overall Big Picture context of Christian truth, or in terms of existential, or post-modern truth? Just because you may be a little fuzzy on the definitions of "existential," and "post-modern," it doesn't mean that you may not be living according to their erroneous philosophies, instead of according to the true ethics of the Bible. Both existentialists and post-moderns absolutize each day, because for them, truth, if it exists at all, is only "what works for them at the moment." Since they don't believe in absolute truth, and scoff at the very idea, they can't refer to historical events to learn lessons from actions and decisions that were either successful or unsuccessful. The only thing they have that is meaningful to them is today.

So, what about your approach to each new day? Granted, it is the only "day" over which we have control, because we can't undo our mistakes of yesterday, and we aren't guaranteed a "tomorrow." Yet, in order to make the most of today we need to be careful that we are living it in the context of the wisdom of historical lessons, and with the confidence of God's promises for us (promises that apply to both today and tomorrow).

Our belief in absolute and unchanging truth, enables us to know that if we repeat our bad decisions of yesterday, we will continue to get unpleasant consequences. On the other hand, by learning from our bad decisions of yesterday, which were based upon thinking our thoughts, we can make good decisions today by re-thinking God's thoughts, which will bring about pleasant consequences.

As discussed, we must not forget that the world in which we are living has been negatively affected because of Adam & Eve's decision to prefer their thoughts, to God's thoughts. Their decision was an attempt to transfer their allegiance from the Creator to the creature, and the consequence of this disrespect of and disobedience to God's will has been that everyone is born with the mindset of "I want to do things my way, not God's way," with our allegiance being to ourselves, instead of God.

God Demands Our Allegiance

Once we become Christians, our first order of business is to transfer our allegiance from ourselves to our Creator. This requires that we take a full spiritual step, not a hypocritical half-way step. Since Jesus has freed us from being slaves to Satan, we should joyfully recognize that we are now slaves of our Lord, Savior and King, and consequently, the motivation behind all of our thoughts, words and decisions is to bring "glory to His name." [2] By the same token, any glory that we seek should be "from

God." [3] As we go about our daily duties Satan will put several temptations in our path. Four of the most common ones are:

- The temptation to "establish our own righteousness, instead of submitting ourselves to the righteousness of God." [4] Paul spoke about this to the church at Rome.
- The temptation to avoid impending temporal judgments from others, as was the case when Israel's evil King Ahab fasted in sackcloth. [5]
- The temptation to use God's judgment on your enemy for personal gain, as when King Jehu wiped out King Ahab's family along with the worshippers of Baal. [6]
- The temptation to escape from an unpleasant situation or circumstance, as did the Jews in Babylon who fasted and mourned for 70 years. However, the major influencer in their decision-making was to get rid of their captivity, instead of getting rid of their sins. [7]

The renowned 17th Century nonconformist preacher Thomas Brooks explains

It is the end that dignifies or debases the action, that rectifies it or adulterates it, that sets a crown of honor or a crown of shame upon the head of it. He that commonly, habitually, in all his duties and services, proposes to himself no higher ends than the praises of men or rewards of men, or the stopping the mouth of natural conscience, or only to avoid a smarting rod, or merely to secure himself from wrath to come, he is an hypocrite. [8]

Brooks continues with his devastating description of hypocrites.

Hypocrites love to share with Christ in His happiness, but they don't love to share with Christ in His holiness. They are willing to be redeemed by Christ, but they are not cordially willing to submit to the laws and government of Christ. They are willing to be saved by His blood, but they are not willing to submit to His scepter. Hypocrites love the privileges of the

147

Gospel, but they don't love the services of the Gospel, especially those that are most inward and spiritual. But now a sincere Christ, he owns Christ in all His offices, he receives Christ in all His offices, and he closes with Christ in all His offices. He accepts of Him, not only as a Christ Jesus, but also as a Lord Jesus; he embraces Him, not only as a saving Christ, but also as a ruling Christ. ....An hypocrite is all for a saving Christ, for a sin-pardoning Christ, for a soul-glorifying Christ, but regards not a ruling Christ, a reigning Christ, a commanding Christ, a sanctifying Christ; and this at last will prove his damning sin (JOHN 3.19-20). [9]

Giving our complete allegiance to Jesus is what the message of the Bible is all about. Parables, slices of history, sermons, psalms and prophetic visions are all used to drive home the point that the Creator is smarter than His creatures, and because of that, our efforts will only be successful if we are careful to conform our thoughts, decisions and actions to His inerrant Word. The fact that He is in complete control of His creation, and is guiding and directing all events and circumstances toward that purpose, means that His will and His team will win in history.

Question 49. What is the criteria you use to make your best decisions?

   a. The "prevailing opinion" of other Christians, plus my common sense and logic.

   b. God's Word is the primary authority, but for those topics about which I haven't studied, I comply with what other Christians suggest.

Q. 48 NOTES

1 Romans 12.2
2 Psalm 115.1
3 2 Thessalonians 2.4-6
4 Romans 10.3
5 1 Kings 21; Jonah 3
6 2 Kings 10
7 Zechariah 7.5-6 8

8 From "A Cabinet of Jewels" in *The Works of Thomas Brooks*, Vol. 3, (Banner of Truth Trust), cited in *Free Grace Broadcast*, Issue 193, Fall 2005, p.15 www.mountzion.org
9 Brooks, ibid., *Jewels*, p.19

What's the best decision you ever made? How about your "Fabulous Five" all-time decisions? The reason I ask is because I saw a hair replacement commercial the other day and a customer said, "This is the best decision I've ever made!" That got me to thinking about the best decision I ever made. In coming up with the answer to that I began writing down what I'll call, "Significantly Good Decisions" in order to select the right one. Since we're discussing decision-making, it's only fair if I ask you to write down not only your "best decision," but your all-time "Fabulous Five," or if you really get on a roll, your all-time "Top Ten."

The number of "Significantly Good Decisions" you come up with doesn't matter, but the process of thinking about and writing them down is very important, as will be explained. Besides, it's private and you don't have to show them to anyone, so take a few minutes and go for it. The following chart has ten lines in case you think of ten Significantly Good Decisions. Again, it's the process, not the number of decisions that's important. Write down the decisions as you think of them, then go back and rank them by filling in the numerical number in the right-hand column.

My Very Own Private All-Time Significantly Good Decisions

DECISIONS	RANKING
------------------------------	----------
------------------------------	----------
------------------------------	----------
------------------------------	----------
------------------------------	----------
------------------------------	----------
------------------------------	----------
------------------------------	----------
------------------------------	----------
------------------------------	----------

The Enlightenment popularized the idea that it was culturally acceptable to separate Christian principles from everyday decision-making. Its basis for promoting this heresy was the idea that man's autonomous reason enabled him to make accurate decisions. In other words, the Enlightenment philosophers didn't believe in The Fall of Man and so had no reason to believe it had adverse consequences on man's reasoning. We, however, know better, and regardless of the topic being discussed or debated, we must ask:

Upon what authority are we basing our decisions?

If the decision we make depends upon man's reasons instead of God's, we will lose the discussion, because when God's Word is not upheld, the "glory and honor" that results from the decision will go to man, not God. Since we serve a "jealous God," [1] we are inviting His wrath by doing anything that does not bring Him the honor He deserves. [2]

In all instances, we should recognize that any "solution" that is not based upon biblical ethics is only dealing with the fruit that is falling from man's "poisoned cultural tree," instead of the root cause that is enabling man's poisoned cultural tree to continue to grow. Why would we want to make such a compromised "solution," when we say, "God is smarter than man?" If we are ultimately going to base our decisions upon man's word, instead of God's Word, why do we need God? Put another way, if God's Word (truth/reality) is not our exclusive reference point for making our daily decisions, then we are simply hallucinating when it comes to developing solutions. This is so because God created all things, so obviously, nothing can have meaning if separated from its origin, and it's Creator. The definition for "hallucination" is to "visualize unreal things," and for a person to attempt to come to an understanding of something by viewing it apart from God, means that he has eliminated all hope of truly understanding the issue. This is why it is absolutely necessary to filter our decisions through the grid of absolute biblical truth, otherwise all we have is a "sense" or a "feeling" that something is the best course of action to take. The fallacy of reasoning in this manner is that there is no way to reconcile the "sense," or "feeling" of others who have a different "sense," or "feeling."

150

The issue comes down to whether we, as creatures, want to submit ourselves to God, the Creator. It is obvious why non-Christians don't want to do that, but what excuse can we have for our unwillingness to be ruled by our Lord, Savior and King, Jesus Christ?!

The effective temptation that Satan uses on us is to suggest that we can "help God out" by adding pragmatism and common sense to our decision-making. When faced with this temptation, we must recall that "we are not sufficient in and of ourselves to arrive at correct decisions, but our sufficiency is from God. [4]

In order for anyone to truly understand anything apart from God, he would have to have an exhaustive knowledge, which, of course, no human has, but Christians, by re-thinking God's thoughts and definitions, can have true understanding. [3]

In other words, "He is the vine and we are the branches." [5] Our calling is to "Fear God and keep His commandments, for this is man's all." [6] For "whether we eat or drink, or whatever you do, do all to the glory of God."[7] Our decision-making should be based exclusively upon

> *Whatever things are true, whatever things are noble,*
> *whatever things are just, whatever things are pure,*
> *whatever things are lovely, whatever things are of good*
> *report, if there is any virtue and if there is anything*
> *praiseworthy—meditate on these things.*
>
> PHILIPPIANS 4.8

May we never forget that such biblically obedient behavior as just described is commanded, not simply suggested by our Creator God. Let's rejoice that we are no longer "dead in our sins" [8] and are no longer "slaves of sin," [9] and that we have been "made free" by Jesus' perfectly sinless life, death on the cross which paid for our sin debt, and His victory over death! [10] And may our daily goal be to conform each of our decisions to the biblical truths that we profess to hold so dear, by asking ourselves whether this decision is "holy and just and good." [11]

Return to your Significantly Good Decisions. Look back over your list and see if what we've discussed changes your list either by adding dif-

151

ferent decisions or deleting others, or by re-numbering them. Most likely your list includes decisions about your spouse, children, vocation, or an investment. Did you list your decision to become a Christian? After all, what could be more important than that? How about your decision to make all decisions conform to biblical truths? What could be more important than that?

The point is it's only natural to think about decisions you've made about the people you love, the vocation at which you spend such a large portion of your life, or even an investment that has produced a significant return. Each of these, however, represents natural things: things which we can see, feel, touch, taste and smell. However, as Christians, we now inhabit this natural (physical) world in a supernatural and spiritual way. The Holy Spirit has graciously written God's law on our hearts so that we no longer think in exclusively natural terms as we did when we were non-Christians. Thanks to God's grace we have replaced our natural and sinful wisdom with supernatural and holy wisdom. Therefore, our list of Significantly Good Decisions should not only include natural items as it would have when we were non-Christians, but should now include some supernatural items as well. Yes, you are still a physical person who is living in a physical world, but as a Christian, you should be making your decisions in a supernatural way, based upon your spiritual insights and holy wisdom.

By conforming our decisions to God's Word we are keeping His commandments and showing our love for Him. In the words of Jesus

He who has My commandments and keeps them, it is he who loves Me. And he who loves Me will be loved by My Father, and I will love him and manifest Myself to him."

JOHN 14.10

Q. 49 NOTES

1 Exodus 20.5; 34.14
2 Deuteronomy 4.24; 32.16
3 Rushdoony, R.J., *By What Standard?* (Thoburn Press, 1958), pp. 10-11

4 2 Corinthians 3.5
5 John 15.5
6 Ecclesiastes 12.13 See Van Til, Cornelius, *Christian Theistic Ethics*, (P & R Publishing, 1980), pp. 28-29

7 1 Corinthians 10.31
8 Ephesians 2.1
9 Romans 6.17
10 John 8.36
11 Romans 7.12

Question 50. Do you lean on your understanding, or upon God's?

a. Are you going to mirror the way non-Christians live, making your daily decisions according to your wisdom, while adding moralistic principles to your lifestyle in an external effort to win points with God? Or,

b. **Are you going to mirror the way the Bible commands you to live, with your external actions founded on the internal motivations of your new spiritual heart?**

In presenting such a godly antithesis for our non-Christian neighbors, we won't have to make external efforts to impress them with our periodic charitable works, because they will see a consistently different lifestyle that is based upon an all-encompassing ethical behavior that is not limited to going to church, hosting a small group Bible study, or going on a short-term missionary trip to distribute Bibles or build a Christian school.

The next pivotal question is whether our daily decisions demonstrate that we are on God's meaningful and victorious "A Team," or on man's meaningless and losing team? Make no mistake. We are at all times and in all circumstances serving either God or man. None of us ever acts in a neutral manner. Every decision we make shows that we are either for something, or against something. It is a truism that our actions betray our words, so in answering to whom we are partial in our daily decisions: yourself or God, we must be careful to answer it according to what our actions portray.

> *And whatever you do in word or deed, do all in the name of the Lord Jesus, giving thanks to God the Father through Him.* COLOSSIANS 3.17

Otherwise we will run the risk of being the type of individuals Jesus speaks about in the following verse:

> *You are they who justify yourselves before men; but God knows your hearts: for that which is highly esteemed among men is abomination in the sight of God.* LUKE 16.15

153

As the only people on the face of the earth to have the sin-clouded "veil lifted from our eyes" 1 so that we can know the truth, our duty is to:

Cast down imaginations and every high thing that exalts itself against the knowledge of God, and bringing into captivity every thought to the obedience of Christ.

2 CORINTHIANS 10.5

Instead of continuing to "lean on our own understanding," 2 we have the honor and privilege of leaning on God's understanding by "walking in the law of God with all of our heart." 3 To refuse to obey God's law is to be in rebellion against Him, since it is idolatrous to make decisions that do not conform to His Word. Of course, none of us needs practice in being disobedient to God's law, since that's what we did consistently in our sinful state, when we were eager to prove to our neighbors that we hated God and His rules. In our redeemed state, however, we "keep His law" in order to demonstrate to our neighbors that we "love God." 4 This is why it is in particularly bad taste to prefer man's law to God's law once we become Christians. After all Jesus has done for us, why would we want to show such disrespect for Him and His Word? When Israel repeatedly failed to live according to God's laws, the prophet Hosea recorded these words from Jehovah:

My people are destroyed for lack of knowledge. Because you have rejected knowledge, I also will reject you from being priest for Me; because you have forgotten the law of your God, I also will forget your children. HOSEA 4.6

These are really serious words, because God is really serious about us living in conformity to His Word, and He really judges individuals, families, and countries, that repeatedly disrespect and disobey His Word. 5 May we all be diligent to incorporate biblical ethics into our worldview so that neither we, nor our children are rejected and forgotten by God! Our authority for making decisions in God's four ordained self-governing spheres of the individual, family, church and state is derivative (from God). At our (physical) birth we were original sinners, who longed to think our original thoughts and act in original ways. Our reference point was exclusively our thoughts, which meant that our worldview and lifestyle was formed by the information we perceived from various ideas and events. As the 5th Century B.C. philosopher Protagoras wished: "Man is the measure of all things."

Opposing this self-worshiping attitude is the God-worshiping attitude that comes with our second (spiritual) birth, where we see ourselves as derivative copies of the holy triune God of Scripture, who are now motivated to re-think God's holy thoughts so we can make holy decisions. Before our conversion we did our best to image Satan, and after our conversion we are doing out best to image Jesus. This change in our reference point from ourselves to God means that we now should be (emphasis on should be) seeing the world through God's eyes, instead of our eyes, which should bring about drastic changes in our worldview and lifestyle.

> *Nevertheless the solid foundation of God stands, having this seal: "The Lord knows those who are His," and, "Let everyone who names the name of Christ depart from iniquity."*
>
> 2 TIMOTHY 2.19

Q. 50 NOTES

1 2 Corinthians 4.3-4; John 16.8
2 Proverbs 3 5; Hosea 5 11-12
3 2 Kings 10.31-32
4 John 14.15

5 See *This Is Not A Drill! Real Lessons for Real People from the Real God on How to Live and Govern Ourselves, Really!*, Buddy Hanson, (Hanson Group, 2008)

Refocusing Your Worldview

Has the information in this section revealed that you may have been looking at the world through blurred lenses? If so, how does this information help you to change your mantra as you approach each day in Christ's Kingdom? Yes, I said, "mantra," and yes, that usually means something that is chanted, but for our case we're using it as an unspoken mantra, or that "frame of reference" we bring to our daily decision-making that enables us to either accept or dismiss proposals that don't conform to our predisposed way of viewing the world. The upside of having such a mantra, or frame of reference is that we don't have to start from scratch in evaluating each decision, which means it saves us a lot of time. The downside is that if our mantra needs changing, and we don't realize it, then we will, with the best of intentions, make decisions that are not in our best interests.

Both Satan and Jesus have a mantra that they would prefer us to use in our daily decision-making. Take a look at both mantras to decide which one is currently dictating your decisions. The clearer your focus becomes with each area of decision-making, the sharper your decisions will reflect God's will, instead of Satan's.

What's in Your Mantra?

Satan's Version: Salvation & Frustration

"You are losers in the here-and-now, but winners in the hereafter."

"Jesus loves us and came to save us from our sins so that when we die (or are raptured!) we will be freed from the shackles of Satan's dominion upon the earth, and will joyfully spend eternity with fellow believers worshiping the triune God of the Bible. Until that time Jesus' Word encourages us to save as many people as we can and comforts us in our trials on this evil-infested earth by giving us a 'hope to cope' with all that Satan throws at us."

156

Jesus' Version: Salvation & Occupation

"You can be winners in both the here-and-now, and in the hereafter (by living according to My Word!)."

"Jesus loves those whom the Trinity chose before the foundation of the earth (EPHESIANS 1.4,17; 2.8) and came to earth to perfectly fulfill the Law (JOHN 1.1,14; MATTHEW 5.17; HEBREWS 4.15; 1 JOHN 4.10) and pay our sin debt by dying and overcoming death (JOHN 10.17-18; 1 CORINTHIANS 15.45) and has given us His Word to instruct us in how to live and govern ourselves (PSALM 119.105; JEREMIAH 31.33; JOHN 17.17; COLOSSIANS 3.16; RO-MANS 8.9, 14, 16; 2 TIMOTHY 3.16-17) and complete Jesus' victory over Satan (1 JOHN 3.8; 4.4; COLOSSIANS 2.13-15; HEBREWS 2.14) by taking dominion over the earth (GENESIS 1.26-28; 9.1-4; MATTHEW 28.18-20; ROMANS 8.37) and restoring God's will "on earth, as it is in heaven." (MATTHEW 6.10; REVELATION 11.15).

Fifth Cut

Eliminating Rationalizations & Pragmatism

Now that you have taken the Personal Worldview Checkup and have read the explanations of the answers to see in which ways the collective non-Christian cultural agenda has been "pulling your strings," you're just about ready to begin re-assembling your spiritual musical instrument so that your worldview and lifestyle can demonstrate some sanctified string music. Part Two will discuss exactly how a Christian worldview should impact your lifestyle, by offering five Replacement Strings. Each Replacement String will take an in-depth view of some of the important concepts addressed in the answers to the Personal Worldview Checkup questions. A little more "meat" is added to those skeletal foundational truths as well as the inclusion of practical applications. To set the table for that, this chapter cuts off any lingering rationalizations for not exiting our children from the public schools. It also summarizes some of the non-negotiable elements that should be in a Christian worldview.

Each of us can rejoice that, as Christians, we are no longer a puppet of Satan. [1] The Holy Spirit has written the Law of God on our hearts [2] so that we know how God commands for us to live, and are motivated to frame our daily decisions in accordance with His revealed counsel. In other words, now we are a puppet of God, and the "strings" that are attached to us enlighten us to the truth, are righteous and holy, and result in personal freedom and liberation from Satan's strings. [3] This is a major contrast to our former "strings" which were sinful and prevented us from the truth of how to correctly live and govern ourselves.

The Knowledge Contrasted chart shows at-a-glance the distinctive differences between a Christian and non-Christian education,[4] and should go a long way toward eliminating any rationalizations and/or pragmatic reasons that a Christian parent may have regarding the question of whether they should continue to send their children to God-hating public schools.

Emotions run deep on the issue of whether we should "EXIT"* our children from the public schools, but it should be remembered that there was a lot of emotion at the Alamo, and we all know the result of that battle. So, encourage your Christian brothers and sisters to carefully consider the ten contrasts on the Knowledge Contrasted chart and remind them that standing for Jesus is often unpopular, but is still our commanded duty.

If they are still hesitant, challenge them to give you a description of what they would like the public schools to be, and then ask them what expectation they could possibly have that such changes could take place, especially when the public schools were founded to de-Christianize American students.

Many people and various organizations have suggested one or more of the first eight suggestions, however, a school that adopted each of them would still not be providing a Christian education, much less a school that refused to adopt the ninth item. For example, how pleased do you think our Creator God would be for a school to teach creationism as merely an "alternate" theory of how the world began? Or, what good would the Ten Commandments do hanging on the classroom walls if they were

NOTES

1 Ephesians 2.2   3 2 Corinthians 4.3-4
2 Jeremiah 31.33   4 Hanson, Buddy, *It's Time to Un-Quo the Status*, (Hanson Group, 2006), p. 140

See EXIT Strategy: A Handbook to Exponentially Increase Your Service for God, (Hanson Group, 2005)

Knowledge Contrasted

True Education	False Education
1. King Solomon, "The fear of the LORD is the beginning of knowledge." Proverbs 1.7	1. Karl Marx, "Man is the creature of the natural order only."
2. (Analogical) Thinking God's thoughts after Him.	2. (Unilogical) Thinking man's thoughts.
3. Regenerate reasoning.	3. Unregenerate reasoning.
4. Error is the result of sin.	4. Errors are decreasing as man's knowledge increases.
5. Restating the truth of the Bible.	5. Comprehension increases, but the pursuit of "new truth" fails because ALL FACTS are needed.
6. Total sufficiency of God.	6. Self-sufficiency of man.
7. The natural PLUS the supernatural.	7. The natural only (what can be seen, felt, measured, tested).
8. Absolute proof.	8. Relative truth.
9. Biblical justice.	9. Poetic justice.
10. Practical application of biblical truths to an absolute and unchanging value standard.	10. Practical application of knowledge learned to relative values.

never referred to? The Ten Commandments and various other biblical verses are plastered on building after building in Washington, D.C., but are seldom, if ever, referred to by those who work in those buildings and what kind of civil government has that brought us! And, while every parent would probably vote for stricter discipline in the schools, upon which ethical standard would "good and bad behavior" be determined? In the midst of our current collective non-Christian worldview, which is based upon the multicultural hogwash of political correctness, who could

What Would They Look Like?

- Would they teach creationism as an "alternate" idea of how the world was created?

- Would there be no sex education?

- Would the pro-homosexual agenda in the curriculum be eliminated?

- Would Easter and Christmas be observed instead of Spring break and Winter Holidays?

- Would the Ten Commandments be displayed on classroom walls?

- Would there be more discipline (or any discipline)?

- Would the principles of biblical capitalism be taught instead of the Marxist principles of socialism?

- Could a student, teacher, coach, or administrator pray publicly in Jesus' name at school events?

- Would the ethics that were taught be based upon the monotheistic triune God of the Bible, or upon a politically correct mixture of various religions?

seriously imagine that a public school's ethical standard would be the monotheistic standard of the Bible?

When all of the rationalizations and pragmatism is cut through and you come to the bottom line of this discussion, the lingering question is whether a parent wants their children to receive an education that is founded upon truth or upon lies. Non-Christian parents won't consider such an idea for one minute, but it shouldn't take that long for Christian parents to realize that they need to EXIT their children and either begin to home school them, or find a Christian day school.

Part One concludes with some Core Biblical Strings to refresh your memory about what types of elements are "non-negotiable" for your worldview. However, before that, I want to assist you in making the educational decision that is best for your family, by presenting five Proposed

Solutions, a "Bad Company Corrupts Good Morals," chart and a Parents' Resource page that gives a biblical "filter" for any Christian curriculum. Hopefully these ideas will enable you to think of just how and where to educate your children!

Proposed Solutions for Educating Our Children

1. Explain to your Christian brothers and sisters what Christian education is and how it *totally differs* from that of the government schools.
2. Explain to members of your church why it is dishonoring to God and in direct disobedience of Deuteronomy 6.6-7 to send our children to government schools.
3. Inform prospective new members to your congregation these biblical ethics so they will know where you stand.
4. Meet with other pastors in your city to ask them to go through the same instruction with their congregations.
5. Support Christian Education
   - Begin a Christian school in your church (or join with other churches to do so). Ask Exodus Mandate (www.exodusmandate.org) about how to start a Christian One Room Schoolhouse.
   - If you already have a Christian school, consider "planting" another school in another part of town. It's common for churches to plant "sister" churches, so what about "sister" Christian schools?
   - Join a Home School network in your community and subscribe to one of the excellent Home School magazines for your families.
   - Appoint a Vocational Networking committee to place Christian teachers and administrators in government schools in Christian schools so they will have jobs to go to when they leave their current positions.
   - Make the children of your congregation your top missionary financial priority, setting up full and partial scholarship aid so that money is not a factor for your families. Ask your church officers what is more important to the youth in your church than assisting fathers to obey their responsibility to "train up their children" in a Christian education. Could a foreign missionary have a higher priority? Should a new gym or a new sound system, or some other addition to your current physical facility have more of a priority?

"Bad company corrupts good morals."
1 Corinthians 15.33

The reasons to EXIT our children from government schools are not:

- Violence
- Lack of discipline
- Anti-American curriculum
- Over-crowded classrooms
- Drugs
- Dumbed-down textbooks
- Illiterate high school graduates
- Teaching socialism and reliance on civil government instead of capitalism and self-government

These are simply the results of a system of indoctrination that is based upon the foolish ideas of non-Christians. Proverbs 1.7

The reasons to EXIT our children are these:

- We are dishonoring and disobeying God's command to "train up" our children.
- We are promoting the worship of false gods and the idolatry of the state.
- Government school teachers and administrators who are Christians are "unequally yoked" with non-Christians (and their congregations should help them find other employment).
- Because of the blatant disrespect for and disobedience to His Word, God is not listening to our prayers. Proverbs 15.29; 28.9; 1 Samuel 8.18

Opprobrious Objections Refuted

OBJECTION: The church usurps its authority by telling families how to educate their children.

We are commanded to "demolish arguments" against our Lord, Savior and King, Jesus Christ, and this includes instructing our children in how to do this.
2 Corinthians 10.5

OBJECTION – We must reach out to all members.

We're commanded to "come out from them and be separate."
2 Corinthians 6.14-17

SUPER
NATURAL
Glue

A Biblical "Filter" for any Christian Curriculum
(Home School or Christian Day School)

Lesson Preparation: How Does This Lesson Demonstrate:

S The sovereignty of God over His creation.
U The unique advantage of having a Christian worldview and lifestyle.
P Our purpose and calling to bring about God's will on earth as it is in heaven.
E The historical excellence of God's plan for the earth.*
R Our need to re-think the God's wisdom before making decisions.

NATURAL

G Get your children out of the government schools, n-o-w!
L Learn how to bring glory and honor to our Lord, Savior, and King, Jesus Christ.
U Upload biblical ethics to all situations and circumstances.
E Extend Christ's Kingdom with the biblical ethics learned.

In the government schools if students are taught anything about thinking, they are taught to think naturally, since that is the only way non-Christians think. We all come into the world in rebellion to the triune God of Scripture and desire to be our "own gods" by thinking our thoughts and basing decisions upon them. This is why Christian education should teach students how to think supernaturally, since we have the blessed advantage of the Holy Spirit to guide and direct our thoughts into the truth. What better, then, to hold our Christian curriculum and our thoughts together than Supernatural Glue?

For example, the personal liberty of Western Civilization, which is based upon God's word; and the tyranny of Eastern Civilization, which is based upon man's word.

The idea is for the acronym SUPER to be used by the parent-teacher after the lesson to elicit some reflective thinking from the child. In the early years, this could be a discussion, and later it could be a one-page written assignment. Thoughts, rather than length should be the important consideration. The parent simply asks:

"How does this lesson demonstrate one of the topics in the acronym SUPER?"

The GLUE acronym cites reasons for not having children in the government schools (reasons that home schooling parents already know, but might like to share with their friends who are still sending their children to be brainwashed by the weapons of mass instruction).

What Does God Say?*

Having seen what man's word states about educating our children, let's listen to what God's Word says:

Do not provoke your children to wrath, but bring them up in the training and admonition of the Lord.   EPHESIANS 6.4

Do not learn the way of the Gentiles.   JEREMIAH 10.2

Do not be conformed to this world, but be transformed by the renewing of your mind, that you may prove what is that good and acceptable and perfect will of God.   ROMANS 12.2

Do not be unequally yoked together with unbelievers. For what fellowship has righteousness with lawlessness. And what communion has light with darkness?
                                        2 CORINTHIANS 6.14

* Taken from It's Time to Un-Quo the Status, Buddy Hanson, (Hanson Group, 2006), pp.130–32

My people are destroyed for lack of knowledge. Because you have rejected knowledge, I also will reject you from being priest for Me; because you have forgotten the law of your God, I also will forget your children. HOSEA 4.6

Any curriculum that does not have the law of God as its centerpiece is not true education. God's Word is the foundation of how we should live and govern ourselves. It is our final authority over our conduct and beliefs.

The following chart provides a comparison between a Christian education and a non-Christian education. The first three items under Christian education are blank so that you can add what you would consider critically important. Items four through fifteen are listed to get your mind in gear. As we've seen, since God's Word is true, any educational system that is not based upon biblical ethics is "false." So the contrast between Christian education and non-Christian education boils down to a contrast between a true and a false education. Or, put another way, a true and a false worldview. With approximately 90 percent of Christian parents sending their children to public (government) schools, is it any wonder that approximately the same percentage of adult Christians don't have a developed Christian worldview?

Educated...For What?

Christian Education Goals	Non-Christian Education Goals
1.	1. "The philosophy of the classroom shall become the philosophy of the government in the next generation." ABRAHAM LINCOLN
2.	2. "Take away the heritage of a people and they are easily persuaded." KARL MARX
3.	3. Teachers are "the prophets of the true God and the usherer of the true kingdom of God." JOHN DEWEY, *MY PEDAGOGIC CREED*

continued on next page

4. Christ-centered. Creatures of God, who are born sinners and need His salvation so we can image Him and bring Him glory and honor.

5. Preparation for life. Happiness comes through being missionaries to our neighbors by incorporating biblical ethics into every aspect of our lifestyle and doing the best we can at all times and in all places (to serve God and our neighbors.)

6. "The end of learning is to repair the ruins of our first parents."

   JOHN MILTON, *OF EDUCATION*

7. To clearly comprehend the distinctives of the biblical worldview (self-government, low taxes, obey God's rules)

8. There are "good and bad" values/ethics/behavior.

9. We are personally responsible for our actions.

10. Teachers share your worldview.

11. Develop the mind.

12. Reliance on self-government.

13. Know why the biblical worldview makes more sense than any other worldview. = be able to defend the faith

14. Bring about God's will on earth in all areas of life.

15. Disciple the nations.

4. Child-centered. Biological accidents who need self-esteem and social promotion so we can "do our own thing" and bring glory and honor to ourselves.

5. Preparation for a paycheck. Happiness comes through material possessions. We're "worker bees."

6. Teachers are not instructors, but "facilitators, guiding students as they try out various pragmatic strategies to discover "what works for them."

   JOHN DEWEY

7. To teach students how to construct their own knowledge. Postmodern truth is "made" (subjectively), not "found" (in the objective truths of the Bible).

8. No values; teach only basic facts/skills.

9. Collectivism. The group is more important than the individual.

10. Teachers don't want to know your worldview.

11. There is no mind. Anything that cannot be "touched, seen, smelled, or objectively measured" doesn't exist.

12. Reliance on central government.

The Necessity of Giving Our Children a Christian Education

A Final Call to Fathers

Did you ever make the statement while you were in public school: "What good is [name the subject: i.e., history, algebra] going to do me in real life?" I certainly did. I just couldn't figure out how all of the different and apparently disconnected curriculum subjects could relate to whatever I would do once I grew up. Since I had no inclination to work for the railroad, how would being able to figure out how soon two trains going toward each other at 60 mph would collide? Or, of what practical benefit would I gain by knowing who won the War of 1812, or even who fought it? To me, school seemed to be a never-ending contest to see who had the best memory and could regurgitate random facts back on test papers.

Never was I taught the difference between "holy and unholy" behaviors, [1] or even that there was such a distinction, much less to "repent, and turn away" from unholy behaviors. [2] Never was I instructed in "the statutes of the Lord." [3] Never was I told that "the word of Christ" should "dwell in me" so that I and my friends could "admonish one another in psalms and hymns and spiritual songs." [4] Or that God's Word was "profitable" for anything other than Sunday school, worship service, weddings and funerals. [5]

Looking back on my school days I can understand why I was confused. Public schools, which are founded on separating the ethics of parents from their children, don't believe in a unifying absolute truth and therefore intentionally teach the various curricula subjects as being separate from each other. Students are asked to regurgitate random facts, because without a belief in a transcendent God, all facts are random, and have no ultimate meaning to which they can be attached. No wonder John Dewey said that the overall goal of public schools was to socialize students. What other option could he have had, because once He dismissed the belief in God, he also dismissed any ultimate meaning of any facts!

The next thought that pops into my brain is that no one seemed to question the authority of the state to teach what it was teaching. There was no home schooling then and while there was a Catholic elementary school, I don't recall there being a Protestant school. The chief priests and elders of Jesus' day certainly did not provide godly role models of behavior, but at least they asked Jesus after first hearing Him teach in the Temple: "By what authority are You doing these things? And who gave You this authority?" [6] If a Christian were to ask his civil rulers "By what authority is the state mandating that children attend public schools?" the answer would probably be "Our state constitution." But should that be the end of the discussion? Should we not begin a plan to amend the constitution of our state to give parents the freedom to carry out their God-given responsibility to educate their children?

This brings up one other thought. Where did fathers get the idea that they were no longer commanded to be responsible for the education of their children? King Solomon says, "Hear, my children, the instruction of a father, and give attention to know understanding. [7] Solomon adds, "A wise son heeds his father's instruction, but a scoffer does not listen to rebuke." [8] Fathers are to teach their children "when they sit in their house, walk by the way, lie down and rise up," [9] which is to say that we are to teach our children in the ways of God everywhere and at all times.

So conclusive is the Bible's case made for the father being responsible for the education of his children, that we are told: "A fool despises his father's instruction, but he who receives correction is prudent." [10] And that if a child "ceases to listen" to his father's instruction, "he will stray from the words of knowledge." [11] Does all of this mean that the Mother has no biblical warrant for instructing children? Not in the least. Once more we can turn to the wise words of Solomon: "My son, hear the instruction of your father, and do not forsake the law of your mother." [12]

As we've seen,

God's Word is Truth, and Man's Word is False

This means that unless we obey God by bringing our children up in the knowledge and wisdom of the Lord [13] we are subjecting them to little more than foolish fables in the public schools, plus the very real possibility that they will develop a non-Christian worldview and lifestyle. We've also discussed the conclusion that,

ONLY God's Word Works, and Man's Word ONLY Fails

By refusing to exit our children from the public schools, are we preparing them for failure in life? If that is not our intention, then what reason do we have for continuing to send them there? Let's face it. Non-Christians have all of the pragmatic and rationalistic reasons for sending their children to public schools.

✓ They don't believe in God.
✓ It's convenient to shift the responsibility of raising their children to other people.
✓ Instead of taking the time to raise and instruct their children, mothers can earn their own money and be their own person.

However the question remains, what do any of these pragmatic and rationalistic reasons have to do with our commanded responsibilities from God?

• Are we Fathers not commanded to teach our children to be able to discern "holy" from "unholy" activities?
• Are we not commanded to teach our children to repent from their self-centered desires and to turn their lives over to Jesus who is not only their Savior, but their Lord and King, as well?
• Are we not commanded to teach them all of the statutes of the Lord, so that they will not only live according to them, but urge others to do so?
• And finally, are we not commanded to instruct our children that God's Word is completely sufficient for all aspects of our daily decision-making, and not just for Sunday school, worship service, weddings and funerals?

NOTES
1 Ezekiel 44.23
2 Ezekiel 14.6
3 Leviticus 10.10 11;
Matthew 28.18-20
4 Colossians 3.16
5 2 Timothy 3.16
6 Matthew 21.23
7 Proverbs 4.1
8 Proverbs 13.1
9 Deuteronomy 6.7;
11.19
10 Proverbs 15.5
11 Proverbs 19.27
12 Proverbs 1.8
13 Proverbs 22.6

The following list of core "Biblical Strings" is far from complete, and are in no particular order, but are listed to serve as a reminder of just how blessed we are as people who are set apart for the work of extending Christ's Kingdom. (PSALM 4.3)

Core Biblical Strings

BIBLICAL STRING 1
You are a redeemed creature of God.

BIBLICAL STRING 2
The Bible instructs you in the only true way to live.

BIBLICAL STRING 3
God's appointed manner of bringing about His will on earth as it is in heaven is through the four self-governing spheres of: individual, family, church and state.

BIBLICAL STRING 4
Parents are responsible for the education of their children and the curriculum should be Christ-centered, because it is an essential part of Jesus' Great Commission.

BIBLICAL STRING 5
Since God's Word is true and applies to all areas of our life, our civil laws should be based upon biblical ethics.

BIBLICAL STRING 6
We are in the obedience business, and God is in the results business, so when we vote, as when we do anything else, our primary goal must be to do the right thing, and trust-in God to bring about the correct results in His perfect timing.

BIBLICAL STRING 7
God's Word is completely sufficient to provide us with all the wisdom we need in living a satisfying life.

BIBLICAL STRING 8

We live in a universe, not a biverse, which means that God's ethics should be used in all of our situations and circumstances.

BIBLICAL STRING 9

The Ten Commandments provide an outline upon which all of the teaching of the Bible rests. This means that our dealings with each other should be conform to the Second Table of God's law (commandments 5-10), and should be based upon the authority of the First Table of God's law (commandments 1-4).

BIBLICAL STRING 10

We are commanded to EXIT our beliefs from our homes and churches and to walk in all the ways God has commanded us, and not merely in those ways that fit most comfortably to our current worldview and lifestyle.

A psalmist urges us to, "Praise the LORD with the harp; make melody to Him with an instrument of ten strings." (PSALM 33.2) The spiritual musical instrument we will be building in Part Two is designed to not only tug at your heart, but make obedient music to God's ears by harmonizing our thoughts, words and actions so that we will present a distinctively different and God-honoring lifestyle to our non-Christian neighbors that testifies how God would have them live.

Let's make some sanctified soul music!

Refocusing Your Worldview

Has the information in this section revealed that you may have been looking at the world through blurred lenses? If so, how does this information help you to change your mantra as you approach each day in Christ's Kingdom? Yes, I said, "mantra," and yes, that usually means something that is chanted, but for our case we're using it as an unspoken mantra, or that "frame of reference" we bring to our daily decision-making that enables us to either accept or dismiss proposals that don't conform to our predisposed way of viewing the world. The upside of having such a mantra, or frame of reference is that we don't have to start from scratch in evaluating each decision, which means it saves us a lot of time. The downside is that if our mantra needs changing, and we don't realize it, then we will, with the best of intentions, make decisions that are not in our best interests.

Both Satan and Jesus have a mantra that they would prefer us to use in our daily decision-making. Take a look at both mantras to decide which one is currently dictating your decisions. The clearer your focus becomes with each area of decision-making, the sharper your decisions will reflect God's will, instead of Satan's.

What's in Your Mantra?

Satan's Version: Salvation & Frustration

"You are losers in the here-and-now, but winners in the hereafter."

"Jesus loves us and came to save us from our sins so that when we die (or are raptured!) we will be freed from the shackles of Satan's dominion upon the earth, and will joyfully spend eternity with fellow believers worshiping the triune God of the Bible. Until that time Jesus' Word encourages us to save as many people as we can and comforts us in our trials on this evil-infested earth by giving us a 'hope to cope' with all that Satan throws at us."

Jesus' Version: Salvation & Occupation

"You can be winners in both the here-and-now, and in the hereafter (by living according to My Word!)."

"Jesus loves those whom the Trinity chose before the foundation of the earth (EPHESIANS 1.4,17; 2.8) and came to earth to perfectly fulfill the Law (JOHN 1.1,14; MATTHEW 5.17; HEBREWS 4.15; 1 JOHN 4.10) and pay our sin debt by dying and overcoming death (JOHN 10.17-18; 1 CORINTHIANS 15.45) and has given us His Word to instruct us in how to live and govern ourselves (PSALM 119.105; JEREMIAH 31.33; JOHN 17.17; COLOSSIANS 3.16; ROMANS 8.9, 14, 16; 2 TIMOTHY 3.16-17) and complete Jesus' victory over Satan (1 JOHN 3.8; 4.4; COLOSSIANS 2.13-15; HEBREWS 2.14) by taking dominion over the earth (GENESIS 1.26-28; 9.1-4; MATTHEW 28.18-20; ROMANS 8.37) and restoring God's will "on earth, as it is in heaven." (MATTHEW 6.10; REVELATION 11.15).

PART TWO

Building Your Own
Spiritual Musical Instrument

Replacement String

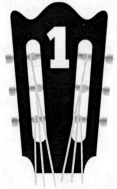

Where Could We Get Enough Bread in the Wilderness
to Feed such a Great Multitude?   MATTHEW 15.33F

After a victory over a tough opponent coaches like to tell their team, "We can see what kind of a team we can be if we continue to work hard to improve." With this first Replacement String we're going to get a glimpse at what kind of "team" we're on as members of Christ's Kingdom. To do that, I'm going to place some mental pictures in your brain about what God's will is for our earth. Now you may think that my referring to the earth as our earth sounds a little presumptive, since David tells us "The earth is the LORD's and the fullness thereof," [1] but the remarkable and inescapable truth is that He has put us in charge of His earth and commanded us to "subdue and rule over it." [2] This is not a common way of looking at the Christian's calling today, but it is exactly the way the Protestant Reformers viewed it, and it is exactly the way the founders of

America looked at it. The words of the Mayflower Compact provide an excellent example.*

> *In the name of God, Amen. We, whose names are under-* **written,** *the* **Loyal Subjects of our dread Sovereign Lord, King James, by the Grace of God, of England, France and Ireland, King, Defender of the Faith,** *etc. Having* **undertaken** *for the Glory of God, and Advancement of* **the Christian Faith, and the Honor of our King and Country,** *a voyage to plant the first colony in the northern parts of Virginia; do* **by these presents,** *solemnly and mutually in the Presence of God and one of another, covenant and combine ourselves together into a civil Body Politick... In Witness whereof we have hereunto subscribed our names at Cape Cod the eleventh of November, in the Reign of our Sovereign Lord, King James of England, France and Ireland, the eighteenth, and of Scotland the fifty-fourth. Anno Domini, 1620.*

Should we not be more than a little interested in what earlier Christians believed who willingly died at the stake, were drowned, tied to horses and torn apart as the horses ran in opposite directions, had their heads chopped off, and so forth? Why were these people willing to give their lives, if necessary, in order to uphold the truths of the Bible? If the civil authorities, or the church authorities (since it was the Catholic church that was behind these atrocities) came to you and said, "Unless you publicly admit that you don't believe that the Bible is the Word of God we will hang you in the courthouse square," what would you do? Would you even have to think twice about making such a decision? If your answer is, "Well, yes, I would have to think about my answer," then listen up, because what we're about to discuss should clear any doubts you may have about what Christianity is all about.

* The words in bold print were omitted from the public school textbook Triumph of the American Nation, *(Harcourt Brace Jovanovich, 1986) without indicating to either the teacher or students that it had been "edited." This also provides an excellent example of the type of misinformation that public school students are subjected to daily in the name of "education."*

The ideas we'll be discussing have fallen on hard times over the past 150 years, but that doesn't make them untrue. All-in-all, we'll be discussing some topics you were prevented from discussing in the government schools, so they may sound too good to be true, but hang in with me and I believe you will see that there is more than enough Scripture to support our optimism.

What would life and our culture be like if we consistently obeyed God, instead of consistently disobeying Him?

We're in the midst of a "total cultural war" yet most of us are giving only a "marginal" effort in fighting it. On the back burner of our minds we know that at any moment we are either imaging Christ or imaging Satan with our decisions, words and actions. Most of us are comfortable with keeping that truth on the back burner of our minds, and most of us don't like someone like me coming along to "meddle" by saying that we need to move this truth to the front burner. But, better that I or another Christian remind you than God, because one way or another, He's gonna remind you. As Blondie sings, He's "Gonna git cha, git cha, git cha." [3] That's just the way God operates. He is a most loving and patient God, but if after patiently waiting for us to get our act in gear, we continue to disregard His counsel, He will bring an unpleasant circumstance or event into our lives to remind us to get back on track. The reason for this is that as we go through our lives, we're either Christ's assistants, or Satan's assistants. There isn't a third category. With every thought, decision and action we make we're either extending Christ's Kingdom, or we're pretending that Satan is ruling the earth, and that Jesus failed to "destroy the works of the devil" [4] when He was on the earth. This would mean that Jesus' second return to earth would be to set-up His kingdom, and then return a third time for the final judgment before handing His Kingdom over to His Father (I challenge you to find any Scripture to support the myth that Jesus will return to earth a third time!).

As we view the world, our attitude and resulting lifestyle will reflect whether we are living according to *Calvary*, or *Cavalry*. Calvary or Cavalry. If our worldview reflects *Calvary*, we understand that in dying on the cross, Jesus empowered us to complete His victory over Satan which means that we are to make a bold stand toward Christianizing our culture by doing what we can to conform it to biblical ethics. On the other

181

hand, if our worldview reflects *Cavalry*, we will abandon the culture war and imagine that Jesus will have to rescue us as His supernatural cavalry swoops down from the heavens and beams us up to safety, rescuing us from the responsibilities He has commanded us to do. That's an interesting concept isn't it? The consistent message throughout the Bible is for us to obey His instructions. In the Old Testament Jehovah sent prophet after prophet to call the disobedient Jews back to a biblically obedient worldview and lifestyle. In the New Testament we're told

> *All Scripture is given by inspiration of God, and is profitable*
> *for doctrine, for reproof, for correction, for instruction*
> *in righteousness, that the man of God may be complete,*
> *thoroughly equipped for every good work.*
>
> 2 TIMOTHY 3.16-17

From where, then, does the idea come that its OK to ignore "all Scripture" and wait for Christ to do for us what He never did for anyone or any civilization in the Old Testament who lived in flagrant disobedience to His Word (as we are living today)? Certainly such a view contradicts the consistent teaching of Jesus that "If we love Him, we will keep His commandments." [5] Yet, we know that God's Word doesn't contradict itself, because God is perfect and therefore it is impossible for Him to change His mind.

Jesus tells us that we will be "brought before governors and kings for His sake, as a testimony to them and to the Gentiles." [6] What are you going to say when it's your turn to appear before your civil rulers? Will your statement be:

> *Mr. Mayor, or Mr. Governor, or Mr. President, I really have*
> *nothing to say, because I am waiting for Jesus to do my talking.*

I hope your statement won't be something like that because that would surely not be "a testimony to them and to the Gentiles (meaning non-Christians)." Now, before you start getting your dander up, let me make it clear that I am not about to begin a discussion on the subjective speculation about the end times. My focus is 100 percent on obeying what God's objective revelation says about how we are to live. The reason for this is that no matter how fervently I believe in my particular view of the end times, and no matter how fervently you believe in your particular view of the end times, the truth of the matter is that neither of us can absolutely prove it. Why do I say that? Because that is exactly what Jesus says:

> *But of that day and hour no one knows, not even the angels of heaven, but My Father only.* MATTHEW 24.36

Does this mean that we should not diligently study Scripture in an effort to come to an understanding about the end times? Certainly not! Anything in the Bible is most worthy of our study, but the point is that if we're spending all of our time studying what may or may not happen, instead of living according to how God absolutely instructs us to live, then we are not being very effective servants of Christ in His kingdom. Indeed, we're being lousy servants for His Kingdom. J. Gresham Machen, one of the most respected pastors and seminary professors of the 20th century, writes:

> *We may preach with all the fervor of a reformer and yet succeed only in winning a straggler here and there, if we permit the whole collective thought of the nation or of the world to be controlled by ideas which, by the resistless force of logic, prevent Christianity from being regarded as anything more than a harmless delusion. Under such circumstances what God desires us to do is to destroy the obstacle at its root … What is today a matter of academic speculation begins tomorrow to move armies and pull down empires … A revival of the Christian religion will deliver mankind from its present bondage, and will bring liberty to mankind. Such a revival will not be the work of man, but the work of the spirit of God. But one of the means which the spirit will use is an awakening of the intellect.* [7]

The Bible is a very black and white book. There are no shades of gray in it. That's why I'm more concerned with:

- biblical revelation, not biblical speculation
- with application, not abdication
- reformation, not fabrication
- transformation, not capitulation
- Christianization, not contamination
- illumination, not hallucination
- resuscitation, not repudiation
- facilitation, not manipulation

and this is why I focus on God's prescriptions for our culture, not man's mere descriptions! My opinion doesn't count for very much. According to the Bible, I am a despicable sinner whose thoughts are only evil continually. [8] That is why, with God's grace, and the assistance of the Holy Spirit, I make every effort to live according to God's opinion.

Each of us, to a greater or lesser degree, is a "child of our times." Even when we're "on guard," non-Christian viruses can slip into our worldview undetected. While this is a worrisome principle for us as we live in the midst of a collective non-Christian worldview, it will be a "good thing" for us when we take over the direction of the culture. Then, our thoughts will be slipping into the worldview and lifestyles of non-Christians!

What can we do to turn our current collective non–Christian worldview into a collective Christian worldview?

First, we must agree that God's Word is our only ethical standard. Then, we must agree to hold each other accountable to it. Unless we publicly admit that the ethics of our culture depend exclusively upon God's authority, we will, like all other civilizations throughout history, be an easy target for demagogues. Merely saying, "We believe such and such because it's a traditional American value," or a "conservative value" isn't enough. God doesn't command us to hide behind euphemisms, but to boldly give Him the credit He deserves for outlining for us the principles by which we should live and govern ourselves.

Our current generation has been described by many titles, but it has never been described as a "Thinking Generation." We are accustomed to having other people do our thinking for us. When the President addresses the nation, we have a group of "experts" tell us what we just heard. We can't even watch a sporting event without having one of the announcers explain to us what we just saw with our very eyes! We are dependant upon other people doing our thinking. You may think I'm being silly, but test yourself to see how dependant you are on someone else doing your thinking. The next time you are watching a game on TV, turn down the volume and watch the game! See how long you can do that. See if you can really trust your eyes. If you see someone make a touchdown, should you turn up the volume to see if what you saw was real, or was it an optical illusion? The German Chancellor and Dictator, Adolph Hitler, was a very evil person, but he was not stupid. He knew full well the easiest path to taking over a country. He once stated: "It is the luck of rulers when men do not think."

Since research indicates that only one in twenty adult Christians has a developed Christian worldview, I'm very probably going to say some things that may make your blood boil because a worldview and lifestyle that conforms to the Bible is radically different from the one presented to us in the media. So, whenever I say whatever it is that "rings your bell," I would ask that you remind yourself of how gracious and merciful God was to call you from the spiritual darkness in which you came into this world, and made you a new person from the inside out.

> *Christianity, after all, is not simply a nice, polite moralistic "add-on" to our former lifestyle. It is intended to be a complete transformation of our former worldview and lifestyle.*

Granted, this "transformation" doesn't take place overnight, but takes the rest of our lives, yet, the fact is, that we are "new creations" [9] and God expects us to live accordingly. Each of us wants to be successful at what we do and there is no quicker way to get someone's dander up than to point out a mistake in their behavior.

Why does the Bible teach from cover to cover that Christians are to be humble?

The answer, of course, is that humility is a supernatural characteristic, and each of us begins our life with the natural characteristic of being prideful. So if I mention something that points out a behavior that you either need to eliminate from your worldview and lifestyle, or one that you need to incorporate into your worldview, please remember that the non-Christian response is to be offended, but that the Christian response is to be appreciative that you now know that you can be a more effective servant for Christ beginning n-o-w! As football coaches tell their quarterbacks, "Don't think of the last pass (an interception), but think of the next one." If on the next possession the quarterback is still regretting throwing an interception, the chances are he will probably throw another one. The same goes for us; we can't unscramble the eggs of the bad decisions we made yesterday. The great American patriot, Patrick Henry notes, "We are apt to close our eyes to a painful truth," but our new supernatural nature reminds us that our days of covering up are over and its time to reveal the truth and expose the errors of non-Christians. So, as much as constructive criticism hurts, because none of us sets out to dishonor Jesus with our actions, the best thing we can do is repent and focus on our responsibilities from this day forward.

As we begin our discussion, remember this: When we incorporate biblical ethics into our worldview and lifestyle we provide a daily antithesis to the wrong-headed thinking of non-Christians. This is why it is so important for us to force the antithesis! We must be able to demonstrate that God is central to every area of life. [10] We must demonstrate that the Christian religion is a full-time profession, not a part-time hobby.

Why do you suppose that non-Christians present us with a never-ending stream of fads and ideas about how we should live and govern ourselves?

The answer is that non-Christian ideology doesn't work. Never in history has it worked. Just look at the difference between Western civilization (which was founded by Christians) and Eastern civilization (which was founded by non-Christians). Where would you rather live? Some of you are old enough to remember seeing newscasts of Germans dramatically trying to climb over the Berlin wall which separated East Germany from West Germany. Those who are younger may have seen such clips on the History channel. The question is in which direction were Germans going? Correct, they were going toward the West and personal liberty (as reflected in the Ten Commandments) and away from man-centered tyrannical government.

In one of His Kingdom Parables, Jesus says, "The kingdom of heaven is like leaven, which a woman took and hid in three measures of meal till it was all leavened." [11] In Scripture, the terms, "Kingdom of Heaven," and "Kingdom of God" are synonymous and refer to Christ's Kingdom on earth. That is the Kingdom of which all Christians are members, yet instead of "leavening the earth" with Christian principles, we're being "leavened," by non-Christian principles.

How do we turn this around so that we are conforming the world to biblical ethics instead of having the world conform us to its standards? [12]

The answer is that we turn the world "rightside up" [13] when we base our daily decisions upon biblical ethics, instead of on our own wisdom. Thinking is hard, it requires effort and it requires time. Those are two things that our culture doesn't appreciate. We want what we want n-o-w. We don't value the biblical process of planting seeds, and watering them and then reaping the results of our thoughts and actions. Whether or not we like fast food, we do want our food fast. So, in the midst of a culture that demands "instant results," there is a strong temptation to say, "I voted for some good guys and they won, so I'll let them do my thinking for me on cultural issues." I won't go into why such an attitude bodes very dangerous consequences, but I will say that it points up one thing about which you can be certain:

> *When you refuse to think, someone else will be more than happy to do your thinking for you.*

Are you letting God's worldview, or man's worldview frame your thoughts and decisions? The biblical ethics we love and hold so dearly aren't doing our communities any good confined to the inside of our churches and homes. As the credit card commercial cautions: We need to make sure that we don't leave home without them!

We have been called into Christ's Kingdom to bring about God the Father's will on earth as it is in heaven. [14] In and of ourselves this is an impossible task to accomplish. However, with Christ (the Creator and sovereign Ruler of the earth and all People), it is impossible for us not to accomplish our calling. The simple truth is that God is not going to ask us to do something that we can't do. [15] We may think that we can't do it, but when the dust settles, and we've obediently carried out our responsibilities, our conclusion is going to be, "Wow, I did that!" (And I hope we would add, "Praise God!")

Unless we keep this thought on the front burners of our mindset, we will ask: **"Where could we get enough bread in the wilderness to feed such a great multitude?"** [16] But, then, we know the rest of that story, don't we!

Too many of us can't imagine, see, or feel a victory, so we refuse to believe that Jesus is powerful enough to transform the culture through our obedience. As a consequence, we live as though we are on the losing side in the Culture War! This means we are not only disrespecting God's Word, but that we are blaspheming it by living as though what we can observe counts for more than what His Word says! Do we need to remind ourselves of how the divinely inspired writer of the Book of Hebrews defines faith? "Faith," he writes, "is the substance of things hoped for, the evidence of things _____." [17] That's correct, "not seen." Let's think for a second about a couple of other words in this verse: "hoped for." For all you know, I could be hoping for a big fat greasy cheeseburger. After all, I was raised in the South, and we love greasy foods. But if I were holding a big fat greasy cheeseburger, I wouldn't have any need to "hope" for it, because I would already have it. The "hope" I have for the time when America and the entire earth will have a collective Christian worldview, is not something I can presently "see," but I am confident it will come about because God promises over and over in Scripture that it will one day be the case. Indeed, "Faith is the substance of things hoped for, the evidence of things not seen."

William Cowper was an 17th Century lawyer and hymn writer and the following hymn was placed in the Scottish Psalter in 1615. Cowper had bouts of depression and one night decided to commit suicide by jumping off the Thames River Bridge. So he called a cab, but one of the famous London fogs suddenly rolled in and the cab driver became lost and they essentially drove around in a circle, because when the cab driver decided to stop and let Cowper out, to Cowper's surprise he was back at his front door. When he went inside, this is the hymn he wrote:

God moves in a mysterious way His wonders to perform;
He plants His footsteps in the sea And rides upon the storm.

Deep in unfathomable mines of never failing skill
He treasures up His bright designs and works His sovereign will.

Ye fearful saints, fresh courage take; the clouds ye so much dread
Are big with mercy and shall break in blessings on your head.

Judge not the Lord by feeble sense, but trust Him for His grace;
Behind a frowning providence He hides a smiling face.

His purposes will ripen fast, unfolding every hour;
The bud may have a bitter taste, but sweet will be the flower.

Blind unbelief is sure to err and scan His work in vain;
God is His own interpreter, and He will make it plain.

While these words are not divinely inspired, they do reflect the truth that God does perform what He promises, [18] even though to us His ways of bringing them about may look a bit curious. For example, When Jesus' disciples were concerned that He wanted to wash their feet, He replied, "What I am doing you do not understand now, but you will know after this." [19] One of the familiar ways in which God works in "mysterious ways" is in using the meek, in the world's eyes, to confound the mighty. [20]

Let us not forget that we have not been called into Christ's Kingdom to be spectators of history. The idea of culture being a parade, and Christians doing nothing more than standing on the sidewalk to watch it pass in front of us is not biblical! Jesus promises that His followers (us!) will do greater works than He did, [21] and His point is that since the Holy Spirit has written God's law on our hearts, we will be motivated to take the gospel throughout the earth, and not just to a tiny portion of it in and around Jerusalem, as was the case in His day. [22] We are imperfect finite beings who are partners with the perfectly infinite Creator of the universe, so let us not become discouraged that current events and circumstances don't appear to be going our way. The consistent message of Scripture is that God works through our obedience to bring about His will on earth as it is in heaven! [23] As King Solomon assures us

He who sows righteousness will have a sure reward.
PROVERBS 11.18

189

A friend of mine says, "Those who influence culture are the ones who 'show up.'" This is true, but with non-Christians being able to successfully obtain almost complete control of our culture just by "showing up," with themselves, we must ask ourselves what kind of success we can have when we "show up" with God and His perfect rules on how to live and govern ourselves? As mentioned, non-Christians can point to no culture in history that has been able to sustain itself based upon its own ideas. The reason for this is, of course, that God's Word is true, and they hate God's true theology, therefore their cultural "solutions" always fail, because they are based upon their false ideology.

Jesus wouldn't command for us to pray that His Father's will be done on earth as it is in heaven if He wouldn't enable us to do it. Make no mistake: His will will be done, either by us or another country, and since I'm an American by birth (Southern by the grace of God!), I don't want to see America destroyed in order for Jesus to raise up another country to accomplish the eternally perfect plan of the Trinity for the earth!

Reaping His Promises

A popular non-Christian saying is, "The more things change, the more they stay the same." As with most non-Christian sayings, this one is, at best, half right. To make that familiar saying biblical we should say, "Unless we repent, the more things change, the more they will stay the same." Even though technology, living conditions, incomes and education levels may rise over the years, if a community, or nation doesn't repent from its sinful ways, it will continue to experience personal conflicts, strife and sectional wars.

Remember your high school science class when the teacher placed a ruler in a container of water and it looked bent? Of course, no one was fooled by it because everyone knew what the ruler looked like outside the water. But did this optical illusion help you or any of your classmates connect to the biblical truth that perception is not reality? The reality is

> *Satan is a defeated foe and the continued obedience of Christians will complete his defeat (not some random, instantaneous, supernatural act of God).*

Once we begin to view Scripture in this light (the way God intends for us to view it!), we will no longer view the church as a culturally irrelevant institution where Christians gather in retreat from the cruel world once or twice a week. Rather, we will see it as a place to worship the Lord, Savior and King, grow in His grace and knowledge, and become better prepared to extend His kingdom throughout the world. So, when you read of Jesus' victorious promises for His Church, you should not assume they can only be fulfilled in a future age, or as some believe, only in heaven. There is no other age but this one ... it's called "the last days" by Peter, [24] James [25] and Paul. [26]

As Christians, we have four simple options:

- God's inerrant Word tells us how to live and we can strive to consistently obey it.
- If we don't voluntarily adhere to it He will get our attention through unpleasant situations and circumstances.
- If we repent and obey He will end the unpleasant circumstances (although we will still have to deal with the consequences of our previous disobedience)
- If we continue in our disobedience, He will destroy us.

Thanks to our supernatural rebirth, we have no problem recognizing that the triune God of Scripture is the sovereign Creator. What we differ on is where His sovereignty stops and where man's begins. It is hoped that some of the topics we have discussed will enable you to conclude that

> *God's sovereignty doesn't stop—and man's doesn't begin.*

By living in accordance to His instructions and electing Christians to be our legislators and judges, we can expect

- positive consequences
- pleasant living conditions
- increased personal liberty
- fewer and smaller taxes, and
- true justice.

Failure to Present a Godly Alternative, or Biblical Antidote for Our Cultural Issues

In order to exchange God's hand of judgment on the earth for His hand of blessing we need to incorporate biblical ethics into our lifestyle so that those who are looking for a better way of living will see it clearly demonstrated by our daily actions. We need to be a living example of our beliefs. God, through Moses, commands us to conform our communities to His ways rather than conforming ourselves to their ways. [27] Those instructions have never been repealed and are just as applicable today as they were before the Israelites crossed into the Promised Land. Indeed, today, the entire earth is the Promised Land.

By observing how most Christians live today, it appears they are vainly imagining that God will conform to our standards! To imagine that God has given us His inerrant Word just to store it away in our minds is to substitute arrogant intellectualism for holy living. It must be considered that our worldview and lifestyle may be the only Biblical lessons some non-Christians will have ever seen. If our actions do not deliberately and explicitly reflect what God's Word teaches we are failing our mission to be an effectual witness for Him and will suffer great consequences.

When we live as obedient Christians, we will receive from God much more than we can imagine or deserve. But, if we continue in our disobedience by giving little concern about who governs us we will get corruption, higher taxes and less personal freedom instead of the positive results.

Is It Christianity, or Is It Moralism?

Christians and Conservative moralists share a lot of ideology. Some may even think the two camps are synonymous. Moralists keep the reasons for their actions to themselves, preferring to privatize their beliefs, as if they imagine that there is a "secular" realm and a "sacred" realm of life, with never the two meeting. Not so Christians, we are commanded to be ready to provide an answer for our beliefs "in season and out." [28] Christians and Conservative moralists talk alike, often vote alike, are good neighbors and citizens who abide by their community's laws. However, underneath these outward appearances lurks a dramatic difference in how they approach their worldviews. (The Christian lifestyle being based upon the fixed Word of God, and the Conservative moralistic lifestyle being based upon the ever-changing word of man.) Since the worldview of Christians is authentic and that of Conservatives is, at best, a derivative of Christianity, we should not even refer to ourselves as Conservatives.

A worldview describes how a person looks at and interprets reality. In other words, it's how we explain what's going on around us, which means that everyone has a worldview. The foundational difference between the worldviews of Christians and conservatives does not mean the two cannot cooperate in their efforts to improve our cultural situation. All it means is that at some point Conservatives will reach a place at which they say, "Uncle! This far and no farther!" The reason for this is that they have only their own resources on which to depend, and see themselves as being primarily responsible for bringing about the results. We, on the other hand, have the resources of God at our disposal and understand that our calling from God is to consistently and faithfully obey His revealed instructions, leaving the results up to His perfect timing and His unlimited resources. The following eight elements of one's worldview is far from complete and focus only on the differences in the "social" aspects of one's view of life. The Christian column reveals that there is no "cap" on what Christians can imagine God bringing about in His creation. It is very probable that there are those in the Conservative camp who are Christians, but have not fully developed a Christian worldview. Just as it is likely there are those in the Christian camp who are in reality solid, moralistic citizens who are ultimately depending upon their own "good works" to save them more than they depend upon the grace of God.

How is it with you?

? Is your life a testimony to others that you are living by faith in the triune God of Scripture?

? Are you basing your life on the foolish thoughts and imaginations of your fallen mind? Or

? Do you confidently believe that "we can get enough bread" in our current cultural wilderness "to feed such a great multitude?" MATTHEW 15.33F

At a Glance

Distinctive Differences Between a Christian and a Non-Christian Worldview

CONSERVATIVE
1. "Common sense" and intelligence tell us how to manage our families, personal relationships, churches and civil government. (Any "good" or "workable" idea of Conservatives is ultimately "borrowed" from Biblical ethics since only the Bible is truth.)
2. "Go along to get along." Goals are pursued by building coalitions and making compromises, where necessary, and realizing that we won't get all of what we want, but we will at least achieve some, or maybe most, of our goals.
3. Schools should teach "facts," not the meaning behind the facts (because hat would reflect a particular religious view). The goal of education is to produce "efficient" citizens who work well with others. (Parents desiring "more efficiency" send their children to private schools.) Mediocrity and socialism is stressed with an emphasis on the State providing social services.
4. Pay civic rent by volunteering and/or making tax-deductible contributions.
5. Living conditions are seen as being "normal" and it is up to us to improve our conditions as much as possible, leaving our culture "better than we found it."
6. Civil government should have a high profile in the lives of citizens as it guides and directs our lives. A socialistic, communistic and tyrannical "conservative" civil government-based society is the goal.
7. Courts should rule on the basis of laws, not on the basis of judicial opinions.
8. Churches. Sermons should include moral anecdotes, inspiring human interest stories. Social issues should not be addressed because it isn't nice to impose our beliefs on others. How the church has dealt with issues throughout history is of little interest for today's issues.

CHRISTIAN
1. The Bible tells us how to live our lives and govern ourselves.
2. God's plan for how to live is perfect and while making concessions may lead to short-term success, non-Christians will only honor these compromises until they gain enough strength to completely over take us. Culture will be "Christianized" only by a consistent and faithful obedience to God's rules.

194

3. Schools should teach "who we are; where we came from; what our purpose is; where we're going." The goal of education is to produce "wise" self-governing and entrepreneurial citizens. Excellence and capitalism are stressed with an emphasis on the four God-appointed self-governing spheres of the Individual, Family, Church and State being accountable for providing specific needs.
4. Care for widows, orphans and the poor through tithes and offerings.
5. Living conditions are seen as being "abnormal" because of the effects of The Fall of Adam and Eve. Our focus is not on how things "are," but rather how the Bible describes they "could be," namely that we can turn the world "right-side up," thereby normalizing life.
6. Civil government should have a low profile in our lives as its main purpose is to keep our communities safe and protect us from invasion. Social services and education should be provided by the God-appointed self-governing spheres of the family and church. A capitalistic society is the goal.
7. The rule of God's law should be the courts' goal with the intermediate goal of replacing any laws that don't conform to biblical ethics.
8. ALL the Word for ALL of life (expository preaching). The goal is to thoroughly equip the saints for every good work. (2 TIMOTHY 3.16-17) Christians should provide "light" about current events by demonstrating a godly lifestyle to a lost and fallen world. How the church has dealt with issues throughout history is of great interest and the proper lessons should be applied to today's issues so we won't repeat the same mistakes.

NOTES

1 Psalm 24.1
2 Genesis 1.26-28; 9.1-4; Matthew 28.18-20
3 "One Way Or Another," Blondie, 1978
4 1 John 3.8
5 John 14.15
6 Matthew 10.18
7 "Christianity & Culture," the Princeton Theological Review, Vol. 11, 1913, p.7
8 Romans 7.18
9 Colossians 3.9-10
10 1 Peter 2.2' 2 Timothy 3.16-17; Colossians 3.16; Joshua 1.8
11 Matthew 13.33
12 Romans 12.2
13 Acts 17.6
14 Matthew 6.10
15 1 Corinthians 10.13
16 Matthew 15.33f
17 Hebrews 11.1
18 Romans 13.7
19 John 13.7
20 1 Corinthians 1.27-29
21 John 14.12
22 Matthew 28.18-20
23 Matthew 6.10
24 Acts 2.17
25 James 5.3
26 2 Timothy 3.1
27 Deuteronomy 4.5-7
28 2 Timothy 4.2

Has the information in this section revealed that you may have been looking at the world through blurred lenses? If so, how does this information help you to change your mantra as you approach each day in Christ's Kingdom? Yes, I said, "mantra," and yes, that usually means something that is chanted, but for our case we're using it as an unspoken mantra, or that "frame of reference" we bring to our daily decision-making that enables us to either accept or dismiss proposals that don't conform to our predisposed way of viewing the world. The upside of having such a mantra, or frame of reference is that we don't have to start from scratch in evaluating each decision, which means it saves us a lot of time. The downside is that if our mantra needs changing, and we don't realize it, then we will, with the best of intentions, make decisions that are not in our best interests.

Both Satan and Jesus have a mantra that they would prefer us to use in our daily decision-making. Take a look at both mantras to decide which one is currently dictating your decisions. The clearer your focus becomes with each area of decision-making, the sharper your decisions will reflect God's will, instead of Satan's.

What's in Your Mantra?

Satan's Version: Salvation & Frustration

"You are losers in the here-and-now, but winners in the hereafter."

"Jesus loves us and came to save us from our sins so that when we die (or are raptured!) we will be freed from the shackles of Satan's dominion upon the earth, and will joyfully spend eternity with fellow believers worshiping the triune God of the Bible. Until that time Jesus' Word encourages us to save as many people as we can and comforts us in our trials on this evil-infested earth by giving us a 'hope to cope' with all that Satan throws at us."

"You can be winners in both the here-and-now, and in the hereafter (by living according to My Word!)."

"Jesus loves those whom the Trinity chose before the foundation of the earth (EPHESIANS 1.4,17; 2.8) and came to earth to perfectly fulfill the Law (JOHN 1.1,14; MATTHEW 5.17; HEBREWS 4.15; 1 JOHN 4.10) and pay our sin debt by dying and overcoming death (JOHN 10.17-18; 1 CORINTHIANS 15.45) and has given us His Word to instruct us in how to live and govern ourselves (PSALM 119.105; JEREMIAH 31.33; JOHN 17.17; COLOSSIANS 3.16; ROMANS 8.9, 14, 16; 2 TIMOTHY 3.16-17) and complete Jesus' victory over Satan (1 JOHN 3.8; 4.4; COLOSSIANS 2.13-15; HEBREWS 2.14) by taking dominion over the earth (GENESIS 1.26-28; 9.1-4; MATTHEW 28.18-20; ROMANS 8.37) and restoring God's will "on earth, as it is in heaven." (MATTHEW 6.10; REVELATION 11.15).

Replacement String

Making God's D&P

In baseball, it is said that a pitcher's best friend is the "DP," or the double play, whereby the infield turns a ground ball into two outs. Show me a pitcher, no matter how good, who has an infield who cannot consistently turn the DP and I'll show you a pitcher with a mediocre record.

In life God's Word should be our best friend. The reason for this is because it includes both a description of the various cultural situations in which we will one day find ourselves, and a prescription for how to handle them. God's "D&P," then is His revealed and inerrant Description & Prescription of what life will throw at us. Show me a community or a country that does not include God's Prescription with its Description of its cultural situations, and I'll show you a community or country that is having mediocre results.

Together, God's D&P gives a complete picture, and leads to a definitive conclusion about what to do. Separate, these two essential elements of God's Word give an incomplete picture and lead to confusion. What good does a prescription do when a description of a situation is missing, or what good is a description of a situation if no prescription is offered? Suppose, for example, you go to see your doctor and he says, "Good morning Buddy, I hope things are going well with you and your family. Oh, by the way, here's a prescription for you." And you say, "But doctor, I haven't given you a description of what's wrong!" Or, what if you made an appointment with your doctor, explained a description of your situation and he listened attentively and then gets up and as he walks out of the door, says, "Buddy, I'm glad you came to see me, it's always good to visit with you." And you're saying, "But Doc, wait, you haven't given me a prescription!"

The purpose of going to see our doctor is not to be sociable. We go to get answers, and in the process, hopefully, we are sociable. The main purpose, however, is to either solve a problem or find out how to best deal with it. In a similar manner

> *Jesus does not call us into His Kingdom to be "sociable," but to be cultural "problem solvers."*

Our commanded duty is to provide His answers for how to either solve a cultural issue or explain His counsel on how to best deal with it. Admittedly, as we carry out our calling as culture's "problem solvers" it would be hoped that we would also be "sociable," by not returning evil for evil [1] and by considering the interests of others, [2] but we need to remind ourselves that simply being nice and sociable is not what we have been called to do. Indeed, we can all name several non-Christians who are very nice and sociable.

Whenever we listen to a sermon or attend a seminar or read a book (or the Bible!), we need to ask ourselves

> *"What does this information mean to me and how can I incorporate these biblical ethics into my worldview and lifestyle?"*

If you are in a small group study, ask the leader to provide that answer. Without that answer, at best (!) all we are doing is accumulating additional interesting biblical ethics in our brain without a clue of how to use them.

- Why would our Lord, Savior and King, Jesus Christ, reveal these inerrant ethics for living and then preserve them over the centuries if He didn't want us to incorporate them into our everyday decision-making?!
- Why should we look upon His Word as being worth little more than biblical trivia to be recited in an internet blog or around fellow Christians in order to impress them with our vast knowledge of an ancient collection of writings that has been miraculously preserved over the years?
- Why should you be impressed with a person who has spent a lot of time studying the Bible, and who can spout out chapter and verse on a wide variety of issues, but who views God's Word as merely an amazingly interesting collection of anecdotes?

Such a person certainly wouldn't impress me. Indeed, I would probably ask them to get a life and do something meaningful.

Now, let's turn our attention to your weekly worship service. If the sermon does not include both elements of God's equation for successful living (the D&P), then you've heard a speech instead of a sermon. The "speech" may have been very motivating, and it may even have been an accurate exegesis of the description of a current cultural condition, but if it didn't tell you what to do about it by applying biblical ethics to the condition, it's not going to do you much good. For example, let's use another baseball example: Suppose your coach tells you that as a base runner you need be off and running at the "crack of the bat." This is very good advice if there are two outs, but it could be very bad advice if there are less than two outs, because you may find yourself running into a double play. The same principle holds, whether you are a base runner, or a person who steps out of your home each morning: you not only need to know *what* to do, but *when* to do it.

A good speech can inspire you, it can pump you up and motivate you with the best advice that an imperfect and sinful man can provide, but a sermon goes beyond that by inspiring you with God's perfect and inerrant counsel on how to be a cultural "problem solver." And, never forget that God has called you to be a cultural problem solver in Christ's Kingdom, not an irrelevant slave on Satan's plantation.[3]

To imagine that God the Father, Jesus, and the Holy Spirit went through all they did to reveal, preserve and make their inerrant Word understandable to us only to have us use it in what amounts to a biblical trivia game is the same as concluding that God has called us to live trivial and uneventful lives as slaves on Satan's plantation, with the best scenario being that some of us will strive to be the smartest slaves on Satan's plantation. What a blasphemous thought!

- Can you think of one verse that says we have been called out of spiritual darkness and into God's spiritual light to repress that light?

I didn't think so.

- Can you cite one verse that says Christians should, in effect, be Satan's assistants in promoting a non-Christian worldview and lifestyle?

I didn't think so.

Brothers and sisters, don't think for a second that at any moment you are not either promoting Christian ethics, or non-Christian ethics. At any moment you are either a living as a servant of Christ or a servant of Satan. At any moment you are living either as a member of Christ's Kingdom or Satan's kingdom. As Joshua once said, "Choose this day who you will serve." [4]

Are you making God's D&P in your everyday life? You are if you are incorporating His description of what our culture should be into your worldview and lifestyle, and are including His prescription for solving the various issues and events which you are facing. Both halves of God's equation must be included in your worldview and lifestyle in order for you to be effective servants for Christ in His Kingdom. I don't know who was the first to say: "Both halves make a whole," but whoever he or she was, they were on to something. To prove it, let's play a word association game. (The answers are at the conclusion of this section, following the notes.)

- If I say "Romeo," what would you say _____
- If I say "Bacon," what would you say _____
- If I say "Love," what would you say _____
- In talking about sports, if I say "Offense," what would you say

  _____
- In talking about our Christian witness, if I say "Salt," what would you say _____
- If I say "Trust" what would you say _____
- If I say "Repent," what would you say _____

In order to make God's D&P, we must include both halves. What this means is that when we hear someone "describe" how bad culture is getting, we should ask them what God's prescription is for solving it. Saying this will do something positive for us and for the person with whom we are talking:

- It will remind us to re-think God's thoughts, instead of attempting to come up with our own solutions, and [5]
- It will remind them that God is smarter than we are, and that He has already given us the solutions for whatever situation or cultural issue that is facing us, and that the only way we are going to be able to successfully deal with it is to do so according to His Word. [6]

Who Are We?

The first step to take in moving away from the current man-centered worldview and toward a God-centered worldview is to frame our cultural discussions according to biblical ethics. In doing so we should refer to ourselves as Christians, not Conservatives. The title "Christian" outranks every other title we have.

- ✓ **Reflect on the process** the Trinitarian Godhead used "before the foundation of the world" [7] to call to Itself a people.
- ✓ **Consider what a great privilege** has been given to us by God in His infinite mercy and grace, in calling us to carry out His will on earth.
- ✓ **Consider what a great price** had to be paid by the Trinity in order to redeem us so we can bear the name of Christ.

Then ask yourself why it is that we hesitate to refer to ourselves as Christians at all times: whether at work, at play or anywhere else?

- Do we have any reason to be ashamed at being personally selected by God to be a member of His family?
- Do we have any reason to be embarrassed that God's Holy Spirit has enabled us to be the only group on the face of the earth to discern the Truth?
- Do we have any reason to feel intimidated by non-Christians who are operating according to the infinitesimal smallness of their fallen intellect? There are some brilliant people who are Christians, and there are some brilliant people who are non-Christians, but even Christians who have average intelligence can do something the most brilliant non-Christians can't do. Thanks to the Holy Spirit, we can understand the truth! This means that there is no reason for any of us to be intimidated by any ideological arguments that non-Christians fire at us … because, brothers and sisters …*they're firing blanks!* [8]

> *We must not be ashamed to bear the name of Christ, nor should we bring shame to the name of Christ by carrying His banner unworthily.*

Scripture is clear that God chose us, rather than the other way around, so we have no reason to proudly flaunt the fact that we are a Christian, but neither do we have any reason to keep our light hidden inside our homes and churches.

Now that God has saved us from eternal damnation by graciously calling us out of our fallen estate, what are we supposed to do?

The answer is to finish the work of Adam and Eve. Since God knows everything and never makes mistakes, there should be no other conclusion than that mankind's purpose remains the same as it has always been, namely to "subdue and rule over creation." [9] Our receptiveness to His will and eagerness to obey Him are proof that He has called us. Through

Moses God warns us to be careful to walk our talk: "If you walk contrary to Me, I will walk contrary to you." [10] For those who are not taking their calling of serving God seriously, Isaiah has this somber statement:

> *The Lord says: "These people come near to Me with their*
> *mouth and honor Me with their lips, but their hearts are far*
> *from Me. Their worship of Me is made up of only rules taught*
> *by man. Therefore once more I will astound these people with*
> *wonder upon wonder; the wisdom of the wise will perish, the*
> *intelligence of the intelligent will vanish." Woe to those who*
> *go to great depths to hide their plans from the Lord, who do*
> *their work in darkness and think, "Who sees us? Who will*
> *know?" You turn things upside down, as if the potter were*
> *thought to be like clay! Shall what is formed say to him who*
> *formed it, "He did not make me?" Can the pot say to the*
> *potter, "He knows nothing?"*   ISAIAH 29.13-16

Rev. Joe Morecraft writes:

> *The point at where the battle rages today is the issue of*
> *sovereignty and jurisdiction. Who has the right of total claim*
> *on a person's life and property—Christ or Caesar? To whom*
> *does a person owe his total allegiance—Christ or Caesar?*
> *To whom do your children belong—Christ or Caesar? Who*
> *declares the law, whose word is the binding authoritative*
> *word for the sphere of politics—Christ or Caesar? Who*
> *is the head of the church—Christ or Caesar? Who is the*
> *ruler of the kings of the earth, [in other words] all political*
> *institutions—Christ or Caesar?* [11]

God has given each of us a very important mission and we and our leaders need to be careful not to trifle with it. In Martin Luther's words:

> *If I profess with the loudest voice and clearest exposition every*
> *portion of the truth of God except precisely that little point*
> *which the world and the devil are at that moment attacking, I*

am not confessing Christ, however boldly I may be professing Him. Where the battle rages, there the loyalty of the soldier is proved, and to be steady on all the battlefield besides, is mere flight and disgrace if he flinches at that point. [12]

Playing Baseball by Softball Rules

Perhaps by relating our behavior to a sports analogy it will be easier to see the un-winnable corner into which we have painted ourselves. Take, for example, the games of baseball and softball. Both have many similarities, yet both also have their distinctive differences. They both have:

- similar bats
- similar gloves
- identical batter's boxes
- dirt infields and grass outfields
- similar uniforms
- three bases and a home plate
- a pitcher's rubber
- the grandstands and fences are similar
- most of the rules are the same – each team has three outs per inning; the offense hits the ball and runs the bases; the defense catches the ball and tries to throw-out the runners

Even though baseball and softball have many similarities, if a baseball player attempted to play by softball rules, he would most likely lose every time. The biggest hindrance to his success would be the distance between the bases. In baseball, the distance is 90 feet, and in softball its 60 feet. So a baseball player operating under softball rules would be out virtually every at bat since he would be stopping 30 feet short of the base. (Unless, of course, if he hit a home run.)

For these reasons no baseball player would attempt to "play baseball" according to softball rules. It's simply not logical. However, how many Christians are there who insist on living (and governing) according to Conservative non-Christian rules? It's as blatantly illogical to do so as our baseball/softball analogy, yet we continue to do so ... and we wonder why we continue to get thrown out at first base!

What about Our Rules for Living
   …does it matter which ones we use?

Yes. The only way for us to improve our communities for our children and grandchildren is to begin living by God's rules, applying them to every area of our life. As the hymn goes, "There's no other way, but to trust and obey." Indeed, why should we even think there is "another way?" God wrote the instructions!

- Shouldn't we expect to fail if we neglect to live by them?
- Shouldn't we expect to fail if we continue to elect non-Christians to office and continue to send our children to, or to teach in the ungodly public schools?
- If we continue to fear our employer or customers or congregation more than we fear the triune Creator God and live by their rules, instead of by His, should we expect anything but failure?
- Shouldn't we expect to be laughed at, ridiculed as a "fringe group" and dismissed as being "culturally irrelevant" when all we do is deal with the various falling fruit from man's sinful tree, like abortion, gambling and pornography, instead of attacking the root of man's tree (sin) by instituting programs and policies based on God's rules?

> *The way a person looks at the world will greatly affect their decision-making and their entire approach to life.*

The reason Paul tells us not to "conform ourselves" to the worldview of non-Christians [13] is that Christians and non-Christians approach life from opposite viewpoints. Christianity completely transforms our lifestyle. Each of us recognizes the eternal consequences of being a Christian, or a non-Christian. Christians go to heaven and non-Christians go to hell. That's as stark a contrast as you can get, which is why non-Christians attempt to dismiss the idea of such a place as "hell." However, there is not only a stark difference between Christians and non-Christians in the hereafter, but also in the here-and-now. For example,

- We know who we are and why we are here, and what to do.
- We have meaning and direction for our lives. Non-Christians don't know how they got here and neither do they know their purpose.
- We have confidence in an objective set of instructions for living. We have truth. They have no confidence in any view of life because they don't believe in unchanging and universal truth. They would love to have truth, but unless and until the Holy Spirit changes their heart, they have no way of arriving at it. *Since they don't have a transcendent Creator-God providing answers on how to live, they make up their own philosophy.*

Throughout history non-Christians have tried every way they could imagine to arrive at truth. First they attempted to disprove the teachings of the Bible, and failed miserably. Then they said, "Lets don't go there anymore, instead we'll redefine 'truth.'" So they came up with the idea of relative truth, which meant that truth depended upon one's situation or circumstances, or the environment in which one was raised. That probably sounded like a good strategy to them, because what it did was, in effect, give everyone "license" to live pretty much the way they wanted, and to justify it by saying that their worldview was based upon "relative truth." The only negative thing about it was it didn't work. It still didn't provide the irrefutable answers to how they got here, and why they are here, or how they should live.

In the current postmodern fad, truth is either said to be non-existent, or that it is whatever works for me. Others say, perception is reality. Non-Christians will sooner or later discover through experience what we already know through God's gracious enlightenment of our minds, that this attempt to find the truth will also fail miserably.

- Can you see why we are a major irritant to non-Christians?

We not only know what the "ought" is, we have inerrant instructions on how to bring it about!

- Can you see why all other religious beliefs gang up on Christianity in an effort to remove our voice from the public square?

They don't want us to engage in the public discussion because they know we have the answers they don't have! God has not called us to a Christian intellectual trip. We are supposed to take all of those wonderful truths in which we profess to believe, and that are rattling around inside our brains and connect them to our feet so we can walk our talk. For too long we've confined our Christianity to the inside of our churches and homes, as though God is too small and insignificant to bring about a positive change in society.

- Even though we say we believe that Jesus came into the world to defeat Satan, we live like Satan is the winner.
- Even though we say that Jesus is "Lord as well as Savior," we live as though He is only our Savior, and that our employer, or our customers, our congregation, or the civil government is "lord."

Does it matter which rules we live by? Most certainly. ONLY God's rules work!

Non-Christians are looking for answers. We have the answers, but are keeping them to ourselves! Our mission is to turn the world right-side up and God promises that with the new heart He gave us we will be motivated to do that.[14] Further, the only way we can determine if we have been given a new heart is if we love God's instructions and attempt to consistently live by them. [15] Otherwise, we're only imagining that we are Christians and all our words and actions amount to nothing more than a clanging symbol. [16] The truth is, "those who are according to the flesh set their minds on the things of the flesh, but those who are according to the Spirit, the things of the Spirit." [17]

> *We are God's creatures, living in His creation and He has revealed to us the rules by which we are to live. So why should we expect our efforts to be successful if we conform our behavior to those who are living according to their rules, instead of His?*

Beware of Becoming a Practical Atheist

I doubt if there are any atheists reading this book, because if you are an atheist, you're probably not enjoying it. But could it be that you are a practical atheist? You ask, "What is a practical atheist? To answer that lets listen to the esteemed 20th century Theologian B.B. Warfield:

> Formal atheism denies God; practical atheism is guilty of the possibly even more astounding sin of forgetting the God it confesses. How many men who would not think of saying even in their hearts, "There is no God," deny Him practically by ordering their lives as if He were not? And even among those who yield, in their lives, a practical as well as a formal acknowledgment of God, many yet manage, practically, to deny in their lives that this God, acknowledged and served, is the Lord of all the earth. [18]

Warfield continues:

> Is it true that we can trust the eternal welfare of our soul to God and cannot trust to Him the temporal welfare of our bodies? Is it true that He has provided salvation for us at the tremendous cost of death of His Son, and will not provide food for us to eat and clothes for us to wear? Is it true that we can stand by the bedside of our dying friend and send him forth into eternity in good confidence in God, and cannot send that same friend forth into the world with any confidence that God will keep him there?
>
> How many men do actually think that it is unreasonable to serve God at the expense of their business activity? To give Him their first and most energetic service? How many think it would be unreasonable in God to put His service before their provision for themselves and family? How subtle the temptations? [19]

Wow! May we all have the humility to take Dr. Warfield's words to heart. Let's turn to these familiar words of Jesus:

And He said unto them, 'Is the lamp brought to be put under the bushel, or under the bed, and not to be put on the stand? …Take heed what you hear: with what measure you meet it shall be measured to you; and more shall be given unto you. For he that has, to him shall be given: and he that has not, from him shall be taken away even that which he has.

MARK 4.21-25

I have an announcement to make:

The Kingdom Is HERE!

It is popular to imagine (as did the ancient Jews) that Christ is going to return, set up an earthly kingdom so we can steam roll our non-Christian opponents. Such an idea, however, is clearly at odds with what Jesus told the Pharisees:

Now having been questioned by the Pharisees as to when the kingdom of God was coming, He answered them and said, "The Kingdom of God is not coming with signs to be observed;" nor will they say, "Look, here it is," or "There it is!" for behold, the kingdom of God is in your midst.

LUKE 17.20-21

In Jesus' own words the kingdom already exists …it is "in our midst." His Kingdom is a spiritual one with physical ramifications.

God's promises are to be applied externally. By turning them inward and believing we can't effect positive changes in society is to undervalue Christ's life and to concede the course of earthly events to Satan!

By realizing that we are already members of His Kingdom and that we have at our disposal every resource we need to subdue and rule over this present world, we should get busy doing it and not erroneously think we have to wait for another generation or for another time.

This question goes straight to the heart of a person's worldview. If Satan were the "God of this world," the only thing left for Christians would be to punt. This would mean Jesus was unsuccessful in His mission to defeat Satan and would also mean that His mission for us to "subdue and rule over creation" has been overturned.

Fortunately, Jesus was successful in His earthly mission. In Paul's words, God "delivered us from the domain of darkness and transferred us to the Kingdom of His beloved Son …" While on earth, Jesus assured Christians, "the gates of Hades will not overpower (the work of the church)." [20] So thorough was Christ's victory over Satan that all we have to do is, "Submit to God, resist the devil [and] he will flee …" That's what God's Word says!

Jesus currently sits at the right hand of God the Father where He has "all authority" in heaven and earth. That's what God's Word says. So to stay on the sidelines of life and not advocate and promote God's ethics, is to live as if God's Word is meaningless for day-to-day activities, and to infer that man's will is superior to God's will.

By incorporating the following Six Steps into our lifestyle and holding our Civil Rulers accountable to them we will be able to present God-honoring testimonies and elect God-respecting Civil Rulers.

Six Steps to a Consistent Christian Walk

1. STUDY SCRIPTURE
If we don't take time to study Scripture so that we will know our Lord, we will not know how to serve Him. We may also not forget the many blessings He has given to us.

> *How blessed is the man who does not walk in the counsel of*
> *the wicked, nor stand in the path of sinners, nor sit it in the*
> *seat of scoffers! But his delight is in the law of the Lord, and*
> *in His law he meditates day and night.*　　PSALM 1.1-2

212

2. LEARN HIS LAWS

God has given us His law so that we will know how to live in the world in which He has created. A failure to learn and live by them will result in serious consequences for us and for our children.

> *My people are destroyed for a lack of knowledge. Because you have rejected My knowledge, I will also reject you from being My priest. Since you have forgotten the law of your God, I also will forget your children.* HOSEA 4.6

3. REPENT OF OUR SINS

This is the only way to restore fellowship with God and enable our prayers to be heard and answered. If we are not shamed to repentance, we will be ashamed in our ruin.

> *If they do not speak out concerning these things, reproaches will not be turned back.* MICAH 2.5

> *I will go away and return to My place until they acknowledge their guilt and seek My face; in their affliction they will earnestly seek Me.* HOSEA 5.15

> *Then they will cry out to the Lord, but He will not answer them. Instead, He will hide His face from them at that time, because they have practiced evil deeds.* MICAH 3.4

4. TRUST IN GOD'S SOVEREIGNTY

We should not let current circumstances blind us from the sure and certain hope we have in God. No matter how bad a particular situation is, we must remember that God is in sovereign control of everything and will bring good out of it as long as we remain obedient.

> *But the Lord is in His holy temple. Let all the earth be silent before Him.* HABAKKUK 2.20

> *They will be held guilty, they whose strength is their god.* HABAKKUK 1.11

213

5. LEAD BY EXAMPLE

As has been mentioned, our lifestyles are the only Bibles some people will see. Non-Christians will allow for our mistakes and short-comings, because they know that no one is perfect, but they will quickly see through and reject any type of "Sunday-only" Christianity.

> *Therefore do not be partakers with them; for you were formerly darkness, but now you are light in the Lord; walk as children of light (for the fruit of the light consists in all goodness and righteousness and truth), learning what is pleasing to the Lord.* EPHESIANS 5.7-10

> *By this we know that we are in Him: the one who says he abides in Him ought himself to walk in the same manner as He walked.* 1 JOHN 2.5-6

6. OBSERVE THE SABBATH

God has given us Sundays (The Lord's Day) to rest from our worldly endeavors and spend the day in private and public worship, except for acts of necessity and mercy. It's a great time to spend time with family and friends and to talk about, meditate on and pray over His Word. As our Creator, He knows our frame, which is why He gives us one day in seven to not do the kinds of things we do during the other six days. How far short many of us fall in observing the Christian Sabbath!

Arise and Shine!

Isaiah paints a prophetic portrait of the individuals, civil rulers and nations rushing to worship our Lord, Savior and King. Citizens will live at peace because their civil rulers will conduct their oversight of them in "righteousness" as they govern according to Jehovah's principles. As surrounding nations are converted there will be no reason to close the gates to their cities because disagreements will be solved in accordance to God's Word, not military might. All of this will come about as a result of their living out their faith, reflecting the light they have received from Jehovah of a better way to live (indeed the best way to live). Their faithful obedience to apply the principles of their faith will enable them to bear much fruit for the Kingdom.

It is interesting to note the last verse provides a dramatic difference between the nation that obeys God and the one that is disobedient to His laws. In Isaiah 30.17, which describes Judah's disobedience, we see that "one thousand shall flee at the threat of one," here, in verse 22, we see the role reversed, "a little one shall become a thousand, and a small one a strong nation." [21]

Arise, shine; for your light has come! And the glory of the Lord is risen upon you. For behold, the darkness shall cover the earth, and deep darkness the people; but the Lord will arise over you, and His glory will be seen upon you. The Gentiles shall come to your light, and kings to the brightness of your rising. 'Lift up your eyes all around, and see; they all gather together, they come to you; your sons shall come from afar, and your daughters shall be nursed at your side. Then you shall see and become radiant, and your heart shall swell with joy; because the abundance of the sea shall be turned to you, the wealth of the Gentiles shall come to you. The multitude of camels shall cover your land, the dromedaries of Midian and Ephah; all those from Sheba shall come; they shall bring gold and incense, and they shall proclaim the praises of the Lord. All the flocks of Kedar shall be gathered together to you, the rams of Nebaioth shall minister to you; they shall ascent with acceptance on My altar, and I will glorify the house of My glory.

Who are these that fly like a cloud, and like the doves to their roosts? Surely the coastlands shall wait for Me; and the ships of Tarshish will come first, to bring your sons from afar, their silver and their gold with them, to the name of the Lord your God, and to the Holy One of Israel, because He has glorified you. For in My wrath I struck you, but in My favor I have had mercy on you, therefore your gates shall be open continually; they shall not be shut day or night, that men may bring to you the wealth of the Gentiles, and their kings in procession. For the nation and kingdom which will not serve you shall perish, and those nations shall be utterly ruined.

'The glory of Lebanon shall come to you, the Cypress, the pine, and the box tree together, to beautify the place of My sanctuary; And I will make the place of My feet glorious. Also the sons of those who afflicted you shall come bowing to you, and all those who despised you shall fall prostrate at the soles of your feet; and they shall call you The City of the Lord, Zion of the Holy One of Israel. ... I will also make your officers peace, and your magistrates righteousness. Violence shall no longer be heard in your land, neither wasting nor destruction within your borders; but you shall call your walls Salvation, and your gates Praise. The sun shall no longer be your light by day, nor for brightness shall the moon give light to you; but the Lord will be to you an everlasting light, and your God your glory, your sun shall no longer go down, nor shall your moon withdraw itself; for the Lord will be your everlasting light, and the days of your mourning shall be ended.

Also your people shall all be righteous; they shall inherit the land forever, the branch of My planting, the work of My hands, that I may be glorified. A little one shall become a thousand, and a small one a strong nation. I, the Lord, will hasten it in its time.

ISAIAH 60.1-14, 18-22

NOTES
1 Romans 12.17
2 Philippians 2.4
3 Genesis 1.26-28; 9.1-4; Matthew 28.18-20
4 Joshua 24.15
5 Psalm 36.9; 73.24; Romans 12.16; Ephesians 4.4
6 Isaiah 55.8-9; Mark 8.38
7 Ephesians 1.4
8 See *Spiritual Bullets for Daily Physical Battles,* Buddy Hanson, (Hanson Group)
9 Genesis 1.26-28
10 Leviticus 26.24
11 Morecraft III, Rev. Joseph, *With Liberty & Justice For All,* (Onward Press, 1991), p.147
12 Luther's Works. Weimar Edition. *Briefwechsel* [Correspondence], Vol. 3, pp. 81f.
13 Romans 12.2
14 Acts 17.6
15 John 14.15
16 1 Corinthians 13.1
17 Romans 8.5
18 Warfield, B.B., *Faith & Life,* (Banner of Truth Trust, 1916, 1974), p.249
19 Warfield, *ibid., Faith,* p.251
20 Matthew 16.18
21 Matthew 13.31-32 The Parable of the Mustard Seed

Answers to Questions on pg. 203:
Juliet, Eggs, Marriage, Defense, Light, Obey, Believe

Has the information in this section revealed that you may have been looking at the world through blurred lenses? If so, how does this information help you to change your mantra as you approach each day in Christ's Kingdom? Yes, I said, "mantra," and yes, that usually means something that is chanted, but for our case we're using it as an unspoken mantra, or that "frame of reference" we bring to our daily decision-making that enables us to either accept or dismiss proposals that don't conform to our predisposed way of viewing the world. The upside of having such a mantra, or frame of reference is that we don't have to start from scratch in evaluating each decision, which means it saves us a lot of time. The downside is that if our mantra needs changing, and we don't realize it, then we will, with the best of intentions, make decisions that are not in our best interests.

Both Satan and Jesus have a mantra that they would prefer us to use in our daily decision-making. Take a look at both mantras to decide which one is currently dictating your decisions. The clearer your focus becomes with each area of decision-making, the sharper your decisions will reflect God's will, instead of Satan's.

What's in Your Mantra?

Satan's Version: Salvation & Frustration

"You are losers in the here-and-now, but winners in the hereafter."

"Jesus loves us and came to save us from our sins so that when we die (or are raptured!) we will be freed from the shackles of Satan's dominion upon the earth, and will joyfully spend eternity with fellow believers worshiping the triune God of the Bible. Until that time Jesus' Word encourages us to save as many people as we can and comforts us in our trials on this evil-infested earth by giving us a 'hope to cope' with all that Satan throws at us."

217

Jesus' Version: Salvation & Occupation

"You can be winners in both the here-and-now, and in the hereafter (by living according to My Word!)."

· "Jesus loves those whom the Trinity chose before the foundation of the earth (EPHESIANS 1.4,17; 2.8) and came to earth to perfectly fulfill the Law (JOHN 1.1,14; MATTHEW 5.17; HEBREWS 4.15; 1 JOHN 4.10) and pay our sin debt by dying and overcoming death (JOHN 10.17-18; 1 CORINTHIANS 15.45) and has given us His Word to instruct us in how to live and govern ourselves (PSALM 119.105; JEREMIAH 31.33; JOHN 17.17; COLOSSIANS 3.16; ROMANS 8.9, 14, 16; 2 TIMOTHY 3.16-17) and complete Jesus' victory over Satan (1 JOHN 3.8; 4.4; COLOSSIANS 2.13-15; HEBREWS 2.14) by taking dominion over the earth (GENESIS 1.26-28; 9.1-4; MATTHEW 28.18-20; ROMANS 8.37) and restoring God's will "on earth, as it is in heaven." (MATTHEW 6.10; REVELATION 11.15).

Replacement String

God-Honoring Decision-Making
"It Never Occurred To Me To Do *That*!"

I think its safe to say that each of us, when brainstorming possible solutions to a problem, have said, "It never occurred to me to do *that*!" Or, from another perspective, when was the last time you said, "It never occurred to me that he (or she) was thinking *that*!" Hopefully, the ideas presented in this chapter will result in your having several "It never occurred to me" moments. Let me begin by asking a disturbing question:

> *What if you were to find out that up to now you have*
> *been spending the majority of your time and resources*
> *on peripheral issues, instead of their root causes?*

In other words, you've been a "fruit inspector," of the bad fruit that is falling from man's poisoned tree, instead of a "root extractor" of man's tree? For example, you have volunteered to help "reform" the quality of the public schools in your town. Perhaps, you've volunteered your

219

time at the school doing various things, or even been elected to the local school board. "The class size is too large," you say, or "They need to teach creationism along side of evolution." It doesn't really matter what your well-intended reasons are for wanting to help the children in your town receive a better education; the point is that the public schools were founded to *de-Christianize* the education of our children, therefore, even though your efforts may succeed in small victories, the school system will never change its curriculum to *teach the truth*. If improving the education of children in your town is your passion, the biblical thing to do is to encourage your Christian friends to withdraw their children from the public schools and either home school them, or send them to a Christian Day School.

Your reaction to what I've just said could well be, "Buddy, with all due respect, I don't think I agree with your 'solution.'" And, if that's what you're thinking, hold that thought, because we'll come back to it later.

While the vast majority of Americans profess to be Christians, research shows that 95 percent of us do not have a developed Christian worldview, and without such a worldview a person is more likely to view Jesus as his or her personal *Savior*, rather than also being their *Lord* and *King*. Such an attitude could also indicate that they are merely good moralistic people, rather than true Christians. If so, they will make their daily decisions as though they are mini-gods who have the capability to think things through according to their wisdom, instead of relying exclusively upon God's wisdom.

However, the truth is that we are creatures with a distorted ethical view of the world and we need to rely upon God's counsel in order to correctly make our decisions. [1] From cover to cover, God's Word tells us that true Christians not only acknowledge that the triune God of the Bible is the real God, but they *abide in His truth*. To quote Jesus' half-brother James, "You believe there is one God. You do well. Even the demons believe and tremble! But do you want to know, O foolish man, that faith without works is dead?" [2] James is telling us that instead of merely making a *mental assent* that the God of the Bible exists, we should make a *physical consent* to His truths.

Since the triune God of Scripture created a cause-and-effect universe whereby the actions we take cause consequences, it behooves each of us to be careful that our decisions reflect God's will, or put another way, that

220

they conform to biblical ethics. As Christians, we have been given the perfect standard for determining "good" actions, from "bad" actions: that standard, of course, is God's inerrant Word. The apostle Paul instructs us that everyone is "cursed who does not abide by all things written in the Book of the Law to perform them," [3] Paul adds that since we "were once darkness, but are now light in the Lord, "we should "walk as children of light." [4] He explains that we are "the one's slaves whom we obey, whether of sin leading to death, or of obedience leading to righteousness." [5]

The Old Testament prophets also talked of the positive consequences of making decisions according to God's Way, not our way:

You shall walk in all the ways which the LORD your God has commanded you, that you may live and that it may be well with you, and that you may prolong your days in the land which you shall possess.   DEUTERONOMY 5.33

Who is wise? Let him understand these things. Who is prudent? Let him know them. For the ways of the LORD are right; the righteous walk in them, but transgressors stumble in them.   HOSEA 14.9

If you are willing and obedient, you shall eat the good of the land.   ISAIAH 1.19

Is This Decision the Biblical Thing to Do?

The best "decision" we can make before making any decision is to remind ourselves that the purpose of our decision-making is to bring about God's will and agenda, and not our will and personal agenda. In other words, what is the motivation behind the reason we are about to make this particular decision? Will it help to expand Christ's Kingdom, and bring honor to Him, or will it help us to expand our personal kingdom and bring honor to us?

Since only God's Word is true, the only way for us to come to the correct definition of an issue is to frame it in terms of biblical ethics. We have not been called into Christ's Kingdom to live according to our definitions; that's the way we lived before we were saved. We need God's definitions. The reason for this is that, ethically speaking, we "see through a glass dimly" [6] This means that the situation we observe is not necessarily what we think it is, but rather what God says it is.

We should be most thankful that we don't live in a subjective world, where we're left to our own resources to figure things out. Instead, we live in God's objectively black and white world and have His inerrant and objective counsel to guide and direct us. For proof that our Father "knows best," [7] we only have to remember our reaction after making an ungodly decision. Who has not had occasion to say: "If I would have only acted in conformity to biblical ethics, I wouldn't be in the mess I'm in now!"

Some of our ungodly decisions have, at least, brought personal shame and embarrassment, and perhaps public shame and embarrassment. So

> *Should we not also be ashamed for even thinking about eliminating God's inerrant counsel from our daily decisions?*

Since our daily decisions present a visible testimony to our non-Christian neighbors on how to correctly live and govern ourselves, we could look at them as being "building blocks" of our Christian character. We must never forget that, as Christians, we are "new creatures" who have been "raised up in the heavenly places in Christ Jesus." In our "new life," we have been "created for good works."

> *And you He made alive, who were dead in trespasses and sins, in which you once walked according to the course of this world, according to the prince of the power of the air, the spirit who now works in the sons of disobedience, among whom also we all once conducted ourselves ...*
>
> *But God, who is rich in mercy, because of His great love with which He loved us, even when we were dead in trespasses, made us alive together with Christ (by grace you have been saved), and raised us up together, and made us sit together in the heavenly places in Christ Jesus ...For we are His workmanship, created in Christ Jesus for good works, which God prepared beforehand that we should walk in them.* EPHESIANS 2.1-10

By constructing our Christian character upon the following three Decision-Making Building Blocks, we will be establishing an unshakable foundation upon which we can base our worldview and lifestyle, and we will also be developing "good" habits in which to "walk." [8]

Christian Worldview Decision-Making Building Blocks

Worldview Decision-Making Building Block 1

God's Word is TRUTH, and man's word is FALSE. ONLY God's Word Works/Man's Word ONLY Fails.

PSALM 119.160; JOHN 17.17

Worldview decision-Making Building Block 2

We must be ever conscious that we are operating in God's world and that our efforts will fail unless we consistently live by God's rules. Piecemeal obedience will not enable us, our communities, our State, or America to be the recipients of God's promised blessings.

MATTHEW 22.37

Worldview Decision-Making Building Block 3

We have the assurance from Scripture that as we live-out our faith (by applying biblical ethics to our decision-making) non-Christians will see our successful lifestyles and will be attracted to us.

DEUTERONOMY 4.5-7; ISAIAH 2.1-5

How Your Worldview Influences Your Daily Decisions

In Your Daily Decision-Making

? How far are you willing to let your "spiritual" beliefs take you in the "real world?"

Or,

? At what point are you willing to "set-aside" your trust in God and "take charge" of the situation?

The way you view the world will have a major impact upon the decisions you make. Our purpose, as we exit our home each day is addressed in the first question and answer of the *Shorter Catechism of the Westminster Confession of Faith*.

Question 1: What is the chief end of man?
Answer: Man's chief end is to glorify God (1 COR. 10.31), and enjoy Him for ever (PSALMS 73.25-26).

Which of the following worldviews most accurately describes yours?

• Non-Christian Worldview
Thinking Man's Thoughts
In their collective foolishness they delight in their own wisdom and creativity. They see themselves as being their own boss, doing things "my way." Their life is marked by aimlessly drifting from one fad to another.

• Mixed-up Worldview
Thinking God's Thoughts IF certain
situations/circumstances are favorable
A "results-oriented" view that sees *God and man* running culture's show and reveals the underlying reason of bringing "glory and honor" to ourselves. Included in this worldview are three "isms" that lead the way in losing our culture war: Pietism (confining our beliefs inside our homes/churches); Pragmatism ("There is no clear-cut biblical reason for this decision but this is the best I can do in this situation."); and Euphemism ("I'm a 'conservative' [instead of a Christian]" "I believe in 'tradi-

tional values' [instead of biblical ethics, i.e., both tables of the law]" "We need to have 'character education' taught in schools [instead of Christian education]")

- **Christian Worldview**
Thinking God's Thoughts. (PERIOD!)

An "obedience-oriented" view that sees God running culture's show and reveals the underlying reason to bring "glory and honor" to God. We "reason together" (ISAIAH 1.18) with our Lord, Savior and King as "We speak...not the wisdom of this age, nor of the rulers of this age, who are coming to nothing." (1 CORINTHIANS 2.6) We know that we are not our own; that we are God's property and should "present our bodies as acceptable living sacrifices" (ROMANS 12.1-2), consecrating all of our actions for His glory and honor. We keep a steady course of advancing God's Kingdom, by being anchored by His absolute and unchanging promises and encouraged at the assurance that we, and our children, will be blessed for our obedience to His revealed truths for living.

Decision-Making Wheels

The Decision-Making Wheels illustrations at the end of this chapter are provided to assist you in making godly decisions. In order to give you a side-by-side comparison of the two decision-making processes (OUR Way and GOD'S Way), both Decision-Making Wheels have been reduced in size. As you work through a decision, you will probably want to use a full sheet of paper for each "Wheel" in order to give yourself room to write out your strategies and tactics. The steps to completing the "Wheels" are as follows:

OUR Way
1. Write the Core Issue about which you are making a decision in the center of the sheet of paper.
2. Draw a circle around it.
3. Draw four lines extending out from the four "corners" of the circle. This is where you will write your strategies and tactics for dealing with the Core Issue. If you only have two or three strategies and/ or tactics, that's fine. If you have more, add more lines. When you finish listing the strategies and tactics, "connect" them with an

outer circle. Now you have a Decision-Making Wheel with your strategies and tactics serving as the Wheel's "spokes."

4. Next, list the Consequences that may result by making your decision according to OUR Way.

5. Finally, list the reasons you think your decision will solve the issue.

Step 1
Core Issue

Step 2
Strategies & Tactics

Step 3
Circle to "connect"

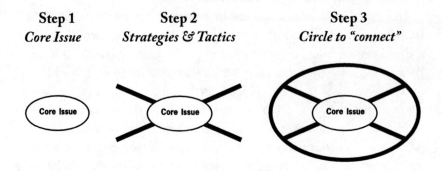

Step 4
List consequences of making
decisions according to OUR way

Step 5
How will this decision help solve
the issue before us?

GOD'S Way

1. As you did in the OUR Way Wheel, write the Core Issue about which you are making a decision in the center of the sheet of paper.

2. Draw a circle around it.

3. As you begin to compare what God says to what man says, you may find that the Core Issue in the OUR Way Wheel, is really a "spoke" on the GOD'S Way Wheel. You may also find that only some, or perhaps none of the "spokes" in the OUR Way Wheel, apply to the GOD'S Way Wheel. (Since only God's Word is truth, why bother wasting your time, efforts and resources on any strategies and tactics that do not conform to God's Word?!)

4. Next, list the Consequences that may be caused by making your decision according to GOD'S Way.

5. Finally, list the reasons you think your decision will solve the issue.

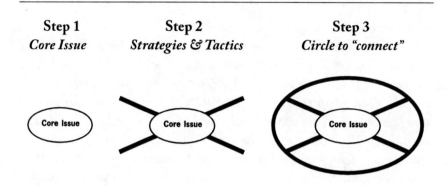

Step 1
Core Issue

Step 2
Strategies & Tactics

Step 3
Circle to "connect"

Step 4
*List consequences of making
decisions according to GOD's way*

Step 5
*How will this decision help solve
the issue before us?*

The Process for Making Godly Decisions

1. Compare what God's Word says to OUR Way.
2. Determine if we can, or should, incorporate any of OUR Way strategies/tactics into GOD's Way.
3. Should the Core Issue for OUR Way more accurately be a "spoke" (tactic/strategy) for GOD's Way?
4. If none of the OUR Way strategies and Tactics conform to GOD's Way, why should we waste our time, efforts, resources on them?

It cannot be emphasized too strongly that since God's Word is truth:

> *All decisions, whether in the home, on the job, in the halls of our legislatures, or on the judicial benches, in the classroom, or wherever decisions are made…if they don't conform to biblical ethics, they are, FALSE, and we shouldn't expect them to work, regardless of how much money, time, effort or good intentions we devote to them!*
> PSALM 119.160, 2 SAMUEL 7.28;
> JOHN 14.6; COLOSSIANS 1.2; 2 TIMOTHY 2.25

Decisions • Decisions • Decisions

As with anything, the best way to develop a new habit is to practice it. Following are five topics for which you should be able to present a Christian "solution." Fill-in the OUR Way Wheel first, using only man's reasons, then fill-in the GOD's Way Wheel, using biblical reasons for your "spokes." For your convenience, some suggested Scripture references are discussed and listed in the form of DMC's (Decision-Making Concerns). As you are working through these five sample topics, you will no doubt think of other issues facing Christians for which you can "build" an answer that God would approve. Two completed Decision-Making Wheels at the end of this chapter offer illustrations of what your completed Wheels may look like.

TOPIC 1 **Submitting to Civil Rulers: Where do we draw the line between submitting to Caesar and submitting to Christ?**

DMC 1-1 Paul tells us civil rulers are "appointed by God" to "do what is good." [9] In this context, "good" is defined as legislating and enforcing laws that conform to Scripture. Is what you are objecting to an issue that is merely irritating, and/or unpopular, or is it unbiblical? It is unbiblical when a civil ruler commands us to do something that is contrary to Scripture (Hebrew Midwives Exodus 1.15-22; Shadrach, Meschach and Abednego, Daniel 3.10-18), or when he commands us not to do something that is biblical. (Peter and the apostles, Acts 4.18-20; 5.29)

DMC 1-2 Since God created an orderly universe, anarchy and individual resistance are unbiblical methods of dealing with unjust civil rulers.[10] God's approved method of civil resistance is through the interposition of another civil ruler (a Lesser Magistrate). For example, if you have a problem with a policy of your Mayor, instead of approaching him, you should take your concerns to a City Councilman and have him interpose on your behalf.

228

This way you are objecting to a particular issue, but are still obeying God by "submitting" to the authority of the civil ruler (i.e., paying a fine and/or going to jail, if necessary).

TOPIC 2   **Educating our Children: What's a Christian to do?**

DMC 2-1   The esteemed 17th Century author John Milton states that the goal of education is "to repair the ruins of our first parents." Certainly, no Christian can argue that Adam and Eve's disobedient decision has wreaked havoc upon our world. Milton's statement agrees with Jesus'command to "teach them all things I have commanded you." [11] King Solomon also proclaims that "the fear of the Lord is the beginning of knowledge." [12] We are not to be "tossed to and fro" with every opinion that comes down the pike, [13] yet that is exactly what upwards of 90 percent of adult Christians are experiencing because they were not taught how to live-out their faith during the 12 years they spent in public (government) schools. Government schools are educating our children according to man's wisdom, which is the opposite of how we are commanded to teach them:

In all your ways acknowledge Him, and He shall
direct your paths.   PROVERBS 3.6

The goal of public (government) education is nothing less than Christian ethic cleansing, or the extermination of the Christian mind and way of life.

DMC 2-2   The first commandment is to "have no other gods before Me." [14] The public (government) schools turn this commandment on its ear by worshiping all gods, except the one true triune God of Scripture. As a Christian parent, how do you reconcile your association in any way with the public (government) schools?

229

DMC 2-3   Fathers are commanded to be responsible for the education of their children,[15] teaching them when they "sit in their house, when they walk by the way, when they lie down and when they rise up." [16] While it is biblically acceptable to delegate the carrying out of this responsibility to a wife to home school, or to a Christian day school, the father is still personally accountable to God for the curriculum that is taught, which means there is no biblical warrant for sending our children to a school that openly states that it hates God (or to a Christian Day School that says it loves God, but teaches from the same God-hating textbooks the public schools use)!

DMC 2-4   What is Christian education? What is Christianity? Christianity is not simply a pretty add-on to our otherwise ugly lifestyle; it is a complete transformation of our lifestyle, a completely different way of living. By the same token, Christian education is a completely different way of teaching. We have absolutely no biblical basis to expect that it will please God for us to add creationism to an ungodly curriculum. Or to eliminate pro-homosexual instruction from the curriculum. Or to add prayers. Who do we think we are, and with whom do we think we're dealing? I don't think many of us have thought about this because to purposely think that we can con God by saying, in effect:

Lord, I'm not going to follow Your commands completely, but I am going to follow those that "fit-in" to my current worldview and lifestyle. Tell You what I'm going to do: As a favor for what You've done for me by rescuing me from an excruciatingly painful eternal existence in Hell, I'm going to do what I can to elect Christians to the school board.

Or

I'm going to spend my spare time and resources attempting to have creationism taught as an alternative (!) view of how the world began.

230

Think about what I've just said, repeat said. Perhaps if we said what we're thinking, we would hear how silly some of our thoughts are. God gave us His Son who gave His all for us. In return for this unspeakable and undeserving gift that we have received, such thoughts as I have just described reflect that we are negotiating with God by stating:

Lord, I'm not going to give you my all, but I am willing to give you a portion of my life ... a portion that conveniently fits into my current worldview and lifestyle and allow me to still share my personal lordship of my life with Your lordship of my life.

Where on earth do we get such an idea that the Creator of the universe is going to negotiate with us in order to partially share His lordship of our lifestyle? I challenge you to find such an idea in your Bible. I shouldn't have to tell you that you won't be able to, because if there were such an idea in your Bible, you might as well burn it because such a "god" couldn't save you and would be a worthless, powerless fraud.

DCM 2-5   We are commanded "not to learn the way of [non-Christians], [17] to "come out from them and be separate," [18] that "bad company corrupts good morals," [19] and to "have no fellowship with the unfruitful works of darkness." [20] As a Christian parent, how do you reconcile these verses with your association in any way with the public (government) schools?

DMC 2-6   We are commanded to "walk in all of God's ways, [21] and not in only those ways that fit into our self-serving agenda. Are you willing to pay the consequences of being "rejected by God" [22] for being in such blatant disobedience to the clear teaching of Scripture by sending your children to the public (government) schools, (or teaching, coaching or serving as an administrator in them)? Jesus tells us that the

231

student "will be like his teacher," [23] upon what basis do you believe that Jesus is lying to us?!

DMC 2-7 If you could "fix" the government schools, what would they look like?

- Would they teach creationism as an "alternate" idea of how the world was created?
- Would there be no sex education?
- Would the pro-homosexual agenda in the curriculum be eliminated?
- Would Easter and Christmas be observed instead of Spring Break and Winter Holidays?
- Would the Ten Commandments be hung on classroom walls?
- Would there be more discipline? (or any discipline)
- Could a student or teacher or coach or administrator pray publicly in Jesus' name at school events?

In your mind's eye, exactly what does your idea of a public school look like? Do you know that I have never had anyone answer that question for me! The only answers I get are reactions against some of the distasteful "pieces" of the public education pie. But, as we have seen, adding a few biblically delicious "pieces" won't serve to correct the distasteful public school pie mix. What needs to be done is to throw the entire pie away and start over from scratch with God's recipe.

TOPIC 3 **Preaching the Whole Counsel of God: Is there a biblical reason for a church to incorporate with the state?**

DMC 3-1 God has appointed four self-governing spheres to bring about His will "on earth as it is in heaven": Individual, Family, Church and State. Each of these self-governing spheres has been given specific accountabilities and should not attempt to usurp any of the responsibilities of the other spheres. There are two problems with the state's 501c3 "tax-exempt" program for churches. In the first place, the state is usurping the church's commanded responsibility to preach the whole counsel of God (by restricting it in the matter of endorsing political candidates). In the second place, the church is guilty of voluntarily relinquishing its commanded duty to preach the whole counsel of God and to disciple its members in how to live-out their faith by applying biblical ethics in all situations and   circumstances.

DMC 3-2   20th Century seminary professor B.B. Warfield comments on some of the excuses Pastors give for not preaching and teaching the whole counsel of God's Word.

> *Sometimes they mean that the world will not receive this or that. Sometimes they mean that the world will not endure this or that. Sometimes they mean that they cannot so preach this or that as to win the respect or the sympathy or the acceptance of the world. The Gospel cannot be preached? Cannot be preached? It can be preached if you will believe it. Here is the root of all your difficulties. You do not fully believe this Gospel! Believe it! Believe it! And it will preach itself! God has not sent us into the world to say the most plausible things we can think of; to teach men what they already believe. He has sent us to preach unpalatable truths to a world lying in wickedness; apparently absurd truths to men, proud of their intellects; mysterious truths to men who are carnal and cannot receive the things of the Spirit of God. Shall we despair? Certainly, if it is left to us not only to plant and to water but also to give the increase. Certainly not, if we appeal to and depend upon the Spirit of faith. Let Him but move on our hearts and we will believe these truths; and, even as it is written, I believed and therefore have I spoken, we also will believe and therefore speak. Let Him but move on the hearts of our hearers and they too will believe what He has led us to speak. We cannot proclaim to the world that the*

house is afire — it is a disagreeable thing to say, scarcely to be risked in the presence of those whose interest it is not to believe it? But believe it, and how quickly you rush forth to shout the unpalatable truth! So believe it and we shall assert to the world that it is lost in its sin, and rushing down to an eternal doom; that in Christ alone is there redemption; and through the Spirit alone can men receive this redemption. What care we if it be unpalatable, if it be true? For if it be true, it is urgent. [24]

DMC 3-3   The first amendment to the U.S. Constitution automatically gives every church "tax-exempt" status as soon as it is organized, so there is no reason to incorporate with the state in order to secure tax-exempt status.

Congress shall make no law respecting an establishment of religion, or prohibiting the free exercise thereof.

DMC 3-4   Even if the preceding consideration were not true, ask your church officers whether the main priority of a church is to secure a "tax-exempt" status, or to preach and teach all of God's Word. If their answer is tax related, dust off your shoes and leave that tax-exempt moralistic social club behind, and find a real church of God.

DMC 3-5   What do tax-exemptions have to do with it? I'm as much for tax-exemptions as anyone, but where does Scripture say that a person should become a Christian so that he can get a tax-exemption? Don't we become Christians to put Jesus' will first, and to stop being self-centered, and begin being others-centered? Isn't it about time we replaced "economics" with "evangelism" as our first priority in our Christian walk? [25]

TOPIC 4   **Property Tax: Does God or the State own the land?**

DMC 4-1   King David and the apostle Paul tell us "the earth is the Lord's and all its fullness." [26] This means that when the state imposes a tax on property, it is breaking the eighth commandment, (You shall not steal, Exodus 20.15) and the tenth commandment (You shall not covet, Exodus 20.17).

DMC 4-2   The prophet Samuel makes it clear that state's authority to tax only extends to the head tax. [27] All other taxes by the non-Christian state are unbiblical because the state has no biblical warrant for providing social services, since such services are to be carried out by the self-governing spheres of the individual, family and church. The state is assigned only two responsibilities: to protect us from invasion and to keep our communities safe so that we can live, work, play and raise our children in Christian liberty. [28]

TOPIC 5   **What are we to do regarding illegal immigrants?**

DMC 5-1   For I was hungry and you gave Me food; I was thirsty and you gave Me drink; I was a stranger and you took Me in; I was naked and you clothed Me; I was sick and you visited Me; I was in prison and you came to Me. ...

And the King will answer and say to them, "Assuredly, I say to you, inasmuch as you did it to one of the least of these My brethren, you did it to Me."   MATTHEW 25.35-36, 40

As you know, these are not the words of a Mexican, or an Iranian, or anyone else who happened to casually stroll across our border, but the words of the Creator of the Universe. So what are we to make of them? Does this mean, to quote the old Coca-Cola commercial, "We are the world," and we should allow every person who wants a better life to come to America? The answer is two words, and to avoid

235

the suspense, I'll give the answer to you, then backup and explain it. The answer is: ABSOLUTELY NOT!

DMC 5-2   Someone may object by saying, "Buddy, aren't we supposed to love our neighbor? Again, it's a two-word answer: ABSOLUTELY YES! Let's take a minute to remind ourselves about the episode of the Good Samaritan. This is described in the 10th chapter of Luke's gospel. A lawyer, was attempting to justify himself, and asked Jesus *"Who is my neighbor?"* Jesus describes a situation where a person was beaten up, robbed and left on the side of the road. A priest and a Levite walked past him without helping, and a Samaritan came by, tended to him, took him to an inn and paid for his stay. Jesus then asked the lawyer who he thought was a neighbor to this person. The lawyer answered "He who showed mercy on him." Then Jesus said to him, *"Go and do likewise."* [29]

"Hanson," some may ask, "how are you going to reconcile this text with your 'ABSOLUTELY NOT answer?" To begin with, let's consider the context. There is an old saying about interpreting the Bible: "A text without a context is a pretext." In order to find the context of the Good Samaritan we need to answer three questions:

First, *who is our neighbor?* The answer to that is anyone and everyone with whom we come in contact.

Second, *how do we "show mercy," or how do we "love" our neighbor?* The definition of the word "Love" in the Bible is not the same as our 21st century definition of some emotional feeling, but rather, as the apostle Paul says in Romans 13.10, "The fulfilling of the law."

This raises the third question: which laws is the apostle Paul talking about. The answer to that is the 2nd Table of Law, or commandments 5-10. The first four commandments, the 1st Table, describe our relationship to God, and provides the authority upon which our laws are based, while the 2nd Table describes our relationship to each other: honor those in authority, don't kill, cheat, steal, lie or covet.

236

DMC 5-3 One of Satan's most effective tactics against Christians has been to "sell" us the myth that we now live in an age of "grace," because the days of the "law" of God are long gone. This is a brilliant tactic by Satan because it appeals to our old nature of wanting to live according to our will, instead of God's will. Satan's worst nightmare is that we will live according to God's laws, because he knows that this will ultimately lead to his defeat. He is well aware that if he can get us to live according to our own wisdom, common sense, logic and pragmatism, we will continue to mess things up. [30]

DMC 5-4 Let's think about God's law for a minute. If we don't have "law," neither will we have "justice." The Bible is all about "justice," and justice is defined by God's law. Jehovah instructed the Israelites to

Neither mistreat a stranger nor oppress him, for you were strangers in the land of Egypt.
        EXODUS 22.21; 23.9; LEVITICUS 19.33-34

How are we going to define "mistreat," and "oppress" if God's Law no longer applies? We've seen the results of letting non-Christians define these words: In Canada they call them hate crimes if pastors teach that it is wrong to be a homosexual! These "hate crimes" will be coming to a church near you real soon if we don't get off our duff and get out of the pew and obey God!

DMC 5-5 In the Bible, citizenship depended upon a person's faith. If a person wasn't a Jew or a Christian, they could still enjoy the benefits of working and raising their family, but they couldn't vote or hold office. In our current non-Christian culture we are going to have to think long range as far as having the requirement for citizenship as being a Christian, but we can today require that all citizens have faith in American values.

237

There was also no "instant gratification" when it came to achieving citizenship in Israel. Depending upon the particular situation, foreigners who came to live with the Jews, or who were captured in battles with them, were required to live and work from 3-10 generations before being allowed to become citizens and receiving any benefits of being a citizen. Hard work, long-term goals and a desire to live according to God's rules were required, not an instant proclamation that they were citizens.

Again, today we could say, "Hard work, long-term goals and a desire to live according to American values are the requirements to becoming American citizens.

In opposition to this, Rome granted citizenship to everyone with no stipulations. This degraded the status of being a citizen, and eventually helped lead to Rome's destruction. Granting citizenship with no strings or accountability to anyone would be similar to baptizing everyone who visits your church without requiring a profession of faith. What would your church become if that were practiced! I submit to you that the same thing would happen to your church that will happen to America if we don't attach accountabilities to citizenship!

DMC 5-6   What should we do? We should do exactly what Jesus did 2,000 years ago, and it is the true meaning of the Parable of the Good Samaritan: *Keep the law.* The laws we have regarding granting citizenship to immigrants should be followed, and if we disagree with them, there are constitutional ways to change them.

Hopefully, this biblical approach to decision-making has helped you to have some "It never occurred to me" moments, and that you will re-think some of your current decisions to see if they are in sync with God's counsel. I also hope this approach to decision-making will assist you in focusing your thoughts on the why behind today's issues so that you can deal with them according to God's wisdom, instead of your wisdom. For example:

✓ Why do we continue to elect the wrong people, and/or why, when we elect the right people, do they govern in the wrong way? (i.e., as Conservatives, instead of Christians)

✓ Why do we continue to oppose the various cultural issues in the wrong way, which guarantees that our efforts will fail?

In order to begin answering these "whys," and to get to the "how" of successfully dealing with these issues it is necessary to get a clear picture of where we are in our cultural crusade. That's why the Decision-Making Wheels will help you to clarify the biblical approach we need to take, by focusing on God's Big Picture for how His earth is supposed to work, and not being consumed by our immediate circumstances. This way our "immediate" decisions will not only include ways to deal with the issues facing us today, but also what to do today that will positively affect tomorrow so that we may not have to face these particular issues again.

So, how about it? As you have traveled your way through these pages, did you have many "It never occurred to me to do *that*!" moments? I hope so, and I also hope that you had an equal number of "It never occurred to me to *think that*!" moments, because, as has been mentioned, thinking is where our decision-making begins. This being the case, may we all begin our daily decision-making by thinking Christian thoughts, so we will arrive at Christian decisions!

NOTES

1　Isaiah 55.8-9
2　James 2.19-20
3　Galatians 3.10
4　Ephesians 5.8
5　Romans 6.16
6　1 Corinthians 13.12
7　Job 21.22; Romans 11.34
8　Isaiah 30.21
9　Romans 13.1-7
10　Romans 13.2; 1 Peter 2.13, 21-23
11　Matthew 28.18-20
12　Proverbs 9.10
13　Ephesians 4.14-15
14　Exodus 20.3
15　Ephesians 6.4
16　Deuteronomy 6.6-9
17　Jeremiah 10.2; Romans 12.2
18　2 Corinthians 6.14-17
19　1 Corinthians 15.33
20　Ephesians 5.11
21　Deuteronomy 10.12
22　Hosea 4.6
23　Luke 6.40
24　Warfield, B.B., *Faith & Life*, (Banner of Truth Trust, 1916), pp.241-242)
25　Matthew 25.40, 45
26　Psalm 24.1; 1 Corinthians 10.26
27　1 Samuel 8.9-18
28　Romans 13.1-5
29　Luke 10.29-37
30　Genesis 8.21; Jeremiah 17.9; Romans 7.18; Mark 7.21-23

Decision-Making

OUR Way	GOD'S Way
Man's Word is *False*	**God's Way is *True***

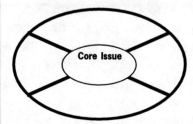

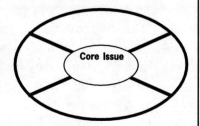

Consequences of making decisions according to OUR Way

1.

2.

3.

How will this decision helps solve the issue before us?

1.

2.

3.

Consequences of making decisions according to GOD'S Way

1.

2.

3.

How will this decision helps solve the issue before us?

1.

2.

3.

Decision-Making Wheels

OUR Way

1. Write the ISSUE in the center circle.
2. List strategies/tactics on the spokes

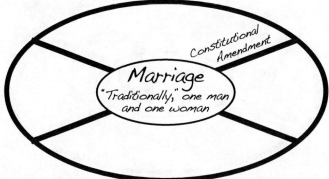

CONSEQUENCES

1. *Who's "traditional values" are best?*
2. *Are our traditional values old-fashioned and need updating?*

GOD'S Way

1. Compare what God says (in the Bible) to **Our Way**.
2. Determine if we can, or should, incorporate any of these strategies/
   tactics into **God's Way**.
3. If none of the **Our Way** strategies/tactics conform to **God's Way**,
   why should we waste our time, efforts, and resources on them?

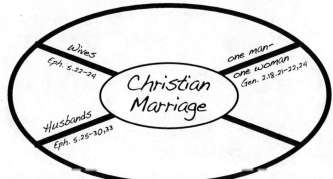

CONSEQUENCES

*"Blessed are those who do His commandments, that they may have the
right to the tree of life."* REVELATION 22.14

Decision-Making Wheels

OUR Way

1. Write the ISSUE in the center circle.
2. List strategies/tactics on the spokes

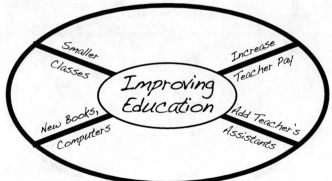

CONSEQUENCES

1. *Students may become more "technically proficient," but they still do not learn how to live and govern themselves, what their purpose is in life, how they got here, or where they're going.*

GOD'S Way

1. Compare what God says (in the Bible) to **Our Way**.
2. Determine if we can, or should, incorporate any of these strategies/ tactics into **God's Way**.
3. If none of the **Our Way** strategies/tactics conform to **God's Way**, why should we waste our time, efforts, and resources on them?

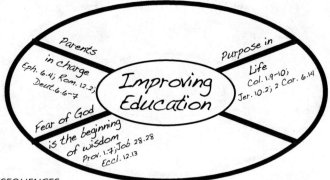

CONSEQUENCES

"Blessed are those who do His commandments, that they may have the right to the tree of life." REVELATION 22.14

242

Has the information in this section revealed that you may have been looking at the world through blurred lenses? If so, how does this information help you to change your mantra as you approach each day in Christ's Kingdom? Yes, I said, "mantra," and yes, that usually means something that is chanted, but for our case we're using it as an unspoken mantra, or that "frame of reference" we bring to our daily decision-making that enables us to either accept or dismiss proposals that don't conform to our predisposed way of viewing the world. The upside of having such a mantra, or frame of reference is that we don't have to start from scratch in evaluating each decision, which means it saves us a lot of time. The downside is that if our mantra needs changing, and we don't realize it, then we will, with the best of intentions, make decisions that are not in our best interests.

Both Satan and Jesus have a mantra that they would prefer us to use in our daily decision-making. Take a look at both mantras to decide which one is currently dictating your decisions. The clearer your focus becomes with each area of decision-making, the sharper your decisions will reflect God's will, instead of Satan's.

What's in Your Mantra?

Satan's Version: Salvation & Frustration

"You are losers in the here-and-now, but winners in the hereafter."

"Jesus loves us and came to save us from our sins so that when we die (or are raptured!) we will be freed from the shackles of Satan's dominion upon the earth, and will joyfully spend eternity with fellow believers worshiping the triune God of the Bible. Until that time Jesus' Word encourages us to save as many people as we can and comforts us in our trials on this evil-infested earth by giving us a 'hope to cope' with all that Satan throws at us."

Jesus' Version: Salvation & Occupation

"You can be winners in both the here-and-now, and in the hereafter (by living according to My Word!)."

"Jesus loves those whom the Trinity chose before the foundation of the earth (EPHESIANS 1.4,17; 2.8) and came to earth to perfectly fulfill the Law (JOHN 1.1,14; MATTHEW 5.17; HEBREWS 4.15; 1 JOHN 4.10) and pay our sin debt by dying and overcoming death (JOHN 10.17-18; 1 CORINTHIANS 15.45) and has given us His Word to instruct us in how to live and govern ourselves (PSALM 119.105; JEREMIAH 31.33; JOHN 17.17; COLOSSIANS 3.16; ROMANS 8.9, 14, 16; 2 TIMOTHY 3.16-17) and complete Jesus' victory over Satan (1 JOHN 3.8; 4.4; COLOSSIANS 2.13-15; HEBREWS 2.14) by taking dominion over the earth (GENESIS 1.26-28; 9.1-4; MATTHEW 28.18-20; ROMANS 8.37) and restoring God's will "on earth, as it is in heaven." (MATTHEW 6.10; REVELATION 11.15).

Replacement String

**Making the non-negotiable attitude change from
"What's in this for me?" to
"What's in this for Christ's Kingdom?"**

Before we begin, indulge me for a few seconds while you ask those in your house: Who's going to win the World Series (or Super Bowl)? Before asking them, ask yourself so you can compare your answer with theirs. If there is disagreement, ask those with different answers why they believe that their predictions will be accurate, instead of your predictions? And, if everyone agrees, ask yourselves, "How can we be absolutely certain that our predictions are correct?"

"Loosen up, Hanson!" someone may say, "We're only talking about sports!" Fair enough, but let's change the topic to "life," and whether we can be absolutely certain about which is the correct way to live, raise your family, and govern yourselves, your community, your state and country? Non-Christians live according to how they think they should live, which means that whether the question is who will win the World Series, or how to raise their family, or how to govern themselves, their answers will reflect an equal amount of uncertainty. Still, such an attitude to life's burning questions is perfectly understandable for them, since they don't believe in a triune, transcendent God who provides revealed answers to how we should live. We, on the other hand, should live according to how God wants us to live. This, too, is perfectly understandable, since we do believe in God. By the end of this chapter, perhaps you may be reminded that you need to re-focus your thoughts on the kinds of decisions you make because the consequences of those decisions are causing you to live in ways that are dishonoring to God. If so, don't worry about it, or get your feelings hurt, but rather praise God it's been brought to your attention and, repent and begin making your daily decisions conform to God's thoughts, rather than according to your thoughts!

If I were to ask: "What's the most effective way to deal with a particular cultural issue?" you would probably say, "The answer is not to turn to the editorial page, or to an internet blog, but open the Bible and see what God has to say about it." And, of course, that would be the correct answer, but the next question is "Why aren't most of our Christian brothers and sisters (you and I included) doing that?" Because, if we were applying the biblical truths we know to our situations and circumstances, we wouldn't have nearly the amount of negative cultural issues that we are currently facing. *Knowledge* isn't our problem; *application* is, so during this chapter we'll focus on ways we can match our walk with our talk. On Judgment Day, Jesus isn't going to give us an oral exam, He's going to give us a physical exam. Not a medical physical, but an ethical physical as He examines how worn our spiritual shoes are. Sadly, too many of us are wearing spiritual shoes that have been barely broken in. Even though we "talk" Christian, we "walk" non-Christian. As the 19th Century American philosopher Ralph Waldo Emerson puts it: "What you do speaks so loudly that I cannot hear what you say."

So the next time a Christian brother or sister proposes a "solution" for an item in the news, say to them, "I have a question about what you just said, and it may be a little shocking, so let me preface it with the request that you ask me the same question whenever I give you my thoughts on an issue. Fair enough? The question is: 'What Scriptural support do you have for your solution?'"

> *What Scriptural support do you have for your solution?*

By using these nine words to assist our Christian friends re-focus their daily decisions according to biblical ethics, and have them use the same question to assist us in re-focusing our decisions according to biblical ethics, how distinctively different will their and our worldview and lifestyle be to that of our non-Christian neighbors? And, isn't that exactly how we're supposed to be living? When God tells us that His Word is true, what He is also telling us is that our word is false. So what do we do? We go around saying, "God's Word is true. It's inspired, and contains no errors or contradictions," and we might even add, "He is the Creator, and we are the creatures; He's the Boss," but all the while we're saying this, we are making decisions according to our word and rarely, if ever, step back from a decision to consider if it conforms to those biblical ethics in which we profess to believe! Our goal seems to be to fit God's standard into our standard, and replace *His* plan and cultural agenda with *our* plans and cultural agenda.

I'm tempted to say, "Go figure," but it could be that "figuring" is precisely our problem. Instead of "Going and doing what we know, we seem to prefer to "figure out" ways to avoid obeying God.

Nonsensical	God's Word is true, but that particular
Rationalization 1	teaching is meant for an agrarian and nomadic
	people who lived in the desert centuries ago.

To such a nonsensical rationalization, you might ask, "So you are saying that God's Word was true, but it is no longer true?"

Nonsensical	Yes, God's Word is true, but that particular
Rationalization 2	teaching is describing something that's
	going to take place in heaven.

To which you might ask, "So are you saying that we should be so heavenly minded, that we become no earthly good?"

Long story short, we must do whatever we can to develop the habit of re-thinking God's thoughts, and admit that if we can't find any Scriptural support for a proposed solution, there's no true reason for continuing to approach it in that fashion, because to do so would be to advance a lie. To highlight how important our daily decision-making is, let's say that

I'm not a Christian, and I decide to rob a bank. I get caught, convicted and sent to prison, where I become a Christian. Now, even though Jesus will welcome me with open arms in heaven when I die, I still have to serve my prison sentence while I am alive. Actions cause consequences. If our decisions and actions are biblical, the consequences will be positive, and if our decisions and actions are unbiblical, the consequences will be negative.

The point is that there is a Christian way to think and make decisions, and a non-Christian way to think and make decisions, and just as non-Christians wouldn't want to be accused of thinking and living like Christians, neither should we want to be accused of thinking and living like non-Christians. Since we serve a God who has given us objective rules for living, our evaluations on how biblically we are serving God should be based upon His objective standards of conduct. By continuing to depend upon our ideas instead of God's, and to have more faith in our abilities to bring about particular solutions, the less faith we will have in God's abilities to bring about His perfect solutions. Once again, let's remind ourselves of what we all profess: God's Word is True. This means that for our words to be true they must reflect His words. When our words don't reflect God's words, the decisions we make will be based upon sinful hallucinations! To break this down a little further, let's return to our theological coin. Since God's Word is true one side of the coin is inscribed with

ONLY God's Word Works!

Now, that has a good ring to it, but what would the flip side of the coin say?

Man's Word ONLY Fails!

As we've discussed, this doesn't have a good ring to it, but it is true nevertheless, and until we admit this and factor it into our decision-making process, we will continue to be rebellious in our service to Jesus. Isaiah records these poignant words from Jehovah to his neighbors:

248

Woe to the rebellious children," says the LORD, "Who take counsel, but not of Me, and who devise plans, but not of My Spirit, that they may add sin to sin; who walk to go down to Egypt, and have not asked My advice, to strengthen themselves in the strength of Pharaoh, and to trust in the shadow of Egypt! Therefore the strength of Pharaoh shall be your shame, and trust in the shadow of Egypt shall be your humiliation.   ISAIAH 30.1-3

Unless you became a Christian at an early age, you can remember how as a non-Christian, your worldview and lifestyle was constructed on a foundation of sand, and to use Paul's words, you were "tossed about with every wind of doctrine" [1] as you based your decisions on whatever the latest public opinion poll said, or if you were in school, whatever the "in crowd" thought. In those days, if someone had asked, "Buddy, are you accomplishing what you should be accomplishing in life?" you would have had no way of definitively answering. About the best answer a non-Christian can have to that question is: "I *think* so. Or, "I guess so." Now, however, we have been given absolute (definitive) truths about what our purpose in life is, and specific strategies and tactics to accomplish that purpose. While we may not be where we want to be, we know that we are on the right track and that we are headed in the right direction. This enables us to have a vision of where we're going. Hockey great, Wayne Gretzky liked to say, "I skate to where the puck is going to be, not where it has been." As Christians, we should live and make decisions according to what we will be in heaven, which is perfect, rather than what we used to be, which was imperfect sinners. Since we're living in an imperfect world and are imperfect individuals, we will not come close to achieving perfection, but we can advance toward that goal, because we are no longer imperfect sinners, but redeemed sinners.

How do we develop an explicitly Christian approach to Decision-Making?

As discussed in the previous chapter, the two-fold answer to this pivotal question is: Make certain that we have a reverential fear of God's

249

Word, and not simply a respect for it, and then we must identify what is the "Chief Influencer" of our decisions.

Tactics to Use with Christians who hold No Positive Hope for the Future of the Earth

Instead of writing off these Christian brothers and sisters, we can attempt to turn their thinking around by discipling them in the following ten biblical tactics. This is by no means a complete list, so you may think of additional tactics as you read through them.

TACTIC ONE
Point out the numerous portions of Scripture in both the Old and New Testaments that promise that our obedience will be rewarded in space and time, and not just in eternity.

TACTIC TWO
Have them consider whether the activities and projects in which they are involved will impact the "root" of a cultural issue, which will lead to a complete long-term victory, or whether it is merely dealing with a "fruit" of the underlying issue, which would mean that, at best, any victory would be incomplete and short-term. For example, why try to get prayer back in the public school classrooms, if they deliberately teach that Christianity is no better or worse than any other religion? The Decision-Making Wheel described earlier can be effectually used to illustrate the core issue and root causes of cultural issues in addition to assisting us in developing a biblically-based decision with which to "solve" the issue.

TACTIC THREE
Ask them whether Statement A, or Statement B more accurately describes the reason behind their decisions:

Statement A: "This is what my friends (research, teachers, etc.) say."
Statement B: "The biblical example upon which I'm basing this decision is _____."

TACTIC FOUR

Ask them to not only consider the best biblical option, but to also list one or two other biblical options in the likelihood that they will have to "make adjustments" in their original plan in order to accomplish God's desired results. For example, every football team begins each game with a Game Plan designed to attack their opponent's tendencies. However, once the opponent makes adjustments in their play calling to counter the original Game Plan, the coach makes "adjustments" to their adjustments. This doesn't mean that they have watered down their Game Plan, but rather that they have made solid adjustments to deal with a changing situation. While God gives us the absolute ethics by which we can attack the current collective non-Christian cultural agenda, He doesn't limit us as to exactly how we should incorporate His ethics into our situations and circumstances.

TACTIC FIVE

The more "connected" you can get them to feel about their biblically obedient efforts and resulting positive results on culture, the more motivated they should be toward living for God in all areas of their lifestyle.

TACTIC SIX

Remind them that we are not a bunch of "Lone Rangers." Emphasize the necessity of "trusting" each other's contributions toward accomplishing the goal. On the athletic field, for example, when teammates establish confidence in each other, the defensive end doesn't have to look over his shoulder to see whether the linebacker is covering his back. Neither will the cornerback have to worry about whether the safety will be there to help him in pass coverage. He knows the safety will be there, just as the safety knows the cornerback will be where he is supposed to be, therefore each of them can concentrate on carrying out their assignments.

TACTIC SEVEN

Since we are responsible for bringing about God's will on the earth, through our faithful and consistent obedience, and decision-making, we should establish some checkpoints to objectively measure our level of obedience.

TACTIC EIGHT

Make a list of the blessings God promises for obedient worldviews and lifestyles and periodically review it to remind ourselves of how important our obedience is and how it will be used by God to bring about His will, "on earth as it is in heaven." [2]

TACTIC NINE

Develop the awareness and understanding of how a God-oriented lifestyle is superior to a man-oriented lifestyle.

TACTIC TEN

Consistent preparation and practice are essential: Former NFL Coach Mike Ditka says, "The will to win is meaningless without the will to prepare." Just as athletic teams physically prepare to meet and beat (!) their next opponent, so should we mentally prepare ourselves to meet and beat the various elements of the collective non-Christian worldview. Athletic teams never leave details unattended. "How many successful people have you ever heard say, 'I just make it up as I go along?'" Ditka explains that teams are successful because of "Execution of basic plays, not innovation." By the same token, we should spend time daily refreshing our mind about how to deal with a particular issue from God's standpoint, and not based upon some idea we invent. It is only by doing this that our decision will bring glory and honor to Him. NFL Coach Norv Turner agrees "You must practice at a high level to compete at a high level," and former NFL Coach Bill Walsh adds, "Preparation precedes performance."

When we turn on the TV, pick up a newspaper or magazine, or step outside our homes, we see a culture that is being conducted according to a non-Christian ethical agenda. What we should focus our thoughts on, however, is the kind of culture that we will have when we begin to consistently conform our daily decisions according to God's ethics. The following chart provides ten components of a Christian civilization. Each component reflects a concept in one of God's Ten Commandments, beginning with the tenth commandment and ending with the first commandment. As you pause to think about each of these components hopefully you will begin to frame a mental "picture" toward which you base your decisions. Obviously, none of us is perfect and we will fall far short of perfectly achieving these godly goals, but I think everyone will agree that we can do a whole lot better in our Christian walk than we are currently doing!

Ever imagined what life on earth would be like had Adam and Eve not disobeyed God?

X   Everyone would get along with each other.   No military; no jealousy; worldwide peace.

IX   We would "mean what we say," and "say what we mean." Isaiah 32   No public relations spin doctors would be needed.

VIII No Stealing
&
VII   No cheating   No police; no insurance; no security systems.

VI   No death.   No dangerous animals. Plenty of collective wisdom and historical anecdotes from family members.

V   We would respect parents, teachers, public officials, and each other.   The entire earth would demonstrate "Southern Hospitality."

IV   Honor and keep holy the Lord's Day.   Increasing our knowledge of and appreciation for the Creator God whom we serve.

III   Self-governing and personal accountability.   No large central "nanny" government.

II   We would worship God only in the way He prefers, not in ways that we imagine He prefers   God would listen to and honor our worship.

I   We would worship only the (true) Triune God of Scripture, not a   God would listen to our prayers and honor them.

EXODUS 20.3-17

The Big Picture

Are we currently under God's judgment and thereby losing the religious war? YES. Are we fighting the war in an unbiblical manner? YES. Can we expect God to hear our prayers and intervene on our behalf? NO. How, then, can we get out of this mess and win the religious war? There has only been one answer to this question throughout Scripture and throughout time: Repent and begin to consistently incorporate the Biblical truths we know into our lifestyle. James points out that by living in this manner we will be able to keep our channels of communication open to our Lord, Savior and King. James writes, "The effective fervent prayer of a righteous man avails much." [3] We can also be confident that God will reward our obedience in His perfect timing by bringing about

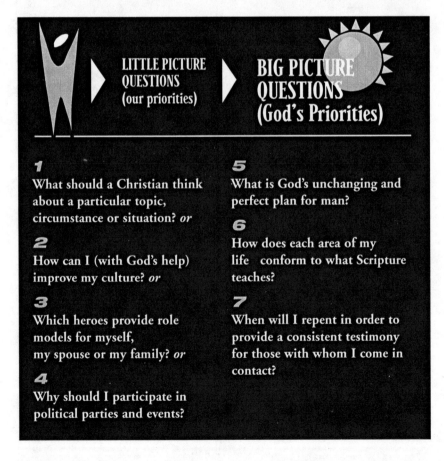

LITTLE PICTURE QUESTIONS (our priorities)

BIG PICTURE QUESTIONS (God's Priorities)

1
What should a Christian think about a particular topic, circumstance or situation? *or*

2
How can I (with God's help) improve my culture? *or*

3
Which heroes provide role models for myself, my spouse or my family? *or*

4
Why should I participate in political parties and events?

5
What is God's unchanging and perfect plan for man?

6
How does each area of my life conform to what Scripture teaches?

7
When will I repent in order to provide a consistent testimony for those with whom I come in contact?

BIG PICTURE QUESTIONS
(God's Priorities)

1

What should a Christian think about
a particular topic, circumstance or situation? *or*

2

How can I (with God's help) improve my culture? *or*

3

Which heroes provide role models for myself,
my spouse or my family? *or*

4

Why should I participate in political parties and events?

5

What is God's unchanging and perfect plan for man?

6

How does each area of my life conform to what Scripture teaches?

7

When will I repent in order to provide a consistent
testimony for those with whom I come in contact?

the exact results He has promised. He has appointed us to be in the obedience business while He brings about the results. [4]

This divinely perfect formula cannot be improved upon by our stepping over into the results arena. No matter how well-intentioned we may be, such efforts to "help out God" in a particular event or circumstance will result in failure. There are two things we must do in order to successfully carry out our calling:

1. Think God's thoughts after Him (stay in His Word)
2. Fit our LITTLE PICTURE (our immediate circumstances) into God's BIG PICTURE (His revealed will for earth) so that we are certain we are attacking the taproot and not just an isolated branch.

Jesus intends for us to go about our daily tasks by viewing the world through God's eyes, not our own. This is the only way we will be able to shift our focus from one that is primarily concerned with the LITTLE PICTURE that focuses primarily on our situations and circumstances, to God's BIG PICTURE that focuses on His plan for a redeemed earth.

When we view life through our eyes, it is a horizontal view with our time-oriented priorities nearest to us. We know that God's life-oriented priorities are "out there," but since they are obscured from our line of sight they remain fuzzy in our thought processes. Questions 1-4 focus on our priorities and questions 5-7 are oriented toward God's priorities. All are good questions and need to be asked and answered. However by beginning our focus with questions 1-4 our tendency is to try to fit God's priorities (questions 5-7) into our overall thoughts and plans as best we can. For proof that such an approach will fail, we only have to think about our daily quiet time. Anyone who has attempted to "add" a few minutes with God to either the beginning or end of a day has likely experienced unsatisfactory "hit and miss" results. God is not some subjective Being on the periphery of our life. He is our life. There is no Scriptural justification for beginning each day with a "To Do" list that does not have God at the top. Hoping to fit God in "between the cracks" of our routine demonstrates that our priorities come first, and His come in a distant second. Such an attitude clearly demeans God's importance in our life and testifies to our non-Christian neighbors that He really has nothing important to do with our daily actions and decision-making, since our lifestyle is so similar to theirs.

Little picture questions serve to block out the BIG PICTURE QUESTIONS by conning us into thinking we're living for God, when we're really only being "busy" for Him.

The reason we so easily con ourselves is because when our focus is on Questions 1-4 we are, in essence, looking at life through our eyes, rather than through God's eyes. The BIG PICTURE Illustration shows the preferred way of viewing life and these seven questions. Looking upon them from a vertical perspective enables us to constantly have all seven questions clearly in view. This way we are reminded to sift our various daily decisions and priorities through God's overarching priorities to make certain that our actions conform to His revealed principles for living. By doing this we are not only able to carry out His will, but we also present to our neighbors a lifestyle that is distinctively different (and attractive!).

We should never forget that God is concerned first and foremost about His will being done on earth. He's interested in our being "more than conquerors through Christ," [5] not busying ourselves in church-sponsored activities and events that have little, if anything, to do with bringing about His will on earth. God doesn't simply want a portion of our valuable time, He demands and commands our entire life! Since questions 5-7 are life-oriented, keeping a clear focus on them enables us also to deal consistently with questions 1-4. This is much better than the attitude shown in LITTLE PICTURE Illustration where we place our primary focus on questions 1-4, thereby valuing "time spent" with God, over "results achieved for God." May we therefore view life through God's eyes, from a vertical perspective, instead of from the fallen horizontal perspective of our non-Christian neighbors. The apostle Paul says we should be

Casting down arguments and every high thing that exalts itself against the knowledge of God, bringing every thought into captivity to the obedience of Christ, and being ready to punish all disobedience when your obedience is fulfilled.
2 CORINTHIANS 10.5-6

Where Are We?

Where We Were *Before* The Messiah (BC)	Where We Are *Now* (AD)

1. There was worldwide
  a. slavery
  b. polygamy
  c. low social position of women and children
  d. political oppression and poverty of the masses
  e. brutal physical persecutions
	1. The growth of the church from 120 members in Jerusalem to millions throughout history.

2. The Gospel was mainly limited to the physical nation of Israel and to a few proselytes	2. The Gospel has spread throughout the world via:
	  a. radio, TV, internet
	  b. audio/video/DVDs
	  c. print
	  d. missionaries
	  e. Bibles translated into many languages.

	3. Commentaries and Bible study aids assist our growth in God's Word.
	4. Early church councils which correctly applied Scripture against certain heresies.
	5. Advances in medicine & health care.

In other words, our every action should be designed to bring glory and honor to God and to provide a Christian alternative for everyone with whom we come in contact. Instead of "baptizing" our lifestyle with an unending flow of church-sponsored meetings and activities, while continuing to conform the remainder of our actions to those of our non-Christian neighbors, we need to fulfill our calling to "subdue and rule over" our neighborhoods and communities, which is obeying Christ's command to disciple the nations.

Where We Want To Be

IMAGINED Hope	BIBLICAL Hope
1. The establishment of an earthly kingdom that will provide: a. More material wealth b. Less trial/temptations c. Worldwide peace because Jesus' army are capable of to any task in will be superior to Satan's army.	1. To continue to multiply and to subdue and rule over all creation. To bring glory and honor to God by giving the best effort that we which we are involved. 2. To train up our family in God's Word. 3. To evangelize/disciple our acquaintances as we assist in conforming the world to live according to biblical ethics. 4. To live for God, not our selfish desires.

The preceding chart assists you in forming a mental biblical picture of where we are, in comparison to where we've been, and where we're going to be follows. It's easy to turn on the news and conclude, "There's no way things could get better!" But when you compare the lifestyle conditions of the 21st Century to the 1st Century, I think you will agree that while we may have a long way to go, we've certainly come a long way!

What is the Gospel?

Jesus tells us through Mark's letter, "The time is fulfilled, and the kingdom of God is at hand. Repent, and believe in the gospel." [6] So, exactly what is it that we are supposed to believe? The English word "gospel" comes from the Anglo-Saxon "god-spell," and has been popularized with the phrases, "Good tidings," and "good news." Does this "good news" from God apply only to a person's:
- Individual salvation, or does it also apply to the
- Restoration of the behavior of individuals (and consequently their culture and the earth), or, both?

259

Uh oh, there's that question again! Isn't it so much easier to make decisions strictly according what we think, rather than digging into the Bible to find out what God thinks? That's the way Satan would have us reason, but as we've seen, when we depend exclusively upon our reason, we quickly become (biblically) unreasonable. Besides, the effort and concentration required to search the Scriptures serves as our "practice" to sharpen our biblical skills and to reinforce God's truths upon our minds, in the same manner as repetitive practice on the athletic field reinforces the skills for the players to use on game day.

The gospel is certainly "the power of God to salvation to everyone who believes," [7] but in addition to telling about Jesus' life, death and resurrection, it also tells us the good news about how to live and govern ourselves. Isaiah records Jehovah's message that "the nation and kingdom which will not serve you shall perish, and those nations shall be utterly ruined." [8] This knowledge of God that the Holy Spirit writes on our hearts [9] which leads us to repent, is far more than a mere sorrow for the way in which we have lived up to that point, but rather is a decision to turn away from our previous worldview and lifestyle, and turn to Jesus and to begin to live according to His will, and not ours.

As we've seen, this "free gift" of forgiveness that Jesus gives us is the costliest gift we will ever receive, because it demands that we give up everything from our former lifestyle. Anything less than that may result in our having a more moralistic lifestyle, where we are valued as "good neighbors" and upstanding, law-abiding citizens, but it does not represent a true profession of faith in Christ.

Three Pivotal Questions

ONE   Whether intended or not, can your lifestyle be characterized as including a lot of disconnected "religious" activities and projects, or is your lifestyle directed toward bringing about God's will on earth through a series of interconnected activities and daily decisions?

Don't Compromise Your Testimony

The next time you are tempted with the suggestion to "loosen up a little" in your application of God's ethical standard to your lifestyle, consider the following questions:

✓ How will conforming God's ethics to the world's (even in a small way) affect your testimony to your non-Christian neighbors that God is "The way, the life and the truth," (John 14.6) since you are now saying there is another way and another truth?

✓ Where is an example in history of any people consistently succeeding by conforming to the ways of the world's non-Christian agenda?

✓ Why won't your compromise with the non-Christian way of doing something, bring "glory and honor to God?" (1 Timothy 1.17; 1 Peter 1.7; Revelation 4.11; 21.24) In what ways do you think you are demonstrating that you are trusting in God's wisdom, when you conform to man's wisdom?

✓ If you don't strive to live in strict conformity to God's will, since you believe that it is truly the correct way to live and govern yourself, then what incentive does a non-Christian have to stop living according to their will and begin to follow God's will? Why should they change their worldview and lifestyle for a Christian one, if there is no hard and fast ethical standard of behavior by which to live?

✓ How will your efforts at following the will of non-Christians demonstrate that you love and respect the ways of God more than you love and respect the ways of man? (2 Chr. 19.2)

✓ How does your behavior testify that you "hate sin" (disobedience to God's Word) when you willingly and voluntarily choose to live in sin? (Ephesians 2.12)

✓ How will your disobedient actions demonstrate that you are ultimately no different than those who hate God? (Psalm 9.17; 10.4)

✓ Given that the major tenet of the Bible is that God rewards those who obey Him and punishes those who disobey Him, (Leviticus 26; Deuteronomy 28) why do you expect to be able to "walk on hot coals without having your feet burned?" (Proverbs 6.28)

✓ Do you consider yourself to be more able to avoid denying God by being less careful in your walk? (Matthew 26.69-75)

✓ Why do you imagine that you can strengthen your case for living according to God's will by blatantly disobeying it? (Exodus 32.26; Judges 5.23; Mat. 12.30; Numbers 23.9; John 17.16)

✓ Since you are going to spend eternity with fellow Christians, shouldn't your main desire upon the earth to be to spend it in fellowship with them, and to live and govern yourself according to God's will, rather than spending your time with non-Christians, and living and governing yourself according to their will? (Hebrews 12.22-24; 2 Corinthians 6.17-18)

261

TWO   In evaluating your worldview and lifestyle, what are some things you can either stop doing or start doing to enable you to present a holier testimony to your non-Christian neighbors?

THREE Where's Your Passion?
  • Since God offers us such great things as:
  • The correct way to live
  • How to raise our families
  • How to govern ourselves
  • Providing us with the most meaningful purpose in life (assisting in bringing about His will on earth as it is in heaven), and
  • Eternal fellowship with all Christians throughout history once our life on earth is completed …

Why are so many of our Christian brothers and sisters so lifeless and careless in their service in Christ's Kingdom? Could the reason be that they have Jesus "in their heart," instead of having Him "occupying the throne" of their heart? As our generation lives in the midst of a collective non-Christian cultural agenda, there is tremendous pressure, either explicit or implicit, to be a little "compromising" with God's instructions. The following chart may be helpful in fighting through this common temptation.

By now, you've probably thought several times, "Hanson, you sure are optimistic, but it's hard for me to believe that the Bible really says what you say it says!" I can well understand why you may be thinking along those lines, since there is so much pessimism spewing from the pulpits, radio, TV and books, however, let me respond with two words: "Believe it!" The Civilization's Scorecard chart should help you overcome your doubts.

After you have thought-through the positive promises from God on the Scorecard, do this: Take a blank sheet of paper and make your own Civilization's Scorecard, with a W and an L column. Fold it and place it in your Bible. Then as you are studying through various portions, when you come to a verse that promises a victory for Jesus and His followers, write it on your Scorecard. And, when you run across a promise that describes where Satan will defeat us, write it down. HINT #1: You will find a lot of "Ws." HINT #2: You won't find any "Ls!"

Civilization's Scorecard

Christ Wins (Ws)	Christ Loses (Ls)
Let them have dominion...over all the earth. Genesis 1.26-28	
Is anything too difficult for the LORD? Genesis 18.14	
One of you routs a thousand, because the LORD your God fights for you, just as He promised. Joshua 23.10-13	
Ask of Me, and I will make the nations your inheritance. Psalm 2.8	
What is man that You are mindful of him...You made him ruler over the works of your hands; You put everything under his feet. The LORD foils the plans of the nations; He thwarts the purposes of the peoples. Psalm 8.4-6	
But the plans of the LORD stand firm forever. Psalm 33.10-11,13-19	
The highest heavens belong to the LORD, but the earth He has given to man. Psalm 115.16	
The wealth of the sinner is laid up for the just. Proverbs 13.32	
The government shall be upon His shoulder, and...of the increase of His government and peace there shall be no end. Isaiah 9.6-7	
He will not falter or be discouraged till He establishes Justice on earth. Isaiah 42.3-4	
His dominion is an everlasting dominion. Daniel 7.14	
For My name shall be great among the nations. Malachi 1.11	
Your kingdom come, Your will be done, on earth as it is in heaven. Matthew 6.10	
All authority has been given to me in heaven and on earth. Matthew 28.18	
The time is fulfilled and the kingdom of God is at hand. Mark 1.15	
The Kingdom of God is not coming with signs to be observed; not will they say, "Look, here it is!" or "There it is!" For behold, the Kingdom of God is in your midst. Luke 17.20-21	
He who believes in Me, the works I do he will do also; and greater works than these he will do. John 14.12	
For He must reign [in heaven] until He puts all enemies under His feet. 1 Corinthians 15.24-25	
Resist the devil and he will flee from you. James 4.7	
Have made us kings and priests to our God; and we shall reign on earth. Revelation 5.10	

Let's Review Our Calling

- Christianity is not a part-time "job;" it's a fulltime "profession."
- The answer to what we are supposed to "get done" with our life is: We are members of God's "A" team, and are cultural winners, not caretakers. We've been called to "take Christian dominion," not live by non-Christian opinion.
- As redeemed sinners who have mercifully been called into Christ's Kingdom, our service for Jesus should not merely be "church busyness," but Kingdom building.
- We "build" Christ's Kingdom through the four God-appointed self-governing spheres of: Individual, Family, Church and State. This bottom-up, divinely appointed division of labor will lead to personal liberty and the Christianization of our culture, in contrast to the tyrannical top-down central governing ideas of man.
- We grow in God's grace and knowledge through consistent Bible Study, prayer and with the help of a Christian brother or sister who disciples us in how to incorporate biblical ethics into our worldview and lifestyle.
- Only Christians can definitively answer the six core questions about life. By God's grace we know the Who, What, Where, When, Where, Why & How answers. (See Six Questions chart at the end of the Third Cut)

NOTES
1 Ephesians 4.14
2 Matthew 6.10
3 James 5.16
4 Psalm 33.10-11, 13-19; 138.7-8
5 Romans 8.37
6 Mark 1.15; Matthew 3.2; 4.17
7 Romans 1.16
8 Isaiah 60.12
9 Jeremiah 31.33

Has the information in this section revealed that you may have been looking at the world through blurred lenses? If so, how does this information help you to change your mantra as you approach each day in Christ's Kingdom? Yes, I said, "mantra," and yes, that usually means something that is chanted, but for our case we're using it as an unspoken mantra, or that "frame of reference" we bring to our daily decision-making that enables us to either accept or dismiss proposals that don't conform to our predisposed way of viewing the world. The upside of having such a mantra, or frame of reference is that we don't have to start from scratch in evaluating each decision, which means it saves us a lot of time. The downside is that if our mantra needs changing, and we don't realize it, then we will, with the best of intentions, make decisions that are not in our best interests.

Both Satan and Jesus have a mantra that they would prefer us to use in our daily decision-making. Take a look at both mantras to decide which one is currently dictating your decisions. The clearer your focus becomes with each area of decision-making, the sharper your decisions will reflect God's will, instead of Satan's.

What's in Your Mantra?

Satan's Version: Salvation & Frustration

"You are losers in the here-and-now, but winners in the hereafter."

"Jesus loves us and came to save us from our sins so that when we die (or are raptured!) we will be freed from the shackles of Satan's dominion upon the earth, and will joyfully spend eternity with fellow believers worshiping the triune God of the Bible. Until that time Jesus' Word encourages us to save as many people as we can and comforts us in our trials on this evil-infested earth by giving us a 'hope to cope' with all that Satan throws at us."

265

Jesus' Version: Salvation & Occupation

"You can be winners in both the here-and-now, and in the hereafter (by living according to My Word!)."

"Jesus loves those whom the Trinity chose before the foundation of the earth (EPHESIANS 1.4,17; 2.8) and came to earth to perfectly fulfill the Law (JOHN 1.1,14; MATTHEW 5.17; HEBREWS 4.15; 1 JOHN 4.10) and pay our sin debt by dying and overcoming death (JOHN 10.17-18; 1 CORINTHIANS 15.45) and has given us His Word to instruct us in how to live and govern ourselves (PSALM 119.105; JEREMIAH 31.33; JOHN 17.17; COLOSSIANS 3.16; RO- MANS 8.9, 14, 16; 2 TIMOTHY 3.16-17) and complete Jesus' victory over Satan (1 JOHN 3.8; 4.4; COLOSSIANS 2.13-15; HEBREWS 2.14) by taking dominion over the earth (GENESIS 1.26-28; 9.1-4; MATTHEW 28.18-20; ROMANS 8.37) and restoring God's will "on earth, as it is in heaven." (MATTHEW 6.10; REVELATION 11.15).

Replacement String

Are ALL These Days Are Included In Your Worldview?
The Seven Days of Christians

Day One **Euphoria!**
Ecstatic about being a member of Christ's Kingdom.

Day Two **Decision-Making**
How can I base my worldview, lifestyle and decision-making upon biblical ethics?

Day Three **Substituting God's Thoughts for Our Thoughts**
Living by God's rules, instead of by man's rules.

Day Four **Are Non-Christians Really In Control?**
Am I on the winning team on the earth, or only in heaven?

Day Five **Our Worldview & Lifestyle:**
What's Scripture Got To Do With Them?
Focusing on obedience and leaving the results to God.

Day Six **Inside the Winners' Locker Room**
We're the only ones who know the triune God of Scripture, and His truth.

Day Seven **R-e-s-t & Worship**
We can put our world "on hold" for a full day and worship our Creator because we know that He is in sovereign control of His creation.

Introduction

Every Christian knows that it is necessary to live according to a Christian worldview. Technically speaking, every Christian does live according to a Christian worldview, but, pardon the pun, in many instances, it is very holey! The reason there are so many holes in the worldviews of most of us is because very little, if any, time is spent by churches on instructing their members in how to live for Christ. Instead, they spend their time informing them of biblical truths, but fail to provide instructions on how to incorporate those truths into their worldview and lifestyle. There are several reasons for this, some of which will be discussed in Day Four.

Since a complete Christian worldview includes several key components The Seven Days of Christians divides those components over one complete week in a chronological order. This is designed to assist you in determining where you are in your progression toward demonstrating a consistent Christian worldview and lifestyle, and it can also be used in helping a friend see how, even with good intentions, their decision-making will not be honoring to our Lord, Savior and King, Jesus Christ, unless they eliminate any remnants from their former non-Christian thought processes. (See Day Three)

The Seven Days of Christians is presented in terms of a new Christian's first week with the Lord. Even though your "first week" with the Lord may have occurred several years ago, and even though it may have taken you several years to work through these seven essential elements of the Christian walk, you will probably recall having some of the same kinds of questions and "new realizations" about what the Christian life is all about.

> *Once Satan deceives us into believing that a "conservative" lifestyle is synonymous with a "Christian" lifestyle he has for all intents and purposes rendered us ineffective servants for Christ's Kingdom.*

With research showing that only one in twenty adults who profess to be Christians actually has a developed Christian worldview,* The Seven Days of Christians

---

* *The respected Christian researcher George Barna reports that only one in twenty adult Christians has a developed Christian worldview and only one in two pastors.* www.barna.org

can be most helpful in overcoming what may be the most effective weapon that Satan has in his arsenal.

The reason for this is that the discussion over cultural concerns becomes one of a liberal man's opinion versus a conservative man's opinion. Obviously, the missing element in that debate is God and the inability of sinful man to arrive at the truth apart from God's perfect counsel. The ramifications of this will be discussed in Day Four, but for now it is worth noting the disturbing possibility that many of our "Christian" friends may, in fact, only be "conservatives" and on their way to living in eternal torment in Hell, unless someone explains the situation to them and they repent.

While such an unfortunate situation is hopefully not the case for you, it may be for someone you care about, and if so, The Seven Days of Christians would be an ideal way for them to recognize the true state of their eternal condition. Others may find The Seven Days of Christians helpful in identifying and tying down any "loose ends" regarding their walk with Christ. Since all of us are "works in progress," there is no shame in identifying the habits from which we need repenting. Indeed, how blessed are we when someone, some sermon or some book points out a way in which we may be unintentionally bringing dishonor to Christ. Any "shame" should be reserved for those who are hesitant to seriously examine their Christian walk in order to keep their strong areas strong and to strengthen their weak areas.

Jesus gave His all in redeeming us from our former sinful lifestyle, and we should give our all (our whole heart) in living for Him in as consistent a manner as we can.

> *And now, Israel, what does the LORD your God require of you, but to fear the LORD your God, to walk in all His ways and to love Him, to serve the LORD your God with all your heart and with all your soul, and to keep the commandments of the LORD and His statutes which I command you today for your good?* DEUTERONOMY 10.12-13

> *Blessed are those who keep His testimonies, who seek Him with the whole heart!...With my whole heart I have sought You; Oh, let me not wander from Your commandments!* PSALM 119.2, 10

269

Blessed are those who hunger and thirst for righteousness, for they shall be filled. MATTHEW 5.6

Brethren, I do not count myself to have apprehended; but one thing I do, forgetting those things which are behind and reaching forward to those things which are ahead, I press toward the goal for the prize of the upward call of God in Christ Jesus. PHILIPPIANS 3.13-14

Each "day" should help you gain greater clarity in how to use your God-given abilities to bring glory to Christ's Kingdom in all phases of your lifestyle and in all the situations in which God chooses to place you. Regardless of where you are in your Christian walk, The Seven Days of Christians will very likely highlight some areas that need improving.

Enjoy the walk!

EUPHORIA!
Ecstatic about being a member of Christ's Kingdom

We begin this day with an attitude that is most thankful and most grateful for God's undeserved mercy toward us. For the first time ever, and only as a result of the Holy Spirit's work in our heart, we see how vile we are in God's sight. We also realize how far we have strayed from God's will. [1] Man, whom God made perfect in Adam and Eve, has made himself and his creation imperfect through his disrespect of God's laws. [2] We also see how we had previously viewed ourselves as "the potter," when in reality, we are nothing more than "clay in the potter's hand." [3]

In the fast-pace of the 21st century we may not take much time to reflect on what it means to be a Christian (since few people take any time to reflect on anything in our culture), but the esteemed independent Pastor Jeremiah Burroughs lived during times when people did think and meditate upon God's Word, and in 1654 he penned these electric words:

> *That we should be called "the sons of God" – that we wretched, base, vile sinners; that we, not angels, should be called not servants, not friends only, but that we should be called the sons of God; even we who were the children of the devil, as firebrands of hell in ourselves; that we should not only be plucked out of the fire, but be called the sons of God, not only be sons, but this should be made known that we should be called the sons of God; this excellent and blessed state of ours*

271

is spiritual, and is hidden from the world. ...The truth is,
we know but very little ourselves of the blessedness of this
condition....but we know that when He shall appear we shall
be like Him. [4]

During Burroughs' lifetime people didn't try to con themselves about how horrible they were in the sight of God as non-Christians. Neither did they attempt to deceive themselves about how desperately they needed His redeeming hand to pluck them out of the tormenting fires of hell. Since they were aware of their "old" condition, they were most appreciative of their "new" condition. We would do well to recapture that attitude by reminding ourselves that no matter how "moral" and "socially acceptable" our non-Christian lifestyle was, it was still putrid in the sight of God.

Before receiving their supernatural heart transplant, non-Christians don't see themselves as God sees them, and without a belief in a transcendent Creator God, they view themselves as nothing more than "biological accidents." For them there is no "meaning" for being alive, so they attempt to create meaning out of their work, or their possessions, or their relationships, or their lifestyle. They make such statements as: "If I can make a certain amount of money," or "If we could move into a certain neighborhood," or "If I could attend a certain school, then I would be happy." Yet, with the achievement of each goal, non-Christians find the hoped for "satisfaction" missing, so they set higher goals and throw all of their energies into achieving them, only to discover that, once achieved, there is still no lasting satisfaction. In King Solomon's words, the non-Christian lifestyle is "vanity and grasping after wind." Solomon, is described as being "wiser than all men," [5] and certainly no one has ever had more resources at his disposal than he to attempt to achieve satisfaction and peace of mind. Yet, in spite of his wealth and resources, he failed to achieve peace of mind apart from God.

I made my works great, I built myself houses, and planted
myself vineyards. I made myself gardens and orchards, and I
planted all kinds of fruit trees in them. I made myself water
pools from which to water the growing trees of the grove. I
acquired male and female servants, and had servants born
in my house. Yes, I had greater possessions of herds and flocks

than all who were in Jerusalem before me. I also gathered for
myself silver and gold and the special treasures of kings and of
the provinces. I acquired male and female singers, the delights
of the sons of men, and musical instruments of all kinds.
So I became great and excelled more than all who were
before me in Jerusalem. Also my wisdom remained with me.
Whatever my eyes desired I did not keep from them. I did not
withhold my heart from any pleasure, for my heart rejoiced
in all my labor; and this was my reward from all my labor.
Then I looked on all the works that my hands had done and on
the labor in which I had toiled; and indeed all was vanity and
grasping for the wind. There was no profit under the sun.
ECCLESIASTES 2.4-11

Solomon continued to reflect on the meaninglessness and vanity of a non-Christian lifestyle by explaining how he "hated" his labor because once he died the fruits of all of his hard work would be passed into the hands of someone who may squander all that he worked for during his life.

Then I hated all my labor in which I had toiled under the
sun, because I must leave it to the man who will come after
me. And who knows whether he will be wise or a fool? Yet
he will rule over all my labor in which I toiled and in which
I have shown myself wise under the sun. This also is vanity.
Therefore I turned my heart and despaired of all the labor in
which I had toiled under the sun. For there is a man whose
labor is with wisdom, knowledge, and skill; yet he must
leave his heritage to a man who has not labored for it. This
also is vanity and a great evil. For what has man for all his
labor, and for the striving of his heart with which he has
toiled under the sun? For all his days are sorrowful, and his
work burdensome; even in the night his heart takes no rest.
This also is vanity.   ECCLESIASTES 2.18-23

Solomon concludes his chapter on the vanity of life without God by adding how life as a Christian dramatically changes one's worldview. Yes, Christians can enjoy the world, and we do that by focusing on what

273

we can control today, and not worry about what may or may not happen tomorrow. He writes that, as Christians, we can comfort ourselves with the truth that God is in complete control of His creation which means that the burden we once carried around to effect specific results by taking specific actions has been lifted from us by God's strong hands. Our only responsibility now is to incorporate the biblical ethics in which we profess to believe into our daily decision-making and let God take care of the when and how of effecting the change He desires. So, at days end, even though we may not achieve our desired results, we have helped to achieve His desired results through our faithful obedience. In addition, we also have the assurance that our successes or failures during that day did not come as a surprise to God and that He is working "everything together for good to those who are called according to His purpose." [6]

> *Nothing is better for a man than that he should eat and drink, and that his soul should enjoy good in his labor. This also, I saw, was from the hand of God. For who can eat, or who can have enjoyment, more than I? For God gives wisdom and knowledge and joy to a man who is good in His sight; but to the sinner He gives the work of gathering and collecting, that he may give to him who is good before God. This also is vanity and grasping for the wind.* ECCLESIASTES 2.24-26

19th century British pastor Charles Bridges explains that Solomon's words, at first glance, may sound capricious:

> *Let him give diligence to prove his character – "good before God;" and then, in the confidence of the Divine favor, let him rejoice in his temporal blessings. This pleasure of "eating and drinking" is totally distinct from the mere animal appetite. It recognizes the Christian principle —"Whether you eat of drink—do all to the glory to God." (1 Corinthians 10.31) The world, with all its legitimate enjoyments, is the Christian's portion, 1 Corinthians 3.22 making its pleasures subordinate, not primary.* [7]

Bridges continues to place our current situations and circumstances in the proper context of God's Big Picture with these encouraging words:

> *Say then —Christian sufferer —does thine heart rebel, to*
> *see the wicked prosper, and thyself in woe? Say, wouldst thou*
> *change? Is he better off than thou? Are his earthly blessings*
> *better than thy grace? Is not Jesus more than silver and gold*
> *to thee? Hast thou the lesser portion, because thou hast the*
> *Lord? Leave thyself with God, and be at peace. Let this*
> *living faith preserve thee from that brooding discontent,*
> *which seems to throw a cloud upon the goodness of thy most*
> *gracious God. (Chapter 2.24; 3.12; 5.18; 1 Timothy 4.3-5)*
> *Never suppose that the overflow of temporal enjoyments*
> *can form the chief good. Enjoy the gifts of God—whatever*
> *portion of them be allotted to thee, as the stream from the*
> *fountain of his special interest in thee. (Genesis 33.5) This*
> *enjoyment can never be in unholy sensualism, or unrestrained*
> *indulgence —but with that Christian mirth—cheered—as*
> *in the bright era of the Church (Acts 2.46)—with the smile*
> *of Divine acceptance, which makes "a continual feast." Let*
> *this be our abiding portion all the days of our life—every*
> *new day bringing a fresh gift of God for his service and glory.*
> *Whatever we may lose, the grand interest is secured.* [8]

Solomon next reminds us that as members of God's chosen army who will "inherit the earth" through our obedience, [9] we have no biblical reason to exhibit anything but an upbeat attitude, because even though we will encounter "days of vanity," the gospel on which we base our lives includes, "glad tidings of great joy." [10]

> *Go, eat your bread with joy, and drink your wine with a*
> *merry heart; for God has already accepted your works. Let*
> *your garments always be white, and set your head lack no*
> *oil. Live joyfully with the wife whom you love all the days of*
> *your vain life which He has given you under the sun, all your*
> *days of vanity; for that is your portion in life, and in the labor*
> *which you perform under the sun.* ECCLESIASTES 9.7-9

Bridges explains why we have no reason to complain:

> *The charge of melancholy is a libel upon religion. The man that is an heir to "a lively hope, anchored within the veil"[11] —what ground has he for melancholy? Why—we find him "greatly rejoicing," even in the midst of "heaviness."[12] A sinner has no right—a Christian—supported by Divine strength, favor, and consolation, has no reason – to complain. His treasure includes the promise of all that he wants, in deep sense of his own unworthiness, and of his Father's undeserved love.*

Even though we know that we can't "do enough" to repay the debt that we owe to Jesus for redeeming us, we are nevertheless determined to give our best effort toward bringing glory and honor to Him in everything we say and do. While we feel that a great weight has been lifted off of us, we are not certain exactly what's expected of us as new members of Christ's Kingdom.

- What books or DVDs should we buy to help our growth in God's grace and knowledge, and which church and/or Bible study should we join?
- Should we change jobs?
- What about our friends, do we need to replace them with "Christian" friends?
- What about our parents, and/or our brothers and sisters who may not be Christians; how should we meet with them to discuss our new faith?

Questions such as these can be addressed by the officers of your church. Each of them has been exactly where you are, and have in all probability assisted other new Christians in getting their brand new supernatural legs ready to walk with Christ. However, there is one large caution to keep squarely in mind: While Christ has gained a member of His Kingdom, Satan has lost a member, and even though he can't "undo" your divine membership, he can and will do all that he can to minimize the effectiveness of your service for Christ. Satan well knows that the more obedient you and other Christians are, the quicker his work as the Great Deceiver will come to an inglorious end.

Satan has thousands of years of experience honing his tactics of lies and deceit, but you, as a rookie in Christ's Kingdom have the Creator God in your corner. And, among other things, the Creator God of the universe has spelled out in clear detail how to accomplish the purpose for which you have been called. So, let the Bible be your guide as you encounter Satan's various tactics. Following is a listing of some of his most successful deceptions. They are discussed in detail during Day Four

DECEPTION 1 Personal salvation is the main goal of the Bible.

DECEPTION 2 The certainty of cultural defeat and that we will only "stir things up," and cause a commotion by attempting to obey God by incorporating biblical ethics into all aspects of our lifestyle.

DECEPTION 3 Attempting to "reform" public schools is much better than providing a Christian education for our children.

DECEPTION 4 Imagining that the 1st Table of God's Law (commandments 1-4) is optional to the events and circumstances happening outside our homes and churches.

DECEPTION 5 The myth that life has two mutually exclusive realms: "religious" and "real life," and that we can rely on our common sense and wisdom to successfully solve cultural issues.

DECEPTION 6 Conservative moralism is encouraged to convince us that we can "legislate" our way out of our cultural problems by substituting the central government of the state for the divinely prescribed self-governing spheres of the individual, family, church and state that provide personal liberty.

Each of these Satanic deceptions is premised on the idea that Christianity is merely a "moralistic add-on" to your former lifestyle. Satan could only wish that this were true, because that would mean he was still in control of your life (and this earth). As he knows from first-hand experience, however, his kingdom came crashing down when Jesus defeated him during the first century. [13] The mission that each Christian has had since the first century has been to help "mop up" Jesus' conclusive victory through our consistent obedience to His Word. [14]

The Parable of the Mustard Seed:

Jesus instructed His first century followers in how His Kingdom would slowly but surely spread over the entire earth, from a few disciples in one geographic region to millions of disciples in all the nations of the earth.

The kingdom of heaven is like a mustard seed, which a man took and sowed in his field, which indeed is the least of all the seeds, but when it is grown it is greater than the herbs and becomes a tree, so that the birds of the air come and nest in its branches.   MATTHEW 13.31-32

The Parable of the Leaven:

The kingdom of heaven is like leaven, which a woman took and hid in three measures of meal till it was all leavened.
      MATTHEW 13.33

These parables of Jesus echo the prophecies of Ezekiel, [15] Daniel [16] and Habakkuk, whose optimistic and encouraging words are familiar to us all:

For the earth will be filled with the knowledge of the glory of the LORD, as the waters cover the sea.   HABAKKUK 2.14

So, as you begin your relationship with Christ, do so with every assurance that you are on the "winning team." (See Day Six) You can also expect your worldview and lifestyle to undergo a complete transformation. Some of your former habits will be easily and quickly replaced with God-honoring ones, and others will require a longer and much more difficult battle to discard. But, with the Holy Spirit's guidance, direction and assistance, you can be certain that you will be able to bring glory and honor to God in all areas of your lifestyle.

•The lifestyles of a Christian and a conservative, law-abiding, moralistic, good citizen are similar, but the motivation for why each lives as he does is very different (and will ultimately determine whether they live forever in heaven or hell).

•What is this "dramatic difference" and why do Christians have it and conservative non-Christians don't?

•Now that you know that you are "clay in the Potter's hands," instead of being the potter, how should this realization change the way you make decisions?

•Why is it critically important for you to understand that Christianity is not a "moralistic add-on" to your worldview and lifestyle, but a complete transformation of it?

•As a Christian, you are "more than a conqueror through Him who loves you." [17] In what ways do you think that this truth will impact your worldview and lifestyle?

NOTES

1 Isaiah 53.6

2 Genesis 1.31; 3.11; Psalm 19.1; 101.2-3; Lamentations 4.1

3 Jeremiah 18.6

4 Burroughs, Jeremiah, *Hope*, (Soli Deo Gloria, [1654], 2005), pp. 1-2

5 1 Kings 4.31

6 Romans 8.28

7 Bridges, Charles, *Ecclesiastes*, (Banner of Truth Trust, [1860], 1961), pp.45-46

8 Bridges, *ibid.*, *Ecclesiastes*, pp.206-207

9 Psalm 37.11; Matthew 5.5

10 Luke 2.10

11 1 Peter 1.3; Hebrews 6.19

12 1 Peter 1.6

13 Matthew 4.1-11

14 Matthew 28.18-20

15 Ezekiel 17.23-24

16 Daniel 4.22

17 Romans 8.37

DECISION-MAKING
*How can I base my worldview, lifestyle and
decision-making upon biblical ethics?*

ractically overnight everything's changed. Our old non-Christian
processes of thinking and making decisions need to be replaced by
new processes of Christian thoughts and actions (remember that our actions flow from our thoughts). [18] Like a first day on a new job, we want
to begin our Christian calling by putting our best foot forward, but we
find that there are two bumps in our path on which we can easily stub
our toes.

Bump 1   For the first time in our life we are motivated to put the
interests of others above our self-interests. We also are motivated to study the Bible so that we will know more about
how God wants us to live and govern ourselves. But when
we begin looking for fellow Christians to serve as role models, we have a difficult time identifying them. Most of the
Christians we see have worldviews and lifestyles that are
identical to non-Christians with the exception that they go
to church and are more moralistic in their behavior and ethics (Satan's Deceptions 1 & 6).

Bump 2   Most of the worldviews and lifestyles of the Christians
we meet indicate that God created two separate realms of

life that must be kept apart at all costs. One is a "religious realm" which is where we talk about how great it is to be a Christian and this realm, we discover, is to be confined to the inside of our home and church. The other is a "real life realm" where we act in a moralistic manner, and make decisions according to our rules and our wisdom, instead of according to God's revealed wisdom. (Satan's Deception 5)

For many of us, the consequence of our new Christian lifestyle is not very much different than our old non-Christian lifestyle. We've just "added" the 2nd Table of God's Law (commandments 5-10: honor those in authority, don't kill, steal, lie, cheat, covet) to our behavior and we attend church and talk about God in our home, but we still approach our daily decision-making the same way we always have by trusting-in and relying-upon our own wisdom, logic and pragmatism.

Notice I said this scenario describes *many* of us. There are a few who feel compelled to "live" for Christ in all of their situations and circumstances, and not just "act" favorably toward Him inside their homes and churches, and/or when they are around fellow Christians. Since these brothers and sisters see the rest of us separating "religion" from "real life," they mistakenly think that the only way they can live fulltime for Christ is to either go into the ministry, become a missionary, or else by starting or joining a business that has "Christian" in its name. These brothers are held in high esteem by us and we refer to them as being "dedicated Christians," or "devoted Christians" to the faith.

As for the rest of us, we do what we can on Sundays and Wednesdays inside our homes and churches to bring glory and honor to our Savior with those "religious" parts of our lifestyle. Pause and think about what you just read ... "With those 'religious' parts of our lifestyle ..." That doesn't sound very good does it? Is this what Christ had in mind when He called us into His Kingdom? Before the Holy Spirit performed supernatural heart surgery on us we had both feet planted firmly in Satan's kingdom. Does it sound acceptable for us now to have one foot planted in Christ's Kingdom with our other foot still in Satan's kingdom? I hope not!

On Day Two none of us has very much personal holiness, because that is a character trait that we will develop, cultivate and improve upon for the remainder of our life on earth. The ultimate goal of personal holiness is to "hate every false way," [19] and the more we study Scripture, the more we will recognize how all-encompassing that goal is for our worldview and lifestyle. For example, a common high priority for new Christians is to share their new faith with others. However, they may be puzzled about how to do that, since they have never had any "evangelism training." What follows is not to be taken as a slam against such training. Indeed, I whole-heartedly encourage evangelism training, but a person shouldn't feel "unqualified" to be a witness for Christ if he hasn't had such formal training.

When Moses was giving the Israelites advice for how to live in the Promised Land, he told them that they had been instructed by Jehovah through him in how to live and govern themselves and if they were careful to live according to those truths they would not only have successful lives, but would have their new non-Christian neighbors come to ask them how to become Christians! In essence, Moses told them:

> *Since there are no Christians in the Promised Land, you may be tempted to compromise the biblical ethics you know in order to build a relationship with them, imagining that after you've established a 'friendship' with them you can present the gospel. However, don't fall for this temptation because such rationalistic and pragmatic thinking reflects man's thoughts, not God's thoughts. Whereas man has to manipulate people and circumstances in order to get people to act in a certain manner, God's Word and the Holy Spirit simply changes their heart! You know this, so live according to what God has taught you and trust in His sovereign control of your non-Christian neighbors.*

Let's listen carefully to the inspired words of Moses:

Surely I have taught you statutes and judgments, just as the LORD my God commanded me, that you should act according to them in the land which you go to possess. Therefore be careful to observe them; for this is your wisdom and your understanding in the sight of the peoples who will hear all these statutes, and say, "Surely this great nation is a wise and understanding people. For what great nation is there that has God so near to it, as the LORD our God is to us, for whatever reason we may call upon Him? And what great nation is there that has such statutes and righteous judgments as are in all this law which I set before you this day? Only take heed to yourself, and diligently keep yourself, lest you forget the things your eyes have seen, and lest they depart from your heart all the days of your life. And teach them to your children and your grandchildren. DEUTERONOMY 4.5-9*

God's message to the Israelites is identical to His message to us:

> *By consistently basing our worldview and lifestyle upon the biblical truths in which we profess to believe, we will provide godly role models for our ungodly neighbors. We will also be providing godly role models for new Christians to follow in their everyday behavior.*

Sadly, with only an estimated one in twenty adult Christians having a developed Christian worldview, there are not many Christian role models for new Christians. But we still have God's inerrant Word, which clearly spells out how we should live, so if you are having trouble finding a suitable Christian brother or sister to serve as your "discipler," turn to the true and perfect Discipler, the triune God of the Bible and your personal Lord, Savior and King, Jesus Christ and He will light your path with His priceless wisdom in His revealed Word.

The purpose of **The Seven Days of Christians** is not to point out the fact that someone is sinning by either doing or not doing something, because we're all guilty of that. Rather, the point is to explain why certain behaviors we are demonstrating to our non-Christian neighbors are not presenting Christianity in its true light, and since we are the only "Bible" they may read, we need to be careful that our testimony to them is accurate.

DAY 2 THINK ABOUT

How's your walk with Christ?

Before you answer, allow me to help you begin your answer by asking: "How has your thinking process changed since you became a Christian?" If your answer doesn't include the phrase: "My thinking and the resulting decision-making process has changed 180-degrees from what it used to be," you are very likely not honoring Christ with your walk.

As you work your way through all seven "Days" it should become clear that you cannot honor Jesus with your walk when you, in essence, confine Him to a "Jesus Backpack" that you carry throughout your life. According to this mindset, we have several "Christian Actions" that we periodically pull out of the backpack in order to show non-Christians that we really do believe what we say we believe. After a few weeks, however, we tire of demonstrating for a cultural issue, or letter writing, or legislative lobbying, so we put that particular "Christian action" back into our backpack and continue to demonstrate a lifestyle that is virtually indistinguishable from our non-Christian neighbors.

The following illustration shows how dealing with the "fruit" of the collective non-Christian worldview in which we are currently living will not affect the change in our culture that we desire. To achieve that goal we must deal with the "root" cause.

The Jesus Backpack

The "Fruit"

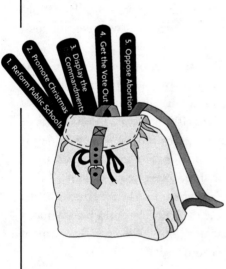

1. Reform Public Schools
2. Promote Christmas
3. Display the Commandments
4. Get the Vote Out
5. Oppose Abortion

The "Root"

1. Instead of obeying the 1st Commandment to worship only the triune God of Scripture.
2. Instead of objecting to ungodly politically-correct policies (and curriculum).
3. Instead of encouraging churches to counsel (and perhaps discipline) members who are legislators, judges and CEOs for making decisions that do not conform to Scripture.
4. Instead of churches instructing their members in how Christian civil rulers should govern.
5. Instead of promoting the idea that our civil laws should be based upon biblical ethics. (or do we want to give the impression that man is smarter than God when it comes to determining how we should live and govern ourselves?).

What must be recognized is that our "Jesus Backpack" mentality conforms to the way non-Christians approach life. For them, there is no definitive way to live, so their worldview and lifestyle is characterized by different aspects of a person's life that are "acted out" in whatever ways that are supported by the latest opinion polls. Rather than attempting to carry Christ around on our back, we need to obey His commands that we carry Him around inside our heart. [20] The difference between these two lifestyles is dramatic:

- ✓ If Jesus is in our backpack, we periodically act for Him.
- ✓ If Jesus is in our heart, we consistently live for Him.

This is not to imply that any of the isolated "actions" in the Jesus Backpack are not worthwhile in and of themselves. What they demonstrate is indignation among Christians for having Jesus' truths blasphemed in the media, in the workplace and in the state-mandated school system. The main reason our brothers and sisters are periodically "acting" for Jesus, is that few Pastors are explaining to them how to continuously "live" for Him.

Where did Christian employees and Christian college students learn to think like this? Did their parents teach them? Probably not. Did their churches teach them? Maybe. Did the public schools teach them. Definitely.

What other reason could explain some of America's largest corporations dishonoring God with their decisions? Do we think that 100 percent of their employees are non-Christians? Why would university students be more concerned about a "Christmas" tree being called a "Holiday" tree when, for the remainder of the year, they are subjected to a blasphemous curriculum and deferential treatment just because they are Christians?

The apostle Paul tells us that, as Christians, "the spirit of the world" that we used to have has been replaced with the "Spirit who is from God so that we might know the things that have been freely given to us by God." [21]

Explain why you think it is that some of your Christian friends
(who, by the very definition of Christianity, "know" the truth)
refuse to incorporate biblical ethics into their daily decision-making?

Ask them for their reasons and you will see that they will either be based upon pragmatism, rationalizations, or a misinterpretation of Scripture. Do you think you can assist them in recognizing the need for externalizing their faith? (By the way, how are you doing in "exiting" your beliefs from your home, church and/or small group Bible study into all areas of your lifestyle?)

- What message are you sending to non-Christians who observe your daily decisions (which result from your worldview)?
- Review your most recent decisions to determine whether they were based upon biblical ethics, or non-biblical ones (pragmatism and/or rationalization)?
- Have your decisions today, and their resulting actions "taken ground for Christ's Kingdom" by bringing glory and honor to God? Or has the motivation behind them been to bring glory and honor to yourself?
- Ask yourself: "Is this decision a conservative response to a liberal action, or a Christian response to an ungodly action?"

In bringing all of this together, it might be helpful to recall that since we are children of God, how does our Father in heaven view your day-to-day decisions? Asked another way: How is it with your children? Would you prefer that they "acted" for you in certain isolated situations because that's what they knew you expected, or would you prefer that they "live" for you in all situations and circumstances because they can't imagine any other acceptable way to live in order to bring "honor" to you? [22]

The euphoria of Day One has led to some puzzling questions on Day Two, but you will discover a realization on Day Three that will provide a pivotal point in your service for Christ.

NOTES
18 Matthew 15.19
19 Psalm 119.104; See *Return to Sender*, Buddy Hanson, (Hanson Group) for a detailed study on how to live a biblically obedient (holy) lifestyle.
20 Jeremiah 24.7; Ezekiel 11.19; Matthew 5.8; 6.21; Colossians 3.15
21 2 Corinthians 2.12
22 Exodus 20.12

SUBSTITUTING GOD'S THOUGHTS
FOR OUR THOUGHTS
Living by God's rules, instead of man's rules

ay Three begins, appropriately enough, at "the beginning" as we look at how Adam and Eve fell for Satan's temptation to base their worldview and lifestyles upon their wisdom, logic and pragmatism. Adam and Eve loved God, but they wanted to live according to their rules instead of His rules. Every aspect of our life has rules:

✓ **Vocation.** There are particular office hours, and both written and unwritten rules for conducting ourselves as we carry out our duties.
✓ **Sports.** All sports have referees and/or umpires to see that the games are played according to the rules.
✓ **Computers**. Computers will do what we ask of them as long as we ask them according the rules of how they are programmed.
✓ **Driving.** Road signs and traffic signals guide and direct us to safety on the highways and byways.

God gave Adam and Eve the ability to choose, just as He gives us the ability to choose. We are not pre-programmed robots; we make our own choices. The difference, however, between our choices and the original choices of Adam and Eve is that they had the ability to make the correct decision. As we all know, they didn't make the correct decision and as a result, everyone who has been born after them has come into this world unable (because of sin) to make God-honoring (correct) decisions. Yes, we make decisions according to our "free will," but the Bible tells us that until the Holy Spirit gives us a new spiritual heart, our will is "free" only to make God-dishonoring decisions. In the inspired words of "the Preacher"

> *God made man upright, but they have sought out many*
> *schemes.* ECCLESIASTES 7.29

Let's go back to the first conversation God had with Noah and his family as they stepped out of the ark and onto dry land:

> *I will never again curse the ground for man's sake, although*
> *the imagination of man's heart is evil from his youth.*
> GENESIS 8.21

Now, let's fast forward in time to the sixth century B.C. and hear how the prophet Jeremiah describes the human decision-making condition:

> *The heart is deceitful above all things, and desperately*
> *wicked; who can know it?* JEREMIAH 17.9

King Solomon similarly decries

> *Truly the hearts of the sons of men are full of evil; madness is*
> *in their hearts ...* ECCLESIASTES 9.3

If we look to New Testament examples, we will find corroborating statements by Jesus and Paul:

> *For out of the heart proceed evil thoughts, murders,*
> *adulteries, fornications, thefts, false witness, blasphemies.*
> MATTHEW 15.19

> *For I know that in me (that is, in my flesh) nothing good*
> *dwells.* ROMANS 7.18

Paul continues by stating

> *Because the carnal mind is enmity against God; for it is not*
> *subject to the law of God, nor indeed can be. So then, those*
> *who are in the flesh cannot please God.* ROMANS 8.7-8

Obviously, this is not a pretty picture. Indeed, it's a very disturbing one. As Christians, we want to bring honor to Jesus with our decisions, yet throughout Scripture we are told that by depending upon our wisdom, logic and pragmatism, it will be impossible to honor Jesus with any decision we make! Jeremiah characterizes such self-centered thinking by Christians as having their heart "depart from the LORD." [23] Since the only way that any of us becomes a Christian is for the Holy Spirit to "write the law upon our hearts," [24] the thought of having our heart "depart from the LORD" should be one that is most unsettling. Isaiah adds this "woe" for those who think their own thoughts:

> *"Woe to the rebellious children," says the LORD, "Who take*
> *counsel, but not of Me, and who devise plans, but not of My*
> *Spirit, that they may add sin to sin; who walk to go down*
> *to Egypt, and have not asked My advice, to strengthen*
> *themselves in the strength of Pharaoh, and to trust in the*
> *shadow of Egypt! Therefore the strength of Pharaoh shall be*
> *your shame, and trust in the shadow of Egypt shall be your*
> *humiliation.* ISAIAH 30.1-3

Notice that Jehovah tells the Israelites that if they want to trust in the wisdom and strength of the state, instead of in His wisdom and strength, then that's exactly what their wisdom and strength shall be and the result will be "humiliation" instead of "holiness." Jesus' half-brother James makes the same point by stating that if we lean on our own wisdom we will be "double-minded" and "unstable in all of our ways." [25]

As these verses teach, the deceitfulness of our sinful heart means that the only way we can be certain that our decisions are "true" and God-honoring is for us to re-think God's thoughts. When Jehovah asks Job: "Who is this who darkens counsel by words without knowledge?" [26] His meaning to Job (and the rest of us) is: "You may think that you are smart, but without filtering your thoughts and knowledge through my revealed Word, you are foolish!" We may not like to be reminded of this, and certainly non-Christians would dispute it, but the truth is "if the light that is in us is darkness, then so will our view of the world be dark."[27] Non-Christians have no excuse for the "darkness" of their worldview, because in their unredeemed state of being separate from God, it's the natural way for them to view things. We, however, know better and by consistently comparing our decisions to the biblical ethics in which we profess to believe, we can keep from falling prey to Satan's temptations to make our decisions based solely upon our wisdom. So, as we approach each decision, may we remind ourselves that it is in "Christ's light that we see light." [28]

We are in need of sound biblical instruction, and one of our top priorities should be to look for someone to "disciple" us and not hesitate to provide caring correction to our daily walk. In addition to not being "self-willed" [29] we need to demonstrate a humility that is appreciative of the instruction and correction we receive. [30] In other words, we need to change our mindset from looking for excuses not to obey God's instructions to one that looks for excuses to obey His Word. We should eliminate from our worldview and lifestyle such rationalizations as:

- ❖ The Bible is true, but that principle was meant for another time. Since we are living in modern times, we are smarter than those who lived in the agrarian culture of the first century.
- ❖ I know that's what the Bible says, but there is no way we could live that way today. It would be nice if we could, but there's just no way.

If we could only make ourselves repeat such thoughts out loud we would see how lame and dishonoring to Jesus they are, because what both are presupposing is that we are smarter than God and our wisdom is all that is needed to live successfully in 21st century America. Adam and Eve would be proud of our self-centered thinking! So may we all begin today with a passion to look for reasons to obey God's Word, not for reasons to disobey it.

Dramatic Changes in Our Walk with Christ

- Instead of being a completely self-centered individual, you have begun to notice that you are sincerely concerned for the welfare and the priorities of others. PHILIPPIANS 2.4

- In addition, when you have a decision to make you find yourself filtering it through the biblical ethics you know, which inspires you to want to study Scripture so you will learn additional ethics to incorporate into your worldview. MICAH 6.8; HEBREWS 5.13-14

- You realize that you can base your lifestyle upon the truth, while your non-Christian neighbors only have lies. Their pluralistic approach to life, where they refuse to publicly profess to follow any particular god, leads them to walk "in the futility of their minds" (Romans 1.21-22) because they are excluding God's perfect wisdom from their decision-making. Their vain, purposeless and meaningless existence was well stated in Day One by King Solomon. ECCLESIASTES 2.4-26

- You also know that you will be able to spend eternity with fellow Christians and every time you think about how glorious and enjoyable that will be you marvel at why Jesus would have given His life to pay for your sin debt so that when God the Father hears your prayers, He views you through Jesus' perfectly obedient lifestyle. GALATIANS 3.13

- You have learned not to lean on our own understanding. PROVERBS 3.5

- You are learning to look at the things which are not seen. 2 CORINTHIANS 4.18

- You have contentment. 1 TIMOTHY 6.6; PHILIPPIANS 4.11-12

- You have lasting satisfaction. JOHN 6.35

- You have true rest for your soul JEREMIAH 6.16; MATTHEW 11.28

- You love God's law PSALM 119.113

- You hate every false way PSALM 119.128

- You have been given righteousness PROVERBS 11.18

During the first three "Days" of your walk with Christ you have been the recipient of some profound changes. Twelve of those changes are highlighted in the "Dramatic Changes in Our Walk with Christ" chart. As you read through it, note how many of those changes you have already made an integral part of your daily walk. Don't be surprised if you think of additional biblically ethical changes that you can incorporate into your lifestyle!

The point is that with all of your trust in the work that God has done inside your heart, why are you hesitant to extend your trust in His wisdom to the circumstances and situations happening outside your heart. After all, how "wise" is it to lean on your faulty wisdom for living when He has delivered to you the perfect instruction manual? Doesn't David urge us to "trust in the LORD and do good…and He shall give you the desires of your heart. …Commit your way to the LORD, trust also in Him…and He shall bring forth your righteousness as the light, and your justice as the noonday." [31] And doesn't David's son, Solomon, admonish us to

> *Trust in the LORD with all your heart, and lean not on your own understanding; in all your ways acknowledge Him, and He shall direct your paths. Do not be wise in your own eyes; fear the LORD and depart from evil.* PROVERBS 3.5-7

The Chronicler provides another advantage for "leaning on the LORD by stating: "The eyes of the LORD run to and fro throughout the whole earth to show Himself strong on behalf of those whose heart is loyal to Him." [32] On the one hand we have our Creator's perfect wisdom and resources to back up our daily actions, and on the other hand we have our faulty wisdom and our limited resources. Each of us knows that we should trust in our Creator more than ourselves, or in fellow creatures, so why are we so inconsistent in doing that? I believe the answer is that we are "finicky" trusters. Instead of viewing God's Word as a full meal of wisdom and having the attitude of eating everything on our plate, we view the contents and only choose to eat those portions that "look like" they taste good. That means that in some aspects of our lives, we are prone to trust in God, while in other areas, we rarely give His wisdom any consideration and trust-in our own wisdom and resources.

The fault in such "finicky trusting" is discussed by several inspired writers. Solomon informs us we should not condition our obedience upon being able to "figure everything out."

> *For though a man labors to discover it, yet he will not find it;*
> *moreover, though a wise man attempts to know it, he will not*
> *be able to find it.*　　　　　ECCLESIASTES 8.17

Paul proclaims that God's wisdom and knowledge, as well as His judgments are "past finding out." [33] So, rather than attempt to bring God's mysteries down to our level of understanding, we should attempt to raise our level of reasoning toward His level. Instead of making our logic and wisdom the norm for whether we should live according to a biblical ethic, we should make God's wisdom and logic the norm. Otherwise we will, in Jeremiah's words, be "following the counsels and the dictates of our evil hearts, and will go backward and not forward." [34]

By reminding ourselves that God is the Creator, and makes no mistakes, and we are creatures who are full of mistakes, we should have no problem in following the advice of Jehovah to the sons of Korah to

> *Be still, and know that I am God.*　　　　　PSALM 46.10

Whether or not a person is successful in "being still" will depend upon what they "see" on God's "plate of wisdom." Non-Christians like to say, "Seeing is believing," and since they can't "see God," they don't believe in Him. But Christians view the world through "supernatural" lenses which come with our supernatural heart transplant, and therefore "see" an entirely different world. The issue, then, is how do we view the world, because how we look at it will determine what we see. Christians are commanded to live by "faith" in the way God sees the world and describes it to us in His Word, [35] not by physical sight alone. By failing to do this we open ourselves up to being influenced by human logic and pragmatism, which will result in our looking for excuses (and circumstances) to disobey God, rather than looking for excuses (and circumstances) to obey Him. Solomon, in addressing an audience that was predominantly farmers, used the following analogy:

He who observes the wind will not sow, and he who regards
the clouds will not reap.   ECCLESIASTES 11.4

This was Solomon's way of saying, "You know that in order to bring forth a harvest you must sow your seeds. Some of you, however, who would rather not work today may decide that because it is windy your seeds will be blown away. Others may say, 'It looks like its going to rain, and since that might wash the seeds away, I'll wait until tomorrow.'" His point being that Farmer A will "see" the end result of not doing what he knows to do and, in order to avoid those unpleasant consequences, will sow his seeds and be blessed with a harvest. On the other hand, Farmer B will "see" numerous excuses for not doing his duty because his focus is on today instead of the consequences of what will happen tomorrow if he doesn't fulfill his duty, with the result being he will "beg during harvest and have nothing." [36]

When we "put a cap" on God's sovereignty by stating, "I know the Bible says that, but that couldn't mean for our times!" We should remind ourselves that God doesn't make mistakes and has put us on the face of the earth to accomplish His will, and has given each of us specific skills and abilities by which we can successfully carry out our duties. This means that there will never be a better or more opportune time for us to do so than n-o-w! Our duty is to guard against having "an evil heart of unbelief:"

> *Beware, brethren, lest there be in any of you an evil heart of*
> *unbelief in departing from the living God; but exhort one*
> *another daily, while it is called "Today," lest any of you be*
> *hardened through the deceitfulness of sin.*
> HEBREWS 3.12-14

Bridges warns us to not be "The slothful man" planting "his hedge of thorns" [37] or crying out in cowardly fear, "There is a lion in the way—a lion in the streets." [38] Bridges continues

> *The trifling discouragements of the "winds and the clouds"*
> *are the appointed trials of faith. And when does our God*

295

honor faith, till he has first tried it? Or when does he fail to honor it, either in the trial or out of it? How little should we have known of the power of faith, the privilege of prayer, the preciousness of the promises, the faithfulness and sympathy of the Savior, if difficulties had not shown to us our weakness, and made the Gospel a Divine reality to our souls! ... Still an halting spirit quenches the glow of Christian energy. Feeble effort ensures defeat. [39]

Once again, we turn to Solomon to provide a simple analogy to explain a complex subject.

> *If the ax is dull, and one does not sharpen the edge, then he must use more strength; but wisdom brings success.*
>
> ECCLESIASTES 10.10

Who would want to argue with this piece of advice from King Solomon? "If you're going to chop wood and your axe is dull, you will have to use more strength," he tells us. "But if you use your wisdom, you will have success." And just what is that "wisdom" that will enable us to have success in chopping wood? Obviously, the answer is to "sharpen our axe" before we begin work. So what does this have to do with the way we approach our daily situations and circumstances? The answer is the same: to sharpen our wisdom and attitude by praying for specific direction and guidance before we take on our daily duties.

Instead of depending upon God to be the exclusive "sharpener" of our axe, and to therefore make us "perfect in our weakness," [40] we often attempt to use His sharpener only part of the time, all the while complaining about how terrible our culture is becoming the other part of our time. We see the seemingly insurmountable mountain the non-Christians have built by capturing control of every institution of cultural influence, then we look at ourselves, and conclude there's no way we can be "more than conquerors through Him who loved us." [41] Our error in reaching this conclusion is to focus primarily upon ourselves and not on God's counsel.

- Does not the prophet Isaiah promise that God:

  Gives power to the weak, and to those who have no might He increases strength.   ISAIAH 40.29

- Are we not "children of God" [42] who have been commanded to pray that our Father's will "will be done on earth as it is in heaven?" [43]

- Have we not been given the Holy Spirit to lead and direct us in our decision-making? [44]

- Doesn't the "sufficiency" for us to successfully accomplish our calling as members of Christ's Kingdom come from God, and not ourselves? [45]

- And whenever we need perfect wisdom and counsel concerning a particular situation or circumstance, hasn't God promised to give it to us? [46]

An axe doesn't sharpen itself. Its owner must take the time and effort to do it, but as we've discussed, such time and effort pays off in huge dividends. Each of us became a member of Christ's Kingdom as a result of the effort of the Holy Spirit upon our hearts, but after that it took our effort to repent and place our faith in Christ. But that only placed us into the Kingdom, and as members we are expected to live according to God's will, not our will (the horribly flawed one from which we were mercifully rescued). God's will commands that we "knock down the gates of hell"[47] and that cannot be done without effort. It means taking a public stand for Christ, which could cost us friendships, our job or even our life. Again this equates to effort. In addition, Satan sets daily enticements to tempt us to revert to making decisions according to the way we made them when we were non-Christians. The following aphorism is often used by sales managers to stress the importance of their sales staff being aggressive in their pursuit of business, because their prospects are going to buy their product or service from someone else, if they don't get to them first. The principle it teaches, however, also applies to us as every morning when we step outside our home. Satan begins tempting us to keep our

297

"old" (non-Christian) habits, and if we are not diligent to put on "new" (Christian) habits we will not win the day. [48]

> Every morning in Africa, a gazelle wakes up. It knows it must run faster than the fastest lion or it will be killed. Every morning a lion wakes up. It knows it must outrun the slowest gazelle or it will starve to death. The moral: It doesn't matter if you are a lion or a gazelle, when the sun comes up, you better be running.

Our calling to expand Christ's Kingdom requires that we do so aggressively, not passively. [49] 20th century seminary professor and biblical commentator William Hendriksen describes it like this:

Therefore it takes vigorous men, men who are eager to fight and to conquer, to overcome Satan and thus to take possession of the kingdom, of all the blessings of salvation. The kingdom, then, is not for weaklings, waverers, or compromisers. It is not for Balaam (2 Peter 2.15), the rich young ruler (Matthew 19.22, Pilate (John 19.12-13), and Demas (2 Timothy 4.10). It is not won by means of deferred prayers, unfulfilled promises, broken resolutions, and hesitant testimonies. It is for strong and sturdy men like Joseph (Genesis 39.9), Nathan (2 Samuel 12.7), Elijah (1 Kings 18.21), Daniel and his three friends (Daniel 1.8; 3.16-18), Mordecai (Esther 3.4), the Peter of Acts 4.20, Stephen (Acts 6.8; 7.51), and Paul (Philippians 3.13-14). And here let us not forget such valiant women as Ruth (Ruth 1.16-18), Deborah (Judges 4), Esther (Esther 4.16), and Lydia (Acts 16.15, 40). [50]

We live in a dynamic universe; a universe in which nothing is "nailed down," because no area of our lives exists in a vacuum. Whether we're a parent, a student, a Christian, or all three, we will never reach a state in which we can say "I've arrived" and can therefore turn our attention to other areas without periodically reviewing our overall walk with Christ to see whether we're still on course.

> *Because of laziness the building decays, and through idleness of hands the house leaks.* ECCLESIASTES 10.18

Solomon gives the example of a building, and even though he wrote this approximately 2,600 years ago, we can still identify with it. The older buildings become, the more frequently repairs are going to become necessary. Roofs wear out and need to be replaced, central heat and air conditioning systems will wear out, rooms will need to be re-painted, etc. Since Solomon is not writing specifically to building contractors, but rather to sinners, we can relate his advice to our personal conduct. We sin both by commission (by our actions) and by omission (by our inaction). As we strive to honor those in authority, and to not lie, cheat, steal, kill or covet [51] our attempts to avoid such ungodly behavior should be focused not only on our actions and our thoughts, but on the actions of those under our authority. James tells us, "To him who knows to do good and does not do it, to him it is sin." [52] Just as through "idleness of hands a house leaks," so does the failure of church officers to discipline their members, or the failure of parents to see to it that their children receive a Christian education, or that we make our civil rulers know whether a particular piece of legislation does not conform to Scripture.

We should not forget the lesson of Jesus' Parable of the Minas, where the employee that was given one mina, and failed to invest it because he thought he may make a bad investment, came to his employer and said, "Here is your mina, which I have kept put away in a handkerchief. I feared you, because you are an austere man. You collect what you did not deposit, and reap what you did not sow." The employer replied, "You could have at least put it in a bank and earned interest!" He then took the mina from him and gave it to the employee who had earned the most through his investments. [53]

Throughout the remainder of our life on earth we will be faced with divesting ourselves of old (non-Christian) habits with which we've grown accustomed. Like a pair of old shoes, they are comfortable and our natural inclination is to not exchange them for something new. However, it is precisely because it is our natural inclination to continue in them that should cause concern. As we've discussed, we are no longer in the original and "natural" condition in which we came into this world. As Christians we have been "supernaturally" re-born and along with this "new birth" has come brand new "supernatural" motivations. Since we don't come by these habits "naturally," we have to work at them. Jesus made certain that He approached His daily duties from a biblical perspective by "rising early" and among other things, reviewing how He was going to react to certain situations and circumstances that awaited Him that day.

> *Now in the morning, having risen a long while before*
> *daylight, He went out and departed to a solitary place; and*
> *there He prayed.*   MARK 1.35

DAY 3 THINK ABOUT

As the most fortunate people on the face of the earth; people who have been called into fellowship with our Lord, Savior and King, Jesus Christ, let us strive to "walk in His light."

> *This is the message which we have heard from Him and*
> *declare to you, that God is light and in Him is no darkness at*
> *all. If we say that we have fellowship with Him, and walk in*
> *darkness, we lie and do not practice the truth. But if we walk*
> *in the light as He is in the light, we have fellowship with one*
> *another, and the blood of Jesus Christ His Son cleanses us*
> *from all sin.*   1 JOHN 1.5-7

As we continue to assemble a full-orbed Christian worldview the Day Four dawns on our Christian walk and with it our consciousness is awakened to another truth that appears to be unsettling, but when examined, provides confidence for us on our walk with Christ.

- What does it mean and why is it imperative for Christians to re-think God's thoughts?

- Name one consequence that God promises will happen as a result of our trusting in man's wisdom instead of in His wisdom.

- Why should we seek someone to disciple us in the faith?

- Do you approach your daily decision-making with the attitude that you are going to base your decisions on God's "full meal" of

300

wisdom, or are you being a "finicky" eater as you pick and choose only certain portions?

- Are you tempted to "put a cap" on God's sovereignty by stating, "I know the Bible says that, but that couldn't be applicable for our times!"

- Do you consistently remind yourself, "I am no longer in the natural and sinful condition in which I came into this world and should therefore be careful to no longer make decisions according to the natural inclinations of my heart, but rather according to the supernatural inclination of my supernaturally re-born heart?"

NOTES

23 Jeremiah 17.5
24 Jeremiah 31.33
25 James 1.8; 4.8
26 Job 38.2
27 Matthew 6.23
28 Psalm 36.9
29 Titus 2.7
30 Titus 3.2
31 Psalm 37.3-6
32 2 Chronicles 16.9
33 Romans 11.33
34 Jeremiah 7.24
35 Romans 1.17

36 Proverbs 20.4
37 Proverbs 15.19
38 Bridges, *ibid.*, *Ecclesiastes*, p. 271; Proverbs 22.13
39 Bridges, *ibid.*, *Ecclesiastes*, p. 272
40 2 Corinthians 12.9
41 Romans 8.37
42 1 John 3.2
43 Matthew 6.10
44 John 16.13
45 2 Corinthians 3.5-6

46 James 1.5
47 Matthew 16.18
48 Colossians 3.9
49 Matthew 11.12
50 Hendriksen, William, *The Gospel of Matthew*, (Baker Book House, 1973), p. 491
51 Galatians 5.19-21
52 James 4.17
53 Luke 19.20-27

ARE THE NON-CHRISTIANS *REALLY* IN CONTROL?
Am I on the winning team on the earth,
or only in heaven?

We begin Day Four by noticing that every influential cultural institution is controlled by non-Christians. The news and entertainment media, education, politics, even some of our churches are encouraging us to live according to our rules instead of God's rules. (Satan's Deception 5) What can we, as individuals, expect to do in the face of this non-Christian juggernaut? According to common sense, it appears that Satan is alive and well on planet earth.

But as we learned during Day Three, and as Mark Twain's Tom Sawyer reminds us, "Common sense ain't so common." When we were non-Christians we lived and made decisions as though we were the captains of our ship and masters of our fate. Since we didn't believe in a personal, transcendent Creator God who was in sovereign control of His creation, we approached life in the mode that we, and only we, were responsible for bringing about the desired results for which we hoped.

From a non-Christian point of view, doesn't this make "common sense?" If there is no god, then who else is there to bring about results but man? Indeed, if there is no "god," aren't we, in effect, our own gods, determining "good and evil" [55] according to our own wisdom, logic and pragmatism?

Some examples of successful deceptions Satan uses to cause us to disobey and dishonor Jesus are:

SATAN'S DECEPTION 1
Personal salvation is the main goal of the Bible.

That Jesus would reach down and rescue us out of the helpless pit in which we lived as non-Christians is beyond comprehension. Certainly none of us deserved it. And, if the only reason He did it was to insure that we would spend eternity with Him and fellow believers what more could we ask! However, the Bible tells us of an even greater privilege that He has bestowed upon us: that of doing our part in bringing about His Father's will on earth as it is in heaven. [56] After all, we are commanded to pray for that, and why would Jesus so command us if He wasn't going to bring it about through our obedience!

The first statement the triune God says about humans is that we are created in the image of God and are to "have dominion over ... all the earth." [57] This is repeated to Noah and his family as their EXIT Strategy [58] as soon as they left the ark. [59] And, in His farewell address to His disciples, Jesus tells them to "make disciples of all nations..." [60] Notice Jesus doesn't say, "Make disciples of some people in all nations," but "make disciples of all nations."

Personal salvation, then, as great as it is, is the "beginning," not the "end" of our calling in Christ's Kingdom. The apostle Peter explains that God has given us particular skills and abilities to use with "one another."

> *As each one has received a gift, minister it to one another, as good stewards of the manifold grace of God. If anyone speaks, let him speak as the oracles of God. If anyone ministers, let him do it as with the ability which God supplies, that in all things God may be glorified through Jesus Christ, to whom belong the glory and the dominion forever and ever. Amen.*
>
> I PETER 4.10-11

SATAN'S DECEPTION 2
The certainty of cultural defeat and that we will only "stir things up," and cause a commotion by attempting to obey God by incorporating biblical ethics into all aspects of our lifestyle.

There are two answers for this Satanic tactic. In the first place, those who adamantly teach that a premillennial view of eschatology is absolutely certain are at variance with respected biblical scholars throughout history who say that premilleniallism (the view that Jesus will have to make a physical return in order to defeat Satan) is only one of three legitimate end-time views (amillennial and postmillennial being the other views). So, while there is certainly nothing wrong with advocating and supporting one of these views, we should remember that Jesus, Himself, says "of that day and hour no one knows, not even the angels of heaven, but My Father only." [61] As long as one's end-times view doesn't cause him to neglect his duty to incorporate biblical ethics into all areas of his worldview and lifestyle, then either of the three legitimate views should be appropriate to hold.

A second tactic Satan uses to keep us in our place (inside our homes and churches, instead of outside of them impacting culture) is the "Two Kingdom" view advocated by Martin Luther. This view holds that the kingdom of the "world," ruled by civil magistrates, makes up its own rules of behavior, and the "Kingdom of Heaven" (the church) keeps God's rules. While I have the utmost respect for Martin Luther, he missed it on this point, as we'll discuss later.

A third tactic of Satan is to tempt us to believe that the Christian principles of behavior that we see explained throughout Scripture are meant for us to internalize so that we can improve our spiritual life. Such pietism gives non-Christians a free reign to influence the cultural agenda in any way they can imagine.

A fourth tactic of Satan was promoted by Thomas Erastus, a professor of medicine in Germany during the 16th century. Erastus held that the church is subordinate to the state, and that when Jesus teaches us to give "to Caesar what is Caesar's," He means anything that Caesar asks! The Protestant Reformers, in correcting this false view, explained that there are four God-appointed self-governing spheres through which God enacts His will upon the earth: the spheres of the individual, family, church and state. Each sphere has its accountabilities to God and should not attempt to usurp any accountabilities of the other three spheres.

A fifth tactic used by Satan is to tempt us to be more concerned about what other people may think, than about what the Word of God says is our commanded duty. The inspired writer of the Book of Hebrews rebukes his first-century listeners for their hesitancy to obey God's clear commands:

> *Though He was a Son, yet He learned obedience by the things which He suffered. And having been perfected, He became the author of eternal salvation to all who obey Him, called by God as High Priest "according to the order of Melchizedek," of whom we have much to say, and hard to explain, since you have become dull of hearing.*
>
> *For though by this time you ought to be teachers, you need someone to teach you again the first principles of the oracles of God; and you have come to need milk and not solid food. For everyone who partakes only of milk is unskilled in the word of righteousness, for he is a babe. But solid food belongs to those who are of full age, that is, those who by reason of use have their senses exercised to discern both good and evil.*
>
> HEBREWS 5.8-14

May we never forget that it is not we who are causing a commotion. Non-Christians have already done that by turning the world upside down. [62] It is our commanded duty to turn it rightside up. So, if your end times view is preventing you from "knocking down the gates of hell," [63] get another view!

SATAN'S DECEPTION 3
We should attempt to "reform" public schools, rather than provide a Christian education for our children.

Jesus promises that if we ask Him for anything according to His will, He will hear it and grant it. [64] Since it is His will that parents are responsible for teaching to their children, [65] sending them to a public school system that was established because it hates God is definitely not "according to His will." Therefore, you can pray until you're blue in the face and spend countless hours and money in an effort to "reform" the public schools, but it will be to no avail. We must not forget that when Horace Mann and

305

John Dewey began the push to provide a "cookie cutter" non-Christian education for America's children, it was not for "the love of the children, or the love of literacy, but the spirit of hatred and bad intentions." [66] Mann and Dewey replaced the emphasis of the salvation of the soul, to one on teaching children to focus on a higher economic standard of living. Their stated intention was to "usher in the true kingdom of God" by using teachers to be "prophets of the true God." [67] The devious desires of Dewey and Mann did not fool the 19th century British philosopher John Stuart Mill.

> *A general state education is a mere contrivance for molding people to be exactly like one another. And as the mold ... is efficient and successful, it established a despotism over the mind.* [68]

Time has proven Mill's concerns correct, as today's government school curriculum is indeed a "cruel ruler" (a despot) over the minds of our youth. Of course, we don't need a philosopher to warn us about children receiving an ungodly education, God tells us this throughout His Word. Our commanded duty is to produce "Christianized" children who are warriors for Christ's Kingdom, not "homogenized" puppets of the state who demand one tax-payer subsidy after another.

Finally, to expect to receive from non-Christians that which they don't have to give, is to "spend money for that which is not bread," [69] and is to spend our time, efforts and resources on a fool's errand.

SATAN'S DECEPTION 4
Imagining that the First Table of God's Law (commandments 1-4) is optional to the events and circumstances happening outside our homes and churches.

This Satanic myth holds that we shouldn't insist that our civil laws be based upon God's laws because to do so would offend non-Christians. The result of Christians buying into this myth is that our civil laws are based solidly upon man's word, which means that it doesn't matter what our laws say, but upon what non-Christian men (liberals or conservatives) are legislating. In contrast to this chaotic and ungodly social scene, God says that our civil laws should reflect the 2nd Table of His Law (commandments 5-10; honor those in authority, don't kill, steal, lie, cheat, covet) because the 1st Table of His Law (commandments 1-4) tells us to. Under a Christian form of civil government liberals and conservatives can settle their differences over particular ways to govern themselves by appealing to God's Word. Non-Christian forms of civil governments frequently require much more bloody solutions.

SATAN'S DECEPTION 5
The myth that life has two mutually exclusive realms: "religious" and "real life" and we can rely on our common sense and wisdom to successfully solve cultural issues.

Hitler describes this mindset to a group of German pastors in the 1930s with the statement: "You take care of the things in our churches; I'll take care of things in our culture." Such a worldview implies that Jesus has no clue as to how we should live and govern ourselves and that He is powerless to stop the spread of evil. Certainly, if we believe this myth, we have to dismiss the apostle Paul's counsel to not be "unequally yoked" with non-Christians, [70] since at best we could only interpret this as applying inside our homes and churches. According to this myth, it wouldn't matter whether we were "unequally yoked" everywhere else because that would be the "real world," where we are free to make up our own rules! Can we not recognize how degrading this worldview and lifestyle is to the Creator God of the universe!

SATAN'S DECEPTION 6
Conservative morality is encouraged to convince us that we can "legislate" our way out of our cultural problems by substituting the tyrannical central government of the state for the divinely prescribed self-governing spheres of the individual, family, church and state that provide personal liberty.

Instead of living and governing ourselves according to the bottom-up system of God-appointed self-governing spheres of: Individual, Family, Church and State (what you might call "God's divine division of labor"), we have succumbed to the idol of state government. In the process we have deserted the God-ordained system that introduced to the world the most amount of personal liberty ever known. We have gradually given up our property rights to fund a system of public education that hates God; our family rights and justice in the courts have been lost because we have refused to base our judicial decisions on the absolute ethics of God's Word; and we've forfeited our ecclesiastical rights to preach the whole counsel of God because we've incorporated our churches to the state.

DAY 4 THINKABOUT

- Does the daily testimony that you present to your non-Christian neighbors reflect that you are on the winning or losing team on earth? or
- That Jesus has no advice on how we should live and govern ourselves and that our faith should only be "personal and private?"
- Are your efforts to improve culture directed at their root cause, or the fruit that's falling from man's poisoned tree?
- Are you hesitant to attribute to God (the 1st Table of the Law) the reason for your beliefs, or do you use euphemisms like "traditional values" and "conservative values" to justify your ethics?
- Do you live by two sets of ethics (one set for private portion of you life, inside your home and church; and another for the public portion of your life), or do you live by God's ethics in all your situations and circumstances?
- Do you look to the civil government's help in "legislating" our way out of cultural problems, or do you strive to "live your way" out of them by conforming your daily decisions to biblical truths?

If Jesus was successful in His earthly ministry, you (and He) are winners in space and time. On the other hand, if Satan defeated Jesus, then you (and Jesus) are losers in space and time. The team that you think you're on will manifest itself in your (optimistic or pessimistic) worldview and lifestyle.

In an effort to inspire their players to play with a high level of confidence, coaches tell them: "If you think you can, or if you think you can't, you're right." In other words, "play like a winner, and you'll win most games, play like a loser and you'll lose most games." While this principle may hold true for the athletic field, we can be eternally grateful that it is not theologically correct. As you have seen during the first four "Days" of your Christian walk, your best efforts to save yourself would have fallen miserably short. Praise God for taking the initiative to change your heart so that you could freely decide that you needed to repent and turn your life over to Christ!

Back to our question:

- Since you're on the winning team on earth, why live as though you are on the losing team?
- Why leave your home everyday as though you're on life's second team, when, in fact, you're on life's first team!

Even though non-Christians are controlling the current collective worldview and agenda of our culture, they are not really in control. Since they don't believe in absolute truth they can't even absolutely agree on which is "the right way to be in control." Their ideas are nothing short of pathetic. Nowhere can they point to civilizations that have been successful in implementing their ideas. Of course, even if that were the case, they couldn't cite it because they don't believe in history! They are the "blind leading the blind" [71] and they are going to "fall into their own pit." Living like this is understandable for non-Christians because they have not had the Holy Spirit "lift the veil of evil ignorance" from their mind's eye. [72] We, however, have no such excuse and if we don't repent we will fall into the pit they are currently digging for themselves and suffer the consequences right along side of them. We should be ashamed of ourselves for so living and plead to God to forgive us and grant us time to turn our culture back to Him.

Day Five provides some ideas on how to turn the world "rightside up."

NOTES

55 Genesis 3.1-4
56 Matthew 6.10
57 Genesis 1.26-28

58 See Hanson, Buddy, *EXIT Strategy: A Hand book to Exponentially Improve Your Service for God*, (Hanson Group, 2005)

59 Genesis 9.1-3
60 Matthew 28.18-20
61 Matthew 24.36
62 1 Kings 17.17-18
63 Matthew 16.18

64 1 John 5.14; Luke 11.9

65 Deuteronomy 6.6-8; Matthew 28.18-20; Proverbs 1.7; Exodus 20.3-5; Jeremiah 10.2; Luke 6.40; Romans 12.2; 2 Corinthians 6.11-18; Ephesians 4.14-15; 6.4

66 Isaiah 55.2; ALSO Proverbs 23.5

67 Chodes, John, *Destroying the Republic: Jabez Curryt and the Re-Education of the Old South*, (Algora, 2005), p.5

68 *The Early Works of John Dewey*, (Southern Illinois University Press, 1972), Vol. 5, pp. 254-269, cited in *Biblical Worldview*, January 1990, and in *Choose This Day: God's Instructions on How to Select Leaders*, Buddy Hanson, (Hanson Group, 2003), p. 9

69 Neuhaus, John Richard, ed. *Democracy and the Renewal of Public Education*, (Eerdmans, 1987), p. 51; Isaiah 55.2

70 2 Corinthians 6.14

71 Matthew 15.14

72 2 Corinthians 3.13

OUR WORLDVIEW AND LIFESTYLE:
WHAT'S SCRIPTURE
GOT TO DO WITH THEM?
Focusing on obedience
and leaving the results to God

O n Day Four we began to understand what Paul means by "putting off" our old way of living and "putting on" our new way of living.[73] The Bible presents Christianity as being all or nothing. Nowhere does Scripture hint of Christianity as being a piecemeal and partial moralistic add-on to a person's worldview and lifestyle. Just as Jesus' ministry on earth was to exclusively do His Father's will, so is our mission as members of His Kingdom to do exclusively Jesus' will.

With the thoughts fresh on our mind about the living hell from which we were so mercifully rescued, we should have no desire to return to those "weak and miserable" thought processes which used to characterize our worldview and lifestyle. [74] Now that we have been shone the "straight path," why would we desire to walk in "crooked paths?" [75] As mentioned in Day Four, our calling is one of obedi-

Jesus' primary interest in regard to us is whether or not we are living the right lifestyle, He is not interested in the least that we know the right words to describe how we should live. Do your thoughts conform to Christ's will? If they do, and only if they do, will your actions also conform to His will.

311

ence. This is of utmost importance and should be our top consideration before making any decision.

Does this individual, family, church or civil government decision reflect obedience to a biblical principle?

If we cannot answer "Yes" to this question, we have no ethical basis upon which to make the decision. As a generic theological concept this causes us little concern. "After all," we might reason, "I'm a Christian so why shouldn't I obey my Savior?" The problem comes when we are faced with a specific situation and our first impulse is to make our decisions the way we made them when we were non-Christians … according to our wisdom and whether or not it would lead to the results we desire. In other words, will our decision be pragmatic and practical, or does it reflect "common sense?"

But let's recall why we used to make decisions like this when we were non-Christians. We did so because we saw ourselves as being in control of producing the kind of results we desired. This bears repeating:

Our decision-making process when we were non-Christians was based upon the mistaken belief that we were responsible for bringing about the results we desired.

As Christians, we should no longer think that way. We now know that Jesus brings about the results in His creation. When He called us into His Kingdom, He called us into the obedience business, not the results business. So the next time you are faced with a decision, ask yourself whether you are making it for Jesus' benefit (because it conforms to His will), or is it for your benefit (because it may accomplish your will).

Attempting to approach our Christian life from our former non-Christian results-oriented mindset can cause us to make errors in a variety of situations:

• **Civic Duty.** How often have you heard Christians rationalize, "I don't like either of the candidates, so I guess I'll vote for the lesser of two evils." Whether intended or not, this attitude completely underestimates Christ's sovereign control over His creation. Instead of writing in a name for a candidate who has vowed to legislate according to biblical ethics, or instead of voting for a third party candidate, because in both cases we think our vote will be "wasted," we vote for a candidate who has no intention of bringing glory and honor to Jesus through his legislation. The question to be asked is: "How can we possibly 'waste our vote' when we are voting in conformity with Scripture?"

• **Personal Revenge.** When someone says something about us that is blatantly false, we feel a strong urge to take matters into our own hands in order to bring about "justice." Five days into our Christian walk, however, should be sufficient for us to understand that we are living in God's world and that He is not only perfectly capable of bringing about justice, but promises to do so.

> *Woe to the wicked! It shall be ill with him.*   Isaiah 3.11

> *For God will bring every work into judgment, including every secret thing, whether good or evil.*
> Ecclesiastes 12.14

> *"Cursed is everyone who does not continue in all things which are written in the book of the law, to do them."*
> Galatians 3.10

In no uncertain terms, God assures us that His perfect justice will be done. What He doesn't tell us is *when it* will be done. This means that we have one of two choices by which to live: either we can fear man and put the responsibility for righting wrongs squarely on our backs, or we can fear God and trust Him to bring about His perfect justice at exactly the perfect time. [76] Solomon puts it this way:

> *Let us hear the conclusion of the whole matter: Fear God and keep His commandments, for this is man's all.*
> Ecclesiastes 12.13

If we really believe that our times are "in God's hands," [77] we will not be so fast in attempting to bring about what we imagine to be "justice."

• **An overconfidence in Our Knowledge and Wisdom.** As the saying goes, some people are "legends in their own minds." Solomon has a statement that should stop such arrogance in its tracks:

> *As you do not know what is the way of the wind, or how the bones grow in the womb of her who is with child, so you do not know the works of God who makes everything.*
>
> ECCLESIASTES 11.5

Bridges provides these sobering comments from a 19th Century pastor:

> *Man prides himself upon what he knows, or fancies he knows —the extent of his knowledge. Much more reason has he to be humbled for the far wider extent of his ignorance. ... How little does he know of the things before his eyes! How ignorant are we of our own being! So "fearfully and wonderfully made!"* so *"curiously wrought!"* [78] *...Truly he "does great things and unsearchable; marvelous things without number."* [79] *Our wisdom is but as a drop in the bucket – yea, but a drop in the ocean. Can our drop compare with his ocean? A bucket shall as soon take in the ocean, as man the wisdom of God.* [80]

• **Impatience with our efforts to cause "good things" to happen.** This gets back to the "timing" issue. Just because our obedience doesn't appear to be making a positive difference, it doesn't mean that it won't in God's perfect timing. Solomon assures us that if we "Cast our bread upon the waters, we will find it," even though it may take "many days." [81] "Many days" may mean not until Judgment Day, but if that is the case what complaint could we have? We have done our duty, and God His. [82]

The prophet Habakkuk reinforces Solomon's advice:

> *Though it tarries, wait for it; because it will surely come, it will not tarry.*
>
> HABAKKUK 2.3

And, of course, we're all familiar with the Apostle Paul's encouraging statement:

> *And let us not grow weary while doing good, for in due*
> *season we shall reap if we do not lose heart.* **GALATIANS 6.9**

Some may ask, "Why does God not act immediately?" In answer to that we need look no further than our own life. Had God given us the immediate justice we deserve, we would all be reading this in Hell. But may we never forget to praise Him for being "merciful and gracious, slow to anger, and abounding in mercy," [83] because that "extra time" gave us the opportunity to repent and turn our lives over to Him!

Bridges lists some notable examples from Scripture that have resulted in enormous blessings for Christians throughout the ages:

> *Adam therefore lived more than nine hundred years under the*
> *sentence passed – not executed. (Genesis 2.17; v.5) "The long-*
> *suffering of God waited in the days of Noah." (1 Peter 3.20,*
> *with Genesis 6.3) The ordinary course is to give the sinner*
> *time and space for repentance – to open to him a day of grace*
> *– "An accepted time, leaving him in the neglect of it without*
> *excuse." (Luke 19.42) Were the execution instantly to follow*
> *the sentence, how many glorious manifestations of grace*
> *would have been lost to the Church! We might have known*
> *Paul as "a blasphemer, and a persecutor, and injurious;" but*
> *not as the "chief of sinners, who obtained mercy," as a special*
> *display of "all long-suffering; and for a pattern to them which*
> *should hereafter believe." (1 Timothy 1.13–16)* [84]

As we've discussed, old habits die hard, and living whole heartedly for Jesus may be the hardest habit to add to our "new self." [85] Since Christianity is not an add-on, we have no option but to repent, turn from our former paths (self-serving decisions) and turn to God by making others-serving decisions. [86]

If our profession of faith is real, we will be motivated to work toward this goal of personal holiness and will be eager to increase the consistency of our service in Christ's Kingdom. On the other hand, if our profession of faith is based upon the erroneous presumption that Christianity is merely a moralistic add-on, to our current ungodly worldview and lifestyle, then our profession is false and we will neither be motivated to live for Christ in all of our situations and circumstances, nor will we have supernatural assistance to help us to achieve such a godly goal.

So far we have talked about how we should live in order to show our recognition for and appreciation of Jesus coming to earth to live a perfect life, then dying and overcoming death in order to redeem us from our former way of life. But as has been hinted at, Jesus also fills two other offices toward us. A second office Jesus holds is that of being our Lord, or boss. This is why we must give our best efforts toward consistently obeying His revealed rules in all of our situations and circumstances. A third office Jesus fills is that of King of the universe. A psalmist writes

> *Why do the nations rage, and the people plot a vain thing? The kings of the earth set themselves, and the rulers take counsel together, against the LORD and against His Anointed, saying, "Let us break Their bonds in pieces and cast away Their cords from us." He who sits in the heavens shall laugh; the Lord shall hold them in derision. Then He shall speak to them in His wrath, and distress them in His deep displeasure:*
> *"Yet I have set My King on My holy hill of Zion." "I will declare the decree: the LORD has said to Me, 'You are My Son, today I have begotten You. Ask of Me, and I will give You the nations for Your inheritance, and the ends of the earth for Your possession.* PSALM 2.1-8

The prophet Isaiah adds

> *For unto us a Child is born, unto us a Son is given; and the government will be upon His shoulder. And His name will be called Wonderful, Counselor, Mighty God, Everlasting Father, Prince of Peace. Of the increase of His government and peace.* ISAIAH 9.6-7

> *For the LORD is our Judge, the LORD is our Lawgiver, the LORD is our King; He will save us.* ISAIAH 33.22

The prophet Zechariah explains:

And the LORD shall be King over all the earth.

ZECHARIAH 14.9

The apostle Paul exclaims:

Now to the King eternal, immortal, invisible, to God who alone is wise be honor and glory forever and ever. Amen.

1 TIMOTHY 1.17

And the apostle John writes:

The kingdoms of this world have become the kingdoms of our Lord and of His Christ and He shall reign forever and ever.

REVELATION 11.15

Verses like these help explain why it is so disrespectful for us to send our children to schools that break the first commandment by worshiping more than the one true and triune God of Scripture. It also points up the shame we deserve by not publicly acknowledging His Word as the sole source of our civil laws. Jesus is King and we are His servants, not the other way around.

As we've discussed, our worldview and lifestyle should mirror Christ's. On a much smaller scale we are prophets (teaching His Word), priests (interceding for others in our prayers), and kings (as we rule over various dimensions of our life, household and vocation). Just as Jesus' main priority was to do His Father's will, instead of His will, so should our main priority be to do His will, instead of our own.

Perhaps, most important of all, we should image Jesus' desire to obey His Father, regardless of His situations and circumstances. He was able to do this because He had perfect confidence in His Father's ability to bring about the results that had been planned by the trinity before the earth was created. Jesus has called us into the obedience business, not the results business. It is true that He works His eternally perfect plan through our obedience, but it is still He who initiates and brings about the results.

317

Casting off the idea that we are primarily responsible for bringing about results may be the most difficult part of our "old person" to discard. Yet, in doing so we prove to ourselves that we truly trust-in Jesus' sovereign control of His Kingdom.

- What plans do you have for incorporating biblical ethics into your worldview and lifestyle?
- In order to increase your personal holiness, what are some of the non-Christian ethics in your worldview that you need to eliminate and replace with Christian ethics?
- Are you developing the habit of pausing before making a major decision to ask, "Does this decision reflect obedience to a biblical ethic?"
- Have you reconciled yourself to the truth that, as a Christian, your main goal in decision-making is to obey God, rather than being about results; that you trust in God's eternally perfect plan to bring about His perfect results in *His* perfect timing?
- Are you giving your best effort to "image Christ" by striving to live according to His will, instead of according to your will?

In answering the question posed in the title of Day Five, "What's Scripture Got to Do with It?" the answer is: "Scripture should have everything to do with our worldview and lifestyle. If it doesn't we need to go back to God's drawing board and re-check our calibrations.

NOTES

73 Ephesians 4.20-24; Colossians 3.8-10

74 Colossians 2.20; Hebrews 6.1-3

75 Proverbs 3.5-6

76 Acts 15.18

77 Psalm 31.15

78 Psalm139.12-14

79 Job 5.9

80 Bridges, i*bid., Ecclesiastes*, p. 273, quoting Caryl's commentary On Job

81 Ecclesiastes 11.1

82 Luke 14.14

83 Psalm 103.8; Joel 2.13-14

84 Bridges, ibid., *Ecclesiastes*, p.197

85 Deuteronomy 6.5; Matthew 23.37-39

86 Ezekiel 14.6' Acts 14.15; 1 Peter 3.11

THE WINNERS' LOCKER ROOM
We're the only ones who know the triune God of Scripture, and His truth

T he apostle John tells us that Jesus came to earth to "destroy the works of the devil." [87] Either we can agree with John, that Jesus was successful in defeating Satan's rule over the earth, or we can disagree with his statement, which would mean that Jesus failed in His earthly ministry. I choose to agree with John, which means that Satan only rules over non-Christians. Since we are now "more than conquerors through Him who loved us," [88] and we have Jesus' assurance that "the gates of Hades shall not prevail" against our obedient efforts, [89] let's consider what being a member of Christ's Kingdom means.

First and foremost, we are winners, not losers in space and time. Instead of imagining ourselves as members of Christ's B-Team,* we are full-fledged members of His A-Team who are "working out our salvation with fear and trembling," [90] as well as bringing about God's will "on earth as it is in heaven." [91]

Second, this optimistic worldview does not imply that we will be able to usher in a "golden age of perfection" on earth prior to Christ's victorious return in judgment, because we are sinners living in a sinful

---

* Some imagine that Christians are God's B-Team and should not concern ourselves with attempting to improve culture, because God will raise up His Jewish A-Team to set the world aright.

world. However, the age that we and those Christian brothers and sisters who come after us usher in may seem "golden" in comparison to our current ungodly cultural condition. For example, in the midst of the collective non-Christian worldview in which we are living our adversaries control every influential cultural institution. Because of this it is very difficult for us to keep non-Christian ideas from sneaking into our worldview. But even though we live in what could be described as "non-Christian times," the fact that we are still here, is proof that not everyone is a non-Christian.

The same will hold true when we recapture all of the major cultural influential institutions. Even though at that time everyone will be living in the midst of a collective Christian worldview, it will not mean that there won't be non-Christians among us. The difference between then and now will be that Christians will be setting the cultural agenda. Some people will say, "Hanson, you're a dreamer. Christians will never be able to take the reins of culture." My reply to that is "Not only can we take the reins of culture, but we already have, not only in America, but throughout various Western civilizations."

There was a time when America

- ✓ honored the sanctity of life (Sixth Commandment)
- ✓ showed respect to those in authority (Fifth Commandment)
- ✓ upheld the importance of the marriage vow (Seventh Commandment), and
- ✓ respected personal property rights (Eighth Commandment).

Perhaps non-Christians would like to explain why before Western civilization was Christianized

- there was no concept of or interest in "feeding the hungry, or in helping the poor or disadvantaged (Eighth Commandment)
- there was no concept of or interest in recognizing the worth of all humans (Sixth Commandment)
- there was no concept of or in interest in respecting those in authority (Fifth Commandment)
- there was no concept of or interest in being at peace with our neighbors (Tenth Commandment)

- there was no concept of or interest in the dignity of women and the importance of the family (Seventh Commandment), and
- there was no concept of or interest in honest words/actions in our personal relationships (Ninth Commandment).

History attests to the truth that all of these concepts, along with the concept of capitalism and self-government (Eighth Commandment), were introduced by Christians. Indeed, it was these very values that civilized the Western world, yet, today the Church is doing little in order to convict its members to incorporate them into their lifestyles. As has been discussed, Christianity has become merely something to "add-on" to the periphery of one's already full lifestyle, instead of a life-transforming worldview that God intends.

After a game both teams return to identical locker rooms, yet, there is a world of difference between the attitude of the winners' locker room and the losers' locker room. The winners' locker room is inhabited by the joyfulness and optimism of what is, while the loser's are saddened with thoughts of what might have been. While all of this makes perfect sense, something is happening in 21st century American culture that does anything but make sense. The ultimate losers (non-Christians) are happy and optimistic that they will succeed in transforming America from its outdated and superstitious religious roots, while the ultimate winners (Christians) are pessimistic and saddened at the continuing downward spiral of culture.

Why should non-Christians be absolutely optimistic that they can successfully take over and maintain the reins of culture

- When they admit that they don't believe in absolute truth? Or,
- When they can point to not one single civilization in history that has managed to sustain itself on man's ethics?

Since they can point to no culture in history to support their worldview, they vainly imagine that life is merely a never-ending series of random events. Events that the cultural elites attempt to manipulate to their own self-centered agenda. On the other hand why should Christians be pessimistic about being able to transform our culture:

321

- When God's Word repeatedly assures us that we can successfully do it? Or,
- When we can point to numerous historical examples of civilizations throughout history that have been transformed by biblical ethics?

A comparison between how the Opposing Locker Rooms should look is illustrated in the following chart.

Comparing the Opposing Locker Rooms

The Winners (Christians)

- We have God on our side
- Our worldview has proven time and time again throughout history to "work."

- We have absolute truth

The Losers (Non-Christians)

- They only have themselves
- Their assortment of worldviews combined have no record of even one success! (of a society that was able to sustain itself according to its non-Christian worldviews).
- They have their vain imaginings

DAY 6 THINKABOUT

I would ask "In which locker room you would prefer being?" but since you are a Christian, you are already a member of the winners' locker room. So, perhaps the question should be, why hang out in the losers' locker room?" They don't want you in theirs because your presence only reminds them they are losers.

- Why not leave all that negativity and come into the locker room in which you belong and are welcomed!
- Do you honestly believe that Jesus was successful in defeating the works of Satan during His earthly ministry?
- List two reasons why Christians should be optimistic as they approach each day of life.
- Name the three advantages we have in our Locker Room that non-Christians could only wish they had.

NOTES

87 1 John 3.9
88 Romans 8.37
89 Matthew 16.18
90 Philippians 2.12
91 Matthew 6.10

R-E-S-T & WORSHIP!
*It's OK to put our world "on hold" for a full day
and worship our Creator because we know that
He is in sovereign control of His creation*

*Remember the Sabbath day, to keep it holy. Six days you
shall labor and do all your work, but the seventh day is the
Sabbath of the LORD your God. In it you shall do no work:
you, nor your son, nor your daughter, nor your male servant,
nor your female servant, nor your cattle, nor your stranger
who is within your gates. For in six days the LORD made
the heavens and the earth, the sea, and all that is in them,
and rested the seventh day. Therefore the LORD blessed the
Sabbath day and hallowed it.*   EXODUS 20.8-11

It would be anti-climatic to attempt to improve upon the fourth commandment, because it includes every reason for why Day Seven
should be a day of rest and worship. The "and worship" part is important,
because Day Seven should not be viewed as merely being a "day off," even
though it does provide an opportunity for us to rest from our previous
week's labors and recharge our batteries so we can begin the new week
with renewed vigor and enthusiasm.

Speaking of "rest," approximately 1,600 years ago the North African
Bishop, St. Augustine, remarked that God has made us for Himself, and

"Our heart is restless until it finds rest in thee." [92] So, while God calms our hearts during the week as we reflect on His minute-by-minute care and guidance of our life, on Day Seven we join corporately to praise Him for "resting" our souls. Bridges remarks on the importance of paying careful attention to the sermon. He notes that in too many cases, "We seem to have done with the Word, as it has passed into our ears. But the Word—be it remembered—will never have done with us, till it shall have 'judged us at the last day.'" [93] Bridges made his remarks in relation to King Solomon's counsel to:

> *Walk prudently when you go to the house of God; and draw*
> *near to hear rather than to give the sacrifice of fools, for they*
> *do not know that they do evil.*   ECCLESIASTES 5.1

Not only is careful listening important, but listening "in faith." [94] Jesus, in His Parable of the Revealed Light, picks up this theme, when He admonishes us to

> *Take heed how you hear. For whoever has, to him more will*
> *be given; and whoever does not have, even what he seems to*
> *have will be taken from him.*   LUKE 8.18

Day Seven in **The Seven Days of Christians** example (which is Day One, Sunday, in real life), provides us an opportunity to spend time with those with whom we may not otherwise have time during the week. Parents (or grown children), friends, people who are sick, as well as time spent with our immediate family, discussing the sermon, and some events of the previous week, and/or what the coming week may hold.

All-in-all, Day Seven offers a time to check how serious we are about the sovereignty of God. If we close our business, or refuse to go in to the office for a couple of hours to get a head start on the next week, will God enable us to keep up with our competition? Will He really enable us to make at least the same revenue if our business is open six days, which we would if it were open everyday? Can we really trust-in God's control, or must we trust-in our control?

In every Christian's heart-of-hearts, he knows that the answers to such questions is an unqualified "Yes," so, if you have not already done so, eliminate any remaining tendencies to take direct control of the results of your life: leave them in God's all-knowing hands and focus on demonstrating a lifestyle of complete trust in your Lord, Savior and King's sovereign control of His creation!

At this point in time, Americans appear to take our sports much more seriously than our religion (indeed, a case could be made that sports has become a religion), so perhaps a coaching analogy would be meaningful. Successful football coaches tell their players to not focus on the results of previous plays. Instead they are encouraged to "play every play" with the assurance that sooner or later "good things" will happen.

"Focus on carrying out your responsibilities" is a familiar coaching admonition. The reason for this is if the quarterback continues to dwell on the interception, he may well throw another one, or he will try to "guide" the ball to his receiver instead of using his full throwing motion, which will result in an errant pass. In this example, the quarterback is encouraged to "have a short memory," and take the field on the next set of downs with the mindset that the interception is ancient history. Again, in the words of coaches, "Don't let the things you can't control, control your mindset."

Is this not the same principle for how we should live our lives? God absolutely promises to bless our obedience, but He doesn't tell us when he will bless us.

Occasionally, we will see immediate results, but in most instances the blessings come down the road. Our focus, then, should not be on how badly we disobeyed Him or that we have been faithful to consistently obey Him and haven't seen any positive results come from it, but rather to keep to our knitting and know that in His eternally perfect timetable our efforts will result in a beautiful garment.

Enjoy the day, enjoy God and His creation, and enjoy the time spent with your family. None of us knows how many days we will be allotted on this earth before we are called to glory, so let's do our best to make the best use of our time with those whom we love most, our families!

In using one more coaching maxim, when football teams get in the "red zone" where they are within 20 yards of the End Zone, coaches say that the important thing is not the play they call, but the player. The principle is to get the ball into your key player's hands and let him make a play. This truism also fits well with what our attitude should be about on Day Seven. In order to maximize our enjoyment of the day with our family and friends, let's put the day in God's hands and let Him do with it what He will.

Seven Days without Church Makes One Weak

At one time or another we've all probably seen this message on a church sign as we've driven by and it probably brought a smile to our face. It's debatable whether we'll ever see a sign that reads:

> ## With ALL of the Seven Days of Christians
> ## Your Faith Will Be Strong!

Still, I hope The Seven Days of Christians has helped you see how to have a closer walk with Jesus and to demonstrate to your non-Christian neighbors by your everyday decision-making how Jesus would have us to live and govern ourselves. After all, isn't "enlightening the world with biblical truth" what the Christian life is all about?

> *But you are a chosen generation, a royal priesthood, a holy*
> *nation, His own special people, that you may proclaim*
> *the praises of Him who called you out of darkness into His*
> *marvelous light; who once were not a people but are now the*
> *people of God, who had not obtained mercy but now have*
> *obtained mercy.*   1 PETER 2.9-10

> *You are the light of the world. A city that is set on a hill*
> *cannot be hidden. Nor do they light a lamp and put it under*
> *a basket, but on a lampstand, and it gives light to all who are*
> *in the house. Let your light so shine before men, that they may*
> *see your good works and glorify your Father in heaven.*
>   MATTHEW 5.14-16

For you were once darkness, but now you are light in the
Lord. Walk as children of light (for the fruit of the Spirit is
in all goodness, righteousness, and truth), finding out what
is acceptable to the Lord. And have no fellowship with the
unfruitful works of darkness, but rather expose them.

EPHESIANS 5.8-11

With these verses firmly implanted in the forefront of our memories, may we all heed the prophet Isaiah's call to action:

Arise, shine; for your light has come! And the glory of the
LORD is risen upon you.   ISAIAH 60.1

By following **The Seven Days of Christians** we will neither have a weak week, or a weak faith!

NOTES

92 Augustine, Saint, *Confessions*, Book 1
93 Bridges, *ibid., Ecclesiastes*, p.99; John 12.48
94 Hebrews 4.2

Key Points from
The Seven Days of Christians

- Life as a Christian dramatically changes our worldview and lifestyle.

- We are most thankful and most grateful for God calling us to be members of Christ's Kingdom and giving us the purpose of redeeming His earth.

- As members of Christ's Kingdom will be "more than conquerors" on earth, so there is no biblical reason for us to exhibit a pessimistic, or defeatist attitude as we go about our daily duties.

  –Does not the prophet Isaiah promise that God, "Gives power to the weak, and to those who have no might He increases strength."

  ISAIAH 40.28

  –Are we not "children of God" 1 John 3.2 who have been commanded to pray that our Father's will "will be done on earth as it is in heaven?"

  MATTHEW 6.10

  –Have we not been given the Holy Spirit to lead and direct us in our decision-making?

  JOHN 16.13

  –Doesn't the "sufficiency" for us to successfully accomplish our calling as members of Christ's Kingdom come from God, and not ourselves?

  2 CORINTHIANS 3.5-6

- Our "new life" involves "putting off" our natural habits, and "putting on" our new, supernatural habits.

- We are interested in putting the interests of others above our self-interests and studying the Bible so that we will know more about how God wants us to live and govern ourselves.

- Our calling (and our ministry) is to present a godly role model for our non-Christian neighbors by demonstrating a Christian antithesis of how to live and govern ourselves in all areas of life.

- Rather than attempting to carry Jesus around on our back, we need to obey His commands to carry Him around inside our heart. This means that instead of periodically acting for Him, we will be consistently living for Him.

- We should continually review our decisions to make certain that they are based upon biblical ethics and not pragmatism or rationalization. For example, "Is this a conservative response to a liberal action, or a Christian response to an ungodly action?

The Seven Days of Christians Wrap Up

❖ As you look back over the elements included in each of the Seven Days, which "day" would you consider yourself to be on?

_____

_____

_____

_____

_____

_____

❖ What changes to your worldview and lifestyle do you need to make in order to move to the "next day?"

_____

_____

_____

_____

_____

❖ If you find that you have completed all seven "Days," what can you do to serve Christ better and more consistently in your service in His Kingdom?

_____

_____

_____

_____

_____

Has the information in this section revealed that you may have been looking at the world through blurred lenses? If so, how does this information help you to change your mantra as you approach each day in Christ's Kingdom? Yes, I said, "mantra," and yes, that usually means something that is chanted, but for our case we're using it as an unspoken mantra, or that "frame of reference" we bring to our daily decision-making that enables us to either accept or dismiss proposals that don't conform to our predisposed way of viewing the world. The upside of having such a mantra, or frame of reference is that we don't have to start from scratch in evaluating each decision, which means it saves us a lot of time. The downside is that if our mantra needs changing, and we don't realize it, then we will, with the best of intentions, make decisions that are not in our best interests.

Both Satan and Jesus have a mantra that they would prefer us to use in our daily decision-making. Take a look at both mantras to decide which one is currently dictating your decisions. The clearer your focus becomes with each area of decision-making, the sharper your decisions will reflect God's will, instead of Satan's.

What's in Your Mantra?

Satan's Version: Salvation & Frustration

"You are losers in the here-and-now, but winners in the hereafter."

"Jesus loves us and came to save us from our sins so that when we die (or are raptured!) we will be freed from the shackles of Satan's dominion upon the earth, and will joyfully spend eternity with fellow believers worshiping the triune God of the Bible. Until that time Jesus' Word encourages us to save as many people as we can and comforts us in our trials on this evil-infested earth by giving us a 'hope to cope' with all that Satan throws at us."

Jesus' Version: Salvation & Occupation

"You can be winners in both the here-and-now, and in the hereafter (by living according to My Word!)."

"Jesus loves those whom the Trinity chose before the foundation of the earth (EPHESIANS 1.4,17; 2.8) and came to earth to perfectly fulfill the Law (JOHN 1.1,14; MATTHEW 5.17; HEBREWS 4.15; 1 JOHN 4.10) and pay our sin debt by dying and overcoming death (JOHN 10.17-18; 1 CORINTHIANS 15.45) and has given us His Word to instruct us in how to live and govern ourselves (PSALM 119.105; JEREMIAH 31.33; JOHN 17.17; COLOSSIANS 3.16; ROMANS 8.9, 14, 16; 2 TIMOTHY 3.16-17) and complete Jesus' victory over Satan (1 JOHN 3.8; 4.4; COLOSSIANS 2.13-15; HEBREWS 2.14) by taking dominion over the earth (GENESIS 1.26-28; 9.1-4; MATTHEW 28.18-20; ROMANS 8.37) and restoring God's will "on earth, as it is in heaven." (MATTHEW 6.10; REVELATION 11.15).

Music Maestro, Please!

Play that funky music white boy
Play that funky music right
Play that funky music white boy
Lay down that boogie and play that funky music till you die
Till you die, oh till you die...

As the story goes, Wild Cherry's lead singer, Rob Parissi, was looking for a new sound for his band in the mid-1970s because he could sense that Disco music had peaked. One night someone yelled from the audience, "Play that funky music white boy!" Parissi immediately recognized that his rock'n'roll band needed to stop trying to adapt to Disco and go back to its roots and play some rhythm and blues. And, as they say, "The rest is history."

For 21st century Americans we need desperately to stop trying to adapt to the non-Christian cultural musical agenda and go back to our roots of playing some divinely-inspired and sanctified soul music. So, if Mr. Parissi will excuse the following paraphrase:

Play that sanctified soul music Christian
Play that sanctified soul music right
Play that sanctified soul music Christian
Lay down the basics and play that sanctified music till you die
Till you die, oh till you die...

What's that, you say? You don't consider yourself a "rock" star? Well, not so fast, my friend, because wait until you see what our divine Maestro has to say.

Therefore, to you who believe, He is precious; but to those
who are disobedient, "The stone which the builders rejected
has become the chief cornerstone," and "A stone of stumbling
and a rock of offense."They stumble, being disobedient to the
word, to which they also were appointed. But you are a chosen
generation, a royal priesthood, a holy nation, His own special
people, that you may proclaim the praises of Him who called
you out of darkness into His marvelous light; who once were
not a people but are now the people of God, who had not
obtained mercy but now have obtained mercy.

1 PETER 2.5-10

The apostle Peter is recounting Isaiah's prophecy 700 years before the birth of Christ that both houses of Israel would "stumble" against our Rock, our Lord, Savior, and King, Jesus Christ, their promised Messiah.[1] As Paul states, the Jews refused to "seek Jesus by faith," and attempted to invent works by which they would be accepted,[2] and as a consequence, they would lose their name [3] with believers eventually being called "Christians" at Antioch. [4]

We, however, have been built on the solid foundation "of the apostles and prophets, with Jesus Christ as the chief cornerstone." [5] As such, we're not only "rocks," but "living rocks" who are "built up as a spiritual house and a holy priesthood to offer acceptable sacrifices" of our obedient service for Christ's Kingdom. [6] It is upon this all-powerful, all-knowing and ever-present Rock that "the church is built, and Jesus gives us His Word that we will knock down the gates of Hades" as we conform our daily decision-making to biblical ethics. [7] Let us not forget that this is exactly what Jehovah promised to Adam and Eve with these encouraging words:

I will put enmity between you (Satan) and the woman, and
between your seed and her Seed; He (Jesus) will bruise you on
the head, and you shall bruise His heel. GENESIS 3.15

Surely Adam and Eve were wondering what was going to happen to future generations in light of their recent disobedience, so Jehovah told

334

them that the major consequence would be a battle between Satan's followers and Jesus' followers, with Satan gaining some temporary victories (bruising Jesus' heel), but that the followers of Jesus would eventually take dominion of the earth by delivering a deadly blow to the head of Satan. Approximately 2,000 years later the apostle Paul would encourage first century Christians with very similar words.

> *The God of peace will crush Satan under your feet shortly.*
> ROMANS 16.20

Contemporary rock stars can only hope to "rock the house," with their performances, but our divine Music Maestro has called us to "rock the world" with His gospel opera. Such an optimistic outcome may not look so feasible in our current cultural environment. Satan has performed plastic surgery on our culture and to the human eye it looks very attractive, but God has performed fantastic surgery on our hearts to equip and enable us to carry out our duty of completing the work of Adam and Eve by "crushing Satan" through our obedience and thus restoring Jesus' creation to biblical ethics.

In order to reconcile ourselves with this victorious scenario for the earth, we need to attack the root of the current "culture of defeat" that most American Christians have. If I were to excitedly announce: "Brothers and sisters, listen up, we're losing the culture war!" You would probably say, "Hanson, take a deep breath, of course we're losing the culture war … we're supposed to lose it." My response to that would be: "Jehovah's words to Adam and Eve, and the Apostle Paul's words to the church at Rome don't sound to me like we're supposed to be cultural losers!"

It is exactly at this point that the crux of the problem lies. Research shows that less than 50 percent of Christians read in the Bible once a month. Less than one out of two of us have enough regard and respect and reverence for God's Word to read from it during a 30-day period! During that same 30-day period what do we spend our time reading and listening to? Sadly, you guessed

> *There is nothing more valuable to us than our time, so how we spend it tells a lot about our priorities.*

335

it; we spend our time with the sports section, trade journals, the internet, recipe books, newspapers, magazines, and the evening news.

So we have this myth going around that Satan crushes Jesus, and one out of two Christians take it as "gospel," no pun intended, because there are too many other things in life that they value more than God's Word. Since you are reading this book, you're probably not in the group that doesn't care what God has to say about how we should live and govern ourselves, but I'm sure you know of someone who is, so allow me to offer these two questions that may shock them into opening their Bible:

- Is Jesus clueless about how to deal with the things that happen in "real life?"
- Is Christianity exclusively about eternal salvation and is Jesus "Culturally Irrelevant?"

If they bow up at you when you ask them this, and say: "Jesus, clueless? How can you say such a thing!" Explain that while this sounds like a terrible thing to say, how else can they explain the way so many of their Christian friends act when they step outside their homes and Churches? Why would so many Christians so seldom turn to God's Word, if it were not for the fact that they did not believe it has anything meaningful for their worldview and lifestyle?

The 16th Century French essayist Michel de Montaigne writes, "Nothing is so firmly believed as what we least know," and one out of two of our Christian friends are currently proving him right by so firmly believing in a Satanic myth that they don't bother to open the Bible to see if what they believe has any biblical support. It is hard for me to imagine that anyone who professes to be a Christian would conclude that the Creator of the earth and all knowledge, is "clueless" about anything. So hopefully such a question would drive them to the Bible to verify for themselves that they are on solid ground in believing that Paul missed it when he said we are "more than conquerors through Him who loved us."[8]

The truth is that it is they who are clueless about how to live and govern themselves because not only are they not bothering to study the Bible, but also because practically no one is instructing us in how Jesus commands us to live. The problem with our current culture is we have failed to present a Godly alternative to the non-Christian cultural agenda. Non-Christians know that their life isn't what it should be. They are looking for answers and are finding them in all the wrong places because we, who have been mercifully and graciously given the answers, are being silent!

The culture in which we are living is abnormal because we have not been demonstrating to our non-Christian neighbors what God's antithesis is to their sinful ideas. We have been graciously given supernatural heart transplants by the Holy Spirit, whereby He has written God's Law on our hearts and motivated us to study it and then apply it to our daily situations and circumstances.

Since we live in a cause-and-effect universe, we can have confidence that our obedient lifestyles will result in positive changes in our culture. And since, God created the universe, the earth, all things, people and angels, it is God, and not Satan that is in charge of His creation. Therefore, we can have full confidence in conforming our daily decision-making to God's revealed Word, knowing that God's Word is truth, and that as a result of that ONLY God's Word works!

Four Steps to Redeeming Our Culture

FIRST STEP
Stop going to sources who aren't Christians to find "false answers" to culture's problems.

SECOND STEP
Realize that everyone brings their biases to every fact they encounter. The primary reason we are faced with all of these cultural problems is that we, the Church, have been living as though facts are neutral (even though we know they are not). We should not be upset with the media biasing their reports toward non-Christian agenda items. They're simply being consistent with their worldview. Who we should be upset with is the Church (ourselves) for not living in a consistent manner with our worldview and in not training up Christian journalists, TV anchors and Christian investors to take back the media and bias it toward Christian beliefs.

THIRD STEP

Remind ourselves that even though Christians and non-Christian conservatives use similar vocabularies, both groups are in reality, using different dictionaries. In order to win the Culture War, we must frame the cultural debate between God's ideas and man's ideas, not conservative ideas and liberal ideas.

FOURTH STEP

Remind ourselves that we didn't get into this mess overnight, so we shouldn't expect to correct all of our cultural ills overnight. There is not one non-Christian running around causing all of this cultural turmoil. There are a lot of them and each is focusing only on how they can use their skills and abilities to further their cause. That's how we must approach our tasks as we exit our homes each day. If we think that we have the weight of the world on our shoulders, it will overwhelm us. But, we'll be alright if we develop the habit of simply asking ourselves:

"Does this individual, family, church or civil government decision reflect obedience to a biblical principle?"

By asking this question before making our daily decisions, we'll be well on our way to living in accordance with a Christian worldview. Remember this: All that the non-Christians have accomplished, which is a lot, has resulted because we've offered no opposition to their efforts. Plus, they have captured every influential cultural institution without God.

We've got God!

With His help, why should we not expect to take back all of those influential cultural institutions, as well as our entire culture? After all, Peter tells us that we are a "chosen generation, a royal priesthood, a holy nation, His own special people." If this sounds good, but you still think that its too big of a job for Jesus to work through us to restore His creation, may I call to your remembrance that it was He who created this world in the first place, and if that is still too big a concept for you to grasp, allow me to remind you of something that's as personal as it gets: Jesus saved you! When you were a non-Christian can you remember how unlikely you thought it would be for you to become a Christian, especially when you didn't even believe that there was a God?! Peter also reminds us that "we were once not a people but are now the people of God," and that we at one time "had not obtained mercy but now have obtained mercy."

> *If you still need more encouragement, how about Jesus'*
> *statement to His disciples that "He who believes in Me, the*
> *works that I do he will do also; and greater works then these*
> *he will do, because I go to My Father."9 As to just what those*
> *"works" may be, I'll leave that up to you to decide, but as*
> *Abraham says, "Is anything to hard for the LORD?"10*

The following Worldview Building Blocks were discussed in the answers to our 50 questions and will hopefully provide a good review of those immutable ideas.

Christian Worldview Building Blocks

Worldview Building Block 1	God's Word is TRUTH, and man's word is FALSE. ONLY God's Word Works/Man's Word ONLY Fails.
Worldview Building Block 2	W.Q. (wisdom quotient), not I.Q. (intelligence quotient) is the important thing, just as having a Christian worldview, instead of a non-Christian worldview, is the important thing.
Worldview Building Block 3	When we think of the word "government, we need to remember God's definition of four self-governing spheres working together to redeem culture, with none of the self-governing spheres usurping any responsibilities from the other self-governing spheres.

Worldview Building Block 4	The Bible must be seen and be appreciated as God'slaw-word for all spheres of life, and not just a personal devotional guide. (God is sovereign, not man.)
Worldview Building Block 5	Christianity is not an "add-on" to our lifestyle, but a complete transformation of our lifestyle.
Worldview Building Block 6	Both "Tables" of the Ten Commandments are required for a smooth functioning society
Worldview Building Block 7	It is impossible for any society to be governed by more than one set of ethics.
Worldview Building Block 8	"All Law is 'religious'"
Worldview Building Block 9	We must be ever conscious that we are operating in God's world and that our efforts will fail unless we consistently live by God's rules. Piecemeal obedience will not enable us, our communities, our State, or America to be the recipients of God's promised blessings.
Worldview Building Block 10	We have the assurance from Scripture that as we live-out our faith (by applying biblical ethics to our decision-making) non-Christians will see our successful lifestyles and will be attracted to us. (Deuteronomy 4.5-7; Isaiah 2.1-5)

New Instruments for New Creations

I have been crucified with Christ; it is no longer I who live, but Christ lives in me; and the life which I now live in the flesh I live by faith in the Son of God, who loved me and gave Himself for me.　　　GALATIANS 2:20

Incorporating the ten Christian Worldview Building Blocks into our thinking and daily decision-making requires a new attitude toward life and the only way to have that is for the Holy Spirit to give us a new heart and write God's Law upon it so that we will be motivated to live as new creations in Christ's Kingdom. Without that supernatural heart transplant our attitude won't change. With it, it can't help but change. The following words by the esteemed Geneva Reformer, John Calvin, just about says it all.

The great point is that we are consecrated and dedicated to God and, therefore, should not think, speak, design, or act, without a view to His glory. What He has made sacred cannot, without insult to Him, be put to ill use. But if we are not our own, but the Lord's, it is plain both what error is to be shunned and to what end the actions of our lives ought to be directed. We are not our own; therefore, neither is our own reason or will to rule our acts and counsels. We are not our own; therefore, let us not make it our end to seek what may be agreeable to our carnal nature. We are not our own; therefore, as far as possible, let us forget ourselves and the things that are ours. On the other hand, we are God's; let us, therefore, live and die to Him (Rom. 14:8). We are God's; therefore, let His wisdom and will preside over all our actions. We are God's; to Him, then, as the only legitimate end, let every part of our life be directed.

Oh how great the proficiency of him who, taught that he is not his own, has withdrawn the dominion and government of himself from his own reason that he may give them to God! For as the surest source of destruction to men is to obey

*themselves, so the only haven of safety is to have no other will,
no other wisdom, than to follow the Lord wherever He leads.
Let this, then be the first step: to abandon ourselves and
devote the whole energy of our minds to the service of God.
By service, I mean not only that which consists in verbal
obedience, but that by which the mind, divested of its
own carnal feelings, implicitly obeys the call of the Spirit of
God. This transformation, though it is the first entrance
to life, was unknown to all the philosophers. They give the
government of man to reason alone, thinking that she alone is
to be listened to; in short, they assign to her the sole direction
of the conduct. But Christian philosophy bids her give place
and yield complete submission to the Holy Spirit, so that the
man himself no longer lives, but Christ lives and reigns in
him.* [11]

NOTES

1   Isaiah 8.14
2   Romans 9.32-33
3   Isaiah 62.2
4   Acts 11.26
5   Ephesians 2.20; Luke 20.17; Acts 4.11; Psalm 118.22
6   1 Peter 2.5
7   Matthew 16.8
8   Romans 8.37
9   John 14.12
10 Genesis 18.14
11 Calvin, John, *Day by Day with John Calvin*, (Hendrickson, 2002); Cited on *The Encourager* an e-devotion from the ITR Missions, www.hisglory.us

Foundations of Victory

1. We must trust in and rely on the inerrant promises in the Word of God.

    *O God, You are my God; I shall seek You earnestly; my soul
    thirsts for You ...*   PSALM 63.1 [DAVID]

2. We must focus on "The Promiser," not on the "improbability of the thing promised."

    *Therefore, since we have so great a cloud of witnesses
    surrounding us, let us also lay aside every encumbrance, and the
    sin which so easily entangles us, and let us run with endurance
    the race that is set before us.*   HEBREWS 12.1

3. We must subdue our inner kingdom of the flesh before we can subdue the outer kingdom of the world.

    *...in reference to your former manner of life, you lay aside the
    old self, which is being corrupted in accordance with the lusts of
    deceit, and that you be renewed in the spirit of your mind, and
    put on the new self, which in the likeness of God has been created
    in righteousness and holiness of the truth. ... Let all bitterness
    and wrath and anger and clamor and slander be put away
    from you, along with all malice. And be kind to one another,
    tenderhearted, forgiving each other, just as God in Christ also
    has forgiven you.*   EPHESIANS 4.22-32

4. We must acknowledge our personal inability to do great things for God, before we will be enabled by Him to do great things.

    *And because of the surpassing greatness of the revelations, for
    this reason, to keep me from exalting myself, there was given
    me a thorn in the flesh, a messenger of Satan to buffet me – to
    keep me from exalting myself! Concerning this I entreated the
    Lord, three times that it might depart from me. And He has said*

*to me, "My grace is sufficient for you, for power is perfected in
weakness." …*

*Therefore I am well content with weaknesses, with insults,
with distresses, with persecutions, with difficulties, for Christ's
sake; for when I am weak, then I am strong.*
2 CORINTHIANS 12.7-10

5. We must measure our success by our level of obedience, not by the
results of our obedience.

*I delight to do Your will, O my God; Your law is within my
heart.*   PSALM 40.8 [DAVID]

Well, done, good and faithful servant …   LUKE 19.17 [JESUS]

6. We must always keep Christ uppermost in our thoughts and not tol-
erate evil in any form; if it's from others, we must expose and resist it;
if it's from ourselves, we must repent of it.

Have this attitude in yourselves which was also in Christ Jesus.
PHILIPPIANS 2.5

7. We must remember that God is in complete control and that, sooner
or later, the faith of the church will overcome the rage of men.

*… upon this rock I will build My church; and the gates of Hades
shall not overpower it.*   MATTHEW 16.18

8. We must be more concerned with the consequences of not standing
for Christ, than the consequences of taking a stand for Him.

*Who will rise up for Me against evil doers? Who will stand up
for Me against the workers of iniquity?*   PSALM 94.16

*Stand in the old ways and see, and ask for the old paths, where
the good way is, and walk in it; then you will find rest for your
souls.*   JEREMIAH 6.16

Watch, stand fast in the faith, be brave, be strong.

1 CORINTHIANS 16.13

9. We must understand the political situation. We are living in the age of Politicians. To be successful we need to focus on two actions: (1) Dealing with current Politicians, and (2) Training Statesmen to replace Politicians. Politicians expect you to keep in touch with them (i.e., "the squeaky wheel gets the grease"). Statesmen make decisions based upon God's law (i.e., "it's either God's law, or chaos").

You shall select from all the people able men, such as fear God, men of truth, hating covetousness; and place such over them to be rulers of thousands, rulers of hundreds, rulers of fifties, and rulers of tens.

EXODUS 18.21

10. We must pray.

Rescue me, O Lord, from evil men; protect me from men of violence, who devise evil plans in their hearts and stir up war everyday. ...Keep me, O Lord, from the hands of the wicked; protect me from men of violence who plan to trip my feet. Proud men have hidden a snare for me; they have spread out the cords of their net and have set traps for me along my path. ... Do not grant the wicked their desires, O Lord; do not let their plans succeed, or they will become proud. Let the heads of those who surround me be covered with the trouble their lips have caused. ...Let the slanderers not be established in the land; may disaster hunt down men of violence. I know that the Lord secures justice for the poor and upholds the cause of the needy. Surely the righteous will praise Your name and the upright will live before You.

PSALM 140.1-2,4-5,8-9, 11-13 [DAVID]

In case you may want to re-take the Personal Worldview Checkup and to see how some of your answers have changed, the test is included in Appendix Two.

Appendix One

"Be ye therefore perfect..."

Now that you've replaced the ungodly strings with which Satan was influencing your daily decisions and resulting lifestyle, with God-honoring strings, wouldn't you agree that there should be nothing standing in the way of you living in perfect obedience to God? Did I hear you say, "No, I wouldn't agree, because nobody is perfect!" This reminds me of a statement from a friend of mine: "Nobody is perfect. I am a nobody, therefore I'm perfect." After having a good laugh, I replied, "Nice try, but since you are a special creation of God, you are somebody, therefore you're ethically imperfect."

Since we all agree that we're imperfect beings, how can we fulfill Jesus' command to "be perfect" in our service for Him? [1] In order to find out what Jesus means, we will provide the answer in the form of the acronym GRACE. Hopefully, this brief description of how to carry out our service to God will enable you and your family to understand how you can "stand perfect and complete in all the Word of God." [2]

GOD'S DEFINITION
REQUIREMENT
ASSISTANCE
CONSISTENCY
EXPECTATIONS

GOD'S DEFINITION

*Since we are imperfect inhabitants in an imperfect world,
what does it mean to be perfect in God's sight?*

347

The tendency to view the world through our eyes, rather than through God's eyes, leads us to equate "perfection" with outward behavior, however, we must not forget that God judges our actions by the inclination of our heart. Using the illustration that a tree is known by its fruit, Jesus explains, "For out of the abundance of the heart the mouth speaks. A good man out of the good treasure of his heart brings forth good things, and an evil man out of the evil treasure brings forth evil things." [3] Later, Jesus answers objections from the scribes and Pharisees about His disciples not strictly observing the traditions of the elders.

> *Hypocrites! Well did Isaiah prophesy about you, saying:*
> *"These people draw near to Me with their mouth, and*
> *honor Me with their lips, but their heart is far from Me.*
> *And in vain they worship Me, teaching as doctrines the*
> *commandments of men."*
> *...For out of the heart proceed evil thoughts, murders,*
> *adulteries, fornications, thefts, false witness, blasphemies.*
> MATTHEW 15.7-9, 19

This means that the same outward act could be judged by God to be either righteous or unrighteous, depending upon whether we were doing it to impress others (external motivation), or because we knew it was the right thing to do (internal motivation). The great Geneva Reformer, John Calvin, notes that the Bible consistently calls for "moral integrity... opposed to deceit and vain pretentiousness... We must not only regulate our hands and eyes, and feet, in obedience to his Law; but integrity of heart is above all things required, and holds the chief place in the true definition of righteousness." [4]

It could well be said that "Christianity is an inside out religion. If a person does not have the blessing of having had his heart changed by the Holy Spirit, what comes out of him in the form of words and behaviors, will not be pleasing to God. It is impossible to arrive at Christianity from the outside in. Regardless of a person's efforts of being a good, moralistic conservative neighbor, his behavior will not be sincere because he will still have his sinful heart that prevents him from putting God's will before his will.

Why isn't it OK to mix-in some of our wisdom with God's wisdom?

This question reveals a misunderstanding of who we were before making our profession of faith, and who we are after our conversion to Christianity. We readily agree that we were born sinners, [5] but we may not be so fast in agreeing with the biblical statements that in our non-Christian days, our thoughts and wisdom were "only evil continually." [6] King Solomon puts it this way: "Do you see a man wise in his own eyes? There is more hope for a fool than for him." [7] This means that once we become a member of God's family, we must be aware that our behavior is being affected by some remnants of the unholy character traits we had as non-Christians, and as these raise their ugly head, we must replace them with Christian traits. Unless we establish a goal of analyzing our daily decisions to determine whether they are framed according to the biblical truths in which we profess to believe, we will not be faithful in "casting off the works of darkness, and putting on" godly works. [8]

The result of not seriously evaluating our decisions is that we will con ourselves into thinking that it's alright to keep a few of our most favorite sins in our lifestyle. Such was the familiar case with the rich young ruler.[9] While he was a very moralistic person, he placed personal wealth above following Jesus. Knowing this, Jesus challenged him with the statement: "If you want to be perfect, go, sell what you have and give to the poor, and you will have treasure in heaven; and come, follow Me." [10] The point Jesus is making is not that personal wealth is bad, but that, anything that a person values more than conforming his lifestyle to God's Word is wrong. For some people, this may turn out to be their children, their spouse, or their vocation. Regardless of what it is, and regardless of how exemplary the remainder of a person's lifestyle may be, we must never forget that, as Christians, nothing should hold a more cherished place in our heart than obeying God's Word.

The more determined we are to live a non-compromising lifestyle, the better we will become at presenting a consistent testimony to our non-Christian neighbors. They will recognize that we are "walking" according to God's ethics [11] and that we "love them" (even though they don't deserve for us to), just as God loved us (when we didn't deserve it) before our conversion.[12]

We can see then that "perfection," in God's eyes, is an inside job. It does not mean all of our outward actions are "perfect," but that our new spiritual heart is motivating us to strive for perfection, by obeying biblical truths.[13] In God's eyes, we're all "works-in-progress." This is how King David could say, "The LORD will perfect that which concerns me; Your mercy, O LORD, endures forever; do not forsake the works of Your hands." [14] Being "perfect, just as our Father in heaven is perfect," [15] must be our aim, even though we know we won't be able to attain it. The least we can do for God, in exchange for all that He has done for us, is to give our best efforts at serving Him. Even though we will have our good and bad days in our obedience, we can be comforted to know that "the spirits of just men are being made perfect." [16]

Steps *toward* Perfection
- ✓ The Christian lifestyle is much more than being moralistic.
- ✓ Christianity is an inside out religion.
- ✓ God's will must be first in our priorities.

REQUIREMENT

As mentioned in the episode between the young ruler and Jesus, we must understand that we need to identify whatever it may be that is standing between giving our whole heart to the service of God, and replace it with God's will. Doing this demands that we be diligent and dutiful students of God's Word. Otherwise we will continue to be like children, who are "tossed to and fro and carried about with every wind of doctrine, by the trickery of men, in the cunning craftiness of deceitful plotting." [17] Just as rudders guide the direction of ships, so should God's Word guide the direction we take in life. [18] If we merely worship God's Word, instead of working it, we will be "carried away with diverse and strange doctrines" [19] with our lifestyle resembling "a wave of the sea driven with the wind and tossed." [20]

Becoming a member of God's family and Christ's Kingdom means beginning a lifelong journey toward completely transforming the way we saw the world as non-Christians. This, of course, will greatly affect the way we make our daily decisions. In our unredeemed state, we sought to "fit-in" to the prevailing attitudes of the day so we could be accepted by our friends, associates and neighbors. Since we believed in no objective absolute truths upon which to base our life and daily decisions, we mirrored the attitude of the scribes and Pharisees of Jesus' day by looking to public opinion, or common customs and ethics (e.g. "political correctness"). Now, however, we understand that our former way of viewing the world was completely erroneous, because it was based upon man's word, instead of God's Word. Therefore, we realize that we must "renew our mind" by conforming it to the "perfect will of God." [21] In Paul's words, we must "press toward the goal for the prize of the upward call of God in Christ Jesus." [22]

The apostle John instructs that if we love God, we will "keep His commandments." [23] In addition, our "love" toward one another is further proof that "God abides in us," and that His love is being "perfected in us."[24] When we were unworthy sinners God demonstrated His love toward us by sending His Son to live, die and overcome death for us, which is why it is necessary that we demonstrate love toward our non-Christian neighbors who are also unworthy sinners and, in many cases, are probably just as difficult for us to love, as we were for God to love us! The requirement to love our neighbor[25] is such a tall order that only those who have had a spiritual change of heart could be motivated, or enabled to do this. If we are indeed true servants of God, we will be convicted to love our unlovable neighbors, because when we see in them their hatred of God, we must realize that this is what God saw in us before sending Jesus to redeem us. Let's listen to these words of Jesus:

> *You have heard that it was said, "You shall love your neighbor*
> *and hate your enemy." But I say to you, love your enemies,*
> *bless those who curse you, do good to those who hate you, and*
> *pray for those who spitefully use you and persecute you, that*
> *you may be sons of your Father in heaven; for He makes His*
> *sun rise on the evil and on the good, and sends rain on the just*
> *and on the unjust.*   MATTHEW 5.43-45

Needless to say, this is very difficult advice. Indeed, it flies in the face of everything the non-Christian encompasses. As we recall from our non-Christian days, we were the most important people on the face

351

of the earth, and our view of other people centered on how to manipulate them to help us achieve our self-centered agenda. The idea of approaching the world with an others-centered agenda, while looking for nothing in return for our "good deeds," was completely alien to our former worldview. [26] And the thought of "loving our enemies," was not even on our ethical radar screen. [27]

Even though some non-Christians force themselves to do "good works," in the hopes of earning points toward going to heaven, it is drudgery for them because their sinful heart is opposed to doing the right thing. We, however, willingly obey God, because our sinful heart has been replaced by a holy heart that motivates us to put the interests of others first. [28]

Why should we love non-Christians and consider their interests, when they despise Christian ethics and hate our God?

Do we *really* need to ask this question? Do we not recall how unworthy we were, and how much we despised God's wisdom when He "first loved us?" [29]

- Yes, non-Christians have done nothing to deserve our thoughts, time, or efforts.
- Yes, they are rude and arrogant and consider us to be little more than outdated and superstitious simpletons.
- Yes, it will be impossible for them to understand our biblical reasoning, until the Holy Spirit changes their heart.

But hasn't our gracious and merciful God given us the marvelous privilege of "Making disciples of all the nations, baptizing them in the name of the Father and of the Son and of the Holy Spirit, and teaching them to observe all things that He has commanded us?" [30] Some may object by stating, "This sounds very nice, but let's be real, presenting Christian ethics to people who have not had a supernatural heart transplant by the Holy Spirit, is like speaking to someone in an unknown language. They simply will not be able to understand us!" Such reasoning is theologically true as far as it goes. The problem is it doesn't go far enough. We must remember that at the very moment we are talking to a non-Christian the Holy Spirit may be changing his heart. In addition, we must recognize that, as Christians, we should no longer view ourselves as being in the *results* business.

- Instead of evaluating whether a particular non-Christian may or may not be receptive to the Gospel (results-oriented), we should see ourselves as fulfilling our duties as a faithful servant of Christ's Kingdom (obedience-oriented).
- Instead of seeing ourselves as our own god, whereby we determine good and evil, and are solely responsible for bringing about results, we now should view ourselves as worshiping our Creator God, who perfectly defines good and evil behavior, and brings about His intended results based upon our obedience to His Word.
- Instead of imagining ourselves as being in the results business, we should view ourselves as being in the obedience business, as we do our best to live by biblical truths, and trust-in and rely-upon God to bless our behavior according to His eternally perfect timetable. 17th century Pastor John Davenant writes that "The whole sum of Christian wisdom consists in depending upon Christ alone, and understanding the counsel of God concerning our salvation obtained by him." [31] Davenant adds, "No one is perfect and complete in all the will of God, except he who both knows the will of God, and studies to perform it with all his might. For the will of God is, that we may know those things which he has revealed for our salvation; it is also the will of God, that we should do those things which he commands to be done in obedience to him. [32]

It is absolutely true that we can neither reason anyone into God's family, nor in any way cause them to make a decision to repent and turn their life over to following Jesus, but God can and will work these changes in our non-Christian neighbors as a result of our faithful efforts! As His messengers, we can have confidence that God "will "have mercy on whomever He desires, and have compassion on whomever He desires." [33]

May we not forget the distinctive difference between the manner in which non-Christians see their accomplishments as being of their own making, and/or of their own wisdom, or ingenuity, and the manner in which we recognize that it is only through God's grace and by following His wisdom that we are enabled to accomplish anything that is righteous. By remembering this, and keeping the realization that the Lord will never leave us,[34] we should be able to confidently approach our daily duties.

We all know that we should obey God's Word. The question is "How much does God expect us to obey it?"

As mentioned, when we were non-Christians, our chief and only consideration was to obey our will. Our new spiritual heart, however, has enabled us to view the world in a completely different manner with the result that our chief and only consideration should be to obey God's will. Just as we would have considered it silly to devote some of our non-Christian decisions to God's will, so should we consider it equally silly to devote some of our Christian decisions to man's will. At his dedication of the Temple, King Solomon urged his neighbors to let their heart "be loyal to the LORD your God, to walk in His statutes and keep His commandments." [35] The godly King Hezekiah lived his life by walking in godly obedience, and as he lay on his deathbed, he prayed for an extension of his life with the following words:

> *Remember now, O LORD, I pray, how I have walked before You in truth and with a loyal heart, and have done what was good in Your sight.* 2 KINGS 20.3

As a result of this prayer, Jehovah instructed the prophet Isaiah to tell the King that his life was going to be extended for another 15 years. The next time you make a request to God for assistance and/or wisdom in making a decision, can you approach Him by confidently citing your daily 24/7 walk with Him? Or, would the best testimony you could provide is that you obeyed Him from time-to-time, depending upon the circumstances? If your request would be based upon the latter, how confident would you be that He would hear, much less answer it? When we take our prayers and petitions to God, we can no doubt list some logical reasons for Him to grant our requests, but we should remember that God only hears the prayers of obedient servants. [36]

King David provides an excellent example of "walking with the Lord," both in public and private by promising to "walk within my house with a perfect heart." [37] We can see that the intentions of King David's heart are sincere by his promise to behave in private in the same exemplary manner as he will in carrying out his public duties. Each of us proves to ourselves whether we are holy or wise by all of our behavior, not only by the way we behave around fellow Christians. How we behave "when nobody is looking" is the quickest way to determine our true behavior. Far from being intoxicated with the power of public office, David was intoxicated with the opportunity to demonstrate obedience to God for all to see. So, in answering the question:

What's the big deal about conforming our daily decision-making to the biblical truths in which we profess to believe?

We can list at least three reasons:

- We cannot become all we can be for God by remaining what we are.
- We must realize that God has a desired response for us. It's not up to us to creatively figure out how to live the Christian life. God's revealed plan is clear and specific, and we must do our best to conform our lifestyle to His ethics, since this is the only way to maintain a right relationship with Him.
- Since God's rules are the only ones that count, and since He created a cause-and-effect universe, not a chaotic one, we must be careful that our daily behavior is not something that happens in a random manner, but rather in an intentional manner. In other words, we must intent our actions to conform to His Word.

Steps *toward* Perfection
✓ We must be diligent and dutiful students of God's Word.
✓ In our journey toward completely transforming our worldview and lifestyle, we must "press toward the perfect will of God."
✓ We must "love our neighbors as ourselves."
✓ We must behave in private the same way we behave in public.

```
┌─────────────── Requirements for Perfect Service ───────────────┐
│                       in Christ's Kingdom                       │
│                                                                 │
│   • Put God's will first.                    Matthew 6.33       │
│   • Trust in God's counsel.                  Galatians 3.3      │
│   • Present a brave and bold testimony for                      │
│     Christ's Kingdom by realizing that we are                   │
│     no longer under condemnation.            Romans 8.1; 1 John 4.17-18 │
│   • Demonstrate ethical integrity by not                        │
│     dividing our ethics between God and man. Psalm 119.113; James 1.8 │
│   • Leave elementary principles behind, and                     │
│     growing with solid food.                 Hebrews 5.11-14; 6.1 │
│   • Trust in God's control of His creation.  Proverbs 3.11-12   │
│   • Be patient in relying upon His eternally                    │
│     perfect plan to bring about His will on earth. James 1.4; Matthew 6.10 │
│   • Look for lessons in our circumstances by                    │
│     knowing that all things work together for                   │
│     good to those who love God, and are                         │
│     called according to his purpose.         Romans 8.28        │
│   • Serve God fearlessly, by admitting that                     │
│     our "perfect love for God casts out fear." 1 John 4.18      │
└─────────────────────────────────────────────────────────────────┘
```

ASSISTANCE

Since God has graciously called us into Christ's Kingdom to "crush the head of Satan," [38] we can be confident that He does not send us unarmed to the field of daily combat with non-Christians. 19th century British Pastor John Brown states, "God will fit you for the conflict to which you are called by supplying all your defects." [39] In Peter's words, God will "perfect, establish, strengthen, and settle us." [40]

Meanwhile, Paul reminds us that even the harshest of sufferings are of little consequence when compared to the many and continuous blessings we receive as members of God's family. [41]

How much assistance can we expect for God to provide
in our efforts to live according to biblical ethics?

The short answer is "God will provide us with everything we need to successfully accomplish the purpose for which He has called us!" His inerrant Word unfolds His perfect wisdom for how to live and govern ourselves. Scripture also shows us how He has blessed individuals and civilizations for living in obedience to His counsel, and cursed individuals and civilizations that have disobeyed His counsel. As King David declares, "It is God who arms me with strength, and makes my way perfect." [42] Paul proclaims that the God of all grace also promises to perfect, or mature, us in the faith.

> *Now may the God of peace who brought up our Lord Jesus*
> *from the dead, that great Shepherd of the sheep, through*
> *the blood of the everlasting covenant, make you complete in*
> *every good work to do His will, working in you what is well*
> *pleasing in His sight, through Jesus Christ, to whom be glory*
> *forever and ever. Amen.* HEBREWS 13.20-21

In addition to receiving instruction directly from His revealed Word, God raises up Pastors to formally proclaim His gospel, correctly divide His Word, [43] and to prepare us in how to live-out our profession of faith.

> *And He Himself gave some to be apostles, some prophets,*
> *some evangelists, and some pastors and teachers, [12] for the*
> *equipping of the saints for the work of ministry, for the*
> *edifying of the body of Christ, [13] till we all come to the unity*
> *of the faith and of the knowledge of the Son of God, to a*
> *perfect man, to the measure of the stature of the fullness of*
> *Christ.* EPHESIANS 4.11-13

Correct instruction "lights our path" [44] so that we don't fall into the ditch along side those have been taught by ungodly teachers. [45] By consistently studying God's Word and meditating over how we can apply it into our situations and circumstances, we will be able to discern those who "cheat us through philosophy and empty deceit, according to the tradition of men, according to the basic principles of the world, and not according to Christ." [46]

357

At various points in our Christian walk, each of us serves as either a disciple or a discipler, with the purpose of "presenting every man perfect in Christ Jesus," [47] to bring all kinds of people to that saving knowledge of Christ in which Christian perfection consists.

Steps *toward* Perfection

God fully equips us for each day's battles through:

✓ His perfect counsel on how to live and govern ourselves.
✓ Historical examples of His blessings to obedient individuals and civilizations, and His curses to disobedient individuals and civilizations.
✓ Faithful pastors and Bible teachers.
✓ Discipleship from mature Christians.

CONSISTENCY

As we mature in the faith, our level of consistent obedience to conform our lifestyle to biblical truths should become abundantly clear to everyone who may cross our path. We are promised that our "union" with each other in faithful and consistent obedience to God's will impresses and convicts "the world" of God's love toward us. This explains how presenting a consistent biblically ethical lifestyle is the most effective form of evangelism. [48] "Therefore," as Paul urges us, "having these promises, beloved, let us cleanse ourselves from all filthiness of the flesh and spirit, perfecting holiness in the fear of God." [49]

How much effort does God expect us to put toward faithfully and consistently conforming our lifestyle to His revealed counsel?

If we are not motivated to strive for consistent ethical excellence; if our Christian testimony is one of inconsistent, hit-and-miss, part-time level of biblical obedience, it is a very good indication that we are not recipients of a new spiritual heart, and that we need to repent and get serious about following God's will. In observing the way many Christians live, you would think that they have fallen for the myth of "microwave obedience!" By living according to this myth, they expect long-lasting positive changes in our culture by being on their best biblical behavior for only a few minutes during each day.

It is critical that we realize that we're not apathetic, disobedient caterpillars who are automatically going to turn into energetic, consistently obedient biblical butterflies one day. We are humans that need to be systematically, diligently and patiently taught how to replace the non-Christian behavioral patterns with Christian behaviors.

A hit-and-miss "microwave-type" of Christian lifestyle fails to present a distinctive biblical testimony to our non-Christian neighbors. This results in "the world not knowing that we know the correct way to live and govern ourselves." [50] While it is common for us to say that God's Word is true and perfect, and man's word is false and imperfect, we often don't live as though we really believe it. Sadly, we too often tend to live as though our "perfection" was begun by the Spirit, but that we can now grow in God's grace and knowledge by living according to our own "fleshly" wisdom! [51] Pastor John Brown notes the utter foolishness of such a lifestyle:

> *The religion you at first adopted was a religion which, from its perfection, renders any addition utterly useless. You may—you must—debase it, but you cannot possibly improve it, by any supplement. Your progress is not improvement, it is degeneracy. It is not the child becoming the man, but the man becoming the child. To pass from Judaism to Christianity is— having begun in the flesh—to be perfected by the Spirit. For the Jew to become a Christian, was for the child to become a man—a natural, desirable course. For the Christian to become a Jew, is for the man voluntarily to sink into a second childhood—a most unnatural and undesirable course.*
>
> *They, in receiving the gospel, began with what was spiritual—knowledge, faith, holiness, hope, joy; in submitting to the law, they end in 'meats, and drinks, and divers washings.'"* [52]

Steps *toward* Perfection
Our faithful and consistent ethical obedience.
- ✓ Proves to us that we have received a new spiritual heart.
- ✓ Presents a distinctive biblical testimony to our non-Christian neighbors and convicts them that the best way to live is God's way.

EXPECTATIONS

Talk to the typical American churchgoer and you will find that he has no expectation and/or hope in achieving earthly success. His only hope is in eternal success. As we will see, God's Word expresses much expectation and hope for earthly success. The following familiar words from the apostle Paul emphasize that God's Word "thoroughly equips us for every good work." However, from the attitude of most 21st century Christians, you would think that Paul said the purpose of God's Word is to "equip us to supernaturally escape our work."

> *All Scripture is given by inspiration of God, and is profitable*
> *for doctrine, for reproof, for correction, for instruction*
> *in righteousness, that the man of God may be complete,*
> *thoroughly equipped for every good work.*
>
> 2 TIMOTHY 3.16-17

The esteemed 19th century Southern theologian, Rev. W. S. Plumer, was certainly not pessimistic about the duties to which we are called. He writes, "God will never fail us, provided we follow our calling, keep ourselves within the limits it prescribes, and undertake nothing without the command or warrant of God." [53] Part of Rev. Plumer's optimism can undoubtedly be traced to the fact that he was familiar with the biblical principle that, as we live-out our faith, we will be blessed by God and the "fame" from this will "go out among the nations" and bring honor to God. [54] This is why Christians are referred to as "seals of perfection," and as being "full of wisdom and perfect in beauty." [55]

The widespread pessimism on the part of 21st century Christians causes many of us to automatically translate any "positive" proclamation in Scripture as being something that will happen in heaven, or in a future generation. The puny explanation given for such a belief is that "Things look so bad, and how can God possibly be referring a positive blessing to our times!" However, despite this widely held disbelieving and pessimistic pragmatism, there is no biblical basis to believe that the following optimistic words from King Solomon refer exclusively to eternal judgment.

The hope of the righteous will be gladness, but the expectation of the wicked will perish. The way of the LORD is strength for the upright, but destruction will come to the workers of iniquity. The righteous will never be removed, but the wicked will not inhabit the earth. PROVERBS 10.28-30

We have a "glad" hope because we know that our God cannot lie, [56] and that His many promises to us of earthly victory will be fulfilled. In the words, of Paul, God's hope "does not disappoint." [57] It is common today for many of our Christian brothers and sisters to expect and hope to be supernaturally rescued from our earthly responsibilities, but we see King Solomon telling us that by carrying out our commanded duties we will be "strengthened" so that we can successfully carry them out. The prophet Isaiah agrees: "He gives power to the weak, and to those who have no might He increases strength." [58] May we not forget Who has sent us to do our commanded work! [59] Isaiah instructs that instead of supernaturally flying away from our duties, we will fly into our earthly duties with the strength of eagles, and that we shall also run and not get weary!

But those who wait on the LORD shall renew their strength; they shall mount up with wings like eagles, they shall run and not be weary, they shall walk and not faint. ISAIAH 40.31

There is a truism among sports coaches to "not put a player in a position to fail." By this, coaches refrain from calling a play that the player has not demonstrated in practice that he can successfully perform. But in the "game" of life, our "Coach" promises "not to forsake us" in our efforts, as long as we "don't forsake Him." [60] We should be familiar with the numerous historical examples of God strengthening members of His family to successfully carry out their commanded responsibilities. Here are a few of the more memorable persons:

- Joseph in Potipher's house   Genesis 39.10
- Obadiah in Ahab's house   1 Kings 18.13
- Daniel in the Persian court   Daniel 6.10
- Peter and John at the Sanhedrin   Acts 4.1-20

Do the following statements by Job, King David, Zechariah and Paul indicate that our only "expectation" and "hope" is to be rescued from our calling on the earth?

Yet the righteous will hold to his way, and he who has clean hands will be stronger and stronger. **JOB 17.9**

Blessed is the man whose strength is in You, whose heart is set on pilgrimage. As they pass through the Valley of Baca, they make it a spring; the rain also covers it with pools. They go from strength to strength. **PSALM 84.5-7**

So I will strengthen them in the LORD, and they shall walk up and down in His name," says the LORD. **ZECHARIAH 10.12**

I can do all things through Christ who strengthens me. **PHILIPPIANS 4.13**

Obviously, the answer to our question is that God has no intention of rescuing us from the commanded duties for which He has so completely prepared us to fulfill. Even Jesus prays that we not be rescued, but "kept from the evil one," so that we can complete Satan's defeat. [61] Not only is this very good news for us, it is very bad news for our non-Christian neighbors. While our feet run to righteousness and eventual victory, their feet "run to evil" and their "thoughts to iniquity." [62] The result of this for them is "destruction, misery and no peace of mind." [63] Indeed, not even their worship is recognized by God. [64]

What else could we possibly ask for in order to have an optimistic and confident attitude toward completing the most meaningful work to which God has called us?

Our very Lord promises that even if "the mountains depart and the hills be removed, His kindness shall not depart from us!" [65] Paul poignantly proclaims:

For I am persuaded that neither death nor life, nor angels nor principalities nor powers, nor things present nor things to come, nor height nor depth, nor any other created thing, shall be able to separate us from the love of God which is in Christ Jesus our Lord. ROMANS 8.38-39

- What more can God do for us than He is already doing?
- Why do we persist in our subjective negative and expectations about the earth, when He has revealed such objective and positive expectations? [66]
- Instead of demonstrating to our non-Christian neighbors that we are cowardly hoping to be supernaturally rescued from our commanded duties, why don't we bravely demonstrate to them our obedience to God's commandments, and "declare them to our children?" [67]

Perhaps the answers to these questions can be found in the fact that we:

✓ watch television more than we read our Bible and meditate on ways to incorporate its truths into our lifestyle. Or, that

✓ we spend more time studying our favorite sports team than God's promises to bless our obedience during our life on earth! Or, that

✓ we are more ashamed to explain that we are living according to biblical truths, instead of going with current "politically correct" ideology. [68] Or,

✓ that we are so absorbed with living according to our will that we forget the "endless mercies and compassions" we receive from God on a daily basis. [69]

Whatever the answer may be to the above questions, we should not need to be told how foolish it is to interpret events and circumstances according to our wisdom. As King Solomon exclaims, "There is more hope for a fool than for a person wise in his own eyes." [70]

We should not have to read very far into the Bible to recognize that our expectation" is for God to be our "rock and our salvation and our defense." [71] Paul explains that the "hope of our calling" is to be used by

363

God to put His ethics paramount in the minds of our neighbors, so that "He will be head over all things."

> *[I pray] that the God of our Lord Jesus Christ, the Father of glory, may give to you the spirit of wisdom and revelation in the knowledge of Him, the eyes of your understanding being enlightened; that you may know what is the hope of His calling, what are the riches of the glory of His inheritance in the saints, and what is the exceeding greatness of His power toward us who believe, according to the working of His mighty power which He worked in Christ when He raised Him from the dead and seated Him at His right hand in the heavenly places, far above all principality and power and might and dominion, and every name that is named, not only in this age but also in that which is to come. And He put all things under His feet, and gave Him to be head over all things to the church.* EPHESIANS 1.17-22

How are we to teach God's optimistic hope to our pessimistic brothers and sisters?

First and foremost, we should encourage them to begin reading the Bible, and to stop listening to the erroneous pessimistic teaching from most radio and television preachers (and perhaps, even their own pastor!). Next, ask that they put aside thoughts about what they imagine the Bible is going to say, and to let its message speak for itself. Then, encourage them to find a person who is mature in the faith to answer the questions that will most certainly come as they study God's Word.

In all likelihood, most Christians you talk to will have no idea of how to live-out their faith, because most pastors stop with the exposition of what God's Word says, and not what impact it should be having on the worldview and lifestyle of their members. This unfortunate circumstance makes it difficult for a person who has been used to hearing only negative earthly outcomes from being a Christian, to connect positive results to the biblical truths he reads in the Bible. Before a person is able to apply a biblical truth to his everyday decision-making, he must be able to perceive and conceptualize exactly how he is going to apply it.

Arguably, no one is better at teaching how to do this than sports coaches. Pastors, small group leaders as well as all Bible teachers can learn a lot from their teaching methods. The next time you have an opportunity to listen to a coach talk about how he is preparing his team for an upcoming season, you will probably hear him talk about the "process" he expects his players to go through in their preparations and practices, rather than the number of wins he thinks they might have. Successful coaches know that proper execution is the key to winning games, so instead of talking about winning and losing, they stress the importance of learning how to perform particular plays, and the necessity of carrying out their assignments during the games. The reason for this is that they know that the team that makes the fewest mistakes in a game is usually the victor.

Coaches use the "whole-part-whole" teaching method. First they "show" their players how to perform a play. This can be done by a film, or an actual demonstration. Then they have the players practice the play so that it becomes apparent which parts of the play need further practice. The players then practice their particular "parts," until the coaches feel comfortable that they are performing them correctly, then, the whole team is brought back together to practice the whole play once more.

Since Bible teaching is done verbally, rather than physically, you are going to have to be creative in order to take advantage of the strengths of the "whole-part-whole" instruction method, but it can be done. For example, you can begin by painting a mental picture of God's Big Picture for the particular topic you are instructing, then provide examples of how people with different spiritual gifts can use their abilities to accomplish God's intended purposes. The process could go something like this:

- The "whole:" Introduce God's Big Picture view of how a particular biblical truth will bring perfect wisdom to a cultural issue.
- The "part:" Paint mental pictures and provide examples of how the learners can use their various spiritual gifts to demonstrate this truth to their non-Christian neighbors. (Their Little Picture view.)
- Conclude God's Big Picture view by pointing to a historical example of a civilization that was blessed by God for their obedience, and how your learners can expect similar blessings, since God

never changes. Also provide a handout that summarizes the key points and lists some examples of how to apply the biblical truths. Unless you are lecturing, make note of responses from the learners to determine if you need to meet individually with them to answer any questions or concerns about the message.

Sports coaches "get it."
Sports fans "get it."
But, once again, Christians
are the last group to "get it."

Where is it written that once a person becomes a Christian,
he must put his brain on "hold?"

Such an idea is not to found in Scripture. God, Himself, urges us to "reason together." [72] As sports fans, we "get it" when the coach of our favorite team says that in order to defeat an upcoming opponent "we will have to play a perfect game." We don't question his statement by thinking, "Since none of our players are perfect, how can we expect for them to play perfectly?" We know that what the coach means is that if our players play up to their potential, we have a chance to win. Why, then, do we have such a difficult time "getting" that when Jesus commands us to "be perfect," what He is saying, is that we must have a personal goal to give out best effort at serving Him each day?

By revealing His perfect instructions to us on how we are to conform our worldview and lifestyle to His expectations, not our opinions, God has served His theological tennis ball into our court.

What are you going to do?

Are you going to watch it skip by, as previous generations of American Christians have done, and give non-Christians unfettered access to further de-Christianize our culture? Or, are you going to return His serve by faithfully and consistently conforming your behavior to His ethics? If your decision is to return His serve, then you are serving Him "perfectly." This, of course, doesn't mean that you aren't making mistakes, but rather that you are "in step" with His perfect will for the earth.

Steps *toward* Perfection

- ✓ Our worldview and lifestyle is optimistic because we are confident that God is in complete control of His creation.
- ✓ We have an expectation for success both on the earth and in heaven.
- ✓ We understand that God has called us to redeem the earth and will not substitute anyone to take our place, so that we can know that our consistent and faithful efforts will help bring about God's will on earth as it is in heaven.

A Summary of the Steps Toward Perfection
GRACE

GOD'S DEFINITION
- ✓ The Christian lifestyle is much more than being moralistic.
- ✓ Christianity is an inside out religion.
- ✓ God's will must be first in our priorities.

REQUIREMENT
- ✓ We must be diligent and dutiful students of God's Word.
- ✓ In our journey toward completely transforming our worldview and lifestyle, we must "press toward the perfect will of God."
- ✓ We must "love our neighbors as ourselves."
- ✓ We must behave in private the same way we behave in public.

ASSISTANCE
God fully equips us for each day's battles through:
- ✓ His perfect counsel on how to live and govern ourselves.
- ✓ Historical examples of His blessings to obedient individuals and civilizations, and His curses to disobedient individuals and civilizations.
- ✓ Faithful pastors and Bible teachers.
- ✓ Discipleship from mature Christians.

CONSISTENCY
Our faithful and consistent ethical obedience:
- ✓ Proves to us that we have received a new spiritual heart.
- ✓ Present a distinctive biblical testimony to our non-Christian neighbors and convicts the that the best way to live is God's way.

EXPECTATIONS
- ✓ Our worldview and lifestyle is optimistic because we are confident that God is in complete control of His creation.
- ✓ We have an expectation for success both on the earth and in heaven.
- ✓ We understand that God has called us to redeem the earth and will not substitute anyone to take our place, so that we can know that our consistent and faithful efforts will help bring about God's will on earth as it is in heaven.

NOTES

1　Matthew 5.48
2　Colossians 4.12
3　Matthew 12.34-35
4　Calvin, John, *Genesis*, (Banner of Truth Trust [1554], 1975), p.251
5　Romans 3.23
6　Genesis 6.5
7　Proverbs 26.12
8　Romans 13.12
9　Matthew 19.16-22
10　Matthew 19.21
11　Genesis 6.9
12　John 17.23
13　Philippians 2.13
14　Psalm 138.8
15　Matthew 5.48
16　Hebrews 12.23
17　Ephesians 4.14
18　James 3.4
19　Hebrews 13.9
20　James 1.6
21　Romans 12.2
22　Philippians 3.14-15
23　1 John 5.3
24　1 John 4.12
25　Matthew 22.39
26　Romans 8.1
27　Luke 6.35
28　Philippians 2.4
29　1 John 4.10
30　Matthew 28.19-20
31　Davenant, John, *Colossians*, (Banner of Truth Trust [1627], 2005), p.322
32　Davenant, *ibid., Colossians*, pp. 290-91
33　Romans 9.15
34　Hebrews 13.5
35　1 Kings 8.61
36　1 Peter 3.12
37　Psalm 101.2
38　Genesis 3.15; Romans 16.20
39　Brown, John, 1 Peter, Volume 2, (Banner of Truth Trust [1848], 1975), p. 592
40　1 Peter 5.10
41　2 Corinthians 4.17
42　Psalm 18.32
43　2 Timothy 2.15
44　Proverbs 4.18
45　Matthew 15.14
46　Colossians 2.8; 4.12
47　Colossians 1.28
48　Deuteronomy 4.5-9
49　2 Corinthians 7.1
50　John 17.23
51　Galatians 3.3
52　Brown, John, *Galatians*, (Banner of Truth Trust [1853], 2001), p.111
53　Cited in Plumer, W.S., *Psalms*, (Banner of Truth Trust [1867], 1975), p. 250
54　Ezekiel 16.14
55　Ezekiel 28.12
56　Hebrews 6.17-18
57　Romans 5.5
58　Isaiah 40.29
59　Judges 6.14
60　2 Chronicles 15.2
61　John 17.15
62　Isaiah 59.7
63　Romans 3.16-17
64　Isaiah 1.11
65　Isaiah 54.10
66　Isaiah 5.3-5
67　Psalm 78.6-8
68　Jeremiah 2.25-30
69　Lamentations 3.20-25
70　Proverbs 26.12
71　Psalm 62.5-6
72　Isaiah 1.18

Appendix Two

Your Very Own, Self-Administered, Personal Worldview Checkup*

First Cut | Education

1. What is man?
   a. A biological accident.
   b. A special creature made by God.

2. Should instruction be exclusively based upon absolute truth?
   a. No.
   b. Yes.

3. Should teachers instruct students in "basic and relative ethics" facts," or in "basic facts and absolute ethics?"
   a. Relative Ethics.
   b. Absolute Ethics.

4. Should students be taught the principles of self-government, or should they be instructed in how to work in groups to form a "consensus" or a "synthesis" of opinions through "Group Think?"
   a. Consensus and/or synthesis
   b. Self-government

5. The teaching of history
   a. Actual history should be revised to fit a politicized view that all cultures, at bottom are identical, since all religions are, at bottom, equally irrelevant.

b. The actual history of Western civilization (which is based upon biblical ethics) is contrasted with the history of Eastern civilization (which is based upon non-biblical ethics), because *only* God's Word gives the correct principles on how to live and govern ourselves.

6. Is there such a thing as a "mind," or are the only things "real," those that can be "touched, seen, smelled, or objectively measured?"
   a. There is no "mind."
   b. There is a "mind."

7. Should the curriculum be child-centered, or Christ-centered?
   a. Child-centered
   b. Christ-centered

8. Students should be taught how to bring "glory and honor to God" in everything they do.
   a. False
   b. True

9. Christian education is:
   a. An optional add-on to a child's worldview.
   b. It is an essential part of The Great Commission.
      (Matthew 22.37; 28.18-20)

10. How does a person become "wise?"
    a. Be a good student; go to the best schools and sit under the best teachers, and learn from our experiences.
    b. Study the Word of God.

11. What is the purpose of an education?
    a. Prepare us for a paycheck.
    b. Prepare us for life.

12. Who is responsible for the education of children?
    a. The state
    b. Parents

13. Where is the best place to educate students?
    a. In a structured classroom.
    b. Wherever we "sit, walk, lie down, and rise up."
       (Deuteronomy 6.7)

14. Should teachers get to know the worldview of their students, or should they stick to the curriculum?
    a. Stick to the curriculum.
    b. Learn the worldview of the students.

15. Teachers should pray with and for their students.
    a. False
    b. True

16. When it comes to the issue of Christian education:
    a. Pastors should approach this in a pragmatic manner by not addressing it because it is a divisive issue and they will lose members (or their job!). Besides many churches have members (including officers) who are affiliated with the public schools and/or who send their children to the public schools.
    b. Pastors should approach this in a pious manner by obeying God's clear commands and thoroughly explain the sin of sending Christian children to schools that hate God and only promote the worship of false religions. (Deuteronomy 6.4-7; Isaiah 36.9; 2 Corinthians 6.14; Matthew 15.14, etc.) In the process of doing this, the pastors are providing a testimony to their members that they practice what they preach by trusting-in and relying-upon God's sovereign control of His creation to honor our obedience and curse our disobedience.

17. Is it a sin to submit our children to programs and policies of non-Christians, and/or to join with non-Christians in business ventures?
    a. No
    b. Yes

18. **What does the separation of church and state mean?**
    a. The church shouldn't have anything to do with the state, and the state shouldn't have anything to do with the church. Both should be entirely separate.
    b. God gave each self-governing sphere (individual, family, church, state) particular responsibilities, and neither sphere should usurp any responsibilities of the other.

19. **Should we depend upon the civil government to "legislate" us out of our cultural problems, or should we "self-govern" ourselves out of our cultural problems?**
    a. Legislate
    b. Self-govern

20. **Our civil laws:**
    a. Should be based upon man's opinions and "best guesses," which means sometimes there will be some "gray" areas when the courts administer justice.
    b. Should be based upon God's absolute ethics as revealed on the in errant pages of the Bible, which means there are only "black and white" areas of right and wrong behavior.

21. **Our elected representatives should govern as:**
    a. Politicians
    b. Statesmen

22. **When we vote:**
    a. Do we vote for the "lesser of two evils," or
    b. Do we vote to "overcome evil with good?" (Romans 12.21)

23. **Which economic policies do you favor?**
    a. Those which promote the socialistic "heavy hand" of civil government? or
    b. Those which promote biblical capitalistic principles of self-government?

24. Do you see the role of civil government as:
    a. Providing a wide array of social programs, including education? or
    b. Defending us against attack and keeping our communities safe
    for us to live, work, play and raise our families the way we want?

25. We should "Render to Caesar:"
    a. Everything he asks, because Jesus says so.
    b. Only the things that are Caesar's, because Jesus says so.

26. Should Christians be involved in civil government?
    a. No, all politicians are crooks, and we should not dirty our hands
    in that field.
    b. Yes, a Christian can bring honor and glory to God in all areas
    of life, and since God has given only *one* ethical code by which to
    live, Christian statesmen can help ensure that only biblical
    legislation takes place.

Third Cut | Worldview & Lifestyle

27. What does having a Christian worldview mean to you?
    a. It helps me to know the differences between how Christians and
    non-Christians view the world.
    b. It helps me to know the *descriptions* of the differences between a
    Christian and non-Christian worldview, plus it helps me know
    God's *prescriptions* for how to deal with the various cultural issues.

28. In order to have a satisfying lifestyle:
    a. We can depend upon our self-sufficiency, personal initiative,
    education and the practical application of our knowledge to an
    ever-changing value standard of relative ethics, or
    b. We can depend upon God's Word to sufficiently provide us with
    all the wisdom needed to live and govern ourselves successfully in
    accordance with an absolute and unchanging value standard.

29. When it comes to one's worldview and lifestyle:
   a. There two ethical value standards: a "religious" one to be used in our homes and churches, and a "real life" one to be used in our vocations and/or with non-Christians?
   b. There is only one absolute and unchanging ethical standard for all areas of our life and for all the situations and circumstances in which we may find ourselves?

30. Is your worldview and lifestyle based upon:
   a. The 2nd Table of God's Law: Commandments 5-10 (honor those in authority, don't kill, cheat, steal, lie or be jealous)? Or
   b. Upon both the 2nd Table *and* the 1st Table of God's Law: Commandments 1-4 (worship only the one true God of the Bible, don't make idols, or misuse the name of the Lord, and to keep the Lord's Day holy)?

31. When God tells us to "walk in all the ways that I have commanded you, so that it may be well with you," (Jeremiah 7.23) what does this verse mean to you?
   a. God made a mistake, He really didn't mean it, and we won't be punished if we only make an effort to obey those parts of the Bible that conform to our current worldview and lifestyle. After all, nobody is perfect!
   b. Even though we are imperfect and will never be able to obey God perfectly, we should strive to do that because God never makes mistakes and means what He says. We should put forth our best effort, knowing that we will blessed if we obey God, and cursed if we disobey Him.

32. I believe that:
   a. God exists for us.
   b. We exist for God.

33. Who's "running the show?" Who's in charge of planet earth?
   a. Satan
   b. Jesus

34. As Christians do we have a
    a. Hope to cope?
       Or a
    b. Hope to conquer?

35. It is said that a "text without a context is a pretext," and so is a "worldview and lifestyle without a biblical reference point, pointless." This is why we should always ask before making any decision, or addressing any cultural issue:
    a. Is the *context* of my decision-making man's word?
    b. Is the *context* of my decision-making God's Word?

36. Which statement correctly describes the Christian attitude?
    a. We should keep in our place and not impose our religion on others.
    b. We should "boldly" and "confidently" live by God's ethics at *all* times and in *all* places.

37. Which group of people controls history?
    a. Non-Christians
    b. Christians

38. Are the times in which we are living "normal," or "abnormal?"
    a. Normal
    b. Abnormal

39. God's Word is:
    a. Something soothing for our troubled mind.
    b. A lamp to our feet.

40. How do we "enlarge the place of Christ's tent?" (Isaiah 54.2)
    a. Be seeker-friendly and water down God's Word so that we won't offend non-Christians by using words such as "sin," and "hell."
    b. Teach the whole counsel of God's Word and trust in God's sovereign control to bless the preaching of His Word.

41. **Our duty as Christians:**
   a. Rely-upon and trust-in the advice of *others* when they tell us that we are supposed to live and interpret the Bible within the frame work of current events.
   b. Trust-in and rely-upon God's Word to guide and direct our daily actions.

42. **Are we:**
   a. Armed with God's perfect counsel, and not dangerous?
   b. Dangerous because we have the potential for changing our culture with God's ethics, but don't know *how* to go about it because many of our pastors have done a poor job of teaching us?

43. **Is your daily testimony (lifestyle):**
   a. About the same as the lifestyle of your non-Christian neighbors.
   b. Significantly different than that of your non-Christian neighbors.

44. **Do we live in an orderly, cause-and-effect universe, or in a universe where events happen randomly?**
   a. A random universe.
   b. An orderly universe.

Fourth Cut | Decision-Making

45. **Is it possible for us to make correct decisions by depending upon our own wisdom and common sense?**
   a. Yes, after all, God has given us a brain and the ability to communicate.
   b. No, because Adam and Eve's disobedience impaired our ability to reason correctly. This is why we need to filter all of our decisions through a gird of biblical ethics. Thinking God's thoughts after Him is the only way we can be confident that we will arrive at correct decisions.

46. **What is your opinion regarding God's Word?**
   a. I have *respect* for it.
   b. I have a *reverential fear* of it.

47. **What is the "Chief Influencer" of your daily decisions?**
    a. What's in it for *Me?* or
    b. What's in it for *God?*

48. **What's the Context of Your Worldview?**
    a. It's pretty much the ethics of commandments 5-10: Honor those in authority, don't murder, cheat, steal, lie or covet.
    b. It is a combination of all Ten Commandments, plus the application of the Case Laws that follow them, whereby Moses tells us how to live and govern ourselves.

49. **What are the criteria you use to make your best decisions?**
    a. The "prevailing opinion" of other Christians, plus my common sense and logic.
    b. God's Word is the primary authority, but for those topics about which I haven't studied, I comply with the counsel of other Christians.

50. **Do you lean on your understanding, or upon God's?**
    a. Are you going to mirror the way non-Christians live, making your daily decisions according to your wisdom, while *adding* moralistic ethics to your lifestyle in an external effort to win points with God? Or,
    b. Are you going to mirror the way the Bible commands you to live, with your external actions founded on the internal motivations of your new spiritual heart.

Total of "A" answers   _____
Total of "B" answers   _____

Multiply the "B" answers by 2
to get a numerical score.   _____

Bibliography

Adams, John
The Works of John Adams
Little and Brown

Alderson, Dr. Richard
No Holiness, No Heaven!
Banner of Truth Trust

Alleine, Richard
The World Conquered by the Faithful Christian
Soli Deo Gloria

Augustine, Saint
Confessions, Book 1
Westminster Press

Brooks, Thomas
The Works of Thomas Brooks
Banner of Truth Trust

Bridges, Charles
Ecclesiastes
Banner of Truth Trust

Burroughs, Jeremiah
Hope
Soli Deo Gloria

Calvin, John
Calvin's Commentaries, Vol. XVI
Baker Books

Calvin, John
Institutes of the Christian Religion, Vol. I
Westminster

Chodes, John
Destroying the Republic: Jabez Curryt and the Re-Education of the Old South
Algora

Dabney, Robert L.
Discussions, Vol. One
Banner of Truth Trust

Dewey, John
Experience & Education
Touchstone

Dewey, John
Finding Dewey in the Foxfire Approach
Starnes, Paris, & Stevens

Dewey, John
The Early Works of John Dewey
Southern Illinois University Press

Eastman, Max
Capital, The Communist Manifesto, and other writings of Karl Marx
Carlton House

Flavel, John
Keeping the Heart
Soli Deo Gloria

Hanson, Buddy
Bottom Line Theology: A Bible Study Feast for those who only have Time for a Sandwich
Hanson Group

Hanson, Buddy
The Christian Civil Ruler's Handbook
Hanson Group

Hanson, Buddy
Choose This Day: God's Instructions on How to Select Leaders
Hanson Group

Hanson, Buddy
EXIT Strategy: A Handbook to Exponentially Improve Your Serve for God
Hanson Group

Hanson, Buddy
God's Ten Words: Practical Applications from the Ten Commandments
Hanson Group

Hanson, Buddy
It's Time to Un-Quo the Status
Hanson Group

Hanson, Buddy
This Is Not A Drill! Real Lessons for Real People from the Real God on How to Live and Govern Ourselves, Really!
Hanson Group

Hanson, Buddy
What's Scripture Got to Do with It?
Hanson Group

Hanson, Buddy
Spiritual Bullets for your Daily Spiritual Battles
Hanson Group

Hendriksen, William
The Gospel of Matthew
Baker Book House

Henry, Matthew
Matthew Henry's Commentaries on the Whole Bible, Vol. III
MacDonald

Jordan, James B.
The Journal of Christian Reconstruction, Vol. V, No. 2
Chalcedon

Lewis, C.S.
Till We Have Faces
Fount

Luther, Martin
Luther's Works Weimar Edition
Briefwechsel

Machen, J. Gresham
What Is Christianity?
Eerdmans

Marx, Karl and Friedrich Engels
The German Ideology, "Thesis on Feurbach"
International Publishing

Milton, John
On Education
The Milton Reading Room
Dartmouth College

Morecraft III, Rev. Joseph
With Liberty & Justice for All
Onward Press

Neuhaus, John Richard, ed.
Democracy and the Renewal of Public Education
Eerdmans

Paul, Richard
Critical Thinking: What Every Person Needs to Survive in a Rapidly Changing World,
The Center and Foundation for Critical Thinking

Rushdoony, R.J.
By What Standard?
Thoburn Press

Rushdoony, R.J.
Tithing & Dominion
Ross House Books

Shultz, Dr. Glen
Kingdom Education: God's Plan for Educating Future Generations
LifeWay

Shakespeare, William
Complete Works, "Othello," Act 2, Scene 3
Oxford

Shortt, Bruce
The Harsh Truth about Public Schools
Chalcedon Foundation

Van Til, Cornelius
Christian Theistic Ethics
Presbyterian and Reformed Publishing

Wallen, Ed
Discipleship
Hanson Group

Warfield, B.B.
Faith and Life
Banner of Truth Trust

Connect the "Spiritual Dots" of Your Life's Game Plan

- Everyday Living (Worldview)
- Biblical Basics
- Business & Politics
- Spiritual Growth

Thy Will Be Done on Earth:
Heavenly Insights for Down-to-Earth Living from the Prophet Isaiah

Isaiah's "fifth Gospel" is the most quoted Old Testament book in the New Testament. Isaiah's message offers valuable insights on how to best deal with the situations and circumstances in which we find ourselves. Pastor and author Martyn Lloyd-Jones writes, "[Isaiah] is relevant because it is a book that deals with men and women in their relationships to God ... this is not merely a contemporary message, it is the message of God for the condition of humanity at all times and in all places."

RETURN TO SINNER
Are Your Daily Decisions Betraying Your Christian Testimony?

- What does it mean to be a Christian?
- What is it like to "image" Jesus in what we think, say and do?
- What changes need to be made in the worldview and lifestyle of a new Christian from the worldview and lifestyle he had before his conversion?

If a non-Christian were to ask any Christian these typical questions, he would likely receive some impressive answers. However, when the non-Christian begins to try to find Christian neighbors who are living according to the answers he receives, he may very well conclude that "all of this town's Christians must have gone on vacation." RETURN describes how to "love the Lord your God with your whole heart," and live your life in a God-honoring manner.

This Is Not A Drill:
Real Lessons for *Real* People from the
Real God,
Through His prophets,
On *how* to *live* and govern ourselves,
Really!

This Is Not A Drill is designed to be a resource book for you and your family (and hopefully even a small group study with your friends). With this in mind, the format has been designed more along that of a textbook, than a novel. To help you understand the historical circumstances to which each prophet is speaking, the content is divided into three sections:
- History & Hypocrisy: Conforming ourselves to the world
- Habits: Reforming ourselves to the Word, and
- Holiness or Holocaust? Blessings or Curses: God's sovereignty in History and Prophecy

---

Its Time to Un-Quo the Status
How to normalize the present Abnormal culture of a non-Christian,
Upside-down world and
Turn it right-side up with Christian principles

What does being a Christian mean? Should our lifestyle really be different than that of a non-Christian? And what about our culture: Is "tweaking it" a little with Christian values about the best we can expect, or should we strive to completely transform it? It's Time to Un-Quo the Status addresses these issues by discussing four overarching questions:

- Who Are We & What Are We Supposed To Do?
- Should Christians Be Seen & Not Heard?
- How To Take Ground For Christ's Kingdom
- The Absolute & Positive Hope For The Earth

Just Because Jesus Saves You from the Fire It Doesn't Mean You Get to Drive the Fire Truck!

How the "Me first" brand of Christianity is in fact "No Christianity" at all, and why our Culture will continue to unravel unless and until we "Seek first the Kingdom of God," (Matthew 6.33) by abandoning the idea of there being a God, and begin dealing with the reality of God and the responsibilities that are connected to being a Christian. Fire Truck assists you in

- Answering the question: "Am I getting the job done, as a Christian?" by explaining what you have been called into Christ's Kingdom to accomplish, and by helping you develop a "vision" of how to live as a Christian. We should not forget that God isn't interested that we know His will, but that we do His will.
- Making the non-negotiable attitude change from "What's in this for me?" to "What's in this for Christ's Kingdom?"
- Exchanging subjective conservative moralism for objective Christian reality.
- Developing the awareness and understanding of how a God-oriented lifestyle is superior to a man-oriented lifestyle.
- Striving for consistency in your Christian walk, not complacency.

Hanson Group Books on Biblical Basics

God's Ten Words:
Practical Applications from the Ten Commandments

"Why does humanity need God's law?" First and foremost it serves as a mirror to show us as we really are (fallen and filthy in God's sight), not as we may imagine we are (not quite perfect, but not as bad as others). This helps us to recognize our need of repenting and placing our faith in Christ's words and work.

The principles contained in the Ten Commandments provide a prescription for not only stopping our culture's decline, but of restoring it to God's will. Each Commandment includes a section on what civilization was like before the influence of that Commandment, plus a review and practical application Comments from many of the most respected biblical scholars are included.

FLOWERS for the Christian Worldview Garden

Not quite sure what a Christian worldview is? If so, you're not alone. Only one in twenty Christian adults knows the answer. The seven chapters of FLOWERS discuss the various aspects of a developed Christian worldview. All Christians have one or more of these aspects included in their Worldview Garden, but God desires that we have all seven, because the more "flowers" we have, the less "weeds" we will have. The elements of a developed Christian worldview are:

From Him, through Him and to Him are all things. Romans 11.36
Lean not on your own understanding. Proverbs 3.5
Obedience brings blessings. Leviticus 26; Deuteronomy 28
Word of God is true. Psalm 119.160
Exhibit humility. Matthew 23.12
Repent. Ezekiel 14.6
Saved to succeed, not secede. Psalm 2.8

Making Your Daily READS: Vol. I, II & III
How to READ the Defense of your Opponents' Objections
To Christianity and Make the Right Call to Uphold the Faith

Making Your Daily READS provides 52 "READS," for the various objections the reader is likely to encounter on a daily basis. The READS are categorized into five "audibles:"

R One **religion** is as good as another
E **Editing** God's Word to fit our presuppositions.
A **Apologetics**; defending the faith against common objections
D God is **dead** when it comes to "real life" issues.
S The **State** is exempt from God's authority.

Each audible begins with a Scouting Report that sets the theme for the section. Following that is one READ for each week with a page for the reader to re-write the READ in their own words, and spend the entire week practicing it. As a bonus, a short course in apologetics is included in an appendix.

Divine ComeBacks

How many people do you speak to each day? Whether in an office, on the telephone, through email, or on the street, you have countless opportunities to bring honor to Jesus.

> *What if you could turn every greeting into an opportunity to a non-threatening way to share the gospel?*

If this sounds interesting *Divine ComeBacks* could be the most practical book you'll read this year. *Divine ComeBacks* offers you non-threatening biblical responses to common greetings, such as "How are you doing?" "How are things going?" and "What have you been up to since the last time I saw you?" For the most part, people are not looking for a response that has any substance to it. They are merely using their greeting to be friendly and to initiate a conversation. And, for the most part we reply with such tired and worn expressions, such as, "Pretty good," "Fine," "Great," or "Fair to middlin.'"

Now, whether you're on the job, at the grocery store, at the service station, or walking in your neighborhood, you'll be ready to "put God in play" in your various daily conversations with a creative and thought-provoking *Divine Comeback*.

One *Divine ComeBack* is focused on per week, which means you have six different applications to enrich your answer as you review them from Monday through Saturday. The Lord's Day can serve as a either "catch-up" day, or a day to review the previous week's *Divine ComeBack*.

The *Divine ComeBacks* are grouped among five categories which directly relate to everyday situations and circumstances:

- Dominion/Victory
- Lifestyle/Testimony (Holiness)
- Confident/Optimistic Attitude
- Worldview/Faith
- Consistent Obedience to God's Word

Today is a good day to begin greeting your Christian friends and non-Christian neighbors with a non-threatening, yet convicting *Divine ComeBack!*

Spiritual Bullets for Daily Physical Battles:
How to Crush the Satan-inspired Fallacy
that being "Saved" is the End of the Christian Life,
instead of the Beginning

Spiritual Bullets is written to remind you of (or introduce you to) a few of the remarkable resources that God absolutely and objectively promises to perform as a result of our obedience. The existence of God's Spiritual Bullets is unarguable. Their effectiveness has been proven time and time again throughout history by the Protestant Reformers, America's founding fathers, and others. Revivals have sprouted forth as a result of Christians using them, and revivals have ended because of their misuse.

> *The point is that we have a fully-loaded spiritual weapon, but for one false presupposition or another, we are either not obediently pulling the trigger, or else we're firing man-made blanks.*

Following is a quick look at the five chapters (Lock & Loads).

❖ Lock & Load #1 discusses how you can fulfill your role as a "weapon of righteousness," and whether you are living according to "Life's Time Clock," or according to "God's Clock of Life."

❖ Lock & Load #2 describes how you can contend earnestly for the faith by living exclusively according to God's ethical framework.

❖ Lock & Load #3 defines who you are talking to when you talk to a fellow Christian, and provides some checkpoints for you to get your "talk" about God in sync with your "walk" with Him.

❖ Lock & Load #4 delivers an encouraging "Halftime Talk," reminding you that America's "game" is not yet over, and even though we are trailing at the current moment, we have enough time, Lord willing, to repent and take part in completing Christ's earthly victory over Satan and his followers.

❖ Lock & Load #5 deals a devastating blow to the arrogant presupposition that America is the most important nation that ever was, or that ever will be, and that history and the fate of mankind hangs in the balance of how God deals with us. After a provocative proposal that, instead of being in the "last days," we are living in the "early days" of the earth's existence, 100 objective questions are presented to answer before dealing with the subjective question concerning Jesus' return.

Re-examining Your
Teaching Paradigm

Expanding your approach from Informant to Instructor by advancing from the current "Listening and Learning" mindset of your congregation to the "Listening, Learning and Doing" mindset.

Re-examining Your Teaching Paradigm "repeats" the original approach to the pulpit by the Protestant Reformers, (Puritans), and to some readers this "original approach" may sound so new that they will be tempted to dismiss it. The truth, however, is that what is presented is completely old and proven. Indeed, it was this original way of pastors communicating with their members that helped to "Christianize" the West. Slowly and gradually, pastors have wandered far from the Puritan pulpit model, and as a result, the once solid Christian cultural principles of the West have been replaced by the pluralistic principles from every form of religion except Christianity.

Today's church members are likely to determine the "good guys" in the pulpit from the "bad guys" by how accurate their biblical exegesis is in their sermons. Over the years this zeal to make certain that their members are correctly informed has resulted in a "Listening and Learning" paradigm among Christians, whereby they judge the value of a church according to how solid its teaching is. This paradigm, however, ignores the two most basic questions on the mind of everyone who listens to your sermons:

- What does this message mean for me?
- How should these biblical truths impact my worldview and lifestyle?

Re-examining Your Teaching Paradigm encourages pastors to replace the current "Listening and Learning" paradigm that they are either intentionally or unintentionally presenting to their members, with the "Listening, Learning and Doing" paradigm of their Puritan brothers. As they do this Christians of all ages will be excited to find that they have been called into Christ's Kingdom with a most important purpose, which is to restore our culture to its pre-Fall condition.

From Crying Out in the Stands, to Carrying out God's Plans

Arguably, sports coaches are the most effective teachers in America, and judging by the continuing collapse of our culture, American pastors are arguably the worst teachers. The difference, I believe, is that coaches are held accountable for achieving results, and they therefore take great pains to prepare their athletes to play by teaching them the fundamentals of the game and then having them practice those skills regularly.

For a combination of reasons, (none biblical!) few members expect for the church to achieve any kind of substantial results in our culture. Therefore, pastors are routinely judged for their speaking ability and their entertainment skills (rather than according to their skill to diligently teach their members to completely transform their worldview and lifestyle from their non-Christian days). Attending church is, in too many instances, a place to go to retreat from the everyday cares of the world, rather than being a place to worship and praise the Creator God who repeatedly tells us that He has called us into His family and Christ's Kingdom to "knock down the gates of Hell," and "crush Satan's head!"

For these reasons, *From Crying Out in the Stands*, to Carrying Our God's Plans cites many examples of how coaches teach (which transform the habits of their athletes), and compares them to the ways that far too many pastors teach (which are not transforming the behaviors of most of their members.

- Advance preparation and planning.
- Applying teaching & learning.
- Assimilating Biblical truths and concepts to your learners' current worldview and lifestyle.
- Appreciating how the truths in the message can lead to a more consistent service in Christ's Kingdom.
- Adapting the truths to the learners' worldview.
- Advancing toward the purpose for which God has called us.
- Annulling the idea of waiting for a more favorable time to obey God.
- Admonishing the realities of God's wrath against disobedience.
- Attaining a biblically-based ethical framework.
- Adding God's Word to our lifestyle.
- After the message follow-up tips.

May God's truths about teaching re-awaken you to your calling of transforming lives with God's inerrant and perfect counsel for how to live and govern ourselves!

The Bible Teacher's Daily Primer

Introducing a new kind of daily devotional: One exclusively written for Bible teachers! There are countless daily devotionals, but anyone who teaches the Bible, from pastors to their congregations, to parents to their children, will benefit by getting their mental juices flowing each day with these brief, but broad strokes of effective communication fundamentals that are brimming over with biblical counsel.

Each day's Primer provides specific tactics to involve your learners in the message you present. Each brief, mind-engaging Daily Primer is designed to help you capture your learner's attention by either introducing a proven communication tactic, or reminding you of one that perhaps has become entangled in the cob-webs of your memory bank. Quotes from some of the most respected biblical scholars throughout history are sprinkled in the various Daily Primers. Whether you are teaching from the pulpit, in a small group, or around your kitchen table to your family, these Daily Primers will keep you ahead of the teaching and communicating curve, as you effectively communicate your message.

The Bible Teacher's Daily Primer helps you keep in perspective who you're addressing and what their needs and concerns are ... which is not to accumulate more knowledge about God, but to gain more wisdom in how to live and present a daily Christian antithesis to the cultural agenda of our non-Christian neighbors.

The Bible Teacher's Daily Primer has one goal only: to assist you in becoming a more effective communicator of God's Word. God doesn't call pastors to merely be accurate announcers of His Word. He calls pastors to teach His Word ... to give his best efforts toward making certain that his members "get it." The same holds true for anyone who may be teaching God's Word. From Genesis to Revelation the message is the same: "God's Word works, and man's word fails." However, the continuing decline of American culture during the last century and a half proves that something isn't working, and that something is not God, it's us! If sales managers communicated like us, they would be fired. If sports coaches communicated like us, they would be fired. If military commanders communicated like us, they would be fired. And, we should all be seriously concerned that unless and until we repent and improve our communication and teaching skills, God could immediately fire us, and raise up another country to carry His redeeming message throughout the world.

Non-Christians are not waiting around for us to provide a proof text that tells them their entire view of life is built upon sand! They're waiting around (even though they may not know it) for us to demonstrate that the Christian way of living is better than the non-Christian way of living. Unfortunately, too many Christian teachers think that they have fulfilled their job by accurately presenting a portion of Scripture. It's as though their attitude is, "Hey, I've done my part. If the members didn't 'get it,' that's their problem." Well, we haven't been "getting it," and it's everyone's problem.

You will find:

✓ Devotional thoughts on biblical truths that we need to build into each sermon/lesson.

✓ An explanation of the common false presuppositions that cause many Christians to unintentionally misinterpret God's Word.

✓ Help you install God's vision for your congregation by discussing
   –Your Offense Scheme: Why "The gates of hell will not stand ..." against God's truth. (Matthew 16.18)
   –Your Defense Scheme: How to "Be ready in season and out..." (2 Timothy 4.2)
   –Strategy & Tactics: What each member can do to "Take dominion..." (Genesis 1.26-28; 3.15; Romans 16.20)

May you enjoy and employ God's all-sufficient counsel, and become a more effective teacher, whether from the pulpit, in a small group, or in your home!

Hanson Group Books on Business & Politics

Choose This Day:
God's Instructions on How to Select Leaders

America needs leaders and Choose This Day gives God's formula for selecting them. The civil government policy-making table, like everything else, belongs to God, not man. It should be noted that we're not umpires who "calls'em as we sees'em" when it comes to making our daily decisions, but rather we're players who follow what our coach (God, through His Word) tells us to do. God's duty is to "call the shots," our duty is to obediently follow His game plan. So for Christians to have a goal of being an equal partner in setting society's policies is to greatly demean God. It is exactly because of our refusal to be "salt and light" to our communities that we have lost not only our seat at culture's table, but the entire table, and getting it back won't be easy. Still, it can be done and as soon as we have secured one seat, we need to begin working on a second seat, and then a third, until we have recaptured them all.

The Christian Civil Ruler's Handbook

As important as it is to elect Christian civil rulers (legislators and judges), this is only the first step. Unless the Christians we elect to office have a developed Christian worldview, they will govern no differently than a non-Christian conservative. The Handbook provides a quick read for busy legislators on how to rule according to God's will, instead of according to their own imagination of how God might want them to govern.

Two appendices extend the practical applications discussed in the Handbook. The first one answers common objections regarding religion and politics, and the second one is a multiple choice test on the U.S. Constitution (with an answer key) that Home Schoolers like to use. Get a copy for your Civil Rulers!

The Christian Prince:
Putting Civil Back into Civil Government

The Christian Prince:
- ✓ is the first Christian response to Machiavelli's The Prince in 500 years
- ✓ explains how we can put "civil" back into civil government, and how America can once again attract others-focused statesmen to serve as our representatives, instead of the current self-centered politicians
- ✓ exposes and contrasts the failing ideas of man with the divinely guaranteed-to-succeed ideas of our Lord, Savior and King, Jesus Christ.

Hanson Group Books on Business & Politics

Bottom Line Theology:
A Bible Study Feast for those
Who only have Time for a Sandwich

If Bible study could be thought of as a meal there would be several very wholesome full meals available, complete with veggies, bread and beverage. However, when these lengthy books are boiled down to the bottom line you will find that the biblical ethics that they teach and those that BLT teaches are the same, because there is only one Bible! The advantage that BLT offers is that you won't use up most of your time in searching for the biblical ethics in which you are interested. So, if your current schedule necessitates that you grab a fast spiritual sandwich, then BLT is the Bible study for you. Each of the thirteen sections gets directly to the heart of the Biblical principles discussed.

Daily BLT:
A Daily Arsenal of Godly ammunition
To help you Take Ground for God's Kingdom

DAILY BLT is unique in that it gives practical tools to use according to the way that best fits your personality and schedule. Each Day has three 2-page sections, and depending upon your schedule you can use one (15-minutes), two (30 minutes), or all three (45-minutes) of these 2-page sections. Since Sunday is a Sabbath Day Rest in the Lord, fourteen additional pages are provided.

What's Scripture Got To Do With It?
Connecting Your Spiritual Dots for a More Meaningful Life

Every Christian could list core biblical truths in which he unquestionably believes. Unfortunately, few of us incorporate these beliefs into our lifestyle. How is it with you? Does your lifestyle consistently demonstrate the "answers" you say that the Bible has to life's questions? Are you being salt and light to those with whom you come into contact, or has your salt lost its savor, and is good for nothing else but to be trampled under foot?

Many of us have a lot of "Spiritual Dots" (core Christian beliefs) floating around inside our mind that for one reason or another we have not connected to our everyday lifestyle. *What's Scripture Got To Do With It?* will raise your awareness of those particular Spiritual Dots and stresses the urgency to live in accordance with them.

EXIT Strategy:
A Handbook to Exponentially Improve Your Service for God

If you've been itching for an antidote for the rampant Spiritual anemia that exists throughout your community, EXIT Strategy provides the scratch. Each reader will be able to evaluate a book they're about to buy, or a study they're thinking of joining with thirteen Door Opener worksheets that quickly identify whether they will be involved in simply another form of church "busy-ness," or in an activity that will help them grow in their personal holiness. While every Christian knows we must obey God, EXIT Strategy clarifies that in order to obey God in the way God prefers, we must first know and understand His Word. This is achieved through the exclusive Door Opener worksheets, plus the complete Westminster Larger Catechism (196 questions).

Now That You're A Christian
How and Why You Should Bring Glory and Honor
to God in Everything You Think, Say and Do

The goal of *Now That You're A Christian* is to guide you in answering the many questions that are common to those who are new to the faith. The various elements of a Christian lifestyle are arranged under the following eight topics:

❖ The Absolute Superiority of Christianity
❖ The Absolute Supremacy of Our Triune God
❖ The Absolute Supremacy of God's Word
❖ The Superiority of Your Purpose in Life
❖ The Superiority of the Christian Worldview & Lifestyle
❖ Your Labor Is Not In Vain in the Lord
❖ The Spiritual Superiority of Being a Member of God's Family
❖ What You Can Do Today to Bring Honor to Your Lord,
❖ Savior and King, Jesus Christ

Sprinkled throughout the text are some of Satan's favorite temptations, and an explanation of how to defend yourself against them, and successfully defeat them. There are also helpful charts that summarize key points. Each chapter recaps the main points with a page entitled, "The non-Christian Schlemiel vs. The Christian Real Deal."

Schlemiel is a Yiddish word that refers to a person who is "awkward and unlucky, and for whom things never turn out right." So, in a theological sense, this characterization pretty well describes the non-Christian.

The concluding page in each chapter is a work page entitled "Are You on the Lord's Side, or Are You on Your Side." The four questions provide you with the opportunity to define which non-Christian Schlemiel items are still in your worldview and to note what you can do to eliminate them. Your responses from each of the seven chapters can then be combined on the Life-Plan form in Appendix A. Finally, each chapter ends with a suggested list of resources to help you in your Christian walk.

Each of the topics discussed in these eight chapters are essential in living an obedient Christian lifestyle, but since each of us has been wired with different spiritual hot buttons, one or two of these will automatically come to the top of your biblical hit list. So, as you read through them, prioritize them and begin tackling them one at a time.

The end of the book includes a form for you to compile the basic elements of a LifePlan, plus a two-page self-check that asks: "Are You Willing to Pay the Price for Being a Christian?"

How to Re-Program Yourself
From all of the Blasphemous Ideas You Learned in Public School

For more than 160 years American educators have been turning out Marxist "Manchurian Candidates," who have been subtly indoctrinated to respond to cultural issues in ungodly ways, all the while thinking that they are "card carrying Christians." The operative word here is "think," and it is the way they have been taught to think (or not think) that is the brilliance of the public (government) school movement, and the shame of Pastors to allow their God to be systematically blasphemed on a daily basis.

If you think that it is beyond the realm of possibilities that your "strings" are being pulled in order for you to make your daily decisions according to the non-Christian worldview cultural agenda that is currently in vogue, read this book F-A-S-T!

BUDDY HANSON,
President of the Christian Policy
Network, and Director of the
Christian Worldview Resources
Center frequently speaks to
Churches Homeschool organizations and civic groups about
the necessity of applying biblical principles to every situations,
circumstances and decision-making.
"There are many fine organizations
presenting the descriptions about
how a Christian worldview should
differ from a non-Christian one, but
that's only half of the equation. Our
focus is to present God's prescriptions to reform our culture. Christianity is not an intellectual trip, but
a world-transforming trip as Jesus
commands us to live-out our faith
and bring about 'God's will on earth
as it is in heaven.'" (Matthew 6.10)

For pricing and ordering information contact:*

The Hanson Group
2 Windsor Drive
Tuscaloosa, AL 35404
205.454.1442
bhanson@graceandlaw.com

Bookstores can also order through Ingram Distributors

* Quantity discounts available

LaVergne, TN USA
10 December 2010

208347LV00002B/119/P